American Popular Music

Jazz

D1314299

American Popular Music

Blues
Country
Jazz
Rock and Roll

General Editor: Richard Carlin

Editorial Board:

Barbara Ching, Ph.D., University of Memphis

William Duckworth, Bucknell University

Kevin J. Holm-Hudson, Ph.D., University of Kentucky

Craig Morrison, Ph.D., Concordia University (Montreal)

American Popular Music

Jazz

Thom Holmes

Foreword by William Duckworth,
Bucknell University

Checkmark Books
An imprint of Infobase Publishing

American Popular Music: Jazz

Copyright © 2006 by Thom Holmes

All rights reserved. No part of this book may be reproduced or utilized in any form or by any means, electronic or mechanical, including photocopying, recording, or by any information storage or retrieval systems, without permission in writing from the publisher. For information contact:

Checkmark Books
An imprint of Infobase Publishing
132 West 31st Street
New York NY 10001

Library of Congress Cataloging-in-Publication Data
Holmes, Thom.
   American popular music : jazz / Thom Holmes; foreword by William Duckworth; Richard Carlin, general editor.
     p. cm.
   Includes bibliographical references and index.
   ISBN 0-8160-5316-2 (hc)—ISBN 0-8160-6928-X (pb : alk. paper)
   1. Jazz—Encyclopedias. 2. Popular music—United States—Encyclopedias. 3. Jazz musicians—Biography. I. Carlin, Richard, 1956– II. Title.
   ML102.J3H65 2005
   781.65'0973'03—dc22   2004024218

Checkmark Books are available at special discounts when purchased in bulk quantities for businesses, associations, institutions, or sales promotions. Please call our Special Sales Department in New York at (212) 967-8800 or (800) 322-8755.

You can find Facts On File on the World Wide Web at http://www.factsonfile.com

Text design by James Scotto-Lavino
Cover design by Dorothy M. Preston
All interior photographs courtesy of CTS Images

Printed in the United States of America

VB FOF 10 9 8 7 6 5 4 3 2 1

This book is printed on acid-free paper.

This book is dedicated to Anne,
who is my eighth note,
my quarter note, my half note,
and whole note.

Contents

Foreword   ix

Preface   xiii

Acknowledgments   xvii

About This Book   xix

Introducing Jazz   xxi

A-TO-Z ENTRIES   1

Appendixes   227

Glossary of Music Terms   275

End Notes and Further Reading   283

Editorial Board of Advisers   291

Index   293

Foreword

The Legacy of Jazz

As a kid, I listened to jazz. I loved it; still do. My favorite performers were the pianists Thelonious Monk and Erroll Garner, the big bands of Glenn Miller and Stan Kenton, and the Miles Davis and Cannonball Adderley Quintets. My small town didn't offer much in the way of live jazz, and none of us kids could play it that well, no matter how hard we tried, but I had a radio that, at night, could get WWL New Orleans—all 50,000 watts (clear channel status). They played jazz every night, four to five hours worth as I recall, mostly recorded, but occasionally live, usually a big band on tour, broadcasting from one of the fancier New Orleans hotels. In my world, that radio, and the music it brought to me, was the next best thing to being there; at times, I could almost imagine I was sitting in with the band. And more often than not, for five or six years, I went to sleep listening to jazz, absorbing the history and memorizing the sounds. It was my music; I was its fan.

Now for new listeners to jazz, or to any other style of music for that matter, there is an important distinction to be drawn between a *listener* and a *fan*. I began as a listener—someone turning the dial looking for new sounds—but, drawn in by the music, I stayed to become a fan. And unlike the casual listener, a dedicated fan, more often than not, knows what he or she is talking about and can identify most of the bands and soloists by their sounds. In making that journey with jazz, I learned that in order to truly be a part of an art form, we must not only *know* it, we must *feel* it and sense its subtleties, learning, in the process, to listen and to

grow. Somewhere along the line, most people who enjoy music have a similar experience; many more than once. Because whatever the style of music you now enjoy most, something happened when you first heard it that pulled you in, kept you interested, and made you want to return for more. And much in the same way that I came to know jazz, you learned a lot about the music you like, the facts as well as the sounds. It isn't possible to achieve this degree of musical subtlety and sophistication any other way. Similarly, it is not enough for newcomers to jazz to learn about it intellectually, without also coming to know and appreciate its vast array of sounds. Jazz, after all, is all about sound, and the jazz experience—just as it is with the enjoyment of your favorite music—is incomplete without the use of both the ear and the mind.

Jazz is America's music, no doubt about it; everyone agrees with that. It started here at the end of the 19th century, grew and flourished here throughout the 20th century, and continues to lead the way into the next century, all from here. Although to be fair, in the intervening years, jazz has taken root throughout the world, and there are excellent and highly innovative jazz musicians living everywhere today, all adding their unique voices to the ever-changing artistic mix. But the lineage of jazz, its story, its history—in all its many forms and manifestations—is essentially homegrown American music, speaking a language of hopes and dreams, of aspirations and accomplishments, that are truly and uniquely ours. Ultimately, jazz represents a major strand in the core values of the

American culture, values expressed and preserved in sound.

For the reader and listener just starting to explore this unique and special art form, it is equally important to distinguish, at the beginning, between the unifying *spirit* of jazz and the many and various *styles* of jazz that have occurred since it began. Jazz styles come and go just as over the years fashions in clothes and cars change shape and form. Consider for a moment that within two decades of its beginnings in New Orleans at the turn of the century, Chicago Dixieland emerged in the 1920s, then big band swing in the '30s, bop and cool in the '40s and '50s, and fusion combos after that. Styles change with the times. In the case of jazz, what changed were the special rhythms that moved us, the unique harmonies that spoke to us like no other, and the melodies that made us want to sing. Every new era in jazz stirs and remixes these ingredients to arrive at its own special sound, a sound so unique it gets a name, such as swing or bop or cool.

Spirit, on the other hand—that way of identifying one's self with an ideal, a movement, a way of living life and seeing the world—does not change so serendipitously. And throughout its history, no matter what the style, the spirit of jazz and its way of looking inward and outward simultaneously, its need to express both suffering and pain, hope and joy, has remained more or less the same. Musicians from all styles of jazz recognize this kinship with each other. Some, in fact, were not only active in, but even the stars of, more than one jazz style— from Dixieland to swing, bop, and cool in the case of tenor saxophonist Coleman Hawkins; from swing through bop and cool to fusion for trumpeter Miles Davis, to name but two.

As you begin to use and enjoy this volume on jazz that Thom Holmes has so thoughtfully and carefully put together, remember that you are holding two simultaneous histories in your hands. One describes the many changes of jazz styles that have taken place since jazz began and identifies the men and women who made it all happen; it is about detail. The other history offers a more encompassing and expansive vista, one filled with those ideals of the American artistic spirit; it is the connecting thread. All of the individual stories, from A to Z, make up this broader experience. Successfully understanding the distinction between these two histories, and the stories they tell, is similar, in a way, to knowing and appreciating the difference between a listener and a fan.

Encyclopedias are filled with names, in this case the century-plus group of artists who created jazz, the styles they invented, and the songs they made famous along the way. Some of the artists you will encounter here are household names, such as Louis Armstrong, who changed the way the trumpet was played, or Duke Ellington, who took harmony into territories previously unexplored. Other names may be less familiar, but they are no less important to the mix. All are essential ingredients in the sound. To help make sense of these myriad names, places, and tunes, it might be useful to create a mental grid representing a few key artists and the styles they played. It is a bit like a future generation attaching Elvis's name to early rock and roll, the Beatles to the British invasion, and Snoop Dogg to West Coast rap, before beginning to explore the history of rock. This ever-growing outline is what allows us to listen to something new, connect it to the past, and put it into context. By creating such a grid for jazz, we can, in effect, erect a scaffolding on which to hang the various and sundry new "facts" found along the way. Without such a structure, these facts, devoid of their surroundings, can lose their significance, and the names can lose their sense of time and place. In the pages that follow, Thom Holmes has provided such an overview, and his essay "Introducing Jazz" is an excellent place from which to begin this assimilation.

Additionally, in fall 2004, the Jazz History Museum, located at Lincoln Center in New York, inducted the first group of artists into its Jazz Hall of Fame. All 14 inductees are among the leaders of their eras: Louis Armstrong, Sidney Bechet, Bix Beiderbecke, and Jelly Roll Morton from the earliest days in New Orleans and Chicago; the swing band leader Duke Ellington, the stride pianist Art Tatum, and the singer Billie Holiday; plus John Coltrane, Miles Davis, Dizzy Gillespie, Coleman Hawkins, Thelonious Monk, Charlie Parker, and Lester Young from bop and cool. For a fan familiar with them all, it's nice to see some of our agreed-upon heroes receiving their due. For someone new to jazz trying to make sense of the major styles and the many practitioners, these artists and the styles they embody might also represent a good place to begin. Either way, what is most important is to remember that jazz is really about the sound; you can't go wrong if you choose to start there.

Finally, some music journalists, and jazz musicians as well, are fond of calling jazz America's classical music, measuring its achievements with those made by European classical composers living and writing between the 17th and 19th centuries—Bach to Beethoven to Brahms, essentially—who not only represented but helped to define their times as well. But that comparison, while not exactly wrong, doesn't seem quite right either. In the first place, the two styles (improvised jazz versus composed European classical music) are too different in form and content to justify such a comparison, and in the second, making that comparison can seem demeaning to a whole host of other musical styles that can lay some claim to having been locally born and raised.

Ultimately, however, the worth of 20th-century American jazz is too significant to tie to the coattails of European classical music from a different place and time. Because today, jazz has come to represent more than that comparison can describe or fully convey. Jazz is America's music, its soundtrack—our sound—setting the tone and having carried us through a century filled with depression and prosperity, moon walks and two world wars. And although America is a large place with a rich artistic history and many musical voices, jazz is one of our most important forms of artistic expression, giving voice and helping, as it does, to tell us, as well as the rest of the world, what we feel and who we are. Jazz is not a museum exhibit, filled with memories and information, but a living, breathing art form, growing and changing, defining and redefining itself as it goes. Yesterday, today, and tomorrow. It's not classical music; it's jazz!

William Duckworth

Preface

American popular music reflects the rich cultural diversity of the American people. From classical to folk to jazz, America has contributed a rich legacy of musical styles to the world over its two-plus centuries of existence. The rich cross-fertilization of cultures—African-American, Hispanic, Asian, and European—has resulted in one of the unique musical mixtures in the world.

American Popular Music celebrates this great diversity by presenting to the student, researcher, and individual enthusiast a wealth of information on each musical style in an easily accessible format.

Each volume presents key information on performers, musical genres, famous compositions, musical instruments, media, and centers of musical activity. The volumes conclude with a chronology, recommended listening, and a complete bibliography or list of sources for further study.

How do we define *popular music?* Literally, any music that attracts a reasonably large audience is "popular" (as opposed to "unpopular"). Over the past few decades, however, as the study of popular music has grown, the term has come to have specific meanings. While some might exclude certain genres covered in this series—American classical music leaps to mind—we felt that it was important to represent the range of musical styles that have been popular in the United States over its entire history. New scholarship has brought to light the interplay among genres that previously were felt to be unrelated—such as the influence of folk forms on classical music, opera's influence on jazz, or the blues' influence on country—so that to truly understand each musical style, it is important to be conversant with at least some aspects of all.

These volumes are intended to be introductory, not comprehensive. Any "A to Z" work is by its very nature selective; it's impossible to include *every* figure, *every* song, or *every* key event. For most users, we hope the selections made here will be more than adequate, giving information on the key composers and performers who shaped each style, while also introducing some lesser-known figures who are worthy of study. The Editorial Board and other outside advisers played a key role in reviewing the entry lists for completeness.

All encyclopedia authors also face the rather daunting task of separating fact from fiction when writing short biographies of performers and composers. Even birth and death dates can be "up for grabs," as artists have been known to subtract years from their lives in their official biographies. "Official" records are often unavailable, particularly for earlier artists who may have been born at home, or for those whose family histories themselves are shrouded in mystery. We have attempted to draw on the latest research and most reliable sources whenever possible, and have also pointed out when key facts are in dispute. And, for many popular performers, the myth can be as important as the reality when it comes to their lives, so we have tried to honor both in writing about their achievements.

Popular music reflects the concerns of the artists who create it and their audience. Each era of our country's history has spawned a variety of popular music styles, and these styles in turn have grown over the decades as new performers and new times have arisen. These volumes try to place the music into its context, acknowledging that the way music is performed and its effect on the greater society is as important as the music itself. We've also tried to highlight the many interchanges between styles and performers, because one of the unique—and important—aspects of American cultural life is the way that various people have come together to create a new culture out of the interplay of their original practices and beliefs.

Race, class, culture, and sex have played roles in the development of American popular music. Regrettably, the playing field has not always been level for performers from different backgrounds, particularly when it comes to the business aspects of the industry: paying royalties, honoring copyrights, and the general treatment of artists. Some figures have been forgotten or ignored who deserved greater attention; the marketplace can be ruthless, and its agents—music publishers, record producers, concert promoters—have and undoubtedly will continue to take advantage of the musicians trying to bring their unique voices to market. These volumes attempt to address many of these issues as they have affected the development of individual musicians' careers as well as from the larger perspective of the growth of popular music. The reader is encouraged to delve further into these topics by referring to the bibliographies in each volume.

Popular music can be a slave itself to crass commercialism, as well as a bevy of hangers-on, fellow travelers, and others who seek only to make a quick buck by following easy-to-identify trends. While we bemoan the lack of new visionary artists today like Bessie Smith, Miles Davis, Pauline Oliveros, or Bob Dylan, it's important to remember that when they first came on the scene the vast majority of popular performers were journeymen musicians at best. Popular music will always include many second-, third-, and fourth-tier performers; some will offer one or two recordings or performances that will have a lasting impact, while many will be celebrated during their 15 minutes of fame, but most will be forgotten. In separating the wheat from the chaff, it is understandably easier for our writers working on earlier styles where the passing of time has helped sort out the important from the just popular. However, all the contributors have tried to supply some distance, giving greatest weight to the true artists, while acknowledging that popular figures who are less talented can nonetheless have a great impact on the genre during their performing career—no matter how brief it might be.

All in all, the range, depth, and quality of popular musical styles that have developed in the United States over its lifetime is truly amazing. These styles could not have arisen anywhere else, but are the unique products of the mixing of cultures, geography, technology, and sheer luck that helped disseminate each style. Who could have forecast the music of Bill Monroe before he assembled his first great bluegrass band? Or predicted the melding of gospel, rhythm and blues, and popular music achieved by Aretha Franklin during her reign as "Queen of Soul"? The tinkering of classical composer John Cage—who admitted to having no talent for creating melodies—was a truly American response to new technologies, a new environment, and a new role for music in our lives. And Patti Smith's particular take on poetry, the punk-rock movement, and the difficulties faced by a woman who leads a rock band make her music particularly compelling and original—and unpredictable to those who dismissed the original rock records as mere "teenage fluff."

We hope that the volumes in this series will open your eyes, minds, and, most important, your ears to a world of musical styles. Some may be familiar, others more obscure, but all are worthy. With today's proliferation of sound on the Web, finding even the most obscure recording is becoming increasingly simple. We urge you to read deeply but also to put these books down to listen. Come to your own conclusions. American popular music is a rich world, one open to many different interpretations. We hope these volumes serve as your windows to these many compelling worlds.

Richard Carlin,
General Editor

Acknowledgments

I would like to thank the dedicated and hard-working people at Facts On File, some of whom I have worked with personally and others behind the scenes. I give special thanks to James Chambers, my generous and supportive editor, for turning me loose on this fun project. I am grateful to Richard Carlin, general editor of the series, for recommending me as the author of this jazz volume, a subject he and I have been noodling over for quite some time. Vanessa Nittoli, editorial assistant, did a great job coordinating my input during production. Thanks to Gene Brissie of James Peter Associates, Inc., who served as agent for this series.

There is no substitute for good copyediting and fact checking. I am indebted to William Duckworth, Bucknell University, for his thoughtful review of the manuscript and suggestions. He also wrote the foreword for the volume. The manuscript was copyedited by Jerold Kappes, to whom I offer special gratitude for his incredible work on this lengthy and detailed book.

There are many behind the scenes people at Facts On File who made this book possible. Of these, I would like to especially thank Michael G. Laraque,

chief copy editor; Rachel Berlin, production director; Cathy Rincon, art director; Lisa Broderick, production associate; and James Scotto-Lavino, designer, without whose dedication this volume would not have been completed in so fine a fashion.

As I was writing this book about jazz, I discovered that there was no lack of suggestions for entries from the people closest to me, friends, associates, and even strangers. I am forever grateful to them all but especially to the following people who made effective cases for their jazz favorites: Anne Benkovitz, a bass player herself, for encouraging me to expand my list of bass players and female artists on all instruments and for offering some key editing suggestions; Joseph Benkovitz, for not letting me forget Harry James; Betty Whitford and Jo-ann C. Graham, for reminding me of Alberta Hunter and Johnny Hartman; Gene Bryan Johnson, for our many conversations about modern jazz; Kevin Witt, for his favorite drummers; Maria Romano, for her encounters with New York jazz legends; and the lady behind the counter at the James A. Farley branch of the U.S. Post Office on Eighth Avenue in New York, for playing Lee Morgan while I bought some stamps.

Thom Holmes

About This Book

The World of Jazz: A Guide to Using the Encyclopedia

My love of jazz began with my parents who, during my youth, managed to fill the house with the sound of the most extraordinary jazz vocalists and instrumentalists. My mother, Burt Lou Holmes, was an on-air singer in Detroit during the heyday of radio back in the 1940s. Her favorites included Ella Fitzgerald, Sarah Vaughn, and Nancy Wilson, whose music was always playing in the background when stereo sets were first available. My father, Robert, was an automotive engineer whose taste in jazz favored solo instrumentalists, particularly on Hammond organ and guitar. I can't begin to explain the energizing jolt of inspiration that jump-started my own musical ambitions after hearing his recordings of Wes Montgomery in the mid-1960s. Then there was that secret stash of 78 rpm records that fascinated me as a kid. My parents had been avid record buyers during the swing era. I dipped into their collection regularly to feast on the sounds of Artie Shaw, Benny Goodman, Count Basie, Duke Ellington, Glenn Miller, and others. The scratchy sounds of those 78s left an indelible impression on me. They were a document of jazz history, yes, but those old recordings also seemed to me to be just one stage in the evolution of this thing called jazz that was still all around us. How the music evolved from big bands to small combos and solo artists fascinated me even then, whetting my curiosity about the history of jazz that has culminated in the writing of this encyclopedia.

As a young man my interest turned to rock and roll, jazz, and avant-garde music. My interest in composing took a path toward the creation of electronic music, but my motivation for this work, and my understanding of the nature of improvisation, was always informed by my exposure and love of jazz. I can thank my high school buddy Jimm Wachtel for teaching me about the saxophone. Then there was our mutual friend, drummer Joe Toth, who introduced us to the first recording of the Tony Williams Lifetime. Together we went to Detroit one night to catch a performance of Rahsaan Roland Kirk at the Ibo Cultural Center. After moving to Philadelphia, I befriended an astrophysicist drummer (no kidding) named John Scarpulla who kept up my lessons in jazz. We saw Miles and McLaughlin, and Weather Report, and scores of other jazz greats in and around Philadelphia.

In those formative years of my life, I would have enjoyed reading a comprehensive introduction to the people, history, music, and legacy of jazz. This book is my attempt to write that book. But although it is backed now by 40 more years' experience as a listener, musician, and writer about music, I hope that I have been able to inform this book by the same open-minded curiosity that drew me to jazz in the first place.

The *Jazz* volume of *American Popular Music* is a comprehensive guide to the leading musicians, works, history, and culture that have shaped the history of jazz from about 1900 to the present day.

The majority of this work is an A to Z listing of entries—more than 500 of them. Choosing which entries to include from the entire history of jazz was a huge challenge. A great deal of thought went into these choices so that the encyclopedia could be a valued reference for readers interested in many aspects of jazz—the artists, the history, the slang, the music, and the impact of jazz on American culture. The encyclopedia emphasizes American jazz artists, but acknowledges those artists of foreign birth who have had a great influence on American jazz. More than one-quarter of the biographical entries discuss influential artists outside the United States, many from Cuba, South America, and Europe.

Because jazz is a vital, living art, an effort was made to ensure that the biographies cover the accomplishments of past artists as well as important contemporary musicians. To this end, 40 percent of the biographical entries are about living, working musicians who continue to shape the direction of jazz.

Women's contributions to the world of jazz have long been undervalued in history books and other references. In an effort to correct this inequality, priority was given to including biographies of influential women in jazz, making up about 15 percent of the entries. In addition, a special section of the introduction entitled "Women in Jazz" provides some perspective on the achievements and struggles of women in a musical field historically dominated by men.

The A-to-Z entries cover the following categories of jazz topics:

- Biographies of leading jazz artists, including the musicians, composers, arrangers, and bandleaders who have most influenced the art of jazz during the past 100+ years
- Jazz styles
- Jazz instruments
- Jazz works and important recordings
- Jazz culture, including jargon, landmark places and events, and the impact of jazz on social history
- Jazz terms and musical techniques

The book also includes articles and appendixes to supplement what could not easily be contained in the individual entries:

Introducing Jazz—This introduction provides a definition of jazz and provides additional background on the following:

- **A Brief History of Jazz:** An overview of jazz history and styles of jazz music.
- **Jazz Instruments:** An introduction providing a brief history of jazz instruments. It includes the main listings of instruments found in the encyclopedia, along with their typical role in jazz
- **Listening to Jazz:** Tips for getting the most enjoyment out of listening to jazz
- **Women in Jazz:** An overview of the contributions of women in jazz and the historic difficulties they have faced in achieving wide recognition in this field
- **Quick Guide to Jazz Styles and Artists:** Tips for using the book's entries and cross-references to explore the rich history of jazz and major artists. A subject outline of the major periods in jazz history is provided with the names of key artists of those periods with which to begin one's research

Appendixes—In the back of the book are several helpful references, including

- Appendix I: A Century of Jazz Recordings
- Appendix II: Geographical Time Line of Early Jazz History
- Appendix III: Evolution of Jazz Styles
- Appendix IV: Jazz in the Movies
- Appendix V: Grammy Awards for Jazz
- Appendix VI: Jazz at Lincoln Center Inaugural Hall of Fame Inductees

I hope that this book will interest those who already know jazz as well as those who are new to jazz. In reading it, you will no doubt learn about the musical, historical, and human context of jazz so that you can form your own opinions. However, no book about jazz is complete without listening to jazz. I hope this book will inspire you to do so. Then you will know what all of the excitement is about.

Introducing Jazz

"What we play is life."
—Louis Armstrong

What is jazz? This is a difficult question to answer, but even those people who fall short of finding the words to explain jazz will claim to know it when they hear it.

One of the easiest ways to explain jazz is to say that it's the music made by certain artists and then to name a few. A list might include such greats as BUDDY BOLDEN, LOUIS ARMSTRONG, DUKE ELLINGTON, ELLA FITZGERALD, DIZZY GILLESPIE, MARY LOU WILLIAMS, JOHN COLTRANE, MILES DAVIS, BILL EVANS, KEITH JARRETT, and HERBIE HANCOCK. But what do these names alone tell us about their music?

The artists just mentioned represent more than 90 years in the history of the ever-changing art form called jazz. The music of these artists may be as different from one another as can be; yet, all of it springs from a common source of tradition, discipline, and social and creative values called jazz.

Many music critics and musicians have tried to explain jazz. Some liken it to a language or idea. Others say that jazz is a feeling, a way to express sound. It is the art of the vocalized instrumental tone.

It has been called African-American music, America's classical music, the music of life experience, and just simply America's only original art form.

Some critics offer technical definitions of the music of jazz. To them, jazz is a set of scales and rhythms, a particular way of using melody and beat that are distinctly different from its cousins, the BLUES and rock and roll.

Jazz can also be associated with certain instruments, providing it with a telltale sound.

You can see from these ideas that jazz is both a *kind* of music and *a way of creating* music. One cannot separate the personality of the artist from jazz. Its most distinctive feature is that jazz is unavoidably music of *personal expression*. It is highly interpretive music and *every work of true jazz includes IMPROVISATION,* in whole or in part. You cannot experience jazz by reading a score. You have to listen to it.

Jazz is the soundtrack of African-American life. It is rooted in artistic and cultural traditions that reach back to Africa. The sound of jazz is a history lesson. It expresses the sorrow of repression during decades of slavery in the 19th century. It also reflects the joy of freedom as blacks gained equal rights in a predominantly white America.

Jazz is more than music. It is a way to communicate the emotions that trouble one's soul, the ideas that stir a nation, the love that enlightens a child, and the aspirations of all people to make a better life. It is also about celebrating life, the good and the bad, and all of the triumphs and sorrows that make up human experience. Jazz is a union of the heart with the intellect, a way for the musician to articulate emotion as well as the complex ideas that make a person tick. Expressing oneself through music is at the soul of jazz artistry.

There are many creation myths about the origin of the music as well as the derivation of the word *jazz.* The roots of jazz music go back to the 19th century. It began with music brought from Africa to America during the time of the slave trade. It grew as a fusion of diverse musical and cultural elements, galvanizing aspects of work songs, church music, folk songs, classical, and popular songs. The common thread binding these elements together is that jazz arose noncommercially as an expression of those who were oppressed by poverty and racism. Its history is largely that of the relationship between white and black people in America. It is marked by the repeated imitation of authentic black music by white musicians who gained wealth at the expense of those whose ideas they copied. It is also a history in which black musicians finally gained the commercial and critical success of their white peers.

Jazz may be America's best and most original contribution to world music. As JELLY ROLL MORTON once said, jazz is "the finest music because it's made of all the finest music."[1]

A Brief History of Jazz

If we can say that the cradle of jazz is New Orleans, then its teen years were spent on the road to Chicago. It spent its young adult years in New York City, migrated to Kansas City as it settled down, and then spread across the country, and eventually the world, as it reached maturity. The early history of jazz is one of big cities and musical innovation. It is also one of migrating musicians and a public whose fickle taste sometimes embraced jazz as its most popular music, and other times put it aside as new-fangled musical fads captured its fancy. Here, then, is a capsule summary of the history of jazz. Cross-references are noted for entries in the encyclopedia that expand upon these points.

JAZZ IN THE BEGINNING—1900 TO 1920

The first popular style of jazz emerged from New Orleans around 1900. New Orleans at the time was a freewheeling city with relative racial tolerance and wide musical influences that included Africa, the Caribbean islands, and French-influenced Creole culture. It was here that the earliest jazz ensembles formed. Although the popular myth about early jazz is that the first bands were largely composed of musicians using only marching band instruments, marching bands were not the only tradition from which early jazz drew its influences. A case in point is that of the string bass. The string bass is not a marching band instrument, so it is usually thought that the earliest jazz ensembles must have used the tuba to mark rhythm instead of the string bass. However, there was also a tradition of string bands from which some early jazz drew its instruments, chief among them being the string bass. The string bass was indeed used in the Buddy Bolden band, as the only existing photograph of this group (1905) shows. The use of the string bass in early jazz bands is further born out by other photographs from the time: KID ORY and his Woodland Band (1905), The Peerless Orchestra (1909, 1910); The Original Tuxedo Jazz Orchestra (1910–1913); and The Eagle Band (1916). Parallel to the existence of these groups were brass bands that used the tuba instead of the string bass.

Jazz was a unique distillation of several competing musical forms. In addition to marching bands and string bands, these influences included work songs, spirituals, folk, BLUES, the lively classical idiom of RAGTIME, and songs of cakewalk parties and minstrelsy that were an important part of African-American social life of the late 19th century. From these various influences came the basic instrumentation of jazz: the cornet, trumpet, trombone, or clarinet to play melodies, and guitar, banjo, string bass, tuba, and drums, to play chords and rhythm. By 1915, the tuba had mostly been displaced by the string bass, and the piano had also become a popular part of the rhythm section.

New Orleans groups were mostly African American and excelled at collective improvisation in which melodies were invented on the spot. In NEW ORLEANS JAZZ, musicians improvised at the same time and none took the LEAD or played by himself. Early pioneers of New Orleans jazz included the King Oliver Creole Jazz Band, JELLY ROLL MORTON, Buddy Bolden, and Louis Armstrong.

Around 1915, when the city of New Orleans began to close down many of the night spots and hangouts that employed jazz musicians, the players began to take their music on the road. Some became part of TERRITORY BANDS, transversing the nation and bringing jazz to many new listeners. Some of the most talented New Orleans musicians took their music to Chicago, including Louis Armstrong and "KING" OLIVER. The first recordings of authentic New Orleans Jazz appeared between 1917 and 1920, but were actually recorded in Chicago.

CHICAGO JAZZ made several changes to the style of jazz played in New Orleans. Most important, the collective improvisation of New Orleans jazz gave way to individual solos, largely because of the remarkable skill of Armstrong.

HOT JAZZ (THE 1920S)

From Chicago, jazz quickly migrated to New York City. New York may not be the birthplace of jazz, but jazz first gained widespread popularity because of the attention brought to it in New York. It was there that jazz became popular on the radio, the making of jazz records first became big business, and competition among jazz bands took a prominent position on the stages of New York nightclubs. The 1920s were joyously dubbed the JAZZ AGE, and the Jazz Age was everything New York.

The first important trend in New York jazz was HOT JAZZ. This was the incendiary style brought to the Big Apple by Louis Armstrong. Hot jazz was fast and exciting, open to experimentation, and freely mixed in the rhythms of other cultures, particularly Cuba and Latin America. Armstrong's Chicago recordings with the HOT FIVE AND HOT SEVEN in the mid-1920s provide a document of this exciting new stage in the history of early jazz. By the end of the 1920s, hot jazz had evolved into the larger ENSEMBLE music called SWING.

Jazz gained a new sophistication while coming of age in New York. Composers such as Duke Ellington

and JAMES P. JOHNSON combined elements of European music with jazz from the South. The arrangements became elegant, and jazz matured as a music with many dimensions for many moods.

Jazz also put down roots in Kansas City, where several big names made their mark during the late 1920s and 1930s. Among them were COUNT BASIE, LESTER YOUNG, Mary Lou Williams, and BENNIE MOTEN. KANSAS CITY JAZZ differed from music being played elsewhere. It didn't use the simultaneous improvisation of the New Orleans style. Nor did it feature the sophisticated arrangements of New York jazz. Instead, it was based on short phrases, or RIFFS, that were repeated over the CHORD CHANGES. It was an easygoing, relaxed style of jazz. This new style led to the widespread popularity of swing jazz in the 1930s.

THE SWING ERA (1930 TO 1945)

Swing was an energetic style of danceable jazz that dominated the early 1930s to late 1940s. It was perhaps America's most popular music of the time. Big bands used multiple reed instruments to create a full-bodied swinging sound. But swing was not just a style of BIG BAND music. The word *swing* also denoted a feeling, an energy, that propelled the music of jazz musicians in big and small groups. It relied on driving rhythms and often complex combinations of melodies, chords, and changing keys to create a sensation that was hard for audience members to resist. Representative swing artists included, Count Basie, Duke Ellington, BENNY GOODMAN Quartet, and GLENN MILLER.

LATIN AND AFRO-CUBAN JAZZ (1945+)

The island of Cuba was a hotbed of LATIN AND AFRO-CUBAN JAZZ in the 1940s and the style soon spread to the United States, where it gained wide popularity. It blends African, Latin, and American musical elements. Dizzy Gillespie was largely responsible for introducing Cuban-influenced jazz to the United States during the 1940s. Another influential Latin jazz musician was MACHITO. He was raised in Cuba and came to New York, where he started his own band with brother-in-law MARIO BAUZÁ and directed the music toward jazzier arrangements combining Cuban melodies and rhythms with swing. Other prominent Afro-Cuban jazz artists have included TITO PUENTE, MONGO SANTAMARIA, and GONZALO RUBALCABA.

THE BEBOP REVOLUTION (1940 TO 1950)

As the swing era drew to a close in the late 1940s, a new style of small group jazz emerged that ushered in the era of modern jazz. BEBOP, or bop, for short, evolved from the high-energy playing of swing groups but emphasized instrumental solos rather than hummable melodies. Bebop was the first jazz not intended for dancing. As such, it marked the transition to the modern jazz era. This jazz style was pioneered by CHARLIE PARKER (alto SAXOPHONE) and Dizzy Gillespie (trumpet) and nurtured by small groups in New York City. Considered experimental at the time, bebop dazzled the listener with blazing beats and complex harmonies. But it perplexed some veterans such as Duke Ellington, who declared that, "Playing bop is like playing Scrabble with all the vowels missing." It was jazz for the thinking person and focused on TECHNIQUE, POLYRHYTHMS, and elaborate solos. Representative bebop artists include Dizzy Gillespie, Charlie Parker, THELONIOUS MONK, KENNY CLARKE, BUD POWELL, and MAX ROACH.

MODERN JAZZ (1950+)

After the emergence of bebop, the evolution of jazz is largely marked by the emergence of new styles that were built on a foundation of classic jazz elements. Along with TRADITIONAL JAZZ, these more contemporary styles combine to create the wonderfully multifaceted world of jazz that we know today.

The most important and influential of these modern jazz styles include:

Hard Bop (the 1950s and 1960s): HARD BOP emerged in the 1950s as a popularized version of bebop. It contained the rhythmic vitality of bop, but freely drew from rhythm and blues to forge a captivating, energetic sound. While solos were a part of hard bop, they were often less confrontational than the in-your-face virtuosity of Gillespie and Parker. It became a mainstream style of jazz that remains the bread and butter of jazz musicians to this day. Representative hard bop artists included ART BLAKEY's Jazz Messengers, Max Roach, HORACE SILVER, SONNY ROLLINS, JIMMY SMITH, and STANLEY TURRENTINE.

Modal Jazz (1955+): A style of jazz pioneered in the 1950s by Miles Davis and John Coltrane. In MODAL JAZZ, improvisations are based on different scales, or modes, rather than chord changes and songlike harmony.

Third Stream and Progressive Jazz (1950+): The term *THIRD STREAM JAZZ* was coined by classical musician GUNTHER SCHULLER in 1957 to describe a fusion of classical music elements with jazz. This is generally a highly composed form of jazz with only minor touches of improvisation. Composers who have dabbled in third stream jazz throughout the decades include PAUL WHITEMAN, ARTIE SHAW, Duke Ellington, STAN KENTON, Gunther Schuller, CHARLES MINGUS, and GEORGE RUSSELL.

Free Jazz and Avant-Garde Jazz (1960+): FREE JAZZ is a style that emerged in the late 1950s and is marked by adventurous and unorthodox approaches to harmony, melody, rhythm, and instrumentation. Free jazz often lacks a regular TEMPO and is freely improvised. Alto saxophone player ORNETTE COLEMAN is credited with introducing free jazz in 1959, although SUN RA also worked in this style a few years earlier.

Cool Jazz (1950 to 1960): Also known as West Coast Jazz, COOL JAZZ is a laid-back style of jazz playing that was widely popular in the 1950s. Cool jazz was a reaction against the bebop style, which the uninitiated music fan found difficult to appreciate. Cool was less explosive, but pleasing to the ear. Influential practitioners included Miles Davis, CHET BAKER, GERRY MULLIGAN, the

Modern Jazz Quartet, LENNIE TRISTANO, and DAVE BRUBECK.

Fusion (1969+): FUSION jazz emerged in the late 1960s as the marriage of jazz and rock music. It came at a time when other forms of jazz were losing the younger audience to rock. It is a highly energized blend of electric rock and jazz instrumentation played with jazz virtuosity. Miles Davis was perhaps the most influential leader of the fusion movement. Other important fusion artists include WEATHER REPORT, Herbie Hancock, JOHN MCLAUGHLIN and THE MAHAVISHNU ORCHESTRA, TONY WILLIAMS, CHICK COREA and Return to Forever, SONNY SHARROCK, and PAT METHENY.

Acid Jazz (1990+): This funky combination of hip-hop, rap, and jazz once again proves that jazz music can have wide appeal to a younger generation. Artists associated with early ACID JAZZ include Brand New Heavies, Incognito, Freak Power, and Jamiroquai. Another form of acid jazz combines the talents of a DJ or remixer with classic jazz tracks from the vaults of classic jazz record companies.

Jazz may be America's music, but its appeal spread rapidly around the world as soon as its earliest recordings began to reach foreign lands. Entries in this encyclopedia recount the history of jazz development around the world through the stories of individual musicians from other countries. Individual histories are also provided for several nations and regions where jazz has made a particularly significant impression:

EUROPEAN JAZZ
Latin and Afro-Cuban Jazz
JAPANESE JAZZ
SOUTH AFRICAN JAZZ

Each of these many styles of jazz emerged for a time to take the jazz-loving public by storm, but none ever completely abandoned what had come before. Nor has the history of jazz progressed mechanically from one style to another. It consists of a body of styles that are the source of continuing ideas and inspiration for every practicing jazz musician. Living jazz is an amalgamation of its own history, a music in which all styles continue to play a role in its growth. This richness of tradition pays great dividends to the inquisitive student of jazz.

Following is a complete list of the major styles of jazz that have individual entries in the *Encyclopedia*. From these entries, you can use cross-references to other styles and artists to broaden your understanding of a given kind of jazz and its practitioners.

JAZZ STYLES

Acid jazz
Avant garde
Bebop
Chicago
Contemporary
Cool jazz
Crossover
Dixieland
Free jazz
Fusion
Hard bop
Hot jazz
Kansas City
Latin and Afro-Cuban
Modal jazz
New Orleans
Progressive
Swing
Third stream

Jazz Instruments

Any instrument can be used to play jazz. It is nearly impossible to name an instrument known anywhere in the world that hasn't been played by a jazz musician. This observation alone suggests that jazz is about the musician and not the instrument. This may be true, but it is also clear that the sound of jazz has been closely associated from the beginning with certain familiar instruments.

In its formative stages following the Civil War, the primordial music that would become jazz was first played mostly by small vocal ensembles backed by BANJOS, violins, and homemade percussion instruments such as washboards. By 1890, marching band instruments had been adopted as the melodic and percussive voices of jazz. Early jazz bands played melodies on the cornet (or trumpet), clarinet, and trombone. Rhythm was provided by a combination of guitar or banjo, drums, double bass, or tuba. One of the first acknowledged jazz bands was led by Buddy Bolden in New Orleans from about 1890 to 1907. His group established the makeup of most early jazz bands. Melody was provided by CORNET (played by Bolden), CLARINET, or valve TROMBONE set to a rhythm played on DOUBLE BASS, GUITAR, and DRUMS. While no recordings of Bolden's group were ever made—his group disbanded after he was confined to an insane asylum in 1907 for smashing a pitcher over his mother-in-law's head—many other New Orleans groups imitated the format and sound that it established.

The PIANO was not a part of the earliest New Orleans jazz bands, which had evolved from marching bands and string bands. But the undeniable popularity of ragtime music and the piano slowly edged its way into jazz music. One reason for this was that musicians playing both ragtime and New Orleans jazz began to play together. There are many recorded examples of music from 1900 to 1915 that combined the styles and instrumentation of New Orleans jazz, ragtime, and marching band music. By 1917, when the first popular jazz recording was made, the pianist had become an important member of the jazz ensemble. Some of the best ragtime piano players established themselves in the same hotels, bars, and brothels as the early jazz ensembles. The piano soon became a familiar element in jazz for underscoring the rhythm of the music and providing another melodic voice. To this mix were added new and novel combinations of instruments, often drawing upon the resources of marching band and orchestral players.

Some instruments have seen their popularity come and go in the world of jazz. While banjos and guitars were frequently the keystone of early rhythm sections, their popularity waned after 1910 as the piano, drums, and double bass played too loudly for them to be heard. While the guitar reestablished itself in the 1930s when it could be amplified, the banjo never really made a comeback in mainstream jazz but remains part of the jazz style known as Dixieland.

Both the double bass and tuba were used to mark the rhythm in early jazz ensembles, the tuba being the preferred instrument of marching bands. Although the string bass was commonly found in jazz ensembles as early as that of Buddy Bolden, its low-frequency tones could not be picked up adequately by the earliest sound recording systems. There was a time during the early 1920s that the stalwart string bass disappeared when a group entered the recording studio. In its place was the tuba, whose louder tones and brassy color were more easily recorded. By the late 1920s, once the technology of electrically amplified recordings was in place, the string bass was back for good.

Aside from the human voice, the most popular instruments of jazz are the SAXOPHONE, TRUMPET, double bass, piano, guitar, and drums. Any listener skimming down the liner notes for a jazz CD will notice a host of variations on this combination of instruments. A greater awareness of WORLD MUSIC and the availability of computer music and SYNTHESIZERS have greatly broadened the audio palette of the jazz ENSEMBLE.

How does an alto saxophone differ from a tenor saxophone? What is a B3 ORGAN? Is a VIBRAPHONE a percussion or melody instrument or both? You will find the answers to these questions by reading individual entries in the encyclopedia for the many instruments commonly used to play jazz.

While reading the encyclopedia you will often notice that some instruments, such as saxophones, come in a variety of tonal ranges. Generally speaking, the larger the instrument the lower its pitch range. The following is a quick guide to the comparative ranges of instruments, from the lowest to the highest range.

Low					High
Contrabass	Bass	Baritone	Tenor	Alto	Soprano

Following is a quick guide to entries for jazz instruments that are found in the *Encyclopedia*. They are described according to their familiar roles in a jazz band.

INSTRUMENTS PRIMARILY USED FOR RHYTHM AND ACCOMPANIMENT; SECONDARILY USED FOR MELODIES

Banjo
Bass guitar
Double bass
Drums
Vibraphone

INSTRUMENTS PRIMARILY USED FOR MELODY AND ACCOMPANIMENT

Clarinet
Cornet
Flugelhorn
Flute
French horn
Pocket trumpet
Saxophone
Trombone
Trumpet
Violin

INSTRUMENTS USED EQUALLY FOR RHYTHM, MELODY, AND ACCOMPANIMENT

Electronic keyboard
Guitar
Organ
Piano
Synthesizer

Listening to Jazz

Jazz has an undeserved reputation as being difficult to appreciate, especially if one is not well informed about its artists, history, and influences. While knowing some of those things may make your listening better informed, all it really takes to enjoy jazz is a good set of ears and the ability to feel.

A jazz performance is about as close as you'll ever get to pure emotional expression in music. The instrument becomes a vocalization of the artist's inner self, articulating experience with unmatched clarity of feeling. Those who love jazz, however, also like to explore various styles and periods of the music. After honing good listening skills, knowing more about the traditions and methods that go into creating jazz will certainly further one's enjoyment.

An appreciation of jazz begins by learning how to listen to it. Describing jazz in words is an infinitely more difficult task. The great jazz piano player Thelonious Monk, himself a man of few words, once allegedly proclaimed that "writing about music is like dancing about architecture." This is a challenge for any book about jazz.

This encyclopedia avoids unnecessary jargon but also includes entries for many musical terms that are basic to the language of music and jazz. You will find these terms in the A to Z entries and also as cross-references within the entries themselves. These entries should give you the basic musical vocabulary needed for exploring and appreciating jazz and discussing it with others.

A full appreciation of jazz will come if you listen for certain elements. Jazz is crafty and smart—it embodies the thinking of the musician who crafts an improvisation as it unfolds and the thinking of the listener who can recognize the work that goes into making good jazz. Here are a few tips to keep in mind while listening to jazz.

♦ **Follow the sound of one instrument.** Jazz is composed of several players performing at the same time. It has many layers. Try and pick out one instrument and focus on what that musician is doing. Then listen to another musician. How do the two interact with each other?

◆ **Concentrate on the unity and direction of the music.** A jazz work unfolds step by step. Can you recognize a CHORD pattern, a regular TEMPO, or a melody as it is introduced? Do the musicians repeat certain parts, or CHORUS? Or, is the music free flowing, never repeating a recognizable structure?

◆ **Separate the musical parts.** Jazz generally consists of a rhythm section that accompanies the soloist. A rhythm section may consist only of a bass player and drummer but often has another instrument capable of playing chords, such as a piano or guitar. The soloist, or LEAD voice, is usually a horn or saxophone player, although any other instrument capable of playing notes may be used. Note the interplay between the rhythm section and the soloist.

◆ **How much of the music is composed, how much is improvised?** A typical jazz work begins with a composed section, such as a popular song, that introduces the chords and melody of the piece. After this, one or more soloists may be allowed to improvise over the rhythm and chords established in the opening section. Just how this improvisation unfolds may vary with every performance. Listen for any of the following to occur:

  ◆ A musician may play a written melody but use expression (e.g., attack, volume, VIBRATO, note bending, rhythm) to vary it considerably.

  ◆ The improviser may be free to change the melody radically until it barely resembles the original. However, there is usually some method to what may sound like a radical departure. The musicians may be playing the same notes of the melody, but with different accents. They may be playing against the same chords but adding many of their own notes in between those of the written melody. Even more radical, they may be playing all around the written melody, never hitting one of the

original notes but creating a new melody that is only reminiscent of the written one.

  ◆ Performers may improvise together, or collectively, creating an entirely unique musical performance. The players may establish rules ahead of time about how the improvisation will unfold. For example, the rhythm section may play a persistent chord progression and tempo on top of which two or more players freely improvise.

  ◆ There may be no written music at all, and the players may be free to play whatever they like. However, even in this seemingly out-of-control situation, there are generally a few ground rules laid down ahead of time. Can you tell what they might be?

◆ **Listen to the rhythm.** The beat is the driving force behind jazz. The rhythm often has as much importance as the melody and harmony. This is certainly true in listening to hot jazz, swing, bop, and hard bop. Notice how the ensemble rallies around the rhythm to build excitement and how the soloists inject their own rhythms to complement the rest of the group. There is also some jazz that is essentially without rhythm, at least in the conventional sense. Free jazz may not have a regular beat at all, yet the players can create moments of extreme intensity and drive, moving the music ahead with an organic sense of rhythm. When listening to free jazz, pay particular attention to what the bass player and drummer do, since they are normally required to hold the music together. In the absence of a steady tempo, the ability to play out of beat is perhaps the supreme challenge for a gifted rhythm player.

◆ **Make note of variation.** Music unfolds moment by moment. Remember what has been played and notice whether the same material is repeated in the same way. Jazz musicians can vary the music through a number of techniques: changing the tempo, changing the melody, changing the chords, adding silence, playing louder, adding expression to the notes, and many other methods. How completely does a work get recomposed with each repetition?

◆ **How do the players interact?** Rapport among jazz musicians is essential to quality play. You will note that jazz players are good listeners. They must pay attention to the other players and in some cases are asked to respond in kind with a SOLO or flourish that ties the sound together.

Women in Jazz

Women have been a part of jazz history from the beginning, yet their contributions have almost always been overshadowed by those of male musicians. Open a jazz book or look through a rack of jazz CDs and you will see very few female faces staring back at you. If you were to say out loud to your friends, "There were hundreds of all-woman bands," the reaction you would probably get would be one of disbelief.[2]

But not only have there been many all-female bands, there have been many accomplished women composers, arrangers, bandleaders, and instrumentalists who have worked alongside men and contributed significantly to jazz history.

The first female jazz artists who come to mind are usually the popular singers who rose to prominence in front of big bands during the swing era of the 1930s to 1940s. They include BILLIE HOLIDAY, Ella Fitzgerald, SARAH VAUGHN, BETTY CARTER, and CARMEN MCRAE to name a few. A second group of accomplished women in jazz includes prominent composers and piano players such as LIL HARDIN, Mary Lou Williams, DOROTHY DONEGAN, MARIAN MCPARTLAND, and CARLA BLEY. Their success was made easier because they excelled at singing or playing piano, two musical talents that were deemed socially acceptable for women. But success for women in jazz is never assured. There have been hundreds of other female jazz instrumentalists who never had the same opportunity as men to succeed in this field.

The extraordinary accomplishments of these and other women in jazz did not come easy. Why is this? Common beliefs about a woman's proper role in society were one reason. Another was that men controlled the jazz world and were reluctant to share it with women.

Discrimination by gender is deeply rooted in American culture. Men and women are raised with certain expectations about how best to behave. The roles people play in life as men and women are influenced by the views of family, friends, and the mass media. Why did men put up barriers to women in jazz? Why do they do it still? In the past a woman's success was measured by her accomplishments as a mother, while a man's success was measured by the amount of money he earned. It was not considered ladylike for women to hang out in jazz clubs or travel with male bands. It was okay for women to play piano and string instruments, but it was thought that they did not have the stamina to play wind instruments or drums. But possibly the key obstacle to women working in jazz was this: It was believed that if a woman worked, she did so at the expense of a man who had a family to feed.

While these ideas may seem laughable now, they were part of the inspiration behind the hard-fought women's rights movement that began more than a hundred years ago. During the 20th century, North American women fought to gain equal rights in voting and jobs. Women were successful in achieving equal footing with men in the courts, but even now the battle to experience equal treatment at work and in society is still being fought. Compared to men, women still hold fewer public offices and are paid less than men for doing the same work.

Women have had to fight for respect in jazz for many of the same reasons that they fought for equal rights in the voting booth and workplace. The world of music, especially that of jazz music, has always been a stronghold of male control.

For a woman to succeed in the field of jazz, she not only had to be an excellent musician, she also had to fight an entrenched male culture that challenged her at every turn. The pattern was set during the early days of jazz. Men played the instruments. Men composed the music. Men led the bands. Men managed the jazz clubs where the bands played. The record companies that made jazz records were owned and operated by men. Male critics put their stamp of approval on the music.

Faced with so many obstacles, it is all the more remarkable that women have achieved success during every era of jazz as composers, instrumentalists, bandleaders, and singers.

SHAKING THINGS UP

In the earliest days of jazz records, from about 1920 to 1930, the top-selling artists were female blues singers. MAMIE SMITH made the first blues record in 1920 and was soon followed by other talented African-American singers, including BESSIE SMITH, MA RAINEY, and Ethel Waters. These women not only had drawing power at the box office, but also surrounded themselves with the best male instrumental talent they could find. Many of their recordings featured the hottest jazz musicians around. In a reversal of gender roles, such great male musicians as Louis Armstrong, SIDNEY BECHET, COLEMAN HAWKINS, James P. Johnson, and FLETCHER HENDERSON can be heard playing *backup* on those recordings. The ladies ruled.

Following the success of female singers, other women began to take up instruments and play jazz. Many stuck to the piano, but others took up every conceivable jazz instrument, including the trumpet, saxophone, clarinet, double bass, guitar, trombone, and drums. One of the most accomplished female jazz musicians of the early jazz era was Lil Hardin. She was already a talented piano player by age 19 and joined Joe "King" Oliver's Original Creole Jazz Band in 1917 in Chicago. After leading her own band for a spell in 1920, she toured with King Oliver's band until it returned to Chicago in 1924. While she was with King Oliver, she met and married the second cornetist in the band, one Louis Armstrong. Hardin persuaded

her husband to move to New York to lead his own band, and there he became firmly established as the leading practitioner of hot jazz. Even though Armstrong's rapidly growing fame eclipsed that of Hardin, she succeeded in nurturing her own career as a major songwriter and musician. She was certainly accepted as a player by the guys and performed with Armstrong's outstanding recording groups, the Hot Five and Hot Seven, in the mid-1920s. She led an all-female jazz band in 1931 and opened many doors for female jazz musicians.

Many accomplished female jazz musicians took to the stage during the 1920s and 1930s. Most worked in obscurity, struggling to compete with their male counterparts. In addition to Hardin, other piano players included the New Orleans stylists EMMA BARRETT and Dolly Adams. There was a trumpet playing mother-and-daughter team, Dyer and Dolly Jones. The first all-female COMBO and big bands also sprung up around this time, including Bobbie Howell's American Syncopators, Edna White's Trombone Quartet, The Dixie Sweethearts, and Bobbie Grice's Fourteen Bricktops.[3]

Most of these bands were composed of African-American women, but there soon arose a number of white all-girl bands as well.

During the 1930s, COMPOSER, ARRANGER, and piano player Mary Lou Williams made her mark on the sound of Kansas City jazz. As a composer, she was the equal of Duke Ellington. Her piano playing was as skilled as the best swing and STRIDE players. Her curiosity and intellect guided her through a lifelong adventure of experiment and mastery of many jazz styles. Lesser known jazz women from the 1930s include alto saxophone player Josephine Boyd, tenor sax player Margaret Backstrom, and trumpet players "TINY" DAVIS and Valaida Snow.

During World War II, when many male musicians went off to war, the interest in all-women big bands surged. Some were novelty acts, organized by men, such as Phil Spitalny and his All Girl Orchestra. But others, including the INTERNATIONAL SWEETHEARTS OF RHYTHM and Ina Ray Hutton and Her Melodears were serious big bands that traveled widely. The International Sweethearts of Rhythm were not only all female, but interracial as well, an aspect of the group that made a lasting impression on many who saw them.

After World War II, the craze for all-female big bands died down with the demise of all the big bands. Even so, women had succeeded in breaking the gender barrier in jazz. Society is still trying to catch up with them in many ways. While it is not so shocking these days to see a woman instrumentalist playing jazz, male artists continue to dominate the club scene, concerts, and sales of jazz CDs.

CONTEMPORARY WOMEN JAZZ ARTISTS

Information about many influential women jazz artists can be found in the main entries of this encyclopedia. As a supplement to those entries, the following list is offered of prominent contemporary women jazz artists. Their instruments and group affiliations are shown. All of these musicians have recorded extensively.

The names of players who have their own entry in the encyclopedia are shown in all caps.

TOSHIKO AKIYOSHI (b. 1929) piano player, composer

Astoria Big Band (founded 1986) largely female big band founded by baritone saxophone player Carol Sudhalter

Clora Bryant trumpet player

Terry Lyne Carrington (b. 1965) drummer, composer, and producer

Carol Chaikin alto saxophone player, educator, York Quartet

Kim Clarke double bass and electric bass player, Magnets

Sylvia Cuenca drummer, The Crossing

Jean Davis trumpet player, Big Apple Jazz-women; Jazz Sisters

DIVA (founded 1995) all-female 15-piece big band led by drummer Sherrie Maricle

Akua Dixon cello player

Fostina Dixon saxophone player, educator, Winds of Change Rhythm & Blues Orchestra

Rebecca Coupe Franks trumpet player

Nnenna Freelon (b. 1954) singer

Jane Getter guitar player

Kellye Gray singer

Jane Jarvis piano player

Marian McPartland (b. 1918) piano player, composer

Trudy Pitts organ player

Carline Ray bass player, singer

Rene Rosnes piano player and composer, soloist, the Danish Radio Big Band, The Drummonds

ANNIE ROSS singer

Viola Smit drummer

Sumi Tonooka (b. 1956) piano player, composer, educator

Quick Guide to Jazz Styles and Artists

The history of jazz is contained in the stories of the people who created it. This encyclopedia presents individual entries on the jazz artists, places, and styles that have been most important to its history. The text is rich with cross-references to lead you from one entry to another in order to form a complete picture of a person, his or her music, and the predominant styles of jazz through the years.

The following outline sketches the broad history of jazz by period and some of the corresponding individuals and entries that can be found in the A-to-Z listings. Start with these entries and then use the abundant cross-references to complete your exploration of a given jazz topic. Not every entry in the encyclopedia is included in this list—just the starting points. With some exceptions, the list emphasizes bandleaders rather than sidemen. Some names are repeated for individuals who made a significant impact during more than one era of jazz history.

NEW ORLEANS JAZZ AND EARLY JAZZ
(1900 TO 1920)

EMMA BARRETT
SIDNEY BECHET
BUDDY BOLDEN
JAMES REESE EUROPE
W. C. HANDY
FREDDIE KEPPARD
JAMES P. JOHNSON
JELLY ROLL MORTON
KING OLIVER
ORIGINAL DIXIELAND JAZZ BAND
KID ORY
MAMIE SMITH
FATS WALLER

HOT JAZZ (THE 1920s)

LOUIS ARMSTRONG
LOVIE AUSTIN
BIX BEIDERBECKE
BENNY CARTER
DUKE ELLINGTON
LIL HARDIN
COLEMAN HAWKINS
FLETCHER HENDERSON
EARL "FATHA" HINES
EDDIE LANG
FRANKIE TRUMBAUER

THE SWING ERA (1930 TO 1945)

IVIE ANDERSON
COUNT BASIE
BENNY CARTER
TOMMY DORSEY
JIMMY DORSEY
DUKE ELLINGTON
ELLA FITZGERALD
BENNY GOODMAN
LIONEL HAMPTON
COLEMAN HAWKINS
FLETCHER HENDERSON
WOODY HERMAN
BILLIE HOLIDAY
GLENN MILLER

DJANGO REINHARDT
ARTIE SHAW
BEN WEBSTER
ART TATUM
LESTER YOUNG

THE BEBOP REVOLUTION (1940 TO 1950)

BARBARA CARROLL
CHARLIE CHRISTIAN
KENNY CLARKE
DIZZY GILLESPIE
BENNY GOODMAN
THELONIOUS MONK
CHARLIE PARKER
BUD POWELL
SARAH VAUGHN
MARY LOU WILLIAMS

AFRO-CUBAN AND LATIN JAZZ (1945+)

CHICO O'FARRILL
RUBEN GONZALEZ
TITO PUENTE
GONZALO RUBALCABA
ARTURO SANDOVAL
COMPAY SEGUNDO

HARD BOP ERA (THE 1950s AND 1960s)

ART BLAKEY
CLIFFORD BROWN
BETTY CARTER
JOHN COLTRANE
MILES DAVIS
DOROTHY DONEGAN
BILL EVANS
DIZZY GILLESPIE
THAD JONES
MEL LEWIS
OSCAR PETERSON
CHARLES MINGUS
THELONIOUS MONK
SONNY ROLLINS
WAYNE SHORTER
HORACE SILVER
SUN RA
MARY LOU WILLIAMS

MODAL JAZZ (1955+)

JOHN COLTRANE
MILES DAVIS
GEORGE RUSSELL

THIRD STREAM AND PROGRESSIVE JAZZ (1950+)

DUKE ELLINGTON
GIL EVANS
STAN KENTON
CHARLES MINGUS
MODERN JAZZ QUARTET
GUNTHER SCHULLER
ARTIE SHAW
MARY LOU WILLIAMS

FREE JAZZ AND AVANT-GARDE JAZZ (1960+)

MUHAL RICHARD ABRAMS
ART ENSEMBLE OF CHICAGO
ED BLACKWELL
CARLA BLEY
JOANNE BRACKEEN
ANTHONY BRAXTON
DON CHERRY
ORNETTE COLEMAN
JOHN COLTRANE
ERIC DOLPHY
HERBIE HANCOCK
GEORGE LEWIS
MICHAEL MANTLER
GEORGE RUSSELL
PHAROAH SANDERS
SUN RA
CECIL TAYLOR
JOHN ZORN

COOL JAZZ (1950 TO 1960)

CHET BAKER
DAVE BRUBECK
MILES DAVIS
STAN GETZ
GERRY MULLIGAN

FUSION (1969+)

MICHAEL BRECKER
RANDY BRECKER
CHICK COREA
MILES DAVIS
AL DI MEOLA
HERBIE HANCOCK
JOHN MCLAUGHLIN
PAT METHENY
WAYNE SHORTER
JOE ZAWINUL

CONTEMPORARY (1980+)

CINDY BLACKMAN
MICHAEL BRECKER
RANDY BRECKER
JIM CIFELLI
CHICK COREA
BARBARA DENNERLEIN
DIVA
EITHER/ORCHESTRA
HERBIE HANCOCK
SHIRLEY HORN
KEITH JARRETT
INGRID JENSEN
DIANA KRALL
BRANFORD MARSALIS
WYNTON MARSALIS
KIT MCCLURE
JOHN MCLAUGHLIN
PAT METHENY
MARCUS MILLER
MINGUS BIG BAND
DIANE REEVES
DAVID SANBORN
MARIA SCHNEIDER
WAYNE SHORTER
CASSANDRA WILSON
JOHN ZORN

A-to-Z Entries

AAB

An abbreviation for a song form most commonly associated with the BLUES. It is a 12-bar song, the first A and B being four bars and the second A being eight bars.

AABA

An abbreviation for a song form. It is a 32-bar song divided into four equal eight-bar parts. The letter A stands for the first theme, which is played twice. It is followed by the B part, or second theme, which is played once. The song then concludes with the main theme again.

Abercrombie, John (b. 1944) *American guitarist*

Abercrombie is an accomplished guitarist who blends jazz and rock influences. He is a graduate of the BERKLEE COLLEGE OF MUSIC. Abercrombie learned his licks during the early years of FUSION jazz while playing with several mainstream jazz artists. These included CHICO HAMILTON, GIL EVANS, and GATO BARBIERI. After two successful collaborations with top-notch drummers in the 1970s, BILLY COBHAM and JACK DEJOHNETTE, he started the first of several trios and quartets that he has led over the years. One of the most critically successful of these is the trio Gateway, featuring DeJohnette and bassist DAVE HOLLAND. Abercrombie is a sought-after musician with agility and adaptability. He can play many jazz styles. His use of effects, such as distortion and volume controls, is tasteful and imaginative. Even when using electronic effects, however, the inescapable originality and skill with which he plays always emerges as the focal point of his music. He is also a talented teacher. When faced with playing jazz standards, Abercrombie finds a way to free himself from the ways that these songs have been played in the past. "I still enjoy playing them," he says. "And because I know them so well, I'm very free with them. I'm just as free with them as when I'm playing no chords at all. That, to me, is free jazz."[4]

Abrams, Muhal Richard (b. 1930) *American pianist, composer, educator*

Abrams grew up in Chicago and in the 1960s and 1970s became a leading force in reviving that city's prominence as a laboratory for new jazz sounds. He learned music at the Chicago Music College and was composing and arranging music for bands by 1948. During the 1950s he worked as a SIDEMAN in Chicago for such notables as MILES DAVIS, SONNY ROLLINS, and MAX ROACH.[5]

In 1961 he started his own BIG BAND, The Experimental Band, with Eddie Harris. This outfit was a laboratory for his compositional ideas and his early attempt to combine a European style of classical music composition with TRADITIONAL JAZZ. This led to his growing interest in IMPROVISATION and new jazz sounds.

In 1965 he formed the ASSOCIATION FOR THE ADVANCEMENT OF CREATIVE MUSICIANS (AACM) and expanded access to his jazz workshops to the

Muhal Richard Abrams

came from the BOP tradition, his music has a more surprising feel, using TRADITIONAL JAZZ ensembles to explore new sounds. His tendency to experiment is reminiscent of the tamer work of SUN RA, CHARLES MINGUS, and ORNETTE COLEMAN. At the forefront of Abrams's sound is an unpredictable use of rhythm. Solos and improvisations in his music often project the mood of a work rather than the athletic urgency of bop music. Free improvisation is key to his sound, and each performance is an experiment to which the audience is witness. Abrams's big band work is perhaps his most notable. His compositions in the 1980s echoed his interest in the many traditions of jazz. *Blues Forever* (1981) was reminiscent of DUKE ELLINGTON's ENSEMBLE work. *View from Within* (1985) was colored by the BLUES. *The Hearinga Suite* (1989), for an 18-piece jazz orchestra, resounded with sounds and rhythms from the whole history of big bands.

accent
To emphasize a beat or note by playing it louder or more sharply.

acid jazz
A style of jazz with roots in the 1980s. It fuses elements of TRADITIONAL JAZZ with funk/hip-hop rhythms and techno to produce an infectious, melodious groove. Early acid jazz arose in England as a reaction to "acid house" dance music. Artists associated with acid jazz include Brand New Heavies, Incognito, Freak Power, and Jamiroquai. The evolution of acid jazz in the United States was also influenced by MILES DAVIS's experiments with FUSION jazz and funk/hip-hop–inspired albums *On The Corner* (1972) and *Doo Bop* (1992). Another form of acid jazz combines the talents of a remixer with classic jazz tracks from the vaults of classic jazz record companies. In these cases, the remixer samples parts of classic jazz tracks and adds new rhythms and music to give it a hip-hop beat and contemporary feel. Two successful recordings

broader CHICAGO JAZZ community. Although an accomplished PIANO player and COMPOSER, he is now best known as an important jazz mentor and educator. The AACM sponsored concerts and festivals. It became an influential force in the lives of young black jazz musicians in Chicago during a time of social unrest and racial tension. Abrams encouraged musicians to improve their craft through study and understanding of the whole tradition of jazz. He also gave them hope and a way to rise above the hardships of their poor communities. Many leading jazz groups and musicians got their start with the AACM, including the ART ENSEMBLE OF CHICAGO, LEROY JENKINS, and ANTHONY BRAXTON.

Abrams has composed and performed as a soloist and for many sizes of groups. Although he produced this way include *Hand on the Torch* (1993) by Us3 and *Verve Remixed* (2002), produced by Dahlia Ambach Caplin and Jason Olaine.

Adams, Pepper (1930–1986) *American baritone saxophone player*

The career of baritone saxophonist Pepper Adams ran parallel to that of fellow baritone player GERRY MULLIGAN, and Adams always seemed to be in Mulligan's shadow, despite their uniquely different musical styles. Mulligan was known for the cool, laid-back sound of West Coast jazz. Adams played with explosive power and intensity. During the 1950s, Adams established himself as an important member of the hot Detroit jazz scene. He toured with MAYNARD FERGUSON and STAN KENTON. After moving to New York in 1958, he worked with BENNY GOODMAN and CHARLES MINGUS. He was a stalwart member of the monumental THAD JONES–MEL LEWIS Orchestra of studio musicians from 1965 to 1978. "We called him 'The Knife,'" said bandleader Mel Lewis of Adams, "because when he'd get up to blow, his playing had almost a slashing effect on the rest of us. He'd slash, chop, and before he was through, cut everybody down to size."[6]

Pepper's sharp playing style blended well with the bright, lyrical trumpet playing of DONALD BYRD, with whom he had worked in Detroit. Pepper coled a fiery HARD BOP quintet with Byrd off and on between 1958 and 1962 and again as a reunion effort in 1967, resulting in some of the pair's most brilliant recordings.

Adderley, Cannonball (Julian Edwin Adderley) (1928–1975) *American alto and soprano saxophone player and composer*

Cannonball Adderley was a big man with a big heart and an even bigger sound. He is noted for popularizing a style of music that combined elements of soul music and jazz, a precursor of the funky jazz sound that is so much a part of today's jazz idiom. Adderley grew up in Florida, where he was part of a talented family of musicians. He formed his first jazz band while still in high school. After serving in the army, and leading several military bands, he went to New York in 1955 to seek a career in music. His nickname, Cannonball, is derived from "cannibal," a name once given to him by his friends because of his huge appetite.[7]

In the mid-1950s, Miles Davis made him a part of one of his legendary quintets, with which Adderley played alongside JOHN COLTRANE. He appeared on the landmark albums *KIND OF BLUE* and *Milestones*. Influenced largely by the work of BENNY CARTER and CHARLIE PARKER, Adderley etched out his own identity as a proponent of soul-tinged jazz saxophone. His recording of the song "Mercy, Mercy, Mercy" (1966), composed by his quintet's piano player, Joe Zawinul, was a hit on popular music radio stations. Adderley was a regular winner in popular jazz polls throughout the 1960s, is responsible for getting big breaks for such musicians as WES MONTGOMERY and CHUCK MANGIONE, and was a well-spoken representative of jazz. He sometimes taught jazz workshops at universities. Adderley died young of a stroke, just after completing a recording of *Big Man*, a musical about the life of legendary railroad worker John Henry.

Akiyoshi, Toshiko (b. 1929) *Japanese piano player, composer, and bandleader*

Akiyoshi is an innovative bandleader who successfully blends elements of traditional Japanese music with American-style jazz. Akiyoshi's father was an actor in traditional Japanese Noh drama and encouraged his three daughters to learn PIANO and other arts. Her first exposure to jazz came after World War II through the music played by occupying American troops. By age 16, she was working for a jazz dance band. By 1952 she had founded her own band, and in 1953 made a recording in Tokyo for Norman Granz. Encouraged by piano player OSCAR PETERSON, she came to the United States in 1956 to attend the BERKLEE COLLEGE OF MUSIC on a full scholarship. Like many other female jazz players, she faced racial and sexual prejudice during her early years in America. To counter this reaction from her audience, she recalled playing "clubs and TV wearing a kimono, because people were amazed to see an Oriental woman playing jazz."[8]

After college, she met Charlie Mariano (reeds) and coled a QUARTET with him.

During the 1960s she worked in small group and BIG BAND settings with CHARLES MINGUS, shuttled between Japan and the United States giving performances and holding clinics, hosted a jazz radio program in New York (1967–68), and premiered as a COMPOSER and conductor at Town Hall in New York in 1967. For the latter, she presented works for solo PIANO, jazz trio, and big band. Since marrying her second husband, Lew Tabackin (reeds and FLUTE), in 1969, she has concentrated on composing for large and small ensembles. The Toshiko Akiyoshi Jazz Orchestra features her husband, Lew Tabackin, as featured soloist and has gained worldwide acclaim since its formation in 1973. In 1999 she premiered a big band suite at the MONTEREY JAZZ FESTIVAL marking the 100th anniversary of DUKE ELLINGTON's birth. Akiyoshi has a reputation as a highly original composer on the scale of

Toshiko Akiyoshi

Ellington. Her work uniquely combines elements of Japanese musical scales and traditional instruments with American SWING.

American Jazz Museum

Located in Kansas City, Missouri, the home of early swing, the museum features exhibits, a research center, recording studio, and nightclub. Several exhibits are dedicated to the life and times of LOUIS ARMSTRONG, DUKE ELLINGTON, ELLA FITZGERALD, CHARLIE PARKER and Kansas City jazz. Their Web site is located at http://www.americanjazzmuseum.com.

American Jazz Music (1939)

This book by Wilder Hobson (published by W. W. Norton) is one of the earliest critical studies of jazz in book form.

Anderson, Ivie (1905–1949) *American singer for the Duke Ellington Orchestra from 1931 to 1942*

This elegant lady was arguably the best ever to sing for the DUKE ELLINGTON Orchestra. Her cool style and lively expression were showcased on some of the Duke's most popular recordings. One of these was "IT DON'T MEAN A THING (IF IT AIN'T GOT THAT SWING)". She had a strong voice that blended well with the horn section. As part of the Ellington show, she would trade phrases with the band's drummer. Anderson could also mesmerize audiences with her warm vocal style. According to Ellington, she "stopped the show" during a 1933 performance of the song "Stormy Weather" in London.[9]

She suffered from asthma, which forced her to retire from singing in 1942 and led to her early death.

And His Mother Called Him Bill (1967) *album recorded by Duke Ellington*

The "Bill" in the title was BILLY STRAYHORN, DUKE ELLINGTON's songwriting, arranging, and PIANO playing partner from 1939 to 1967, when Strayhorn died after a prolonged illness. As was often the case throughout Ellington's life, when he was gripped by the sorrow of personal loss, he usually turned to music to get himself back in step again. The result in this case is a touching tribute showcasing a full spectrum of Strayhorn numbers. For the recording SESSION, Ellington assembled many of his band members from the old days. Some of the works have titles that bespeak the final drawn-out months of Strayhorn's life spent in and out of hospitals, "Blood Count," and "U.M.M.G," which stands for the Upper Manhattan Medical Group. The 19 tracks of music range from the rollicking joy ride of "U.M.M.G" to the BIG BAND SWING of "Snibor" and the mournful Johnny Hodges alto SAXOPHONE SOLO

on "Blood Count." Some of the Duke's players on this record might not sound as sharp as they did in the old days, but the sense of loss expressed on these tracks communicates directly and uniquely from the heart.

Armstrong, Lil   See LIL HARDIN.

Armstrong, Louis (1901–1971) *American trumpeter, composer, singer, and bandleader*
Arguably the best jazz trumpeter ever and without argument the most influential musician of the classic era of early jazz, Louis Armstrong's originality and

Ivie Anderson and the Duke Ellington Orchestra

charisma were largely responsible for the growing popularity of jazz across color boundaries during the 1920s and 1930s. He was the first great jazz soloist, an inventor in sound who lifted the voice of the individual above the group. His ability to improvise stunning melodies was unmatched. He was known for both his joyous ways with the TRUMPET and his peculiarly touching and funny vocal style.

The great "Satchmo" began singing on the streets of New Orleans as a teenager. He soon learned to play the CORNET (later the trumpet) and found himself showing off alongside many of the greats of the NEW ORLEANS JAZZ scene. In 1922 he joined a group led by JOE "KING" OLIVER in Chicago, a father figure to Armstrong and possibly the only other musician who was able to teach him something new. By 1925 Armstrong's fame was spreading, and he recorded several landmark 78 rpm records on the OKeh label in Chicago. Soloing with his groups, the HOT FIVE AND HOT SEVEN, these recordings established jazz as a soloist's art. His recording of "HEEBIE JEEBIES" became famous for Armstrong's SCAT SINGING, which he said he did when he forgot the lyrics. He played with big bands until about 1947 and then returned to the small group format. Armstrong's All Stars delighted in playing familiar pop tunes with a classic jazz and New Orleans SWING. Armstrong was a tireless performer, frequently toured Europe where he was equally beloved, and frequently broke into the pop music charts with recordings such as "Hello Dolly" and "What a Wonderful World."

Having grown up with virtually nothing, he aspired to be accepted and exuded joy and humor in his music. His was a big, happy sound, full of round, powerful tones, and unequaled range. He was a testament to the universal appeal of jazz and its leading spokesman throughout his career. How good was he? No less an authority than DUKE ELLINGTON said of him, "There weren't words coined to describe that kind of kick. Louis carried his horn around and sat in and played anywhere he happened to drop in. Everybody on the street was talking about the guy."[10]

WYNTON MARSALIS calls him one of the "most beloved and influential artists in the history of music."[11]

He died in his sleep, reportedly with a smile on his face. When asked about how a person can learn to play jazz, Armstrong quipped, "We all do 'do, re, mi,' but you have got to find the other notes yourself."

arrangement

The written adaptation of a musical work for an ENSEMBLE of musicians. An arrangement will include parts for each musician to play. It determines when an instrument will play, which notes are played when, when harmonies and solos occur, and indicate when IMPROVISATION may take place. An arrangement comprises charts, or individual sheets of music, for each musician, showing his or her parts. One musical composition may have many arrangements, depending on how many musicians are needed to play it and how the ARRANGER wants the music to sound. When a piece originally written for only a few musicians is arranged for a larger ensemble, additional parts may need to be composed for the additional players.

arranger

The person who writes a musical arrangement for a composition. Some of the titans of jazz arrangement include DUKE ELLINGTON, FLETCHER HENDERSON, BENNY CARTER, and GIL EVANS.

Art Ensemble of Chicago

This American AVANT-GARDE jazz ENSEMBLE was formed in 1969 by saxophonist ROSCOE MITCHELL (b. 1940) and trumpeter LESTER BOWIE (1941–99) with bassist MALACHI FAVORS (1937–2004), saxophonist Joseph Jarman (b. 1937), and drummer Don Moye (b. 1946), who joined in 1970. The original AEC was America's foremost avant-garde jazz ensemble for 30 years until the death of Favors in 2004. The group blended FREE JAZZ TECHNIQUE with classic jazz and African music. The group's innovative and ever-changing music is difficult to categorize. Members were as likely to play their instruments in a traditional style as well as embark on surreal squealing and squawking expressions with humor, defiance, and a smart edginess. As experimentalists, they embraced the use of high energy playing punctuated by long silences. They often mixed TRADITIONAL JAZZ instruments with exotic instruments, including piccolo, gongs, African percussion, and baritone and bass SAXOPHONES.

Association for the Advancement of Creative Musicians

During the 1960s Chicago became a hotbed of innovative jazz thinking and experimentation. COMPOSER and musician MUHAL RICHARD ABRAMS founded the Association for the Advancement of Creative Musicians (AACM) in 1965 as a means of joining many local players into a cooperative legion of jazz experimenters. The AACM sponsored concerts and festivals, taught workshops, and supported a loose-knit networks of jazz ENSEMBLES of various sizes, including Abram's own Experimental Band. Abrams encouraged musicians to improve their craft through study and understand the whole tradition of jazz. Musicians who were associated with the AACM included ANTHONY BRAXTON, trumpeter Leo Smith, violinist LEROY JENKINS, and members of the Art Ensemble of Chicago.

"A-Tisket A-Tasket" (1938)

Recorded performance by CHICK WEBB and his Orchestra featuring ELLA FITZGERALD and released by Decca. How does an unabashedly noncommercial bandleader like Chick Webb suddenly produce a hit record? By giving a young singer Ella Fitzgerald a chance to front the band. Webb's hard-driving rhythm and horn section were the perfect complement to Fitzgerald's inspired rendition of a familiar children's song. She breaks form right from the start by varying the melody and never looks back. It's a jumping record that shows off Fitzgerald's great range, coy style, and interplay with the band.

Austin, Lovie (1887–1972) *American piano player, composer, and bandleader*

Lovie Austin (Cora Calhoun) was a trendsetter for African-American women during the early days of jazz. Prior to 1920 she was a popular vaudeville actor and performer on the circuit of the Theater Owners Booking Association (T.O.B.A.). T.O.B.A. booked and promoted African-American singers and entertainers during the heyday of vaudeville. Leading her own group, the Blues Serenaders, Austin became musical director of the Monogram Theater in Chicago and musical director for Paramount Records. Both jobs gave her the chance to accompany many of the top singing stars of the day, including ALBERTA HUNTER, ETHEL WATERS, and MA RAINEY. Austin recorded with the Blues Serenaders and had a long and successful career in jazz. The great MARY LOU WILLIAMS cited Austin as her greatest influence, saying "I remember seeing this great woman sitting in the pit and conducting a group of five or six men, her legs crossed, a cigarette in her mouth, playing the show with her left hand and writing music with her right. Wow! I never forgot this episode. . . . She was a fabulous woman and a fabulous musician too. I don't believe there's a woman around now who could compete with her. She was a greater talent than many of the men of this period."[12]

avant-garde

Jazz music using experimental and nontraditional approaches to musical structure, instrumentation, and performance. Avant-garde composers often borrow ideas from contemporary classical music to alter the way that rhythm, harmony, melody, and ARRANGEMENT are used in jazz. It is largely a composed form of jazz, which distinguishes it from FREE JAZZ. Proponents of avant-garde jazz include ANTHONY BRAXTON, CARLA BLEY, and CECIL TAYLOR.

Bad Plus, The

American jazz trio founded in New York in 2001 by longtime musician friends Ethan Iverson (PIANO), Reid Anderson (BASS), and David King (DRUMS). All three players are rooted in rock music but schooled in jazz, particularly the FREE JAZZ playing of idol ORNETTE COLEMAN. Their sound is driven by Iverson's stylishly athletic piano and is supported by two independently acting rhythm players who lend a rock power to their jazz repertoire. They are apt to cover rock songs and jazz numbers ranging from Ornette Coleman to Black Sabbath and the Pixies, but all with a supercharged jazz trio flair that has impressed jazz and rock fans alike. The Bad Plus is an example of a new stage of FUSION music in which rock, jazz, hip-hop, and popular song join in a seamless mix.

Baker, Chet (1929–1988) *American trumpeter, flugelhorn player, and singer*

Baker got his start playing in U.S. Army bands from 1946 to 1948. After the army, he made a name for himself playing with CHARLIE PARKER and then in the first GERRY MULLIGAN QUARTET. His style was relaxed and bluesy. A good-looking guy, he became one of the centerpieces of West Coast Jazz in the 1950s. The sound of his painfully pure vocals and lonely TRUMPET underlined a tragic life that was often sidetracked by drug problems. He spent much of his last two decades performing in Europe before his untimely death at age 59.

banjo

The banjo was one of the original jazz instruments. It was invented by Africans and introduced to the New World by slaves. The banjo is a stringed folk instrument that was popular in the South following the Civil War. It was used widely as a rhythm instrument by early BLUES and jazz artists. By the 1930s it was replaced by the GUITAR in most groups. It is still associated with early jazz and Dixieland style jazz of New Orleans.

Barbieri, Gato (b. 1934) *Argentine tenor saxophonist, flute player, and composer*

Barbieri is the most famous jazz musician from Argentina. He heard a recording of CHARLIE PARKER when he was a youngster and was inspired to learn CLARINET and alto SAXOPHONE. He first learned to play on instruments borrowed from an orphanage near his home. At age 20 he switched to tenor saxophone. His early music was mainstream jazz. He first came to the attention of jazz fans while playing with two different American artists, Lalo Schifrin and DON CHERRY. Cherry, an experimental player, introduced Barbieri to FREE JAZZ IMPROVISATION. Together, they made several important recordings of AVANT-GARDE music in the mid- to late 1960s.

In 1967 Barbieri began to work with the Jazz Composer's Orchestra. He became interested again in his South American musical roots. Slowly, he began to work the rhythms and melodies of Argentina into his own compositions. He created a warmly romantic fusion of jazz and Latin music that included touches of tango, MAMBO, and South American folk music. His most famous record is the soundtrack he composed for the movie *Last Tango in Paris* (1972). He won a Grammy for this soundtrack, which launched him into international stardom.

His subsequent work continues to fuse Latin music with TRADITIONAL JAZZ and even free jazz improvisational ideas. The sultry sound of Barbieri's warm sax is unmistakably original. His music has been described as fiery, mystical, and passionate. He released his 50th recording, *In the Shadow of the Cat,* in 2003. What makes his music tick? He explains, "The melody is the most important thing, and something I very much love. When I play the saxophone, I play life, I play love, I play anger, I play confusion, I play when people scream; all of these aspects of the world I inhabit become naturally important to me."[13]

Barrett, Emma (1897–1983) *American piano player and singer*
"Sweet" Emma is a legendary figure in traditional New Orleans–style jazz. She first made her mark playing PIANO in the 1920s with Papa Celestin's Original Tuxedo Jazz Band. In the 1960s she became a leader of the NEW ORLEANS JAZZ revival movement as part of the Preservation Hall Jazz Band. She played and sang with a driving, hard-rocking style. She always wore red garters with bells and a beanie. The audience could always hear her jingling while she played piano. After a stroke in 1968 left her partially paralyzed, she continued to play piano, but with one hand! Legend has it that one time in New Orleans, after playing a rousing version of "When the Saints Go Marching In" with her band, elderly BASS player Papa John Joseph turned to Barrett and said, "That one about did me in." Then he fell over and died.

Basie, Count (1904–1984) *American bandleader, composer, piano and organ player*
The high velocity rhythms of the Count Basie Orchestra made it one of the most popular and influential BIG BANDS of the SWING era. Hailing from Red Bank, New Jersey, William "Count" Basie studied PIANO with his mother. As a young man, he went to New York, where he met legendary STRIDE PIANO players JAMES P. JOHNSON and FATS WALLER. Basie got his start playing piano for traveling vaudeville acts but took up with various jazz bands by the late 1920s. In 1929, living in Kansas City, he joined BENNIE MOTEN's Kansas City Orchestra. After Moten died in 1935, Basie formed his own group, the Barons of Rhythm, including LESTER YOUNG among its nine musicians. Radio broadcasts of the group from Kansas City in 1936 brought them fame as well as a record deal. They also made a deal to take the show on the road.

Settling in New York in late 1936, the group expanded to become the Count Basie Orchestra. It was one of the most famous swing bands of the late 1930s. Hit songs included "One O'Clock Jump" and "Jumpin' at the Woodside." The latter was a typical Basie masterpiece with syncopated accents played by muted BRASS instruments, SAXOPHONEs playing in UNISON, and a CALL-AND-RESPONSE between different members of the orchestra. Basie's fame spread worldwide. His philosophy of music was simple. He said, "If you play a tune and a person don't tap their feet, don't play the tune." He continued to make music even into the 1980s after an illness confined him at times to a wheelchair.

bass   See BASS GUITAR; DOUBLE BASS.

bass guitar
Leo Fender introduced the first electric bass guitar in the early 1950s. It was intended to replace the bulky and often inaudible DOUBLE BASS in amplified rock and roll groups. It slowly infiltrated jazz circles and became more widely used during and after the beginning of jazz FUSION music in the late 1960s and early 1970s. Like the double bass, the bass guitar is primarily used for rhythm. Like an electric GUITAR, the standard electric BASS has raised metal frets

along its fingerboard. A player presses a string against a fret to produce a certain note. The fretless electric bass guitar, with a smooth fingerboard more like that of an acoustic double bass, was first popularized by electric bassist JACO PASTORIUS, who removed the frets from his bass guitar himself. The fretless bass provides a more fluid, open style of jazz playing.

Bauzá, Mario (1911–1993) *Cuban composer, arranger, trumpet and alto saxophone player*
Trained as a classical CLARINET player, Bauzá came to New York in 1930. He switched to TRUMPET in 1932, and played with famous bandleaders CHICK WEBB, DON REDMAN, and CAB CALLOWAY from 1933 to 1941. In 1941 he began working in his brother-in-law's Afro-Cuban band. He eventually led ensembles of his own. Bauzá is credited with bringing jazz IMPROVISATION to Cuban music. He also helped DIZZY GILLESPIE get started by introducing him to Cab Calloway.

bebop

The modern jazz era began with the emergence of bebop, or bop, in the 1940s. This jazz style was pioneered by CHARLIE PARKER (alto SAXOPHONE) and DIZZY GILLESPIE (TRUMPET) and nurtured by small groups in New York City. The style evolved

Count Basie Orchestra

from the high-energy playing of SWING groups but emphasized instrumental solos rather than hummable melodies. Considered experimental at the time, bebop dazzled the listener with blazing beats and complex harmonies. The music was built around chord progressions rather than melodies. This was a novel approach to making jazz, especially when the artist was interpreting a popular tune of the day. But it perplexed such veterans as DUKE ELLINGTON, who declared that, "Playing bop is like playing Scrabble with all the vowels missing." It was jazz for the thinking person and focused on TECHNIQUE, POLYRHYTHMS, and elaborate SOLOS. Representative bebop artists include Dizzy Gillespie, Charlie Parker, THELONIOUS MONK, KENNY CLARKE, BUD POWELL, and MAX ROACH.

Bechet, Sidney (1897–1959) *American soprano saxophone and clarinet player*

Bechet was an extraordinary self-taught CLARINET player. He is a true legend of early jazz. After spending several years touring the South in street bands and carnivals, he played with a variety of small jazz groups. Then he joined the Southern Syncopated Orchestra in 1919, which took him to New York and Europe. Other musicians and composers were astounded by what he was playing. On a European tour, he received praise for his playing from Swiss classical music conductor Ernest Ansermet. The conductor described Bechet as "an extraordinary clarinet virtuoso."[14]

By 1921 Bechet had started playing an instrument new to jazz, the soprano SAXOPHONE. His ingenious exploration of this instrument defined the way that the saxophone is played in jazz. Bechet's style had a warm, breezy New Orleans feel with a witty edge. He was a remarkable improviser, composing endless variations to a tune on the spot. In this way, he opened up the imagination of jazz and largely freed it, as did LOUIS ARMSTRONG, from its New Orleans roots.

Beiderbecke, Leon "Bix" (1903–1931) *American cornet player, pianist, and composer*

Although his life was cut short by ill health and alcoholism, Bix Beiderbecke made a lasting impression on the world of jazz. He was the first white jazzman who was widely admired and imitated by African-American players. His CORNET TECHNIQUE, though able, was not as blazing as LOUIS ARMSTRONG's, but he brought delicacy and emotion to his playing that was unheard of for the TRUMPET. His sound was sweet, his phrasing articulate, and the art of his SOLOS had a gripping hold on the imagination. His innovations with melody and harmony were as powerful as those made by Armstrong with rhythm. His soulful style was an important innovation in early jazz. Toward the end of his life he was with the PAUL WHITEMAN orchestra, the premier pop jazz band in the country. Bix was much loved, and Whiteman always kept his seat in the orchestra open even though Beiderbecke's unreliable nature meant that he was often missing in action. One time in haste to join up with the band, he arrived at a train station to catch a 7:00 A.M. train and got on a train going in the wrong direction.[15]

He was often tired and unwell during his performances. Many years later, a musician was working with some of Bix's charts from the Whiteman days noticed a peculiar handwritten note on one of the pages. It said, "Wake up Bix."[16]

His influence can be heard in the work of LESTER YOUNG, CHARLIE PARKER, LESTER BOWIE, and MILES DAVIS, among others.

Bennett, Tony (b. 1926) *American singer*

Tony Bennett (born Anthony Dominick Benedetto) is a popular singer with a gift for the sensibilities of jazz vocalization. He is best known for such pop standards as "I Left My Heart in San Francisco" and "I Want to Be Around," which he made famous in the 1960s during a seemingly endless stream of nightclub and television

"Bix" Beiderbecke (center, with trumpet) and his orchestra

appearances. He has always maintained a close association with great jazz players and after becoming successful, managed to ensure that he was surrounded by the best musicians to showcase his jazz-influenced vocals. In the 1960s he worked with COUNT BASIE, DUKE ELLINGTON, and WOODY HERMAN. He regularly worked with such classic instrumentalists as Zoot Sims (SAXOPHONE) and Bobby Hackett (TRUMPET). He recorded in collaboration with BILL EVANS in 1975 and gradually moved further away from renditions of pop songs to jazz classics, a position he still maintains as one of the most successful CROSSOVER JAZZ artists of all time.

Benson, Ivy (1913–1993) *British bandleader and alto saxophone, clarinet, and piano player*

Few women led BIG BANDs during the SWING era (1932–48). Ivy Benson not only led her own swing band, but did it using all women players. Her father was a musician with the Leeds Symphony Orchestra and encouraged his daughter to take PIANO lessons at a young age. By age nine she had performed on BBC radio as "Baby Benson" and had begun to take an interest in popular music. Her first professional GIGs included three years with Edna Croudson's Rhythm Girls (1928) and a tour with Teddy Joyce and the Girlfriends. She moved to London in the 1930s and eventually assembled her own swing group in 1940, Ivy Benson and her Rhythm Girls. With this nine-member band she performed in the all-girl revue "Meet the Girls" starring the comedienne Hylda Baker. By 1940, and during World War II, Benson led her all-female swing groups of sizes ranging from 12 to 23 members. They struggled to find work at the beginning, playing cafés, movie houses, and seaside piers if need be.[17]

Although good women jazz players were hard to find, she actively recruited musicians through schools and colleges and music teacher acquaintances. Even though her group was talented and could swing with the best male swing bands of the time, if it wasn't for the war it would have been difficult for an all-female band to find work. However, with so many male jazz musicians off fighting, Benson was able to attract a steady following and get regular gigs for her group. In 1943 they were hired as the official BBC radio resident dance band. Another highlight of this period was a 22-week engagement at the famed London Palladium. After the war, beginning in 1946, she took her Ladies Dance Orchestra (sometimes called the All Girl Orchestra) to Europe to entertain American troops stationed in various bases in Germany. They were a perennial favorite of the troops, and Benson continued this work until the early 1960s. The biggest challenge to managing the band was not finding able female players, but keeping them from running off and marrying American soldiers. Benson once remarked, "They seldom seem to marry a fellow musician but playing so often, as we do, for the overseas forces in places like Germany can be fatal. Only last year, one of my best players left the stand one evening, I thought to go to the cloakroom, and was literally never seen again by us. Her elopement would have seemed very romantic, if it hadn't left us a player short!"[18]

Benson was an inspirational figure. She not only led her band but also acted as teacher, adviser, and stand-in mother to its younger members. She achieved great success in the face of harsh criticism and resistance from male bandleaders. But the public loved the music of the All Girl Orchestra and she kept it together, in one form or another, for 35

years. Her selfless dedication to the plight of professional women musicians was evident when she said, "I am always fighting for better terms and conditions not for myself but for my girls."[19]

Berklee College of Music
Founded in 1945, the Berklee College of Music in Boston is the world's largest independent music college and the premier institution for the study of jazz and contemporary music. It offers courses in composition, performance, arranging, and the recording and production of music. A quarter of its students are women and people come from all over the world to study jazz at Berklee. Famous students and graduates from the world of jazz include JOHN ABERCROMBIE (1967), GARY BURTON (1962), AL DI MEOLA (1974), BILL FRISELL (1977), JAN HAMMER (1969), QUINCY JONES (1951), DIANA KRALL (1983), Michael Manring (1979), Michael Mantler (1964), BRANFORD MARSALIS (1980), JOHN SCOFIELD (1973), SONNY SHARROCK (1962), MIROSLAV VITOUS (1967), and JOE ZAWINUL (1959).

big band
Larger jazz ENSEMBLES usually consisting of multiple reeds (three or more), horns (three or more), a RHYTHM SECTION (BASS, DRUMS, PIANO), vocalists, and other possible instruments (e.g., vibes, GUITAR, VIOLIN) to create a solid, pleasing sound of arranged harmony. Big bands are mostly associated with the SWING style of playing, but have been used for all forms of jazz. In classic swing big bands, instrumental SOLOS were minimized in favor of tight harmonies and catchy melodies. Representative big band artists include DUKE ELLINGTON, BENNY GOODMAN, TOMMY DORSEY, GLENN MILLER, COUNT BASIE, and LIONEL HAMPTON.

Birdland
Originally located at 52nd Street and Broadway in New York City and first called the Clique Club, Birdland reopened in 1949 at the height of BEBOP

and was renamed after bop's most important player, CHARLIE "BIRD" PARKER. The first-night performance featured a QUINTET including Parker, Max Kaminsky, LESTER YOUNG, Lips Page, and LENNIE TRISTANO. It was host to many a late night JAM SESSION by the best in jazz. More than 1,000 emerging artists have performed at Birdland. In addition to Parker, Young, and Tristano, the list of performers who played at the club includes such legends as DIZZY GILLESPIE, THELONIOUS MONK, MILES DAVIS, JOHN COLTRANE, BUD POWELL, STAN GETZ, and ERROLL GARNER. The location of Birdland has changed twice since its founding in 1949. After being closed between 1965 and 1986, it reopened in uptown Manhattan. In 1996 it moved to its present location at 315 West 44th Street in midtown. No matter where it has been, Birdland has been one of the most important showcases for new jazz during the last 50 years.

"Birdland" (1976) *recorded performance by Weather Report*

From the album *Heavy Weather* (Columbia), featuring JOE ZAWINUL (keyboards), WAYNE SHORTER (tenor and soprano SAXOPHONE), JACO PASTORIUS (BASS), Alex Acuna (DRUMS), and Manolo Badrena (tambourine). Written by Joe Zawinul as a tribute to the New York jazz club of the same name, "Birdland" was probably the first and maybe only danceable song that came from the FUSION jazz movement of the 1970s. All the elements were there, a funky beat, a rocking bass line, and a bubbling melody that one could whistle. It is important because it marked the beginning of a transition from club and concert hall jazz to urban beats that had great youth appeal.

Birth of the Cool (1948–1950) *album recorded by the Miles Davis Nonet*

The album featured MILES DAVIS (TRUMPET), GERRY MULLIGAN (baritone SAXOPHONE), MAX ROACH (DRUMS), John Lewis (PIANO), J. J. Johnson (TROMBONE), GUNTHER SCHULLER (FRENCH HORN), Lee Konitz (alto saxophone), Al McKIBBON (BASS), and John Barber (tuba). After having worked in CHARLIE PARKER's band playing hot BEBOP music, Davis was inspired to strike out on his own and experiment with a variation of the bop formula. The work of his nine musicians was a satisfying blend of bop's bounce and the solid CHORD accompaniment of SWING bands. The music was more "written" than bebop and placed less emphasis on IMPROVISATION. The result had wide appeal to jazz lovers. It was the first of many influential experiments in jazz style that Davis made in his career. Its impact was immediate. The *Birth of the Cool* (Capitol) recordings led to the growth of both cool and West Coast jazz as well as a revival of the symphonically conceived jazz of DUKE ELLINGTON.

Bitches Brew (1970) *album recorded by Miles Davis*

Featuring MILES DAVIS (TRUMPET), WAYNE SHORTER (soprano SAXOPHONE), Bennie Maupin (BASS CLARINET), JOE ZAWINUL (electric piano), LARRY YOUNG (electric piano), CHICK COREA (electric piano), JOHN McLAUGHLIN (electric GUITAR), DAVE HOLLAND (BASS), Harvey Brooks (electric bass), Don Alias (congas), Jim Riley (percussion), Lenny White (DRUMS), and Jack DeJohnette (drums), *Bitches Brew* (Capitol) is the album that gave birth to FUSION jazz. It signaled the electrification of jazz and the use of rock elements, but it was more than that. Note the peculiar lineup that Davis put together. He had two drummers playing at once, three PIANO players playing at once, and a QUARTET of soloists who could take command of the music at any time. The structure of the music is seemingly free flowing, but careful listening reveals honored structures of jazz form underlying the extended JAMS. Not only was Davis a genius at conceiving new musical styles, he had impeccable taste when it came to choosing sidemen (see SIDEMAN). Note that several of the players on *Bitches Brew* emerged as major influences on FUSION jazz in the years following. JOE ZAWINUL and WAYNE SHORTER formed

WEATHER REPORT. John McLaughlin formed the MAHAVISHNU ORCHESTRA. Chick Corea formed Return to Forever.

"Black and Tan Fantasy" (1927) *recorded performance by Duke Ellington and Bubber Miley*

DUKE ELLINGTON's first masterpiece was his version of New Orleans funeral music, recorded on a Victor release. Opening with muted TRUMPETs and the swinging wail of a CLARINET, the piece quickly morphs into a highly orchestrated SET of swinging horns. The piece literally carried the classic NEW ORLEANS JAZZ sound to the future. Here were the roots, leading into the emerging sound of SWING as defined by the Duke. He did it all in the span of a three-minute song. The result sounds spontaneous, as if it were improvised. The brilliance of Ellington is that he found a way to write most of this down using musical notation.

"Black Bottom Stomp" (1926) *recorded performance by Jelly Roll Morton*

Arrangement for PIANO, TRUMPET, CLARINET, TROMBONE, BANJO, BASS, and DRUMS. JELLY ROLL MORTON was a skilled COMPOSER who made the transition from RAGTIME to jazz, claiming to have invented jazz as he went. Whatever the merits of his claim, there is no denying that he was a brilliant COMPOSER, player, and ARRANGER. "Black Bottom Stomp" is one of his successful orchestrations of classic New Orleans–style jazz. His ARRANGEMENT documented the kinds of free-wheeling IMPROVISATION that New Orleans musicians were known for. The trumpet plays a SOLO over the breaks. Three soloists improvise at the same time.

Blackman, Cindy (b. 1959) *American drummer and composer*

Blackman is one of the most vibrant and powerful drummers on the jazz scene. Her inspiration was BEBOP, and her mentors were ART BLAKEY and Tony Williams. She grew up in Connecticut, where she decided early on to play DRUMS. She studied music and played in school orchestras while attending the BERKLEE COLLEGE OF MUSIC. After Berklee, she headed for New York to practice her craft, first as a subway performer, and eventually as a SESSION drummer for many jazz greats, including JOE HENDERSON, Don Pullen, HUGH MASEKELA, PHARAOH SANDERS, CASSANDRA WILSON, and Angela Bofill. *Code Red* (1992) was her first album as a group leader. Her style is hard-hitting and energetic, her TECHNIQUE flawless. She is one of those rare drummers who can move with ease from jazz to rock. Her greatest fame to date has come while drumming for rock singer-songwriter Lenny Kravitz. She continues to work as a SESSION drummer, tour and record with Kravitz, and release her own SOLO albums, including *Works on Canvas* (2000).

Blackwell, Ed (1929–1992) *American drummer*

Raised in New Orleans, Blackwell became the most prominent drummer of the early FREE JAZZ movement in the 1960s while working with ORNETTE COLEMAN and DON CHERRY. He was not just interested in keeping a beat. He explored the many tonalities of the DRUMS and was a master of shifting rhythms. The reason he succeeded as an improviser was his ability to listen to his fellow musicians and react with alert brilliance with ideas of his own. His most significant work was with Coleman and also Don Cherry. He had several playing stints with Coleman, went to Europe and played on Don Cherry's landmark *Complete Communion* and *Symphony for Improvisers* records, and also played with ERIC DOLPHY, ALICE COLTRANE, THELONIOUS MONK, and ANTHONY BRAXTON. His style combined classic New Orleans TEMPOs with rhythms picked up from Africa, Cuba, and other countries. In the 1970s Blackwell taught music as artist in residence at Wesleyan University and formed the group Old and New Dreams. In 1982 Cherry and Blackwell released a groundbreaking album called *El Corazón*, featuring only the two of them. The record contains more percussion than horn and is highlighted by the use

Ed Blackwell (left) and Don Cherry (right)

of bells, mbira, and other native instruments of Africa, Tibet, and other countries. In the years just prior to his death by kidney failure, he was active with Don Cherry's group Nu.

Blakey, Art (1919–1990) *American drummer and bandleader*

A spirited and rocking drummer, Blakey helped popularize the HARD BOP style with his group the Jazz Messengers. Blakey worked briefly with BIG BANDS in the early 1940s. By the late 1940s and early 1950s, he was a sought-after SESSION drummer for notables including THELONIOUS MONK, CHARLIE PARKER, and MILES DAVIS. Blakey formed the Jazz Messengers in 1954 to play a recording GIG with pianist HORACE SILVER. The group stayed together and did some touring of its own, but several mem-

bers left, including Silver, by 1956. Blakey kept the Jazz Messengers alive by adding new musicians whenever others left. His group soon became a revolving door of opportunity for many up-and-coming players. For 30 years, Blakey's Jazz Messengers was the training ground for an incredible number of musicians who went on to become famous SOLO players. Just a few of them included FREDDIE HUBBARD, WAYNE SHORTER, KEITH JARRETT, WYNTON and BRANFORD MARSALIS, CHICK COREA, STANLEY CLARKE, and JOANNE BRACKEEN.

Blakey was devoted to bringing the driving energy of jazz back to the masses. He believed in the power of music to lift the spirits and give a person hope. That is what he meant when he said, "Music washes away the dust of everyday life." While his drumming TECHNIQUE may not have been as polished as contemporaries GENE KRUPA or MAX

ROACH, his energy and leadership made him a legendary figure in modern jazz. STANLEY CLARKE, who was still in college when he played BASS with Blakey in 1971 and 1972, had great respect for the master's approach to jazz. "He was the swinging-est drummer I had ever played with in my life," said Clarke. "He didn't know anything else but that. He was raw and a true jazz musician in the way he talked and the way he was. . . . He was proud of the contributions that black people made to music and the American art form that is jazz. He always talked about that and really taught us. He made me feel that I should respect myself as a musician, and more so, as a jazz musician; a black jazz musician."[20]

Blanton, Jimmy (1918–1942) *American bass player*

In his tragically short life, Blanton revolutionized the role of the DOUBLE BASS from that of a timekeeping rhythm instrument to that of an important SOLO instrument. In 1937 he moved to St. Louis and joined the Jeter-Pillars Orchestra, a prominent TERRITORY BAND. During the summers he also freelanced as a musician on riverboats with the Fate Marable band. DUKE ELLINGTON, impressed with his style and bold, round tone, hired him in late 1939 and made him a featured player in his orchestra. While working for Ellington and living in New York, Blanton took part in some of the earliest BEBOP jam sessions at MINTON'S PLAYHOUSE. He died of tuberculosis in 1942, leaving behind a legacy of new ideas that were carried on by disciples OSCAR PETTIFORD and CHARLES MINGUS.

He led the BASS into a new era by combining a mastery of the rhythmic bass playing of his predecessors with an agile and tuneful solo style that became a highlight of his performances. Ellington prized Blanton's playing so much that he made special assurances in the placement of microphones to pick up Blanton's sound on stage and in the recording studio. When Ellington first hired Blanton, he already had an older bassist, Billy Taylor Sr., in his orchestra. Duke didn't have the heart to fire him, so he let both players play side by side on stage. Taylor soon became frustrated and quit during one of their performances, proclaiming "I'm not going to stand up there next to that young boy playing all that bass and be embarrassed."[21]

Bley, Carla (b. 1938) *American composer, pianist, keyboardist, bandleader, and record producer*

Bley is not only a prominent woman in jazz but also a leader of the style of jazz known as AVANT-GARDE. Her compositions are technically smart, often whimsical, and always imaginative. Her early love was FREE JAZZ. Her inspirations were MILES DAVIS, THELONIOUS MONK, ORNETTE COLEMAN, and DON CHERRY. Like Bley, these artists all created strikingly original and innovative jazz. In 1964, with Michael Mantler, she formed the Jazz Composer's Orchestra (JCO). The JCO, based in New York, was a showcase for large ENSEMBLE and orchestral jazz works. One of the crowning achievements of the JCO was the production and recording of Bley's composition *Escalator Over the Hill* (1971). This work took her three years to write. It combined jazz and rock musicians and echoed elements of classical, rock, popular, and jazz music. About herself she says, "I find it difficult to be reverent about anything obvious (with the exception of certain musical phrases)."[22]

She continues to compose music for BIG BAND ensembles and has won a Grammy for her achievements. *Escalator Over the Hill* was only intended as a recorded work back in 1971. However, it was produced as a live performance piece for the first time in 1997 in Germany.

blue note

A note in the minor key that is played selectively in the major key. The sound of a blue note lends a sad feeling to the otherwise upbeat major key. Blue notes are used for emphasis, often by singers at the end of a song VERSE. Blue Note is also the name of a jazz recording label and a well-known jazz club in New York City.

blues

A style of folk music dating from the 1800s and first played by African-American slaves. Its TWELVE-BAR STRUCTURE came before jazz but is the foundation of much jazz, rock, and popular music.

Blues and Roots (1959) album by Charles Mingus

Featuring CHARLES MINGUS (BASS), Willie Dennis, Jimmy Knepper (TROMBONE), John Handy, Jackie McLean (alto SAXOPHONE), Booker Ervin (tenor saxophone), Pepper Adams (baritone saxophone), Horace Parlan, Mal Waldron (PIANO), Dannie Richmond (DRUMS), this album released by Atlantic is an exploration of the BLUES, a devotion close to that of Mingus's but not often expressed in his broadly experimental works. His understanding of the roots of African-American music is genuine and heartfelt. The performance has life and soul. He hops up potentially mundane blues numbers, such as "Wednesday Night Prayer Meeting," with a jolt of DOUBLE TIME rhythm. But it all seems normal in the hands of the master juggler.

Blues and the Abstract Truth, The (1961) album by Oliver Nelson

This album is not so remarkable for its compositions—they are all basic BLUES forms. But it is noted for the imaginative arranging of SESSION leader Oliver Nelson and the incredible array of musicians who contributed to the album. Personnel included FREDDIE HUBBARD (TRUMPET), ERIC DOLPHY (FLUTE, alto SAXOPHONE), BILL EVANS (PIANO), Roy Haynes (DRUMS), and PAUL CHAMBERS (BASS). Together, they helped transform Nelson's blues into a HARD BOP showcase. The album established Nelson as a top flight COMPOSER and ARRANGER.

Blue Train (1957) album by John Coltrane

This recording released by Blue Note was one of the early releases made by JOHN COLTRANE as a leader between his stays with MILES DAVIS. It precedes the seminal GIANT STEPS and KIND OF BLUE by two years and catches the tenor master exploring his freewheeling of the blues. Coltrane called this his favorite album as a leader, and it is clear why he felt this way. Despite being the BLUES, this music is pure joy. It is a veritable party of HARD BOP and blues RIFFS played with strength and ambition. It is also one of the most mainstream and accessible of Coltrane's recordings, a straight-ahead style of playing that he eventually left behind as his solos became longer and his musical vision more spiritually aligned. Playing with Coltrane on this SESSION were LEE MORGAN (TRUMPET), Curtis Fuller (TROMBONE), Kenny Drew (PIANO), PAUL CHAMBERS (BASS), and PHILLY JOE JONES (DRUMS).

"Body and Soul" (1939) recorded performance by Coleman Hawkins

This performance by COLEMAN HAWKINS has been called "the most spontaneously perfect of all jazz records."[23]

Released by Victor and apparently recorded as an afterthought at the end of a long SESSION, Hawkins proceeded to effortlessly float through a short, AABA rendition that totally redefined a familiar tune. After playing the start of the melody fairly straight, he quickly departs. He launches into variation after variation, leading his accompaniment to new CHORD patterns, doubling the TEMPO of his SOLO against the slow, balladlike rhythm, never returning to the melody, even at the end of the song. While all of this might sound like a terribly unresolved piece of music, the record was an astounding hit and became Hawkins's most famous tune.

Bolden, Buddy (1877–1931) American cornetist and legendary bandleader

One of the first acknowledged jazz bands was led by Charles "Buddy" Bolden in New Orleans from about 1890 to 1907. His group established the makeup of most early jazz bands. Melody was provided by CORNET (played by Bolden), CLARINET, or valve

TROMBONE set to a rhythm played on DOUBLE BASS, GUITAR, and DRUMS. Bolden was known as a flamboyant and charismatic performer. His group probably played its music by ear. Their musical selections consisted of popular dances, BLUES, and RAGTIME pieces. Bolden's ENSEMBLE disbanded after he was confined to Jackson Mental Institute in New Orleans in 1907 for smashing a pitcher over his mother-in-law's head. Many other New Orleans groups imitated the format and sound that he established. His sound was legendary. DUKE ELLINGTON once declared that Bolden had the "biggest fattest trumpet sound in town. . . . He used to tune up in New Orleans and break glasses in Algiers!"[24]

No recordings exist of Bolden's playing, but echoes of his influence can be heard in the music of his followers, FREDDIE KEPPARD, Bank Johnson, and JOE "KING" OLIVER.

Bona, Richard (b. 1976) *Cameroonian electric bass player, singer, and composer*
Bona learned folk instruments while growing up in his Cameroon village. By age 11 he was playing GUITAR and performing at local weddings and public events. When the proprietor of a local hotel began a jazz club in 1985, he recruited Bona to be a member of his HOUSE BAND. Bona's first exposure to jazz was by playing in this club and listening to the large collection of jazz records kept by the owner. He reportedly switched to BASS playing after listening to the self-titled debut album by JACO PASTORIUS.[25]

Bona was skilled enough to imitate Pastorius's virtuoso style and absorbed much of what he heard in the music around him to school himself in FUSION and jazz styles. By 1989 Bona moved to Paris to work with EUROPEAN JAZZ musicians and African artists, working in particular with the legendary Afropop star Manu Dibango. Bona worked briefly with JOE ZAWINUL in France and came to New York in 1995, soon a member of the Zawinul Syndicate and made two records with the group. He has continued to work with other artists, including CHICK COREA, Larry Coryell, HERBIE HANCOCK, MICHAEL and RANDY BRECKER, PAT METHENY, and BOBBY McFERRIN. His first record under his own name, *Scenes from My Life,* was released in 1999. Bona brings an effortless musicality and world beat to his playing. His style is a high-energy blend of Pastorius and Afropop, a meeting of WORLD MUSIC and jazz tradition. His appearance on Pat Metheny's *Speaking of Now* (2002) was an important new ingredient to the veteran guitarist's revamped sound. While his efforts as a SIDEMAN for others falls more within the normal bounds of jazz and fusion playing, his own records are closer to Afropop than pure jazz, and feature his alluring voice.

boogie-woogie
A jazz PIANO style of the 1920s that influenced the start of rock and roll in the 1950s. In boogie music, the left hand plays BASS as a repeated series of notes "eight to the bar" of the musical staff. It goes round and round like this while the right hand accents the rhythm with repeated patterns of notes and chords. It became popular as dance music.

bop See BEBOP.

bossa nova
This style originated in the 1950s and combined the feel and instrumentation of COOL JAZZ with Brazilian music. It is known for a steady, pulsing eight-note groove and alluring melodies.

Bowie, Lester (1941–1999) *American trumpet and flugelhorn player, composer, bandleader*
Growing up in St. Louis, Bowie learned to play TRUMPET before he was 10 and was leading his own group by age 16. His first GIGS were in pop and rhythm and BLUES sessions. He even toured with a circus band in the early 1960s. After moving to Chicago in 1965, he joined the AACM and later served as its president. With ROSCOE MITCHELL, he

founded the Art Ensemble of Chicago in 1969. This group remained together with its original members until Bowie's death in 1999.

The Art Ensemble was a showcase for experimental jazz with WORLD MUSIC influences. It was one of the most influential groups of the jazz AVANT-GARDE. Bowie's skills as a trumpeter were well rounded. He was just as comfortable playing the kinds of licks that LOUIS ARMSTRONG made famous as well as the sonic experiments that define the outer reaches of FREE JAZZ. As a bandleader, Bowie organized the all-brass Brass Fantasy in 1989. This ENSEMBLE combined Bowie's knack for onstage flair with a rollicking vibe that fused new jazz with the sound of traditional brass band music from the early 1900s. He called his music "avant pop" and summed up his approach this way, "All's fair in love and war . . . and music is both . . . so use anything, as long as it works."[26]

Brackeen, Joanne (b. 1938) *American composer and pianist*

Like CARLA BLEY, who was born in the same year, Brackeen is a pioneering woman jazz artist whose career spans the last four decades. She learned PIANO by listening to jazz records. Although accepted by the Los Angeles Conservatory of Music to study classical piano, she dropped out because her true love was jazz. By age 20 she was playing GIGS in small West Coast jazz clubs. After taking time off from her career to raise a family, she came to prominence in New York from 1969 to 1971 as a member of the Jazz Messengers. Bandleader STAN GETZ is credited with exposing her to a wider audience, especially in Europe. By the late 1970s Brackeen was receiving wide critical acclaim as a SOLO artist. She succeeds in freely combining TRADITIONAL JAZZ elements with the experimental. She is also interested in musical styles from other countries, which she works into her own compositions. She has been influential in expanding the language and texture of jazz beyond its traditional American roots.

Brand, Dollar See ABDULLAH IBRAHIM.

brass

A family of instruments made of brass or other metal. Some have finger valves, such as the TRUMPET, tuba, and FRENCH HORN. Others do not, such as the TROMBONE.

Braxton, Anthony (b. 1945) *American alto saxophone, clarinet, bass clarinet, soprano, and flute player, composer, and educator*

To hear some of the most far-out sounds in jazz, listen to the work of Anthony Braxton. This gifted visionary first studied classical music but was turned to jazz when he was a teenager by ROSCOE MITCHELL. Braxton has been interested in new and experimental jazz sounds from the start. He comes from the 1960s Chicago school of jazz, where he worked early on with the ASSOCIATION FOR THE ADVANCEMENT OF CREATIVE MUSICIANS (AACM) of MUHAL RICHARD ABRAMS. Braxton's influences come from both jazz and modern classical composers such as John Cage and Karlheinz Stockhausen. Among his jazz influences are ERIC DOLPHY, JOHN COLTRANE, Paul Desmond, Roscoe Mitchell, and CECIL TAYLOR. He is noted for having bridged the gap between African-American jazz and modern classical music from America and Europe. The result is a sound that is challenging to the listener and uniquely his own.

His music is impossible to categorize. His theories about composition respect the use of all sounds, even some that many listeners might not consider musical. He composes music of ideas, some of which are mathematical and abstract, using instruments to express the curious and often beautiful workings of his imagination. Although some critics might not consider his roots to be jazz at all, his playing is skilled and challenging. His solos sound nothing like those that listeners might expect from another sax player like Paul Desmond or John Coltrane. There are hints of the more radical sounds of Eric Dolphy and ORNETTE COLEMAN in his music.

In 1971 he released an important album called *For Alto,* a two-record SET of SOLO alto SAXOPHONE compositions originally recorded in 1968. It remains one of the boldest and most unusual recordings in all of jazz history. It came during a period when many jazz musicians were moving toward the more popular sounds jazz-rock FUSION in their music. Braxton's remarkable album was stark in contrast. *For Alto* lacked the kinds of rhythms, melodies, and solos that most people expected of jazz. It was a celebration of purely abstract self-expression, a kind of music that stopped listeners in their tracks. *For Alto* established Braxton as a musician and COMPOSER to be watched.

He worked with a jazz ENSEMBLE called Circle led by CHICK COREA from 1970 to 1972, a group that also included bassist DAVE HOLLAND and drummer Barry Altschul. Since that time, Braxton has continued to work with a variety of ensembles to play his music and has also taught music at both Mills College in Oakland, California, and Wesleyan University in Connecticut, a noted center of WORLD MUSIC studies. He often organizes tours of his musical ensembles that combine lectures with performances. In the 1990s Braxton founded the Tri-Centric Ensemble, a New York–based group organized to stage many of his most ambitious works.

It is not unusual for a Braxton composition to combine elements of opera, computer and video graphics, choral ensembles, and the playing of 30 or more instrumentalists. Of his own music, Braxton has said, "My music, my life's work, will ultimately challenge the very foundations of Western value systems, that's what's dangerous about it."[27]

Some critics question the appeal of his work. Jazz journalist Stuart Nicholson once wrote about Braxton's music ". . . if some performances included moments when he seemed to have perfected the art of playing over the heads of his audience it was because he was not concerned with conveying emotion."[28]

break

A brief, but planned interruption in the flow of a piece during which a SOLO performer usually improvises while the RHYTHM SECTION lays back.

Brecker, Michael (b. 1949) *American tenor saxophone and EWI player and brother of Randy Brecker*

Michael is one of the most accomplished reed players on the CONTEMPORARY JAZZ scene. Like his brother, RANDY BRECKER, he worked in jazz and rock in the early part of his career. By the late 1970s he had carved himself a niche as a powerful, straight-ahead jazz player with a rich sound reminiscent of JOHN COLTRANE. Brecker played with PAT METHENY in 1980–81, HERBIE HANCOCK in 1988, led his own groups, and has worked with pop and rock artists as diverse as John Lennon, Joni Mitchell, and Paul Simon. He has the ability and imagination to apply Coltrane's sometimes radical style to FUSION, pop, and rock music. He is also a skilled player of the Electronic Wind Instrument (EWI), a breath-driven SYNTHESIZER. The EWI was a new and experimental instrument when Becker introduced it while touring with his group Steps Ahead in 1986.

Brecker, Randy (b. 1945) *American trumpet and piano player and drummer*

The older brother of MICHAEL BRECKER, Randy left college and became a member of the jazz-rock group Blood, Sweat, and Tears in 1967, then HORACE SILVER, and eventually found himself in demand as a BIG BAND player. With his brother, Michael, and drummer BILLY COBHAM, he formed the FUSION group Dreams (1969–72). He has since been in great demand with rock and jazz artists and is a sought-after studio musician. He was one of the early jazz players to dabble seriously with rock music and fusion, and continues to straddle the jazz and fusion fence today.

bridge

The third part in an AABA song form. This is normally the third 8-bar section of a song consisting of 32 bars.

Bridgewater, Dee Dee (b. 1950) *American singer and actress*

The multitalented Bridgewater grew up in Tennessee, where she was immersed as a young girl in the music of ELLA FITZGERALD and the jazz playing of her trumpeter father. She has been successful not only as a superb jazz vocalist but in musical theater and stage acting as well. Among her many awards, Bridgewater has earned Broadway's coveted Tony Award (Best Featured Actress in a Musical: *The Wiz*, 1975), was nominated for the London theater's equivalent, the Laurence Olivier Award (Best Actress in a Musical: *Lady Day*, 1987), has won two Grammy Awards (1998), and France's top recording honor, the Victoire de la Musique (Best Jazz Vocal Album, 1998).

Bridgewater made her New York debut in 1970 singing for the legendary THAD JONES–MEL LEWIS Orchestra, an opportunity that opened many doors for the talented vocal stylist. Following her work with the Thad Jones–Mel Lewis Orchestra, she made recordings with DEXTER GORDON, MAX ROACH, SONNY ROLLINS, and DIZZY GILLESPIE. While on Broadway in 1974, she starred in *The Wiz* and is known for her rendition of the song "If You Believe." Her work in jazz continued with projects devoted to the life and music of Ella Fitzgerald (*Dear Ella*) and her acting role as BILLIE HOLIDAY in the play *Lady Day*, and musical tributes to DUKE ELLINGTON and HORACE SILVER. In October 1999, Bridgewater was named an ambassador by the United Nations Food and Agriculture Organization (FAO), on whose behalf she works to combat world hunger. Since 1997, she has also been the host of National Public Radio's weekly jazz program *JazzSet*, featuring live performances from jazz greats. Few artists have found such success as Dee Dee Bridgewater in nearly every medium they touch.

Brilliant Corners (1956) *album by Thelonious Monk*

THELONIOUS MONK wasn't quite BEBOP, wasn't quite FREE JAZZ. He swung to his own rhythm and harmonics and this album is a prized example of his wittiest work. Until the release of this record, Monk was often a SIDEMAN, laboring in the studio for others. With *Brilliant Corners*, he was able to break through as a leader on his own. Monk surrounded himself with a bevy of young jazz lions: CLARK TERRY (TRUMPET), Ernie Henry (alto SAXOPHONE), SONNY ROLLINS (tenor SAXOPHONE), OSCAR PETTIFORD (BASS), and MAX ROACH (DRUMS). Even so, some of these numbers were so difficult to play that they had to be spliced together from various takes. The difficulty of the music, coupled with Monk's own perfectionism, made for tension in the studio. Yet the results are stupendous. Monk crafted a sly and sometimes whimsical SET of five tracks that touch on his experiments with alternative scales ("Brilliant Corners"), playing celeste ("Pannonica"), all embellished by the brilliant play of Roach, who comes closest to matching Monk note for note with some eccentric ideas of his own.

Brown, Clifford (1930–1956) *American trumpeter, composer, and bandleader*

Even though his life was tragically cut short by a car accident at age 25, Clifford Brown played TRUMPET so brilliantly that he is still regarded as one of the major influences of modern jazz. This wonderboy only took up the instrument at age 15. Before he went to college to study music, he was already playing clubs with some of the giants of modern jazz: MILES DAVIS, MAX ROACH, and J. J. Johnson to name a few. Brown's most noted playing was recorded while working with both ART BLAKEY's Jazz Messengers and with Max Roach, with whom he led a QUINTET from mid-1954 until his untimely death. Brown emerged when DIZZY GILLESPIE, Fats Navarro, and MILES DAVIS were the big names in trumpet playing. Rather than imitate their styles, he absorbed what he heard and created a marvelous sound of his own. He could play fast but always sounded relaxed. His use of VIBRATO was gentler and more varied than Gillespie's often frenzied RIFFS. While Miles dabbled in chords and melancholy tones, Brown improvised melodies that dazzled with joy. He also stayed away from making sudden changes, a feature of Gillespie and Parker's bop music. In this way, he reinvented bop and became the most imitated voice of HARD BOP. Upon his death, Dizzy Gillespie affirmed the young man's greatness when he said, "For his artistry, there can be no replacement."[29]

Brown, Ray (1926–2002) *American bass player and composer*

Brown's relaxed but articulate style on the BASS got him work just two years out of high school with DIZZY GILLESPIE's 1946 bop QUINTET. As a founding member of this COMBO with Gillespie and CHARLIE PARKER, Brown was responsible for finding a tasteful yet driving bass style to propel the solos of BEBOP's two biggest stars. He also worked with Gillespie's BIG BAND and later became the musical director for ELLA FITZGERALD (1948 to 1952), to whom he was also married at the time. He spent 16 years as a member of the OSCAR PETERSON Trio and was a familiar player on the JAZZ AT THE PHILHARMONIC tours. His playing can be heard on more than 2,000 recordings. He was a true style-setter in combo bass playing, having shaped the sound of bop and trio RHYTHM SECTIONS in the 1940s and 1950s.

Brubeck, Dave (b. 1920) *American piano player, composer, and bandleader*

Brubeck is a leading practitioner of the West Coast, or California jazz movement that sprang up in the late 1940s as an alternative to BEBOP. The soft melodies and easy TEMPOS of his trademark songs disguised a complex approach to rhythm and harmony that Brubeck adapted from classical music.

Brubeck was brought up in a family steeped in music. His mother was a classical pianist and his music teacher until Brubeck was age 11. His two brothers became music teachers. Brubeck first started playing in jazz COMBOS as a teenager. He received a college degree in music from Stockton's College of the Pacific and after World War II returned to school to study with classical music COMPOSER Darius Milhaud at Mills College between 1946 and 1949. After leading or playing with several groups during his college years, Brubeck formed a trio in 1949 with SWING bassist Gene Wright and drummer Joe Morello. Brubeck's signature sound, however, was not complete until he added a fourth musician to his group in 1951 to form the Dave Brubeck Quartet. The new member was Paul Desmond, with his distinctively bright alto SAXOPHONE sound.

The Dave Brubeck Quartet gained national prominence in a short time, even putting its leader, Brubeck, on the cover of *Time* magazine in 1954. The quartet was largely responsible for the growing appeal of COOL JAZZ or West Coast jazz, an easygoing sound that became widely popular in the 1950s. The quartet consisted of three white and one black musician and their appeal was largely to a white, college-educated audience that was otherwise not so into jazz. Brubeck's classical music training enabled him to decorate his jazz with musical quotes from European composers such as Chopin and Wagner. The dialogue between Brubeck on PIANO and Desmond on saxophone often reminded the listener of Bach's COUNTERPOINT. Some called Brubeck's music "chamber jazz," a friendly nod to classical chamber music. It was, if anything else, *safe* jazz that non–TRADITIONAL JAZZ fans could cozy up to. In 1959, the group released the album *Time Out*, which explored music written in time signatures using five, seven, and nine beats. It became the first jazz album to sell more than a million copies. The quartet placed first in the annual *DOWN BEAT* reader's poll for 10 straight years.

The overwhelming popularity of this combo, symbolized by Brubeck's crowning on the cover of *Time* magazine, didn't sit well with everyone in the jazz community. Many serious jazz devotees, both black and white, considered the Brubeck phenomenon misplaced because he was a college-trained outsider to the real world of jazz. The commercial success of cool jazz came at the expense of more experienced and adventurous black musicians who paid their dues playing clubs and often struggling to make ends meet. Brubeck had no true cultural roots in jazz and seemed to be working in his own world of ideas. But Brubeck shouldn't be criticized for being successful. His accomplishments can stand on the merits of his music alone. He was responsible for exposing a new generation of jazz listeners and players to many unexplored ideas in jazz. His use of uncommon TIME SIGNATURES and song structures borrowed from classical music have had a long-lasting influence on modern jazz. He was certainly not so great a piano player or improviser as many other artists of his time, but Brubeck should be acknowledged as an innovative composer and ARRANGER.

Interestingly, even though Brubeck wrote most of the quartet's works, its signature song, "TAKE FIVE," was composed by Paul Desmond. This gentle, witty, romp was played in the unusual time signature of 5/4. The quartet wasn't the first jazz group to experiment with odd time signatures, but they made more extensive use of them than most other groups.

The Dave Brubeck Quartet played together until 1967. After the end of the original quartet, Brubeck formed another in 1972 that included saxophonist GERRY MULLIGAN. Brubeck also played with three of his sons, Darius, Dan, and Chris, as Two Generations of Brubecks, between 1972 and 1974. Since that time, he has pursued jazz composition in several directions and formed several new quartets. He continued to make regular appearances at jazz festivals, such as the NEWPORT JAZZ FESTIVAL. His musical imagination seems to have no boundaries. He has completed and performed works for jazz combo and orchestra ("Brandenburg Gate: Revisited," 1961; "La Fiesta de la Posada," 1975) works for dance ("Points on Jazz,") four cantatas, an orchestral Mass ("To Hope: A Celebration," 1981), and many smaller pieces. In 1995 he celebrated his 75th birthday by premiering a choral work at the National Cathedral in Washington, D.C. In 1998 he performed his Mass in Russia. He has received many awards and honors including the BMI Jazz Pioneer Award and the 1988 American Eagle Award presented by the National Music Council.

An assessment of "Take Five" by piano player Ray Bryant summed up early reactions from the jazz community to the Brubeck quartet's music. Bryant was a talented "house" SESSION man at Blue Note Records during the early 1960s. He said it plainly when he remarked, "I wouldn't say this swung, but it had a sort of lope to it."[30]

Brun, Philippe (1908–1994) *French trumpet player*

Brun originally studied VIOLIN before taking up the CORNET and then TRUMPET. He was France's first notable jazz trumpeter. He was an accomplished self-taught cornet player by age 21, having occasionally sat in with an American jazz band in Paris that included Bud Freeman and other Chicago players. He closely studied the recordings of LOUIS ARMSTRONG and especially BIX BEIDERBECKE. His first recordings were made in 1929 with the French SWING band Gregor and the Gregorians. Shortly thereafter, he was stolen away from Gregor to play for the Jack Hylton Orchestra, the leading swing band in England. The transition put the young Frenchman in the spotlight. Hylton's was a busy band. In 1929 alone they played 700 performances and sold 3 million records.[31]

The cornet he was playing at the time was a peculiar high-pitched instrument that was only about six inches long. After about three months in England, he switched to the trumpet so that his pitch range was more in keeping with the rest of the band.[32]

The most active years of his career were from 1930 to 1944, during which most of his recordings were made with Ray Ventura's Collegians, Jack Hylton, Bert Ambrose, DJANGO REINHARDT, and Alix Combelle. During World War II Brun left France for Switzerland where he continued to play. After World War II he led his own bands but did little recording.

Burton, Gary (b. 1943) *American vibe player, composer, and educator*

Burton and LIONEL HAMPTON are the two greatest players of jazz VIBRAPHONE, but that is where the comparison ends. Hampton perfected his swinging SOLO vibe style while playing SWING with BENNY GOODMAN in the 1930s. Burton came to prominence in the 1960s with a unique style of his own. Whereas Hampton played the vibes like a percussionist (he was a drummer as well), Burton created his own style of playing that was distinctively PIANO-like. He learned piano during high school and then took up the vibes on his own. Rather than copying the style of other vibe players, like Hampton, he found inspiration in the piano playing of jazz great BILL EVANS. Instead of playing with two mallets, he used four. This allowed him to played pianolike chords as well as melodies. This TECHNIQUE was unheard of in jazz prior to Burton.

He recorded his first album while attending the BERKLEE COLLEGE in 1960–61. He toured as a SIDEMAN with the George Shearing QUINTET in 1963 and with the STAN GETZ QUARTET in 1964–65. He then started his own quartet in 1966 with guitarist Larry Coryell, STEVE SWALLOW (BASS), and Bob Moses (DRUMS). It was with his own quartet that Burton's unique style matured. The sound of the group was clearly grounded in jazz but it also had a flair for rock sounds. Burton's passion for music was equaled by his enthusiasm for teaching jazz. He became an instructor at Berklee in 1971 and later dean of music studies in 1985. Burton's groups over the years have introduced many up-and-coming musicians as well as Berklee alumni, including CARLA BLEY, Larry Coryell, PAT METHENY, TOMMY SMITH, and JOHN SCOFIELD.

Byrd, Donald (b. 1932) *American trumpet and flugelhorn player, composer, and educator*

One might call Byrd "Dr. Jazz" because of his solid schooling in music and his devotion to higher education. Born in Detroit, he attended the exclusive Cass Tech High School, Wayne State University, and then later earned a master's degree in music education from the Manhattan School of Music (1955). This was long after establishing himself as one of the most sought-after and recorded HARD BOP trumpeters. He established his reputation as a spirited soloist while with ART BLAKEY's Jazz Messengers in 1955. After the death of famed trumpeter CLIFFORD BROWN in 1956, many thought that Byrd was his heir apparent. Only 24 at the time, he didn't disappoint with his soulful bop sound.

Byrd gigged with many players during the next decade, including MAX ROACH, Red Garland, JOHN COLTRANE, SONNY ROLLINS, and THELONIOUS MONK. During the 1960s and 1970s he became much more involved in music education. He was instrumental in establishing programs for the study of jazz at the college level, something new at the time. As chairman of the Black Music Department at Howard University, he organized a band and recorded the popular album *Black Byrd* in 1973, a crossover blend of jazz, funk, and rhythm and blues. His 1975 album, *Places and Spaces,* has been lauded as one of the best jazz-funk-soul FUSION albums of all time. It is also one of the most-sampled jazz albums by hip-hop artists and remixers today.

Like MILES DAVIS, Byrd was criticized by his older fans for having become too commercial and straying from his TRADITIONAL JAZZ roots. Continuing his graduate studies, he received a doctorate in education from Columbia Teacher's College in 1982 at the age of 50. He suffered a stroke in the early 1980s but recovered and began making music again in the hard bop style, although without the familiar punch of his earlier music. He continued his studies, adding law to his expertise, spending much of the 1990s lecturing and continuing to encourage the teaching of African-American musical roots at the college level.

Cadence magazine

A comprehensive magazine (without advertising) about jazz and improvised music. Published since 1976, *Cadence* is a great source of interviews and record reviews. *Cadence* started out on a kitchen table over 28 years ago and is still put together with love by enthusiastic jazz nuts.

call-and-response

A musical conversation in which one musician plays in response to another. This can be done by soloists or groups of musicians playing together. It was a popular playing pattern used by SWING bands.

Calloway, Cab (1907–1994) *American bandleader and vocalist*

Calloway was the "hi-dee-ho-man," a high-energy performer and outstanding bandleader of the SWING era. In 1928, after singing in a QUARTET with the all-black revue *Plantation Days,* he took jobs in Chicago as emcee at the Sunset and Dreamland clubs. In 1929 he became leader of the Alabamians and took the 11-piece orchestra to New York City, where they played at the famous Savoy club. Although the Alabamians didn't do so well in New York, Calloway himself succeeded in being noticed. He was soon a much talked about emcee and singer, taking on a role in a revue called *Hot Chocolates* and then becoming leader of another band called the Missourians. Before too long the Missourians had become Cab Calloway and his Orchestra, and the

group was making records for Victor. In 1931, Calloway recorded the hit "Minnie the Moocher," with its famous SCAT SINGING and "hi-dee-hi-dee-hi-dee-ho" CALL-AND-RESPONSE CHORUS. It made him a national celebrity overnight.

Calloway's orchestra was one of the most famous and successful of the swing era. The bandleader was an entertaining sight with his wild hair and white tuxedo. Their music was energized. They played the major clubs in New York, were heard regularly on radio, appeared in many MOVIES, and took their flamboyant act on many successful road tours. Calloway kept his band together until 1948. During that time many rising jazz stars numbered in the ranks of Calloway's bands, including BEN WEBSTER, DIZZY GILLESPIE, and Chu Berry.

Carnegie Hall

Carnegie Hall is New York's most celebrated concert hall. Although it was once reserved for the best players and singers of classical music, jazz became a regularly featured attraction at Carnegie Hall beginning in 1938. It was on January 16, 1938, that the "King of SWING" BENNY GOODMAN shook up the concert-going public with a rocking show tracing the history of jazz and billed as the "first swing concert in the history of Carnegie Hall." Goodman called his tribute "Twenty Years of Jazz." He later wrote, "We were playing for Bix and the fellows on the riverboats, in the honky tonks and gin mills."[33]

When it came time for Goodman's orchestra to play a DUKE ELLINGTON number, they were joined on stage by members of Ellington's band to play the gorgeous "Blue Reverie." After the formal SET was over, COUNT BASIE and members of his band joined them onstage for an informal JAM SESSION. As the driving beat of GENE KRUPA's drum reverberated throughout the old concert hall, audience members got out of their seats and danced in the aisles. It was not only a successful concert, but Goodman's show put authentic jazz in the headlines and gave the general public a taste of the glorious music that had been simmering in small clubs around the country for years. It is also worth noting that the performance featured black and white musicians playing together, an uncommon sight in an America that was still racially divided.

The success of the show led to regular concerts at Carnegie Hall. Other notable swing-era performances at Carnegie Hall included FATS WALLER (1942), Duke Ellington (1943), LOUIS ARMSTRONG (1947), ELLA FITZGERALD and DIZZY GILLESPIE (1947), OSCAR PETERSON (1949), and a 1952 concert featuring players of California "cool" jazz: CHET BAKER, GERRY MULLIGAN, and Paul Desmond. Goodman returned to Carnegie in 1978 for a concert celebrating the 40th anniversary of the historic first jazz performance in this important hall.

Carroll, Barbara (b. 1925) *American piano player and singer*

Often called the First Lady of Jazz piano, Carroll graduated from the New England Conservatory and began making her living as a jazz player in the late 1940s. She is considered the first woman to have embraced the BUD POWELL style of bop piano. In addition to playing jazz, she has appeared as an actress on Broadway. Carroll is known as a talented interpreter of classic songs from the 1930s and 1940s, including those by composers Irving Berlin, Cole Porter, Richard Rodgers, Sammy Cahn, and George Gershwin. Her style is elegant and her TECHNIQUE is perfection. Among her accomplishments have been several high-profile performances in accompaniment of jazz legends, including BENNY GOODMAN at CARNEGIE HALL, and BILLIE HOLIDAY on television. Carroll credits MARY LOU WILLIAMS before her for having helped make it possible for women to succeed in the largely male world of jazz.

Carter, Benny (1907–2003) *American alto saxophone, trumpet, and clarinet player, composer, and arranger*

In terms of talent, Benny Carter had it all. Universally celebrated by fellow musicians, Carter was one of the most important stylists of the alto SAXOPHONE. He also played the TRUMPET, making him one of those rare jazz musicians who successfully mastered both a reed and a BRASS instrument. He grew up in New York, where he took up the CLARINET at an early age but soon switched to saxophone. He was familiar with the HOT JAZZ being played in New York during the early 1920s. He got his start in 1923 playing sax with Willie "The Lion" Smith. He co-wrote his first published song with FATS WALLER, "Nobody Knows," in 1927. His career took off in the later 1920s as both performer and ARRANGER. Bands he worked with included those led by DUKE ELLINGTON, Charlie Johnson, FLETCHER HENDERSON, and later BENNY GOODMAN.

Some of Carter's arrangements for these bands, particularly the Benny Goodman Orchestra, are some of the most memorable and lasting in jazz history. He was probably the most influential arranger of his day. Everyone wanted to copy the Carter sound. He recorded many classic solos on both the saxophone and the clarinet.

Having less success leading his own bands in the 1930s, he went to Europe for three years. His presence was celebrated there, and he played many clubs and resorts. In 1937 he organized the first internationally based interracial band to make a recording.[34]

While in Europe he recorded with the top jazz musicians of Britain, FRANCE, and Scandinavia. Among his European recordings were those with American COLEMAN HAWKINS and Belgian gypsy DJANGO REINHARDT ("Honeysuckle Rose"). Upon returning to the United States, he organized several small groups whose members read like a who's who of jazz greats; DIZZY GILLESPIE, MILES DAVIS, MAX ROACH, J. J. Johnson, and BUDDY RICH, among others.

The second half of Carter's long career was devoted primarily to arranging music. He moved to Los Angeles in 1945 and became the first African-American COMPOSER to forge a career in Hollywood MOVIES and television. This was during a time when black musicians were normally restricted to only playing instruments on soundtracks. Carter not only performed, he also wrote and arranged the music and actually appeared in several films as a musician. During the 1960s Carter was much in demand as a musical director for a variety of singers, including Pearl Bailey, PEGGY LEE, Lou Rawls, and Ray Charles.[35]

In the 1970s he added the title of educator to his many accomplishments, teaching at Princeton University. He continued to compose, teach, and perform into his eighties, touring the world many times and completing several extended jazz works. In 1996 a concert was given in his honor at Lincoln Center, and he received the Kennedy Center Award. In 1961 Miles Davis said of Carter, "Everybody ought to listen to Benny. He's a whole musical education."[36]

Carter, Betty (1930–1998) *American singer*

Born Lillie Mae Jones in Flint, Michigan, she studied PIANO and then took to singing. Inspired by the sultry vocalizations of SARAH VAUGHN, Carter first sang professionally under the name Lorraine Carter at age 16. After some early GIGS with BEBOP COMBOS led by DIZZY GILLESPIE and CHARLIE PARKER, she earned the nickname "Betty Bebop" from bandleader LIONEL HAMPTON. Later calling herself simply BETTY CARTER, she ventured onto a road less traveled by jazz singers.

SCAT SINGING wasn't just a novelty thrown into the middle of her songs; some of her renditions of popular ballads actually began with scat and consisted almost entirely of VOCALESE game play. Her treatment of melody was adventurous. She often used rapid changes in TEMPO, pitch, and volume. Without having known the song she was singing beforehand, it might not have been possible to recognize it. The quality of her voice was rich and warm, as raspy as a SAXOPHONE or as smooth as a softly played TRUMPET. She was as comfortable playing with a QUARTET as she was with a jazz orchestra. Her sound could be considered AVANT-GARDE, but that was a label she never wanted.

Carter's remarkable career also included a temporary five-year "retirement" so that she could raise her children. She came back with a fury, starting her own record label, Bet-Car Records, in 1971. Betty Carter took more artistic risks than any other mainstream female jazz singer. Yet, her warm, authoritative voice had an inviting, irresistible quality. She recorded the hit "Baby It's Cold Outside" with Ray Charles and was awarded a National Medal of Arts by President Clinton in 1997. In 1993 Carter founded an educational program in Brooklyn, New York, called Jazz Ahead to work with a select group of young, talented jazz students toward the staging of a concert. In 1997 the Kennedy Center for the Performing Arts invited Carter to bring Jazz Ahead to Washington, D.C., where it continues. She won the GRAMMY for Best Jazz Vocal Performance, Female in 1988 for the album *Look What I Got!* The remarkable generosity of this giant of jazz was evident when she said, "Creativity and explosive musical minds built this music with the sweat of what inspired them. It isn't the lack of explosive talent that burdens us. We need to create a wider pool for young talent to emerge, to be seen, and to be heard, in order to help them create viable careers of their own."[37]

Carter, Ron (b. 1937) *American bass, cello, and piccolo bass player and composer*

This dynamic jazzman began as a player of cello and DOUBLE BASS in classical music. He graduated from the Eastman School of Music, recorded with the school's Philharmonic Orchestra, and then

and established Cherry as an artist of note. No longer working in the shadow of Coleman or Coltrane, Cherry's punchy POCKET TRUMPET sound emerged as a fresh voice in free jazz. As a technician of his instrument, he was no match for MILES DAVIS or FREDDIE HUBBARD, but the spirit and originality of his sound was often surprising and disconnected from the rules that most players felt compelled to follow.

Cherry's interest in the music of other cultures led him to learn how to play instruments from China, India, Africa, Tibet, and other countries. He began to include these instruments in his music and could be considered one of the first American pioneers of world music, a FUSION of worldwide music cultures.

As an educator, Cherry taught at Dartmouth in 1970, and, with his wife, actively produced education programs about music for children. During the 1980s and 1990s he divided his time between working with several world music ensembles (Codona and Nu), and regrouping with his old friends (Higgins, Blackwell, and others) to lay down more tracks of introspective free jazz. In 1993, only two years before his death, he joined with Ornette Coleman for a reunion tour. Don Cherry was an inspirational spirit with an original jazz voice. He succeeded in bringing the sounds of new jazz and world music to new listeners.

Chicago jazz

Many of the best jazz musicians of New Orleans migrated to Chicago between 1917 and 1920. Chicago was a prosperous industrial city, unlike New Orleans. There were many opportunities for a jazz musician to make a living in Chicago. Some of the best recordings of classic NEW ORLEANS JAZZ were actually recorded by these musicians in Chicago. Chicago-style jazz made several changes to the music of New Orleans. SAXOPHONES were added for the first time, the GUITAR replaced the BANJO, and the music took on a new energy.[40]

Perhaps most important, the collective IMPROVISATION of New Orleans jazz gave way to individual solos, largely because of the remarkable skill of LOUIS ARMSTRONG.

Chicago Underground Trio

Chicago-based American GROUP founded in 1997, the group combines post-bop jazz musicianship with electronica and free IMPROVISATION. Originally a duo founded by Rob Mazurek (CORNET and computer) and Chad Taylor (DRUMS), the current lineup is often a quartet with the addition of Jeff Parker (GUITAR) and Noel Kupersmith (BASS). Their adventurous sound ranges from the ambient to BOP to experimental, recalling an earlier AVANT-GARDE jazz scene in the Windy City led by the ART ENSEMBLE OF CHICAGO. All four of these musicians are fixtures on the underground jazz scene in Chicago. Their music swings freely from melodious jazz to cacophonous experiments, but somehow manages to capture the wide range of styles and instincts that lures today's most eclectic jazz artists. Notable recordings include the MILES DAVIS feel of *Better Together* (1999) and the more radical sonic experiments found on *Flamethrower* (2000).

chops

A musician's technical skill. "The sax player had great chops."

chord

Playing three or more notes at once. Chords are most often used in a repeated sequence as the harmonic structure of a song.

chord changes

Songs consist of a series of chords played one after another. The notes of the melody are played over the chords. Chord changes are also known as the chord progression. The sequence of chords, combined with the rhythm, defines the feel or motion of a piece of music.

chorus

The main body of a song, following the opening VERSE. A song may have several choruses, each subject to a jazz SOLO. A soloist might also be said to be playing a chorus.

Christian, Charlie (1916–1942) *American electric guitarist*

The sweet-faced and mild-mannered Christian was a dynamo on the electric GUITAR. Taught by his father, he first played BASS and acoustic guitar in local combos in Oklahoma, where he grew up. By the time he was 21 he had put down the acoustic guitar in favor of electric guitar. He loved to JAM and soon caught the attention of BENNY GOODMAN, who hired him for his sextet in 1939.

Sometimes called the first modern jazz guitarist, he was noted for playing solos a single note at a time.[41]

This style was different from most guitarists before Christian, who mostly played solos as a series of chords, one exception being EDDIE LANG. Some claim that Christian invented the long, strung-out solos that became the basis of BEBOP. There is much to support this view, given that he played in the same New York clubs as GILLESPIE and PARKER. His SOLO style drifted purposefully away from the horn style of his band mates. He was perhaps the first electric guitarist to give the instrument a new voice. His style was the model for other jazz guitarists until the 1960s, when rock and roll, and WES MONTGOMERY, brought the guitar to the forefront of pop music.

Cifelli, Jim (b. 1961) *American trumpet and flugelhorn player, composer, and bandleader*

Cifelli studied music at New York University and the Manhattan School of Music. He is one of New York's new breed of post HARD-BOP trumpeters. In 1996 he formed the New York Nonet, a jazz COMBO composed of nine musicians. The NONET is unusual but not unheard of in jazz. MILES DAVIS made jazz history with a nonet he formed to record *BIRTH OF THE COOL* back in the late 1940s. Bigger than a combo but not quite a BIG BAND, the nonet offers the bandleader a unique sound that can be both big and small.

Innovative bandleaders from the past that have influenced Cifelli include DUKE ELLINGTON, GIL EVANS, and THAD JONES. Cifelli is an inventive soloist, but gets more notice for his arrangements. The only instruments that are doubled in the New York Nonet are the TRUMPET, FLUGELHORN, and SAXOPHONE. Since no pair of instruments can effectively dominate the sound, the arrangements must rely on interplay, COUNTERPOINT, and textures to convey the soul of the music. Cifelli does this with flair while reviving the hard-bop tradition of classic jazz.

circular breathing

A breathing TECHNIQUE sometimes used by players of wind instruments. The player breathes in through the nose and stores air in the cheeks. Air can then be blown into the instrument while breathing in through the nose again. This allows for playing a note indefinitely without pausing for a breath. It is hard to do. One master of circular breathing was RAHSAAN ROLAND KIRK.

clarinet

The clarinet was the first reed instrument used widely in early jazz. Its popularity as a SOLO jazz instrument began to dwindle around 1921 when SIDNEY BECHET switched from clarinet to soprano SAXOPHONE. Both the clarinet and the saxophone use similar fingering TECHNIQUE, which makes it easy for a musician to switch from one to the other. The clarinet regained popularity as a solo voice when BENNY GOODMAN led his BIG BAND with his snappy and skillfully executed clarinet LEADS. Other noted jazz clarinet players have included ARTIE SHAW and WOODY HERMAN.

Clarke, Kenny (1914–1985) *American drummer, vibe player, and composer*

Kenny Clarke was the architect of BEBOP drumming. He grew up in Pittsburgh, where he learned to play not only DRUMS but also vibes, PIANO, and TROMBONE. He also studied music and wrote songs. His first serious GIGS were with ROY ELDRIDGE in 1935. He toured Finland and Sweden with Edgar Hayes in 1937, his first exposure to the Continent, which would eventually become his home away from America. In New York in 1941 he put together the HOUSE BAND that played MINTON'S PLAYHOUSE. He invited pianist THELONIOUS MONK to play with the group, and together they wrote the early bebop standard "EPISTROPHY." He encouraged other new players to sit in at Minton's Playhouse, including DIZZY GILLESPIE, CHARLIE PARKER, and CHARLIE CHRISTIAN. With Gillespie, he wrote the anthem of bebop, "SALT PEANUTS."

Clarke's drumming style punctuated the work of the soloists but never dominated the music. Instead, he used skillfully placed accents and tasteful razzle-dazzle in the service of the overall sound. He invented a style of ACCENTing that is sometimes called "droppin' bombs" or "klook-mop." This involved rapping off-beat accents on the snare or BASS drum in contrast to the steady pulse of the music. He got his nickname, Klook, from the sound of this drumming TECHNIQUE. Clarke used sublime brush work, patented the accented pairing of a rim shot followed by a bass drumbeat, and you could set your watch to his RIDE CYMBAL.

During his service in the army during World War II, he played TROMBONE in a stage band while in Paris. After the war he toured Europe as Dizzy Gillespie's drummer and began a long and productive career as a SESSION musician for jazz recordings. He loved Europe so much that in 1956 he permanently settled there, where he continued to teach, play, and record jazz with European artists and visiting Americans. He was a founding member of the MODERN JAZZ QUARTET, which he helped organize. He also was coleader of a European BIG BAND with Francy Boland from 1961 to 1972. Although living in France, he made regular visits to the United States and was a respected and much sought-after recording artist for the rest of his career.

Kenny Clarke's drumming was the essence of good taste. He commanded the entire drum set and was the first jazz drummer to liberate the snare drum by using the ride cymbal to keep the steady beat. Another great bebop drummer, MAX ROACH, said of Clarke, "Most drummers are nearly off balance, but Klook had everything right. He had none of the common faults of other drummers; everything was even. That's why everyone wanted to play with him. We younger guys didn't get a break until he went to Europe."

Clarke, Stanley (b. 1951) *American acoustic and electric bass player, keyboard player, composer, and arranger*

Stanley Clarke is one of the most influential and accomplished electric and acoustic BASS players of modern jazz. He first learned bass while in school in Philadelphia. After playing in rock bands in the 1960s, he moved into jazz beginning around 1970. From 1970 to 1972 he worked with various jazz greats, including HORACE SILVER, PHAROAH SANDERS, and ART BLAKEY. Clarke began to receive good reviews and won several listeners' polls during this period. But it was his work as an original member of CHICK COREA's FUSION group, Return to Forever, that brought him to prominence.

Clarke is the most copied electric bassist of the 1970s. He picked up the TECHNIQUE of slap bass playing after hearing Larry Graham of the funk rock group Sly and the Family Stone. What Clarke did with this idea was something else again, adding speed and complex jazz chording to the funk style, making it a staple sound of jazz bass playing to this day.

During and after his stint with Return to Forever, he began to produce his own albums. Teaming up with some of the best jazz and rock performers of his time, Clarke's albums still manage to put the spotlight on the bass. He elevated the bass to a LEAD instrument, applying extraordinary technique, texture, and speed. The personality of his sound can stand on equal footing with solos played on any of the more familiar lead instruments of jazz: SAXOPHONE, PIANO, TRUMPET, and GUITAR. But he has not been without his critics, particularly from jazz purists who dislike the noisy sounds of slap electric bass. Clarke has been one of the most sought-after bassists in jazz and is equally accomplished on both the acoustic upright bass and the electric bass guitar.

His loyalty to Corea was so strong during the Return to Forever days that he turned down offers by both MILES DAVIS and BILL EVANS to play for them instead. This says a lot about his devotion to what they were doing. Fusion was a new idea in the early 1970s, and he and Corea were helping define it. "We were really thinking about changing attitudes about jazz instrumental music," recalls Clarke. "And saying that everything doesn't have to be so pure and follow these rules."[42]

In recent years he continues to record his own albums and tour but has also devoted much of his time to composing and producing music for television and films. He says that writing for films makes him think more about the importance of melody in his music, a confession not often heard from a bass player.

Cobham, Billy (b. 1944) *Panamanian-born drummer, percussionist, and composer*

Billy Cobham was born into a musical family in Panama, surrounded by the sounds of the PIANO, TRUMPET, and steel DRUMS. After moving to New York with his family, he began to learn drums with a passion. At age eight he made his stage debut playing drums for his piano-playing father. After playing with the St. Catherine Queensmen Drum and Bugle Corps, he was accepted to the famed New York High School of Music and Art, where he studied music theory and continued to perfect his drumming TECHNIQUE.

His professional music career got off to a fast start during 1968 and 1969. He toured Europe with HORACE SILVER, played with STANLEY TURRENTINE and SHIRLEY SCOTT, got a job doing drums for the Broadway play *Promises, Promises,* and then joined MILES DAVIS. With Davis, he played on several landmark albums, including *BITCHES BREW, Live Evil,* and *Jack Johnson.* He was getting much critical notice during these outings, but he was still, essentially, a SESSION man.

During the Miles Davis work, he met electric guitarist JOHN MCLAUGHLIN. In 1970 McLaughlin asked Cobham to join his new FUSION group, MAHAVISHNU ORCHESTRA. Arguably the most interesting and influential of all of the fusion groups of that era, Mahavishnu Orchestra often put the spotlight on Cobham's brilliant drumming. Although Mahavishnu only stayed together for three years, Cobham emerged as one of the most popular drummers in jazz. He used the opportunity to launch his own group and SOLO recordings and has been able to sustain a successful solo career ever since.

Cobham's style is dauntingly fast, intelligent, and muscular, an unusual combination for a drummer. He is the most often imitated but most difficult to imitate jazz drummer of the 1970s. He was one of the first to pioneer the use of electronic drum kits in the late 1960s and has been closely associated with new percussion technology over the years. He has taught and conducted clinics, and continues to record and tour with his latest group, Art of 5.

Cole, Nat King (1917–1965) *American piano player, singer, composer, and bandleader*

Cole was the influential leader of a PIANO-GUITAR-BASS trio in 1939 that was much imitated by later jazz piano stylists, including OSCAR PETERSON. Cole's piano style was a little bit of SWING and a little bit of BEBOP. By 1950 Cole had become best known as a singer-songwriter and devoted most of the rest of his career to fashioning pop standards including "The Christmas Song" (1946). Like LOUIS ARMSTRONG, Cole's singing style drew from TRADITIONAL JAZZ.

Coleman, Ornette (b. 1930) *American alto and tenor saxophone, trumpet, and violin player and composer*

FREE JAZZ first came to being in the able hands of ORNETTE COLEMAN. This self-taught musician first learned how to play rhythm and blues while growing up in Fort Worth, Texas. He started with alto SAXOPHONE but was also working with the tenor by the time he left high school. He first became aware of BEBOP and CHARLIE PARKER while still in Texas. This influenced the style of his SOLOS but was not appreciated by his fellow rhythm and blues band mates, nor their audience. He was once beaten up by unappreciative Texans and his tenor sax thrown down a cliff. The fact that he was African American living in the segregated South made matters worse for him.

By 1950 he went to Los Angeles on tour with Pee Wee Crayton's rhythm and blues band, and left the group to stay in California. While working as an elevator operator, he studied music theory and began to form a new approach and philosophy about jazz. He once admitted that as much as he enjoyed CHARLIE PARKER, and could imitate his licks, it was no good just to be able to copy someone else's style. Instead, this intense, thinking young man was seeking a path and philosophy of music all his own. Had he been an automotive engineer, he would have invented a new kind of engine. Being a jazz musician, he invented a new style that came to be called free jazz.

Coleman's major departure from bebop and TRADITIONAL JAZZ was to place higher value on free expression over structure. Bebop was about harmony, and harmony is about chords—playing the right notes. Coleman disengaged his playing from a background of chords, letting solos go where they may.

"Let's try to play the music and not the background," he said, ". . . *expressing* our minds and our emotions rather than being a *background* for emotions."[43]

From 1951 to 1953 he perfected his new ideas while playing various clubs around Los Angeles. Reaction to his unorthodox style was mostly critical, but a few other players began to gravitate toward Coleman.

By 1954 he had begun to find other musicians who shared some of his instincts about jazz. His first QUARTET included trumpeter DON CHERRY, drummer Billy Higgins, and bassist CHARLIE HADEN. Coleman's first record, *Something Else!*, was made in 1958. It revealed the work of an emerging thinker in jazz and was championed by a few, if not most, jazz critics. John Lewis of the MODERN JAZZ QUARTET was influential in getting Coleman a record contract with Atlantic in 1959. This also resulted in Coleman and Cherry being sponsored to attend workshops at the Lenox School of Jazz in Massachusetts. In November 1959 Coleman's quartet opened for a two-week engagement at the Five Spot club in New York. The result was controversial, but successful.

This came at a time when the easygoing COOL JAZZ movement was at its peak. The DAVE BRUBECK Quartet had the biggest selling jazz record in 1959 and appealed largely to a white, college-age audience. In contrast to cool jazz, Coleman and his band mates startled the jazz scene with what seemed like a totally anarchic approach. They ignored chords. They played freely developing solos. They ignored traditional song structures. Consistent patterns of melody, rhythm, and texture were absent in the music. Jazz critics reacted with shock and dismay to the quartet's work. Many leading jazz musicians did a double take. While listening to Coleman's wailing saxophone, the legendary BENNY CARTER once remarked, "I just can't figure it out. From the very first note it's miserably out of tune." But many fans connected with his music. The group's stay at the Five Spot was a sensation, and the two-week GIG turned into 10 weeks. Coleman's quartet then recorded seven albums for Atlantic from 1960 to

Ornette Coleman (right) with Ed Blackwell (drums) and Scott La Faro (bass)

1962, each of which evidenced the young man's bold new vision for jazz. His album FREE JAZZ, recorded with two quartets playing at the same time, gave its name to this new style of jazz.

Surprisingly, Coleman briefly retired from performing in 1963 and 1964, taking time instead to study TRUMPET and VIOLIN. After a successful series of world tours to Japan, Europe, and other places, Coleman settled into another period of study and composing. He opened his Artists House in the SoHo section of New York and gave performances there with his friends for several years. He was writing for orchestra and other nonjazz instrumentation during this time, a highlight being a performance of *Skies of America* for jazz quartet and orchestra, performed at the 1972 NEWPORT JAZZ FESTIVAL. This piece was the first large-scale embodiment of his theory of "harmolodics," a style of composition in which simultaneously played melodies replace the use of traditional CHORD structures. He traveled to Morocco in 1973 to visit a family of traditional musicians living in the remote village of Joujouka, composing music for them and staging some performances.

Coleman was a latecomer to FUSION jazz, but formed an influential group in 1975 called Prime Time. This was his first venture using electric GUITAR and BASS as part of his COMBO. The group became a laboratory for Coleman's increasingly prolific composing and showcased his work into the 1980s. During the 1980s he devoted much time to composing for classical music ensembles, often being commissioned by institutions such as the Brooklyn Academy of Music.

He continues to find time to tour with jazz musicians, compose, and to make adventurous recordings. He has been the recipient of many grants and awards, including the first Guggenheim Fellowship given for jazz composition only (1967) and a MacArthur Fellowship (1994). Coleman will always be known for opening the ears of jazz listeners and musicians to new vistas of sound experimentation. By disconnecting his music from the foundations of traditional jazz, he discovered new kinds of self-expression in his music with which others could connect. His was not an errant journey down a dead-end street. He paved a new highway for himself that others could also follow.

Coltrane, Alice (b. 1937) *American piano and harp player*

Also known as Turiya Sagittananda, Coltrane grew up as Alice McLeod and married JOHN COLTRANE in 1965. She grew up in Detroit, where she studied classical music. She first worked in Detroit with locals such as YUSEF LATEEF. She met John Coltrane while touring with Terry Gibbs in 1962. She became a member of John Coltrane's group in 1966, replacing MCCOY TYNER. Her harp and PIANO playing were well suited to her husband's increasingly experimental music. She was known for using arpeggios, which is the playing of the notes of a CHORD one by one instead of all at once. This fit with her husband's focus on scales instead of chords. With the addition of PHAROAH SANDERS on tenor SAXOPHONE, the sound of the latter work of John Coltrane was increasingly meditative and spacey.

After her husband's death, she led the group herself and produced several albums that extended the style last being explored by her husband. Among

these records is the spiritually uplifting *Ptah, The El Daoud* (1970), a stylistic BRIDGE between the FREE JAZZ sounds of the late 1960s and a more meditative style of jazz featuring drones, suspended tension, and moments of startling beauty. Two of the sons of Alice and John Coltrane, RAVI COLTRANE and Oran Coltrane, became SAXOPHONE players and have performed with their mother. Alice Coltrane heads the John Coltrane Foundation and sponsors annual scholarships for budding jazz musicians.

Coltrane, John (1926–1967) *American tenor, alto, and soprano saxophone player, composer, and bandleader*

There are only a few jazz artists who have had as profound an impact on jazz as John Coltrane. He joins the company of LOUIS ARMSTRONG, CHARLIE PARKER, and MILES DAVIS as one of the most skilled and original jazz musicians of all time. They called him "Trane." His SAXOPHONE playing was as fast and powerful as a locomotive.

Born and raised in North Carolina, Coltrane first played alto saxophone in his high school band. He moved to Philadelphia after high school and studied composition and music theory at the Ornstein School of Music (1944). He played alto sax on his first professional job with a bar band in Philadelphia (1945). Military duty called, and he played alto saxophone for a U.S. Navy BIG BAND (1945–46). After the service, he joined Eddie "Cleanhead" Vinson's rhythm and blues band in 1947–48. Vinson played a hard-driving alto saxophone and asked Coltrane to switch from alto to tenor, the instrument with which he would become most closely associated. Intent on improving his TECHNIQUE, he went back to school briefly in 1951 to study composition and saxophone at the Granoff Studios in Philadelphia (1951). Giving BEBOP a try, he joined DIZZY GILLESPIE's big band (1948–49), playing both alto and tenor. When Gillespie reduced the size of the group to six players, he retained Coltrane for two more years (1950–51).

During the early 1950s Coltrane continued to work with several rhythm and blues bands and then in a group formed by longtime DUKE ELLINGTON sax man Johnny Hodges (1953–55). In 1955 he came to prominence as a player in the reshuffled MILES DAVIS QUINTET. His ascension to stardom as a SOLO artist was fostered by Davis's own experiments. For the first time Coltrane was encouraged to play outside the bounds of the song structure usually dictated by the leader. He exploded onto the scene, recording one riveting performance after another with the Davis quintet. The contrast between the two players was startling enough to serve the needs of the group. Davis, with his introspective, often slowly developing melodies played in stark contrast

John Coltrane

to the fiery whacks of sound that were the stuff of Coltrane's solos.

The relationship between Davis and Coltrane was not always so complementary. Both players competed for the spotlight, a drive that certainly inspired glorious solos but did not always make it easy for Davis to lead a group in which he was the featured artist. A story has been told of Miles and Coltrane jamming one night. Trane liked to play long solos. It seemed that he sometimes played a little too long. When an impatient Miles asked Coltrane why he played such long solos, Coltrane innocently replied, "Once I get going, I just don't know how to stop." Snarling in that raspy voice of his, Davis suggested a way that Trane could stop: "Take the ******* horn out of your mouth!"

Coltrane recorded five landmark albums with the Davis quintet. It was a laboratory for his developing talent. While with Davis, his playing revealed a fascination with CHORD CHANGES that rivaled that of bebop. He might even add chords to a song's already existing CHORD pattern. The Davis quintet also showcased Coltrane's searing solo style. Unlike most saxophonists, he was able to sustain strength and power in all pitch ranges, creating a fullness of tone at all times. His sax screamed for attention. Coming as they did in contrast to the pensive TRUMPET sounds of Davis, Coltrane's solos were electrifying.

Trane was on the verge of mounting a new revolution in jazz, but personal problems overcame him temporarily. During the mid-1950s Coltrane suffered greatly from addiction to both cocaine and alcohol. Davis had to let him go temporarily from the group in 1957 so that Coltrane could enter rehabilitation. Shaken up by the experience, Coltrane not only kicked the drug habit but had a spiritual reawakening. In 1964 he wrote about his rebirth in the notes for his album *A LOVE SUPREME*: "During the year 1957, I experienced, by the grace of God, a spiritual awakening which was to lead me to a richer, fuller, more productive life. At that time, in gratitude, I humbly asked to be given the means and privilege to make others happy through music." Upon coming back, he first played with THELONIOUS MONK in 1956 and 1957 and then rejoined Miles Davis for two years beginning in 1958.

By 1960 Trane's growth as a saxophonist had taken enormous strides. He was the most sought-after SESSION man on the planet. He even added soprano saxophone to his arsenal. His sound had taken on an expansive, otherworldly quality. He took the Davis practice of playing scales rather than chords to even greater heights. The result was blistering "sheets of sound" as jazz critic Ira Gitler called Coltrane's emerging style. With newly earned confidence, Coltrane decided to form his own QUARTET. During its formative stages, he recorded the landmark album GIANT STEPS (1959), his first lasting statement as a bandleader, including seven original compositions. After working with several players in 1960 and 1961, Coltrane settled on ELVIN JONES (DRUMS), MCCOY TYNER (PIANO) and JIMMY GARRISON (BASS) as the basis for his quartet.

For the next six years, this group made some of the most startling and skillfully played jazz ever heard. Coltrane chose his players well. With this group surrounding him, the intensity and purity of his music increased dramatically. Tyner had an uncanny sense for the kind of MODAL JAZZ that Coltrane had learned from Miles Davis. Without such an able and instinctive piano player, Coltrane's music may not have soared so high. Elvin Jones knew how to add texture and rhythm, even when his leader seemed to be flying high above the clouds without a care for song structure and a steady beat. Garrison had the additional challenge of using the bass to follow but also lead the other players when the music moved in his direction.

Gone were the reminders of bebop that had stayed with him since the Gillespie days. Gone, too, was an obligation to play anything as familiar as a song that someone could tap their foot to. To make his point clear, Coltrane recorded his version of a popular song first made famous by Julie Andrews in the movie *The Sound of Music.* "MY FAVORITE THINGS" was a 13-minute romp that unraveled the American popular song idiom. The recording was indeed strange,

but because of the familiarity of the original version, it became the best way for Coltrane to explain, in music, what his music was all about. "My Favorite Things" (1960) was regularly featured in his live sets and made the group famous around the world.

Coltrane and his quartet, however, were not without their critics. Coltrane's solos were thought to be too long. His music was considered by some to be too heady and hard to listen to. The sound of his tenor was at times harsh, like a scream, and almost too intense for many to bear. Yet the group marched on, into history, with a persistence that only the most dedicated artists have to their craft. Except for a few temporary additions or substitutions, including ERIC DOLPHY, Art Davis, Reggie Workman, Roy Haynes, the group remained essentially intact until 1966. Together they recorded 25 live and studio albums. Among these, *Coltrane* (1962), *Live Trane: The European Tours* (1961–63), *A Love Supreme* (1964), and *Ascension* (1965) represent high points of the quartet's recordings.

By 1965 Coltrane's intense spirituality fueled his music with increasingly long and adventurous playing. During this time he married musician ALICE COLTRANE, with whom he had two sons, RAVI COLTRANE and Oran Coltrane, who became saxophone players. His departure from conventional harmony became more extreme and his pieces more unconventional. For the album *Ascension* in 1965, he augmented his quartet with 10 other players, often doubling on instruments. This was Coltrane's version of what Coleman had dubbed the "double quartet" back in 1960. The music was a collective IMPROVISATION triggered by audible signals delivered mainly by Tyner on piano and FREDDIE HUBBARD on trumpet. With each signal, the players could switch scales and introduce new patterns of notes. Unlike Coleman's FREE JAZZ, where soloists periodically rose above the background of the other players, the musicians on *Ascension* kept within the bounds of the overall sonic texture, rarely emerging on their own. The result was a brash new soundscape for jazz. But it didn't sit well with the original members of the quartet. It was clear that Coltrane had, by this time, exhausted the possibilities of his seminal group.

One by one, Tyner, Jones, and Garrison left during 1965 and 1966 while Coltrane put together his new super group to further explore the more spacey music he was conjuring. Among the new members were his second wife, Alice, who played piano, PHAROAH SANDERS on tenor sax, Rashied Ali on drums, and numerous other percussionists. Garrison returned on bass from time to time but was sometimes replaced by Art Davis. This group continued to reach the outer limits of jazz until 1967 with the untimely death of Coltrane at age 40.

The esteem with which Coltrane is held by fellow musicians is summed up by WYNTON MARSALIS, "You listen to Coltrane and that's something human, something that's about elevation. . . . It's about something of value, it's not just loud. It doesn't have that violent connotation to it."

Coltrane, Ravi (b. 1965) *American tenor and soprano saxophone player*

As the son of ALICE and JOHN COLTRANE, the world's most famous and celebrated saxophonist, one might be reluctant to pick up the instrument, but beginning at age 20 Ravi began to show his own individual prowess on the soprano and tenor SAXOPHONES. He gigged with his mother for a time then worked in other bands, including one led by his father's drummer, ELVIN JONES, from 1991 to 1993. Ravi carefully put together a career of his own, not relying on the reputation of his late father to thrust him into the spotlight. His first album as a group leader, *Moving Pictures,* was released in 1998 at age 33. Critics have been careful not to expect too much of him, and he has slowly won them over with the substantial merits of his own playing and composing. His style is forceful but controlled, lending itself well to the interpretation of classics by WAYNE SHORTER, HORACE SILVER, THELONIOUS MONK, ORNETTE COLEMAN and, yes, John Coltrane.

combo

A small instrumental group usually consisting of no more than eight musicians.

comping

Improvising CHORDS to accompany another player's SOLO. A PIANO player might comp while a SAXOPHONE player has a solo. Comping uses accents to stress the interaction of the chords and the solo. One of the earliest musicians to develop this TECHNIQUE was COUNT BASIE in the mid-1930s. It was later widely adopted by bop piano players during the 1940s.

composer

The person who writes a piece of music. The composer may also write the ARRANGEMENT of the piece, but this is sometimes done by an ARRANGER instead.

Conference of the Birds (1972) *album by Dave Holland*

This recording, released by ECM, is a quiet masterwork of FREE JAZZ. DAVE HOLLAND, only 22 at the time, was already known as an accomplished and imaginative free style BASS player. In assembling musicians for this record, he tapped proven innovators ANTHONY BRAXTON (reeds, FLUTE), Sam Rivers (reeds, flute), and Barry Altschul (DRUMS). The result is a collection of Holland compositions that lays out basic patterns upon which the players improvise. The record is an outstanding example of free jazz ENSEMBLE playing. Holland's bass playing alternates between shadowing the others and rollicking freely to weave together the whole. Braxton and Rivers refine the squawks and honks reminiscent of ORNETTE COLEMAN, channeling their energy into several tightly-knit interweaving solos. Perhaps the most outstanding performance of all is that of drummer Altschul, whose free drumming emphasizes textures, not unlike a percussionist in an orchestra.

by black former heavyweight champion Jack Johnson as the Club Deluxe in 1918. It was a casino located above a theater in Harlem at 142nd Street and Lenox Avenue. The failing club was then bought from Johnson in 1923 by a group of mobsters represented by Owney Madden. The extravagant club soon became a mob hangout and a haven for rich white patrons. The Cotton Club employed mostly African-American jazz performers, dancers, and other entertainers. However, the audience was restricted to whites during most of this period. DUKE ELLINGTON's fame grew largely because of his four-year stint at the Cotton Club, which often featured radio broadcasts of his orchestra. The Cotton Club, although not allowing black patrons, succeeded in spreading the music of African-American artists across the country. In 1936 the club moved from Harlem to West 48th Street in midtown Manhattan. The Cotton Club returned to Harlem in 1978, where it is still located on West 125th Street.

counterpoint

Two or more melodies played at the same time and following the same harmonic pattern. In counterpoint, each melody is strong enough to stand alone, but by playing them at the same time, something new and complex is created because of their interplay. The classical COMPOSER Johann Sebastian Bach was one of the first great composers to use counterpoint.

Cox, Anthony (b. 1954) *American acoustic and electric bass player*

Cox was born in Ardmore, Oklahoma, but now makes his home in Minnesota. Bassist Cox has amassed a long list of credits, and has played with just about anybody who is anybody during the last 20 years. As a SIDEMAN, he is adaptable to many styles of jazz, from FREE JAZZ IMPROVISATION to BOP and traditional ballads. As an instrumentalist, his know-how comes from college music studies at the

University of Wisconsin, Eau Claire, (1977–79) and private studies with the legendary DAVE HOLLAND (1981). Cox has frequently worked in Europe, where many of his recording credits originate. He has worked with Charles Lloyd, Sam Rivers, STAN GETZ, JOHN SCOFIELD, Kenny Burrell, Craig Harris, ELVIN JONES, ED BLACKWELL, and Christof Lauer. In 1996 he was a resident guest artist with the NDR BIG BAND in Hamburg, Germany. He has coled two groups: Rios with Dino Saluzzi (bandoneon) and David Friedman (vibes and marimba); and Other Worlds with Friedman and Jean-Louis Matinier (accordion). The unusual combination of instruments in these groups results in a quirky blend of jazz and folk music. Cox's most recent work extends his composing, arranging, and performing skills to vocal, orchestral, and ENSEMBLE work. Cox is a multifaceted player who can work well in any jazz idiom.

crash cymbal

A large cymbal used by a drummer to make a loud, crashing sound. The crash cymbal may have little rivets around its circumference that rattle to make the sound louder. A crash cymbal is used sparingly and does not reverberate as long as a RIDE CYMBAL.

Crispell, Marilyn (b. 1947) *American piano player*

Born in Philadelphia and raised in Baltimore, Crispell studied classical PIANO before beginning her professional career as a player in a rock band. After hearing JOHN COLTRANE, she was inspired to switch to playing IMPROVISATIONAL jazz. In 1978 she toured with another key influence, ANTHONY BRAXTON. She released her first record as a bandleader in 1983 and has been in demand ever since as both a SIDEMAN and group leader. Her taste in music leans toward the AVANT-GARDE. Her richly textured SOLOS suggest a combination of classical music TECHNIQUE singed by exposure to Coltrane's most extreme experimental work. Still, for all of the experimentation, her playing is emotionally powerful and fully engaging. Crispell plays in the great beyond where few improvisers can go. Few of her contemporaries have the imagination, skill, and power of Marilyn Crispell.

crossover jazz

Music with jazz roots that becomes popular with audiences of popular song, rock, and easy-listening music. Artists such as DAVID SANBORN, PAT METHENY, and DIANA KRALL have successfully extended their appeal to audiences of rock and pop without sacrificing the essence of jazz performance. Others, including popular reed player Kenny G have crossed over into a musical genre that might best be described as jazzy mood music.

Cuban jazz   See LATIN AND AFRO-CUBAN JAZZ.

cutting contest

A cutting contest is a competition between individual musicians or bands. It was a popular performance stunt that began during the earliest years of jazz and reached a level of pitched notoriety in the 1920s and 1930s. It all started in the early 1900s in New Orleans, where the popularity of a nightclub often rested on the quality of its musicians. This led to some of the first cutting contests where bands faced off in a public place until one was able to outlast or drown out the other. As famed CLARINET player SIDNEY BECHET recalled about cutting contests, "It was always the public who decided."[45]

Boasting rights generally went to the performers who could incite the most enthusiastic audience response.

One famous rivalry from the early New Orleans days of jazz pitted the loud, brassy sound of BUDDY BOLDEN'S COMBO against the smooth, sophisticated music of the John Robichaux Orchestra. The two groups were often booked to play at the same time in two neighboring public parks. Bolden would sometimes aim his CORNET in the direction of his rival's park and play loudly to "call" his children home. Upon hearing this, many fans would evidently desert Robichaux and run over to enjoy Bolden's band.

Cutting contests often broke out between individual musicians as well. This often happened when PIANO players found themselves playing together on the same program. One of the fiercest competitors was Willie "The Lion" Smith. He described a typical cutting contest like this, "We would embroider the melodies with our own original ideas and try to develop patterns that had more originality than those played before us. Sometimes it was just a question of who could think up the most patterns within a given tune. It was pure IMPROVISATION."[46]

Competition between bands heated up during the heyday of SWING. At the SAVOY BALLROOM in HARLEM, drummer CHICK WEBB's HOUSE BAND rarely lost to any comers. Musicians were so hot to compete in the 1930s and 1940s that they would often go out late at night after their regular GIGS looking for a showdown with a rival. DIZZY GILLESPIE and his friends were known to "ambush" their fellow musicians in this way. "What Charlie Parker and Dizzy would do," recalled musician Duke Garrett, "they would put their horns under their coats and run in on Coleman Hawkins, or run in on Illinois Jacquet and all of them, and start playing. . . . And they would just wipe out the session."[47]

Gillespie himself was haunted by ROY ELDRIDGE. "He was the most competitive musician I've ever seen," recalled Dizzy. "Every time he picks up his horn and another trumpet player's there, he wants to blow him out."[48]

Other famed combatants included tenor SAXOPHONE warriors COLEMAN HAWKINS, LESTER YOUNG, and BEN WEBSTER, who often paired off in late-night duels in the 1930s. Even the somewhat hallowed format of Norman Granz's JAZZ AT THE PHILHARMONIC was often livened up by pitting musicians from the BEBOP style against established swing players. A lot of exciting music was made when the likes of Charlie Parker faced off with Coleman Hawkins during these widely publicized performances. The cutting contest is a jazz tradition that represents the high spirits and exemplary playing necessary to be a great jazz musician.

Cyrille, Andrew (b. 1939) *American drummer and composer*

A native of Brooklyn, Cyrille is a virtuosic drummer with a feel for percussion as the basis of composition. After studying privately with PHILLY JOE JONES, he attended both the Juilliard and the Harnett music schools from 1960 to 1964. He gigged with a multitude of artists during this time, including MARY LOU WILLIAMS, RAHSAAN ROLAND KIRK, and COLEMAN HAWKINS, among others. Cyrille came to prominence while playing with CECIL TAYLOR from 1964 to 1975. While still playing with Taylor's group, he formed a unique DRUM trio called Dialogue of the Drums (1971) with Milford Graves and Rashied Ali.

During the late 1970 and early 1980s he led several groups with more TRADITIONAL JAZZ instrumentation, including the seven-player Moano, the QUINTET The Group, and the QUARTET Pieces of Time also featuring KENNY CLARKE. Cyrille's musical collaborations during the 1980s and 1990s have embraced a wide range of modern jazz stylings. He has worked with artists as diverse as MUHAL RICHARD ABRAMS, ANTHONY BRAXTON, MARILYN CRISPELL, and the Reggie Workman group. As an educator, he was artist in residence at Antioch College in the 1970s and taught at the New School (New York) and the Windham Home for Children during the 1990s.

The one thread that runs throughout all of Cyrille's work is a willingness to experiment. His playing is exceptionally thoughtful and poetic, embracing traditions of jazz, African music, and the mathematically precise rhythms of life in the computer age. He thinks ahead, much like a chess player, anticipating the moves of his fellow players, and providing a percussion backdrop that is nearly symphonic in its breadth and range.

Davis, Ernestine "Tiny" (1907–1994)
American trumpet player and singer

Sometimes called the female LOUIS ARMSTRONG, "Tiny" was an exhilarating TRUMPET player who gained prominence playing with all-women bands during the SWING era. As a young woman, she listened to Louis Armstrong and dug both COUNT BASIE and MARY LOU WILLIAMS. One of her early GIGS was with the HARLEM Playgirls led by Sylvester Rice. She joined the International Sweethearts of Rhythm, a 16-piece, all-female swing band that toured the United States during World War II. This group of accomplished women was groundbreaking in many ways. Not only was it an all-female band in a male-dominated business, but the ENSEMBLE was racially mixed. Members of the orchestra included players who were African American, Mexican, Asian, Puerto Rican, and white.[49]

She remained with the group for 10 years.

In the 1950s she and her longtime partner, Ruby Lucas, who was a drummer and pianist with the Sweethearts, started their own group, the Hell Divers. They also had their own club in Chicago, Tiny and Ruby's Gay Spot. She and Ruby continued to make music for many years, playing festivals and relating the stories of their adventures during the swing years. A short documentary film about them was made in 1988, *Tiny and Ruby: Hell Divin' Women.* Ernestine's playing was top-notch.

Legend has it that Louis Armstrong admired her so much that he once offered her 10 times her salary to join his band, but she refused to leave her ladies.[50]

She was often LEAD player of the group and also excelled at vocals. Her style was pure swing and HOT JAZZ, much in the style of Armstrong. Above all else, she was a swingin' lady. In 1946 she sang the vocal for a recording by the Sweethearts called "Jump Children." The words and rhythms were a prophetic prelude to rock and roll, when she sang, "It takes a long tall Daddy to satisfy my soul, My Daddy rocks me with that steady roll."

Davis, Miles (1926–1991) *American trumpet player, composer, and bandleader*

Davis once said, "I never thought that the music called *jazz* was ever meant to reach just a small group of people, or become a museum thing locked under glass like all the other dead things that were once considered artistic." This sums up the attitude that Miles brought to his music throughout a professional career that lasted 50 years. He was the pied piper of new ideas in jazz. Along with LOUIS ARMSTRONG, CHARLIE PARKER, and JOHN COLTRANE, Davis was one of the four most influential players to ever lay down a note of jazz.

He grew up in East St. Louis, Illinois. He was interested in sports before he took to playing an instrument. As a skinny little kid in a racially segregated community, he learned to box and defend himself from the bullying of white and black kids in his neighborhood. His father was a successful dentist and an activist for the rights of African Americans. His father's nurturing pride and mentorship were a huge influence on Davis, providing

Miles Davis

insisted that his students play Sousa marches and orchestral band music, Davis kept listening to jazz and practicing his CHOPS on his own. Buchanan was a big influence on the early sound of Davis's playing. He recognized the talent in the youngster and wasn't afraid of challenging him, even at the risk of embarrassing Davis. Like his other band mates, the young Davis liked to imitate the VIBRATO sound of popular trumpeters like Harry James. One time during rehearsal, Buchanan stopped the band and scolded Davis, saying, "Look here, Miles. Don't come around here with that Harry James stuff, playing with all that vibrato. Stop shaking all those notes and trembling them, because you gonna be shaking enough when you get old. Play straight, develop our own style, because you can do it. You got enough talent to be your own trumpet man."[52]

Davis took this advice to heart and not only began to smooth out his playing but also began to experiment with other techniques, including the use of scales independent of CHORDs. He began to play GIGs locally and catch the acts of bands that toured the area. He played some dates with the Eddie Randall band, which mostly consisted of SWING music. After leaving Randall because he didn't like their music, he had the chance to play for two weeks with Billy Eckstine's band when they came to St. Louis in 1944. Both CHARLIE PARKER and DIZZY GILLESPIE were a part of Eckstine's band. Playing with them was an eye-opening experience. As a result, Davis decided to go to New York to study music at Juilliard in the fall of 1944.

This was a turning point in Davis's career. Although he attended Juilliard for only a year, he spent most of his free time gigging at clubs like MINTON'S PLAYHOUSE in HARLEM, where BEBOP started. He not only played with Gillespie and Parker, but often with COLEMAN HAWKINS and backed-up BILLIE HOLIDAY. Davis was disillusioned with the teaching at Juilliard. It was steeped in the traditions of European classical music and all but ignored jazz and its African-American roots. He quit Juilliard in the fall of 1945 to devote his time to playing jazz for a living.[53]

him both with opportunity and the drive to exceed at his chosen profession. Davis's first exposure to jazz came from radio broadcasts and recordings. When he was seven or eight years old, he was listening to broadcasts of HARRY JAMES and Bobby Hackett on the radio and absorbing the music of COUNT BASIE, DUKE ELLINGTON, Bessie Smith, Louis Armstrong, and others on record.[51]

Davis started playing TRUMPET at 13. He received his first trumpet lessons from Elwood Buchanan, a friend of his father's who was well acquainted with many professional musicians. Although Buchanan

From 1945 to 1948, Davis played with the Parker QUINTET and established himself as a unique trumpeter with a style and voice that was clearly different from the frenetically exuberant Gillespie. Beginning in 1948, he embarked on his remarkable career as a bandleader. The first fruits of these efforts are today known as the BIRTH OF THE COOL (1949–50) sessions. Davis assembled a NONET, or ENSEMBLE consisting of nine players. Not only was this an unusual size for a jazz group, but its instrumentation was stranger still. In addition to Davis on trumpet, the nonet included players on FRENCH HORN, TROMBONE, tuba, alto SAXOPHONE, baritone saxophone, PIANO, BASS, and DRUMS. This work was not appreciated by audiences at the time and the nonet performed poorly when it attempted to play its work for a live audience. But the recordings have become classics and led to the cool jazz movement, or West Coast jazz style, that became popular in the 1950s.

In 1950 Davis's career seemed poised to take off, and it would have except for his worsening addiction to heroin, a habit he had picked up in 1949. After four years of trying to work and several run-ins with the law, drug abuse seemed to have gotten the better of him. Returning to Illinois and with the help of his family, he finally kicked the habit and returned to New York, where he formed his second important group, the Miles Davis Quintet, in 1955. The group included JOHN COLTRANE, Red Garland, PHILLY JOE JONES, and PAUL CHAMBERS. It was exploding with talent. It was the group that made both Coltrane and Davis famous worldwide. The quintet was prolific, recording six remarkable albums in only 12 months. This spurt of recording was not without an underlying financial motivation: Davis wanted to complete a contract he had with Prestige Records so that he could move on to record on the larger Columbia label.

Davis began to reach out beyond the quintet work during the late 1950s, working with COMPOSER and ARRANGER GIL EVANS. Together they collaborated on several albums combining orchestra and Davis's trumpet, including *Porgy and Bess* (1958) and the remarkably haunting *Sketches of Spain* (1960). Evans's masterly direction allowed Davis to rise to new levels of expression as a SOLO artist. But Davis had not given up COMBO work either. During the same period he reformed his group and added a sixth member, CANNONBALL ADDERLEY, to play alto saxophone alongside Coltrane's tenor. The group released the celebrated album KIND OF BLUE in 1959, a record that has been called the most influential in all of jazz.

The album was Davis's grand experiment in modal IMPROVISATION. In this style of playing, improvisations are based on different scales, or modes, rather than CHORD CHANGES and songlike harmony. It was distinctively different from the song stylings of cool jazz or the breakneck solos of BOP and HARD BOP. *Kind of Blue* painted jazz with a new palette of colors and textures, letting the sound of a note stand on its own, disconnected from the predictable motion of CHORDS, buoyed by supportive interplay of the bass and drums. MODAL JAZZ freed all of the individual players from their usual roles in a combo. Everybody became a featured part of the combined texture of sound.

Coltrane went his own way in the 1960s, and Davis searched for a new direction. The names of players who rose to prominence with Davis during the 1960s reads like a who's who of modern jazz. His quintet from 1963 to 1964 featured piano player HERBIE HANCOCK, bassist RON CARTER, the young TONY WILLIAMS on drums, and WAYNE SHORTER on saxophones. From 1964 to 1968 piano player CHICK COREA replaced Hancock and DAVE HOLLAND replaced Ron Carter. In 1969 Davis began a groundbreaking effort to blend jazz and rock by forming a group comprised of electric instruments. Davis played an amplified trumpet, Hancock, Corea, and newcomer JOE ZAWINUL played electric keyboards, and JOHN MCLAUGHLIN was added on electric GUITAR. They recorded IN A SILENT WAY (1969), an album with only two tracks that paved the way for the astounding BITCHES BREW album recorded the same year and released in 1970. Along with *Live Evil* (1970) and *A Tribute to Jack Johnson* (1970), this quartet of albums defined the outer limits of jazz rock FUSION—the playing of sparse musical figures laid down by Davis and improvised freely by a huge collective of musicians playing onstage.

Davis was radically reshaping the makeup of jazz instrumentation by bringing into play amplified horns and reeds, electronic keyboards, hard-edged and distorted electric guitar, feedback, echo, and a glut of miscellaneous percussion sounds. But Davis's version of fusion was also a complex web of POLYRHYTHMS, modal playing, and free improvisation using multiple rhythm and melody sections playing at the same time. While some critics knocked the jazz great for having sold out to make money from rock, few could really imitate the remarkably complex and unique music that Davis was creating at the time. His 1972 album, *On the Corner,* a blend of funk music and jazz expression, was also panned by critics at the time. It has since been lauded as a prophetic blend of jazz and funk that preceded hip-hop.

After five years of seemingly endless touring and recording, Davis was forced to retire in 1975 due to ill health. He came back in 1980 but suffered a stroke in 1982. Although slowed by health problems, he was able to continue work with PRODUCERS such as MARCUS MILLER who were sympathetic to his desire to create even more new jazz sounds. During this time Davis's talent for arranging and composing became more important as he crafted

The Miles Davis Quintet featuring Herbie Hancock (piano), Wayne Shorter (saxophone), and Miles Davis

several fine albums of instrumental works, including the records *Tutu* and *Amandla*. He toured Europe in the mid-1980s and was the recipient of nationally sponsored music awards in both Denmark and France. At the time of his death, Davis had plans for working with Prince and had been recording tracks with rapper Easy Mo Bee. Although Davis was able to complete only six tracks with Easy Mo Bee, the resulting album, *Doo Bop*, was yet another startling fusion from the imagination of Miles Davis, this time combining rap, hip-hop, and an easy bop swing.

As a player, Davis established a sound for himself that was clearly different from other trumpeters. Although often imitated now, his smooth tone, harking back to the scolding he once received from Elwood Buchanan, remains the signature sound of Miles Davis. He also introduced the metal MUTE sound in the mid-1950s as well as the amplified trumpet outfitted with a WAH-WAH PEDAL, echo, and reverb during his fusion years. His most important contributions to jazz styles included the early evolution of cool jazz, orchestral jazz with Gil Evans, modal jazz, fusion jazz, and the combination of jazz and funk that some might call ACID JAZZ. For a man whose life was often troubled, Davis had an amazing attitude about his work. "Nothing is out of the question for me," he said. "I'm always thinking about creating. My future starts when I wake up in the morning and see the light. . . . Then I'm grateful."

DeFrancesco, Joey (b. 1971) *American organ and trumpet player and composer*
Raised near Philadelphia by an ORGAN-playing father, DeFrancesco took an early liking to the sound of the Hammond ORGAN. He emulates the playing of the legendary JIMMY SMITH. A lot of Smith's TECHNIQUE can be heard in DeFrancesco and, like Smith, Joey tends to be a straight-up TRADITIONAL JAZZ player. His speed on the keys is amazing, and his jamming with other musicians, particularly GUITAR players, shows imagination and

brilliance. He has teamed up with JOHN MCLAUGHLIN and drummer ELVIN JONES for a superb record and a tour (*After the Rain*, 1995), has recorded a CD of Frank Sinatra classics (*Plays Sinatra His Way*, 2004), and released a live album on which he played with Jimmy Smith, his hero (*Incredible!* 2000). Whereas BARBARA DENNERLEIN is known as the consummate experimenter of modern organ style, DeFrancesco is a traditionalist of the pure power sound of the Hammond.

DeJohnette, Jack (b. 1942) *American drummer, keyboard player, melodica player and composer*
DeJohnette studied PIANO and DRUMS while growing up in Chicago. His early playing covered many types of music, including rock, rhythm and blues, and jazz. In the late 1960s he moved to New York and had jobs drumming for singers BETTY CARTER and ABBEY LINCOLN. He played with the Charles Lloyd QUARTET (1966–69), which included KEITH JARRETT. Exposure through Lloyd's performances brought him to the attention of MILES DAVIS, with whom he played on the seminal *BITCHES BREW* (1970), also touring with the Davis FUSION band for two years. Since that time he has worked for Jarrett and developed a reputation as an exceptional SESSION drummer. In 1992, returning to his roots in composition, he wrote music for the Rova Saxophone Quartet. DeJohnette has a ferocious style, akin to the strongest rock drummers, but with the sensibility and intelligence of an old-time jazz master.

Dennerlein, Barbara (b. 1964) *German organ and electronic keyboard player, bandleader, and composer*
Only a handful of innovative keyboard players came to prominence as jazz musicians by playing the ORGAN. Among them, JIMMY SMITH, RICHARD "GROOVE" HOLMES, SHIRLEY SCOTT, and LARRY YOUNG have all been successful. Dennerlein is from the newest generation of keyboard players who feature the organ as their main instrument. With a

nod to Larry Young and other innovators before her, she has kept the organ tradition alive and well in jazz. She plays in a rocking style like Young but can pump out a mean BLUES or a ballad equally well. She also has a knack for composing works in a HARD BOP or classic jazz style that is popular in Europe. Dennerlein is an innovator with the organ and has developed ways to combine its sound with that of MIDI-controlled SYNTHESIZERS, broadening the tones and textures that she can play. Her 2001 CD *Outhipped* showcases her varied styles and technical skills.

Di Meola, Al (b. 1954) *American guitarist, composer, and bandleader*

Born and raised in the Jersey City, New Jersey, area, Di Meola first played DRUMS but then picked up the GUITAR at age eight. By high school he had taught himself to imitate the styles he heard played by the Ventures and the Beatles, but he was already exploring other TECHNIQUEs. His private teacher turned him on to classical, jazz, and BOSSA NOVA styles. In the early 1970s he became enamored with FUSION jazz and the music of guitarist Larry Coryell, who was a major influence on him. Di Meola began studying music at the BERKLEE COLLEGE OF MUSIC in Boston in 1971. In 1974 he was recruited by CHICK COREA to play in his group Return to Forever, the turning point in his fledgling career. Return to Forever put Di Meola in the spotlight. After playing with Corea on three successful albums, he left in 1976 to start his SOLO career. He teamed up with guitarists JOHN MCLAUGHLIN and Paco DeLucia for a flamenco-influenced acoustic guitar tour and subsequent albums in the early 1980s. In the mid-1980s he formed the Al Di Meola Project with Danny Gottlieb on drums, Airto Moreira on percussion, Phil Markowitz on keyboards, and Ron McClure on BASS. He continued to tour on an international basis in the late 1980s and 1990s, often teaming with other stellar players to create an unusual FUSION of jazz, classic, rock, and WORLD MUSIC. In the mid-1990s he toured and recorded with violinist

JEAN-LUC PONTY and bassist STANLEY CLARKE. His 2002 CD, *Flesh on Flesh,* continued his exploration of world music and Latin-infused jazz with guest appearances by Cuban pianist GONZALO RUBALCABA, flutist Alejandro Santos, and World Sinfonia member Gumbi Ortiz on percussion. Di Meola reigns as a guitar giant in jazz and fusion music. Aside from his remarkably fresh work with Return to Forever, his most lasting influence may be in the seamless blend of Latin, American, and world music that he concocts so well. Like McLaughlin, he is a master of both the acoustic and electric guitar and devotes his efforts to exploring new ideas rather than imitating his past successes. About his music, Di Meola explains, "Composing is painful in that you have to avoid the obvious and somehow rediscover yourself. The easiest thing would be to use the same CHORD and progressions of the past. It's much more satisfying to dig down and come up with something new that has deep meaning for you."[54]

"Dipper Mouth Blues" (1923) *recorded performance by the Joseph "King" Oliver Creole Jazz Band*

The Creole Jazz Band was led by one-eyed New Orleans cornet legend JOSEPH "KING" OLIVER. In 1922, he sent for LOUIS ARMSTRONG to join him in Chicago, after which the group became famous for its dueling cornet style of improvisation. The 1923 recording session that resulted in "Dipper Mouth Blues" was the first for this celebrated group and the first for Armstrong as well. The band included Oliver and Armstrong on cornets, Honore Dutrey on trombone, Bill Johnson on string bass, JOHNNY DODDS on clarinet, BABY DODDS on drums, and LIL HARDIN (later Armstrong's wife) on piano. This uptempo blues tune was masterfully arranged with changing textures and combinations of instruments. The banjo dominates the rhythm; the clarinet shifts back and forth from high to low ranges; and the cornets and trombones are often muted. Oliver's classic cornet playing is accentuated by a superb wah wah solo midway through the recording.

With the exception of tracks laid down by KID ORY the year before, "Dipper Mouth Blues" was one of the first popular recordings made by an all-black jazz combo.

dissonance

A combination of notes that does not harmonize, dissonance can be created using CHORDS with unusual combinations of notes, or by playing melodies that conflict with the notes in a chord. Dissonant chords are said to be "unresolved" because we expect the music to harmonize in a more familiar way. Dissonance creates a feeling of tension and anticipation in music.

Diva

Diva is an American concert jazz orchestra consisting of women performers, founded in 1993 by Stanley Kay. He built the ENSEMBLE with the help of drummer and bandleader Sherrie Maricle. The music of the orchestra is written to showcase the talents of the ensemble's soloists. They play PROGRESSIVE JAZZ that is steeped in TRADITIONAL JAZZ sounds. As of this writing, the 15-member BIG BAND included the following roster of players: Sherrie Maricle (DRUMS), Noriko Ueda (BASS), Deborah Weisz (TROMBONE), Chihiro Yamanaka (PIANO), Lori Stuntz (trombone), Karolina Strassmayer (alto), Leslie Havens (bass trombone), Kristy Norter (alto SAXOPHONE), Liesl Whitaker (LEAD trumpet), Anat Cohen (tenor saxophone), Barbara Laronga (trumpet), Scheila Gonzalez (tenor saxophone), Tanya Darby (trumpet), Lisa Parrott (baritone saxophone), and Jami Dauber (trumpet).

Dixieland jazz

Dixieland is a cousin and variant of NEW ORLEANS JAZZ, with the kind of group ensemble playing that characterized early jazz. The term is often associated with white musicians who borrowed the playing style from their black New Orleans counterparts.

Dixieland's early development took place outside of New Orleans as the influence of jazz spread from Louisiana to Chicago. Dixieland is a sincere attempt by white musicians to re-create the classic New Orleans sound as originally practiced by BUDDY BOLDEN, JOSEPH "KING" OLIVER, and others. A notable example of an early white Dixieland group was The Original Dixieland Jazz Band, one of the first to record jazz music. Dixieland reemerged in the 1940s as a revival of classic New Orleans style jazz and again in the 1960s as a colorful, made-for-television semblance of New Orleans riverboat music.

Dodds, Baby (Warren Dodds) (1898–1959)
American drummer

Warren "Baby" Dodds was one of the first exceptional drummers of jazz. Both Dodds and his clarinet-playing brother JOHNNY Dodds played in King Oliver's Creole Jazz Band, which played one of the best representations of early NEW ORLEANS JAZZ. Baby Dodds grew up in New Orleans where he got his start playing in parades and with riverboat bands. He first played with LOUIS ARMSTRONG as a member of Fate Marable's riverboat band from 1918 to 1921. He joined JOSEPH "KING" OLIVER's combo in 1921, playing in both San Francisco and Chicago. In 1923, he was a part of the historic first recordings of King Oliver's Creole Jazz Band, which, by that time, also included Louis Armstrong. He worked with FREDDIE KEPPARD, LIL HARDIN, and other noted band leaders through the 1930s, picking up gigs all over Chicago. He was a sought after drummer for recording sessions, having played on Armstrong's HOT SEVEN recordings and JELLY ROLL MORTON's Red Hot Peppers recordings. During the 1930s and the time of the depression, he helped his brother Bill run a taxi company in Chicago. He remained active as a drummer even after he suffered strokes in 1949 and 1950 but finally retired in 1957.

The sound of early drummers such as Dodds is not very well documented by the first jazz recordings because the drummers were unable to perform

which were the peak years of his success. Jimmy Dorsey's band excelled at crafting pop songs with hummable melodies. They were so immersed in making pop music with standard pop arrangements that their ranking as a genuine jazz orchestra, on the caliber of DUKE ELLINGTON, BENNY GOODMAN, or COUNT BASIE, is questionable. They became the HOUSE BAND for the Kraft Music Hall radio program featuring singer Bing Crosby (1935). Some of their most popular songs included "So Rare" and "Green Eyes." Jimmy's band made musical appearances in several Hollywood movies, and they provided the soundtrack for the popular Fred Astaire–Ginger Rogers film *Shall We Dance?* (1937).[61]

After World War II and the decline in popularity of big bands, Dorsey continued playing with small groups including some work in the Dixieland style.

Dorsey, Tommy (1905–1956) *American trombone and trumpet player and bandleader*

Dorsey grew up with his older brother, Jimmy, in Scranton, Pennsylvania. Of the two Dorsey brothers, Tommy was lauded as the better musician. Some say he was one of the greatest trombonists of all time.[62]

His smooth TROMBONE style made him highly sought after as a SIDEMAN and SESSION musician. With his brother, he first played in early BIG BANDS and orchestras, including that of PAUL WHITEMAN. After forming the Dorsey Brothers with his brother in 1934, the two split over an onstage argument at the Glen Island Casino in May 1935.[63]

Tommy was left without a band. He quickly jump-started his rapid rise to fame by hiring away members of the Joe Haymes orchestra to form his own unit. Tommy had a knack for hiring talented players and a flair for promotion. Whether this was a true jazz orchestra is debatable. The group mostly played pop songs, Broadway hits, and novelty tunes, recording hundreds over the course of the band's existence. Frank Sinatra was one of Dorsey's fabled singers, and it can be said that the band found great success in pop music without

ever having to worry about displaying any serious affiliations with jazz. Although a great trombone player, Dorsey's attempts at playing jazz, especially Dixieland, were robotic.

double bass (string bass)

This large-bodied string instrument provided the rhythmic underpinning of the earliest jazz groups and has been a staple of jazz music ever since. Because the earliest New Orleans jazz groups had a history with marching brass band music, they frequently used the tuba as the bass rhythm instrument. However, many other groups borrowed the upright bass from the string band tradition and used it for the same purpose. BUDDY BOLDEN's band—one of the most influential and popular of the early NEW ORLEANS JAZZ style—used a string bass played by Jimmie Johnson. Also called the upright BASS, it was originally played using only a bow rather than the plucking style that most listeners are now familiar with. The neck of the double bass does not have frets for playing notes. The predominant style in jazz bass playing until the 1960s was the WALKING BASS, where the musician plucked the string once per beat. Another style of playing is slap bass. When playing the slap style, the musician vigorously plucks the string so hard that it bounces off the fret board, making a snapping sound. Musicians including CHARLES MINGUS freed the double bass from its beat-keeping role and transformed it into an evocative SOLO instrument.

double time

When a soloist plays twice as fast as the RHYTHM SECTION.

Down Beat magazine

The history of this influential jazz magazine reaches back to 1935, when it published a collection of articles tracing the history of jazz. It has become an institution, documenting the history, artists, recordings, and performances that have made jazz legendary.

drums

The drums are the heart of the RHYTHM SECTION of a jazz group. Early jazz groups used snare drums, tom-toms, and bass drums such as those found in marching bands. By the late 1920s the basic setup consisted of a bass drum played with a pedal, a tom-tom, snare drum, RIDE CYMBAL, CRASH CYMBAL, and hi-hat. This setup remains the basic drum kit for jazz, although the addition of louder, larger drums, electronic drums, and a wide variety of innovative percussion add-ons continues to evolve. Latin jazz also contributed the conga and timbale (a small snarelike drum) to the repertoire of jazz percussion instruments. New Orleans drummer Arthur "Zutty" Singleton was the first jazz drummer to use wire brushes as well as wooden sticks to play the drums. This added a quieter, softer sound that could be extended by dragging the brush over the surface of the drum.

Early Jazz: Its Roots and Musical Development (1968)

This book by Gunther Schuller is one of the best scholarly studies of the early development of jazz. It was published by Oxford University Press in 1968. Schuller, a working educator and jazz musician, applied a new level of scholarship to the study of jazz. His follow-up to this text was *The Swing Era* (1989), and he continues work on a third volume about modern jazz.

Either/Orchestra

Boston-based BIG BAND founded in 1985 by tenor/soprano saxophonist, COMPOSER, and ARRANGER Russ Gershon (b. 1959). The 10+ piece band blends fiery musicianship, humor, and a quirky selection of numbers, earning its reputation as one of the most celebrated new jazz experiments of the 1990s. Their repertoire includes jazz classics from THELONIOUS MONK, CHARLES MINGUS, and DUKE ELLINGTON but reaches into rock and jazz to deliver sometimes unexpected renditions of familiar songs. Stylistically, the band has evolved from a HARD-BOP, SWING sound to a FUSION of jazz groove and Latin rhythms. Either/Orchestra has recorded more than six CDs.

Eldridge, Roy (1911–1989) *American trumpet, flugelhorn, and piano player, drummer, and singer*

Eldridge was an accomplished soloist on TRUMPET during the days of SWING bands. Although his playing is often thought of as a stylistic bridge between LOUIS ARMSTRONG and DIZZY GILLESPIE, he was first inspired not by Armstrong, but by saxophonists such as COLEMAN HAWKINS.[64]

His early work was with carnivals and regional jazz COMBOS with such colorful names as the Nighthawk Syncopators and McKinneys' Cotton Pickers. By the time he first heard Louis Armstrong in person in 1932, he had already developed an individual style of his own. But Armstrong impressed him in a way that other trumpeters had not. He found fluidity in Satchmo's playing that affected him deeply and transformed his style even more. He made his first recording in 1935 with Teddy Hill's orchestra, and for the next 10 years was a star soloist in many big bands, black and white. He acquired the nickname "Little Jazz" from his musician friends.

What set his improvising apart from others, including Armstrong, were the genuine risks he took and the winner-take-all attitude he had onstage. Whereas other great performers often seemed relaxed in their SOLOS, having often thought ahead about what they were going to play or even mapping out some RIFFS ahead of time, Eldridge always seemed to make it up on the spot. His energy and enthusiasm were catching. When his improvising backfired, as it could, he could always fall back on his marvelous TECHNIQUE to rescue him.

These are the things that inspired other greats to work with Eldridge. Some notable partnerships during his career included stints with FLETCHER HENDERSON's orchestra (1935), GENE KRUPA's band as featured soloist and singer (1941–43), multiple appearances with JAZZ AT THE PHILHARMONIC, a European tour with BENNY GOODMAN (1950), and a host of appearances in America and Europe with notables such as CHARLIE PARKER, SIDNEY BECHET, ELLA FITZGERALD, COLEMAN HAWKINS, BENNY CARTER, and OSCAR PETERSON. In the 1960s he often appeared with the Coleman Hawkins QUINTET and played with COUNT BASIE in 1966. He toured frequently in the 1970s with swing revival shows but also on the small-club circuit with his own group.

In 1980 Eldridge suffered a stroke. This more or less silenced his trumpet playing but he continued to work as a drummer, pianist, and singer until late in his life. Eldridge's brilliant tone, sharp technique, and winning attitude were a great influence on DIZZY GILLESPIE and a host of trumpeters who followed the days of swing and shaped the new jazz sounds of BOP and HARD BOP.

electronic keyboard See ORGAN; PIANO, ELECTRIC; SYNTHESIZER.

Ellington, Duke (1899–1974) *American piano player, composer, arranger, and bandleader*
There has never been a greater jazz COMPOSER than Duke Ellington. Born Edward Kennedy Ellington and given the nickname "Duke" at a young age, he grew up in Washington, D.C., into a middle-class family. The young Ellington showed promise as both an artist and a musician. Although he began PIANO lessons at age seven, his first love was art. He won a poster contest while attending Armstrong High School, but left school before graduation to start a sign-painting business.

All during this time, his interest in music steadily grew. He took private lessons and learned to compose. Music was a vital part of his life in Washington, D.C. He was influenced not only by folk music and spirituals of the time but also by popular RAGTIME artists. In 1919, at age 20, Ellington formed his first COMBO, The Duke's Serenaders,

with his friends Otto Hardwicke (SAXOPHONE) and Arthur Whetsol (TRUMPET). They became a popular local dance band and were soon joined by their drummer friend Sonny Greer. Washington, D.C., however, was not the place to be at that time to make it in jazz. The hot spots for making a name were New Orleans, Chicago, or New York. In 1923 a call came from bandleader Elmer Snowden in New York. Duke and his three friends Hardwicke, Whetsol, and Greer did not hesitate, and off they went to seek their fame and fortune.

Ellington began by playing piano in the group, but soon he was leading the QUINTET as composer, ARRANGER, and manager. The Duke soon began to add members to the squad, experimenting with different sounds. He chose his musicians carefully and always composed music to fit their individual strengths as players. Duke wanted to create a new sound, a swinging sound that featured the energy of LOUIS ARMSTRONG's improvisational combos plus the sophisticated tone of carefully arranged ENSEMBLE works. At one time or another, this band included players on tuba, saxophone, BANJO, trumpet, DRUMS, piano, baritone saxophone, TROMBONES, and even two bassists who played together. His band stayed on at the Kentucky Club for four years, creating a minor sensation. During this same time, Ellington and his band were also making a name for themselves as recording artists. Early recordings from this period included "East St. Louis Toodle-oo" and "BLACK AND TAN FANTASY," both of which hint at the marvelous ensemble writing that was to come from the talented young man.

In 1927 the Ellington Orchestra moved to the prestigious COTTON CLUB, where their fame spread rapidly because of weekly radio broadcasts, recordings, and regular dates in larger theaters. Ellington's first popular hit, "Mood Indigo," was recorded during this period. His sophisticated swing music had become hot, and his band became the one to watch. After their stint at the Cotton Club ended in 1932, Ellington mounted a tour of Europe, where his band was the talk of the Continent. He was following in the footsteps of Louis Armstrong, who had taken his act to Europe the year before. Playing to sold-out crowds wherever they went, the Ellington Orchestra became ambassadors of America's music, and he returned to Europe regularly during the many decades of his extraordinary career.

Ellington's song output during the 1930s and 1940s was dizzying. Some of his most popular hits included "IT DON'T MEAN A THING (IF IT AIN'T GOT THAT SWING)" (1932), "Solitude" (1933), "Sophisticated Lady" (1933), "IN A SENTIMENTAL MOOD" (1935), "Echoes of Harlem" (1936), "Cotton Tail" (1940), and "Take the A Train" (1941), which was the band's signature song. Players who came to play with Duke often stayed for a long time before going on to make a name on their own. Harry Carney, who provided a bellowing baritone saxophone to the Ellington sound, stayed with him for more than 40 years. Ellington once remarked, "The most important thing I look for in a musician is whether he knows how to listen." Duke could make a player with good ears a part of some of the most beautiful jazz ever conceived. Some of the extraordinary players for whom Duke wrote included BEN WEBSTER (tenor saxophone), Cootie Williams (trumpet), and Johnny Hodges (alto saxophone).

The sound of the Ellington Orchestra got bigger and even more distinctive after the Cotton Club days. The orchestra had more BRASS than reed instruments, giving the Duke's sound a defiant punch whenever he needed it. During the 1930s Ellington also began to divide his time between writing popular songs for his band and longer works for the concert hall. The earliest of these included "Creole Rhapsody" (1931) and "Reminiscing in Tempo" (1935). These works were so long that he had to record them on more than one side of a 78 rpm record, the first time a jazz artist had done so.[65]

In later years he wrote for Broadway, the MOVIES, television, and orchestra. His stature as a top-rate composer of serious music was first recognized in Europe, but America finally caught up when from 1943 to 1948 a series of annual concerts held at CARNEGIE HALL featured the Duke and his concert music. Works written for the concert stage include

Duke Ellington

"Black, Brown, and Beige" (1943), "Deep South Suite" (1946), "Night Creature" (1955), "The Far East Suite" (1963), and many more.

In the 1950s and 1960s it seemed that everyone wanted to work with the Duke. During this time he was a frequent guest on television, regularly toured the world, and made regular appearances at jazz festivals around the globe. He collaborated with some of the best-known artists of the day, including JOHN COLTRANE, COLEMAN HAWKINS, CHARLES MINGUS, ELLA FITZGERALD, and MAX ROACH. Ellington was frequently honored, including a 70th birthday bash in 1969 at the White House. He was composing larger works and continued to tour until ill health sidelined him in 1972. The Duke passed away in New York City in 1974. His only son, Mercer, assumed leadership of the band until his death in 1996.

The legacy of the Duke is so big that it is hard to put one's arms around it. While he began his music career with an almost white, pedestrian exposure to "classical" jazz, those members of his bands who admired the grittier sound of Armstrong and KING OLIVER greatly influenced the Duke's perception of his African-American heritage. He took great pride in being a successful black artist. The mere titles of his works were often a bold reminder that jazz was a potent symbol of freedom for African-American people: "Black and Tan Fantasy," "New World A-Comin," "Blue Bells of Harlem," "Deep South Suite," and "Harlem" are but a few examples. As a composer and arranger, Ellington brought a unique sophistication to his works. IMPROVISATION had its place in his music, but it was no more important than the blend of instrumental sounds and his orchestrations. His combination of BLUES harmonies and changes reminiscent of European classical music elevated his jazz over that of most other composers. Not enough is made of the Duke's skill as a piano player. His style was a blend of RAGTIME, the blues, HOT JAZZ, and pop songs, and sometimes as quirky and unpredictable as could be. He was also a genuinely moving interpreter of ballads, setting a high standard for anyone who wanted to interpret his great songs. Duke Ellington was a man who listened to all kinds of music with an open mind and found ways to mix these many ingredients into a sound that was all his own. This is not to say that he liked everything he heard in jazz. He once said that, "Playing bop is like playing Scrabble with all the vowels missing." Even so, the Duke was revered by jazz musicians of all persuasions. As MILES DAVIS so aptly put it, "I think all the musicians should get together on one certain day and get down on their knees and thank Duke."[66]

Ellis, Don (1934–1978) *American trumpeter, composer, arranger, and bandleader*

Ellis was one of the brightest stars of a movement to revive BIG BANDs in the late 1960s. As a trumpeter, he worked in big bands in the 1950s and then played with GEORGE RUSSELL in 1961. Under Russell's

AVANT-GARDE influence, Ellis began to conceive new ways for arranging big band ensembles, incorporating sophisticated TIME signatures and sound textures learned from contemporary classical music. After experimenting with his ideas on several little-known record releases, he knocked the socks off the jazz and rock world with the album *Electric Bath* (1968). It was a FUSION of big band jazz and electric rock with a melange of time signatures and spooky sounds that thrilled hippies and their jazz-loving parents alike. The brash sound of his TRUMPET was a calling card for a new era in big band jazz. Ellis focused on music for motion pictures for much of the early 1970s, but died of a heart attack in 1978.

Encyclopedia of Jazz

Classic encyclopedia series by the late music journalist Leonard Feather (1914–94), in three volumes: *The Encyclopedia of Jazz* (covering early jazz through 1960), *Encyclopedia of Jazz in the Sixties*, and *Encyclopedia of Jazz in the Seventies*. These books are an invaluable source of biographical information about jazz artists and their works. After Feather's death in 1994, work continued on an update to the encyclopedia by longtime Feather collaborator Ira Gitler. The result was the one-volume 718-page reference book, *The Biographical Encyclopedia of Jazz*, published in 1999 by Oxford University Press.

England   See EUROPEAN JAZZ.

ensemble

A small group of performers, usually fewer than 10. Similar to a COMBO.

"Epistrophy" (1948) *recorded performance by Thelonious Monk*

Featuring THELONIOUS MONK (PIANO), Milt Jackson (VIBRAPHONE), John Simmons (BASS), and Shadow

Wilson (DRUMS), Monk's unusual approach to composing can be heard in the classic "Epistrophy," released by Blue Note. While many of his other tunes have a strong rhythm and blues flavor, "Epistrophy" takes directions that are hard to predict. It starts with a repeated round of notes on the piano that spiral slowly upward. The vibraphones complement the piano and then burst into a melody that barely touches the CHORDS being played on the piano. Monk plays with the opening piano PHRASE over and over, trying many variations on it before the song is through. It is the kind of jagged, curious music that marked the genius of Monk. Listen carefully and you will hear echoes of DIZZY GILLESPIE's BEBOP hit "SALT PEANUTS" in the vibes SOLO.

"E.S.P." (1965) *recorded performance by Wayne Shorter with the Miles Davis Quintet*

This instrumental romp taken from the MILES DAVIS album of the same name is a symbol of a rejuvenated Davis with his second QUINTET. Arguably the tightest and most intuitive of Davis's many COMBOS, this quintet was certainly one of the most talented of the 1960s. Composed of Davis, WAYNE SHORTER (tenor SAXOPHONE), HERBIE HANCOCK (PIANO), RON CARTER (BASS), and Tony Williams (DRUMS), each SIDEMAN went on to stellar careers of their own. "E.S.P." is a perfect example of group interplay at its finest.

Europe, James Reese (1881–1919) *American composer and bandleader*

Europe was an instrumental figure in the evolution of jazz from RAGTIME. He was also the first noted African-American musician to lead an ENSEMBLE and make recordings (1913–14 for Victor). Born in Alabama, he was raised in the Washington, D.C., area, where he received his musical education. In 1905 he moved to New York, where he began to earn a living playing ragtime PIANO at nightclubs. In 1910 Europe organized an ensemble of HARLEM musicians, which he called the Clef Club. Under his direction, the Clef Club became a popular fixture on the society dance party scene in New York. By 1914, partly because of a business partnership with the white dance instruction team of Vernon and Irene Castle, Europe conducted the first all-black ensemble to present a concert of ragtime music at CARNEGIE HALL. In 1914 Europe recorded with his ensemble under the name of the Jim Europe Society Orchestra, becoming the first African-American ensemble to make commercial recordings.

During World War I, Europe joined the army and was asked to form a regimental band. The result was an extraordinary orchestra consisting of the finest African-American players that he could muster. Europe's ensemble was part of the first African-American regiment to go to war, becoming known as the "Harlem Hellfighters." His band toured France and became well known for its jazz performances. Europe and his regiment returned triumphantly. His band led the Harlem Hellfighters in a victory parade in New York, up Fifth Avenue to Harlem.

Sadly, Europe was knifed to death by one of his own musicians in a 1919 nightclub incident. The fledgling world of jazz music was devastated by the loss of this talented young man. He received what was possibly the first public funeral for an African American in New York, and was mourned by thousands of fans, black and white. James Reese Europe was a key figure in the transformation of ragtime and marching band music into jazz. About his loss, entertainer Eubie Blake once remarked, "People don't realize yet today what we lost when we lost Jim Europe. He was the savior of Negro musicians . . . in a class with Booker T. Washington and Martin Luther King Jr."[67]

European jazz

Even before the first recordings of jazz had been made in America in 1917, sheet music of RAGTIME and early jazz numbers were already on sale in Europe. The first American jazz artist to make a big splash in Europe was SIDNEY BECHET. He was greatly admired for his CLARINET playing while touring with the Southern Syncopated Orchestra in 1919. He played the New Orleans style of jazz and could improvise long melodies off the top of his head. As early recordings of jazz made their way to Europe, the music became all the rage.

Would-be European jazz artists in Great Britain, France, Germany, and the Netherlands learned their early licks by imitating jazz records. By 1930 several jazz artists and groups had become good enough to strike out on their own. Among the early jazz players in Europe were the Scottish trombonist George Chisholm, the English saxophonist Buddy Featherstonhaugh, and the French trumpeter PHILIPPE BRUN. Their music was skillfully played but could be accused of lacking the spark and originality of their American counterparts. They were mostly copying what they heard.

The education of European jazz artists took a mighty leap forward in the early 1930s, when several prominent big bands from America performed abroad. Following the tremendous success of his recordings in Europe, LOUIS ARMSTRONG was the first to cross the Atlantic. In June 1932 he headlined a show at the London Paladium. It was during this trip that a British journalist mistakenly gave Armstrong the nickname of "Satchmo" when he mispronounced an earlier nickname, "satchel-mouth."[68]

The following year Armstrong returned to Europe and stayed until 1935, cultivating a passionate following. DUKE ELLINGTON swung through in 1933, COLEMAN HAWKINS in 1934.

Even with this added exposure to the most famous jazz artists on the planet, however, jazz remained an especially American phenomenon. In fact, it was so rooted in African-American experience that it appeared condescending, even racist, for white European artists to stake any claim at all to its heritage. This changed with the emergence of a few talented European artists who made no claim to America's music and simply played what they felt with great skill and originality. The most significant of these was the Belgian-Roma (Gypsy) guitarist DJANGO REINHARDT. He managed

to play in a style that combined his own musical traditions with those TECHNIQUES that he heard in American jazz. The result was a uniquely European blend. He partnered for many years with another giant of European jazz, the French VIOLIN player Stephane Grappelli. Grappelli was skilled at classical violin, but his heart was in jazz IMPROVISATION. The contributions and influence of Reinhardt and Grappelli helped make France the first nation outside of the United States to recognize jazz as a serious art form.

Other European nations were not far behind. After World War II many American jazz musicians moved to France and other spots in Europe, where they found a waiting audience. This allowed many up-and-coming European players to play with Americans. By 1960 the jazz scene in Germany was so vibrant and serious that it was said that Germans appreciated jazz as an art form more than Americans.[69]

Jazz exploded in popularity in Europe in the 1960s and 1970s. Some of the old debates about the merits of SWING, BOP, HARD BOP, COOL JAZZ, and FREE IMPROVISATION were played out again to the eager minds and ears of European audiences.

Perhaps the biggest break for European jazz, however, was the export of FREE JAZZ from the United States in the 1960s. Music by the likes of ORNETTE COLEMAN, ERIC DOLPHY, JOHN COLTRANE, ANTHONY BRAXTON, the ART ENSEMBLE OF CHICAGO, and many others introduced a style of jazz that seemed free of cultural barriers. Free jazz seemed disconnected from American history, from the African-American roots of jazz. Although this is far from the truth, free jazz gave European musicians an opening to practice their skills in the more experimental styles of jazz. It also allowed them to recast jazz from the point of view of their own culture. Likewise, jazz FUSION of the 1970s was also a catalyst for many Europeans who were dabbling in both rock and jazz.

From the 1970s come many of the most influential jazz players of Europe. British guitarist JOHN MCLAUGHLIN teamed with Czech keyboard player

JAN HAMMER, Irish BASS player Rick Laird, and Americans Jerry Goodman on electric violin and drummer BILLY COBHAM to form the MAHAVISHNU ORCHESTRA. Keyboard player JOE ZAWINUL, from Austria, combined with American saxophonist WAYNE SHORTER to found the fusion group WEATHER REPORT. Other prominent modern jazz artists from Europe include saxophonists JOHN SURMAN (England) JAN GARBAREK (Norway), COURTNEY PINE (England), STEVE WILLIAMSON (England), TOMMY SMITH (England), ANDY SHEPPARD (England) and Willem Breuker (Holland); French violinist JEAN-LUC PONTY; guitarists ATTILLA ZOLLER (Hungary) and Terje Rypdal (Norway); piano players George Gruntz (Switzerland), MICHEL PETRUCCIANI (France), and organist BARBARA DENNERLEIN (Germany). Jazz is a vital part of the contemporary music scene in Europe. It can now be said that Europe has its own rich roots of jazz that are clearly distinguishable from those of America.

Evans, Bill (1929–1980) *American piano and flute player and composer*

Evans was arguably the most influential jazz pianist since ART TATUM and BUD POWELL. Evans's father was Welsh and his mother Russian. Although neither had a formal background in music, his mother could play PIANO a little and had sheet music in the house. Bill and his brother Harry were encouraged to learn a musical instrument at a young age, both ending up taking piano lessons. Evans played FLUTE and piccolo in his high school band. He listened avidly to music that he heard on the radio and had a talent for reproducing it, note for note, on the piano. By age 12 he was beginning to improvise using BLUES RIFFS. As a teen he became a good BOOGIE-WOOGIE player. He earned a degree in piano performance from Southeastern Louisiana College in 1950 and studied at Mannes College in New York.

While in college studying classical music, he became interested in the jazz piano styles of HORACE SILVER, Bud Powell, LENNIE TRISTANO, and NAT KING COLE. After a stint in the army (1951–54), he was determined to make jazz his life and moved to New York. He first played with a band led by Tony Scott and then worked for a time in 1956 with the AVANT-GARDE jazz COMPOSER GEORGE RUSSELL and his orchestra. Evans recorded his first album as a leader in 1956 with a TRIO that included Paul Motian (DRUMS), and Teddy Kotick (BASS). *New Jazz Conceptions* included 11 tracks, four of which were written by Evans. Among them was "WALTZ FOR DEBBY" (1956), an Evans classic. The small record label that produced the album did not even sell 1,000 copies in the first year, but Evans received some rave reviews from critics.

Evans was fascinated by IMPROVISATION. TRADITIONAL JAZZ improvisation is like a game. The object of the game is to play the most interesting music that you can make up on the spot without having to write it down ahead of time. Rules are established for players to follow and the quality of the performers determines the quality of the result. Evans was forever making up new games for improvisation. By 1958 he had begun to experiment with MODAL JAZZ. In modal jazz, improvisations are based on the notes available in a given musical SCALE rather than a pattern of CHORDS found in an ordinary song. This gives the music a spacious feel because the improviser has all of the notes of a scale to work rather than just those found in a pattern of chords. In 1958 Evans released an album called *Everybody Digs Bill Evans,* which included several modal experiments, particularly "Peace Piece."

Another musician who was experimenting with modal jazz was MILES DAVIS. Davis recruited Evans in 1958 and the piano player became part of one of the most celebrated jazz recordings of all time, *KIND OF BLUE* (1959). Evans and Davis worked as collaborators in composing most of the songs on the album. One of the improvisation games that they devised can be heard on the song "Flamenco Sketches." No melody or chord progression was written for the song. Instead of playing a melody and then inventing variations of it, the players were

Bill Evans

given a sequence of five modes (scales), each of which would serve as the harmonic material for their improvisations. Each player was free to stay with a mode as long as he wanted and then move to the next. The results were not so chaotic as one might imagine because each player seemed to stick only with a given mode for about four measures.[70] It was the kind of grand experiment that Evans relished.

After working with Davis, Evans did some teaching and then led the first of a long line of trios (piano-bass-drum) that would define most of his work for the rest of his career. The style of his trio music could be called conversational. The players interacted freely while supporting an underlying TEMPO. There was nothing entirely obvious or ordinary about their music. Although Evans loved playing rhythm and blues when he was young, he considered the BLUES a limited harmonic structure for his own music. His playing had a rounded, whole tone that few have been able to imitate. He had the SWING of bop, the elusive open sound of modal jazz, and the touch of a classical music pianist whose touch on the keys seemed to have unlimited range in attack and volume.

By all accounts, Evans was a shy, quiet man with a sense of humor about himself and his talents. He reportedly said once that he preferred playing without an audience. He could have stuck with classical music but chose to work in jazz. Evans believed that "you can put all of your musical experience into it, if you approach it right."[71]

Remarkably, he recorded more than 50 albums under his own name. He was also a five-time GRAMMY AWARD winner. Sadly, Evans was also a troubled soul and had a long history of drug and alcohol abuse. He died relatively young at age 51, but not before creating a new style of jazz piano playing that would be embraced by later players, including HERBIE HANCOCK, KEITH JARRETT, CHICK COREA, and many others. For a man who was obsessed with new ideas and TECHNIQUE, he had a remarkably warm sense of what music was all about. "My creed for art in general," said Evans, "is that it should enrich the soul; it should teach spirituality by showing a person a portion of himself that he would not discover otherwise . . . a part of yourself you never knew existed."

Evans, Gil (1912–1988) *Canadian arranger, composer, piano player, and bandleader*

Gil Evans was an innovative jazz ARRANGER and COMPOSER. He ranks with DUKE ELLINGTON, FLETCHER HENDERSON, and BENNY CARTER as one of the most influential forces behind the big sound of jazz orchestras. By age eight the Canadian-born Evans was living with his family in California. A family friend got him started on the PIANO, but he was mostly self-taught. By high school he was playing well enough to do GIGS at a local hotel. He listened intently to LOUIS ARMSTRONG and was greatly influenced by composers and arrangers including Duke Ellington and Fletcher Henderson. Evans formed a 10-piece band with a friend that became the resident dance band at a Balboa Beach ballroom in 1935. In 1937 the band was taken over by

vocalist Skinnay Ennis, but he kept Evans as an arranger and piano player. Claude Thornhill, another pianist and arranger, also joined the group but left in 1940 to start his own orchestra in New York, and eventually took Evans with him. Evans stayed with Thornhill until 1948, taking time out for army duty along the way.

Working with Thornhill was like going to school for Evans. The band had an eccentric mix of instruments with horns aplenty; FRENCH HORNS, tubas, TRUMPETS, you name it. At one time Thornhill even had a CHORUS of seven CLARINETS, a jazzy substitute for VIOLINS.[72]

Evans was set loose in helping Thornhill shape his innovative sound. It was a classically inspired mix of mood music, dance numbers, and BOP SWING. Evans had found his niche as an originator of musically inventive arrangements.

He was a thoughtful man who made fast friends with some of the hottest jazz players in town. Many of them, including MILES DAVIS, GERRY MULLIGAN, and John Lewis, used to hang out at Evans's apartment to talk about jazz. Evans was a generation older than the rest of them, but the other players looked to him as a musical sage and mentor. It was a time of conflicting styles and ideas in jazz. Swing bands were on the wane. Bop was highly charged and making waves. Yet something else was on the verge of happening. Many of these musicians thought it could be found in the quirky arrangements of bop tunes that Evans had been creating for Thornhill. These informal gatherings led to the formation of the Miles Davis NONET and the important *BIRTH OF THE COOL* recordings during 1949–50.

Although Evans arranged only two of the 12 works recorded by the ENSEMBLE, his pieces had a striking sophistication that blended an amazing swing sound with bop. This music was more written out and featured less IMPROVISATION than bop and led to a revival of concert stage jazz after the example of Duke Ellington. For Evans, it led to several landmark collaborations in the 1950s with Miles Davis that used the trumpet player only as a SOLO player in a larger ensemble. It suited Davis's style at the time and put him on the map once again after several years of personal troubles. Together, Davis and Evans recorded *Miles Ahead* (1957), *Porgy and Bess* (1958), and *Sketches of Spain* (1960), with Evans arranging. This music was a far cry from Davis's HARD BOP style. It was big on exposition and orchestration, about as opposite to club improvisation as one could get. The records were popular and gave the careers of both artists a huge boost.

Evans, so long an unsung hero who worked behind the scenes, was suddenly in demand during a time of great innovation in jazz. During the 1960s Evans sometimes led his own bands. But most of the time he was in the studio working on CHARTs for others and arranging music for recording. He became popular on the festival scene and by the late 1960s was widely acclaimed for the innovative sounds he brought to jazz. Like Davis during the 1970s, he added rock instruments and SYNTHESIZERS to his bands to create his own brand of orchestral jazz FUSION. He had planned a collaborative effort with Jimi Hendrix, but the rock guitarist died before they could get into the studio. Still, Evans maintained a couple of arrangements of Hendrix songs, including "Little Wing," in his performing repertoire for many years. He worked with other rock artists, including David Bowie and Sting.

Although not known for his compositions, one could argue that his arrangements of others' works were so original as to have made them his own. His sound was unique in many ways. His classically inspired use of French horn and muted trumpets often gave his work a stately grace. He fondly teased out the lowest sounds that his bands could make, obsessively exploring the movement of bass lines and other bellowing tones. His arrangements had a melodramatic structure, yet it flowed so organically that it rarely felt entirely preconceived. Like the work he did with Thornhill, Evans's productions were made for listening. They could make you jump up and dance at times, but one was usually transfixed by the sheer beauty and originality of his work. Those who played with Gil Evans were tremendously moved by the experience, as were those who listened to his music.

Farmer, Art (1928–1999) *American flugelhorn and trumpet player*

Farmer was a product of the HARD BOP era and was known for his expressive interpretation of melody. Farmer grew up in Kansas City and got his professional start playing TRUMPET in Los Angeles in the late 1940s. He became an important member of the growing West Coast–based bands led by Jay McShann, BENNY CARTER, and others. After touring in Europe with LIONEL HAMPTON in 1952 and 1953, he moved to New York. His cool trumpet sound was in demand, and he found steady work with HORACE SILVER (1956–58) and GERRY MULLIGAN (1958–59). In 1959 he became coleader of the Jazztet, a talented COMBO whose work was largely overshadowed by the work of MILES DAVIS, JOHN COLTRANE, and ORNETTE COLEMAN, all of whom were making historically important music at the time.

During the early 1960s, Farmer took up the FLUGELHORN. Along with FREDDIE HUBBARD and CLARK TERRY, he was one of the most gifted proponents of jazz flugelhorn. Farmer was known for a mellow, sinuous tone and solos that were balanced and beautifully executed. Farmer was well liked and had a deadpan sense of humor. His brother was Addison Farmer (1928–63), a BASS player. Someone once asked Art about his twin brother, "How do you tell yourselves apart?" Without a pause, and with all seriousness, he replied, "When I get up in the morning I pick up the bass, and if I can't play it, I must be Art."[73]

Favors, Malachi (1937–2004) *American bass player and composer*

With LESTER BOWIE, favors was a founding member of the ART ENSEMBLE OF CHICAGO. This group was a leading AVANT-GARDE ENSEMBLE of the 1960s and 1970s. Their music and playing echoed elements of TRADITIONAL JAZZ while also showcasing sounds of WORLD MUSIC, particularly that of Africa. Of his playing, the late Lester Bowie once said, "He plays so much more than the music or the notes of the BASS. His spirit is so heavy, he holds us together."[74]

His jazz roots were solid. He played stand-up bass with DIZZY GILLESPIE and FREDDIE HUBBARD from 1958 to 1960. He led his own groups over the years and collaborated on recordings with other members of the Art Ensemble. In addition to bass, he could sometimes be heard playing zither, melodica, and even BANJO on some of the Art Ensemble works. One of his last recordings was *Tribute to Lester* (2003), produced with the remaining members of the original Art Ensemble after the passing of fellow band mate Lester Bowie.

Feather, Leonard (1914–1994) *British journalist, piano player, composer, and producer*

Feather fell in love with jazz when he first came to America in the mid-1930s. After first producing jazz records, he also became a noted writer about jazz. After moving to New York in 1939, he became one of the most prolific and influential reviewers of jazz music for publications such as *Down Beat, Metronome, Jazz Times, Swing Journal* (Japan), *Los*

around a satisfying and freestanding expression of music without legs.

French horn

A BRASS instrument of medium range, using a coiled tube fitted with valves. It is commonly used in marching bands and orchestras. GUNTHER SCHULLER is a noted French horn player in jazz.

Frisell, Bill (b. 1951) *American guitar and synthesizer player and composer*

Growing up in Baltimore, Frisell gave up the CLARINET for the GUITAR at the tender age of 11. His father and grandfather were both musicians. He attended the BERKLEE COLLEGE OF MUSIC off and on between 1971 and 1977 and also studied guitar for eight weeks with JIM HALL in New York City in 1972. He was influenced by many kinds of music, including rock, jazz, BLUES, and folk, and hints of all of these are audible in his unique playing. Frisell is revered for his TECHNIQUE but also for the breezy romanticism that gives his playing warmth and depth. His influences include blues players and the jazz guitar balladist WES MONTGOMERY. While many jazz guitarists tend to drop a song's melody like a hot potato so that they can get to their SOLO, Frisell uses it to shape every aspect of his performance. "I like to keep that melody going," he explains. "When you hear Thelonious Monk's piano playing, or horn players like Ben Webster, Miles Davis and Wayne Shorter, you always hear the melody in there."[76]

During the 1980s Frisell was heard mainly as the "house" studio guitarist for ECM records, a European-based label specializing in modern jazz. He moved to Seattle in 1989 and has continued to prosper both as leader of his own COMBO and as a collaborator as well. He has recorded with many artists, including JOHN SCOFIELD, Wayne Horvitz, Paul Bley, CHARLIE HADEN, Elvis Costello, and Lyle Mays. His work is consistently great and always interesting. Guitar playing also seems to be his best way of expressing himself. He once said, "I'm basically a pretty shy person and I don't dance or get into fights. But there are all these things inside me that get out when I perform. It's like a real world when I play, where I can do all the things I can't do in real life."[77]

fusion (jazz-rock fusion)

A jazz style that combines rock instrumentation with jazz virtuosity, fusion emerged in the late 1960s during a time when other forms of jazz such as HARD BOP, FREE JAZZ, and TRADITIONAL JAZZ were losing the younger generation of listeners to rock and roll. With rhythm and blues serving as the foundation for both jazz and rock, a merging of the two forms was inevitable. The result was a fire-breathing blend of electric rock effects, heavy rhythms, and the smartness of skilled jazz riffing (see RIFF). MILES DAVIS led the way with a driving rock-style RHYTHM SECTION led by drummer Tony Williams. Williams founded his group Lifetime featuring the incendiary virtuoso electric guitarist JOHN MCLAUGHLIN. Then Davis released *BITCHES BREW* (1970), the most influential of all early fusion albums, and broke open the floodgates. Fusion is often jazz with no horns or reed instruments. McLaughlin's MAHAVISHNU ORCHESTRA used a rock group lineup of GUITAR, DRUMS, BASS, SYNTHESIZER, and electric VIOLIN to play inspired, distortion-heavy jazz. Representative fusion artists include Miles Davis, WEATHER REPORT, HERBIE HANCOCK, John McLaughlin and the Mahavishnu Orchestra, CHICK COREA and Return to Forever, SONNY SHARROCK, and PAT METHENY.

Garbarek, Jan (b. 1947) *Norwegian tenor, bass, and soprano saxophone, flute, and keyboard player* Garbarek is one of Europe's most versatile and articulate jazz players. After having established himself as a disciple of bandleader GEORGE RUSSELL in the late 1960s, he forged his own path in the 1970s by exploring modern BOP sounds with his own groups. He became a frequent guest artist on recordings and performances with CHICK COREA, DON CHERRY, KEITH JARRETT, and others. Garbarek was a member of the Jarrett group in the late 1970s. Most of his own recordings consist of original compositions. His interest in traditional Norwegian and classical music has steadily influenced the evolving nature of his own work over the years. He has been a mainstay of the EUROPEAN JAZZ label ECM since 1971, where he has nurtured a signature sound consisting of long, sustained notes, riveting lyricism, and frequent patches of utter quiet. In the 1990s, straying more from the TRADITIONAL JAZZ axis, he forged a highly successful collaboration with the Hilliard ENSEMBLE, a vocal QUARTET specializing in Renaissance music. This partnership resulted in two successful recordings, *Visible World* (1995) and *Mnemosyne* (1999).

Garner, Erroll (1926–1977) *American piano player and composer*
Garner was a self-taught musician who could not read music; he played by ear. He combined the rhythmic pulse of STRIDE PIANO with his own brand of SWING. He had a remarkable feel for melodies and

melodrama, giving his renditions of standard pop tunes a jazzy, yet orchestral air. By the 1950s Garner had achieved cult status as a creative stylist. He enjoyed great success as a recording artist and nightclub entertainer throughout the rest of his career. He wrote the hit song "Misty" (1963) made famous by pop vocalist Johnny Mathis. He was a frequent guest artist on television and made several tours internationally. The audience delighted in two of his famous quirks; he always sat on a telephone book while he played and could often be heard grunting to the rhythm of his own playing, a sure sign that he was in a groove.

Garrett, Kenny (b. 1960) *American alto and soprano saxophone player*
Garrett has become one of the most noted young alto SAXOPHONE players of the 1990s. His father, a tenor saxophone player, first got young Garrett interested in jazz. By the time he was 18, he was proficient enough to get a GIG with the Mercer Ellington Orchestra. In 1981 he moved to New York City and picked up work with the MEL LEWIS Orchestra and by the mid-1980s he was recording regularly with leaders including ART BLAKEY, FREDDIE HUBBARD, and Woody Shaw. He released his first recording as a leader, *Introducing Kenny Garrett*, in 1984.

The break that made him a well-known name in jazz was working with MILES DAVIS from 1986 to 1989. During this time he recorded four albums with Davis, including the lyrical *Amandla* (1989).

Since that time, Garrett has been a prolific COMPOS-ER, SIDEMAN, and leader. In addition to his own recordings, he has crossed over to guest on rock recordings by Sting and Peter Gabriel. His playing hints at the many kinds of music that he listens to, whether it's HARD BOP, hip-hop, or WORLD MUSIC. He sounds as comfortable playing with Art Blakey as he does with MARCUS MILLER.

For his own groups, Garrett often surrounds himself with players who often provide a stylistic contrast to his own playing, to keep things "fresh and interesting."[78]

The album *Happy People* (2002) was a romp into the heart of bop. His 2003 album, *Standard of Language,* is a focused and energetic excursion into hard bop and FREE JAZZ, with strains of JOHN COLTRANE's "Favorite Things" heard loud and clear in the upbeat and out of kilter key changes of "Kurita Sensei" (2003).

Germany   See EUROPEAN JAZZ.

Getz, Stan (1927–1991) *American tenor, soprano, and baritone saxophone player and bandleader*
Like Dexter Gordon, Stan Getz had a relaxed sound on the tenor SAXOPHONE that flowed smooth as silk. Although considered a BEBOP player, Getz was influenced more by the SWING playing of LESTER YOUNG than by the bop of CHARLIE PARKER. Getz was known for his pretty SOLOS and a cool sound that was accessible to fans of jazz and popular music. He first gained notoriety while playing with the WOODY HERMAN orchestra (1947–49) and was often featured on the band's ballads.

During the early 1960s Getz anticipated the popularity of Brazilian BOSSA NOVA. He worked with the two creators of the style, ANTONIO CARLOS JOBIM and João Gilberto to introduce the sound to American audiences. He recorded several albums of bossa nova music while working with Jobim, Gilberto, and the latter's wife, ASTRUD GILBERTO. These records are classics of this breezy Latin sound called bossa nova. *Jazz Samba* (1962) included remarkable GUITAR work by Charlie Byrd. Astrud Gilberto and Getz recorded *GETZ/GILBERTO* in 1963 and had a smash hit with her vocal of "The Girl from Ipanema." Interestingly, it was the first time Gilberto had sung professionally. Getz took Gilberto and the bossa nova sound on tour, and it became an important part of his repertoire. He led mostly smaller groups during the 1970s and 1980s, dabbled with rock instrumentation for a time, but always returned to his strength as one of the most engaging melodists of the saxophone.

Getz/Gilberto (1963) *album by Stan Getz and João Gilberto*
This is the first classic of BOSSA NOVA jazz. It paired an American bandleader (STAN GETZ) who had been influenced by the sounds of Latin jazz with a Brazilian singer (João Gilberto) who had been similarly influenced by America's West Coast Jazz, or COOL JAZZ. It featured compositions by ANTONIO CARLOS JOBIM and a first-time singing performance by Gilberto's wife, ASTRUD GILBERTO, on "The Girl from Ipanema." This was the second collaboration by these artists, but the one that sparked a craze for Latin jazz with classics such as "Ipanema" and "Desafinado," released by the Verve record company.

Giant Steps (1959) *album by John Coltrane*
Featuring JOHN COLTRANE (tenor SAXOPHONE), Tommy Flannagan, Wynton Kelly, PAUL CHAMBERS (BASS), Jimmy Cobb, Art Taylor (DRUMS), this was John Coltrane's first record to feature his own compositions. Coltrane was avoiding predictable CHORD progressions. This made the music freer and less easy to follow, but allowed the mesmerizing effect of Coltrane's playing to become clear. He seems to move ahead, note by note, playing every possible space in between going up and down his chosen scales.

gig
A job or booking for a musician.

Gilberto, Astrud (b. 1940) *Brazilian singer*
In the early 1960s, when the BOSSA NOVA craze was beginning to start in the United States, Brazilian singer Astrud Gilberto was married to singer and guitarist João Gilberto. João had been the first Brazilian to record a bossa nova song, a style of music created in the late 1950s by songwriter ANTONIO CARLOS JOBIM. Astrud's spare, little-girl voice and smooth delivery became synonymous with the first bossa nova hits, including "The Girl from Ipanema" (1963), which she recorded with her husband and STAN GETZ. Prior to the recording of "Ipanema," Gilberto had never sung professionally. She enjoyed great popularity, toured with Getz, and released several recordings under her own name. In the 1970s she turned to songwriting and wrote "Far Away," which she recorded as a duet with CHET BAKER. She began working with her own COMBOS in the 1980s and continues to tour, often with her musician sons Greg and Marcelo. The shyness heard in her voice was apparently genuine; Gilberto went to acting school in the early 1980s to learn to control her stage fright.[79]

Gillespie, Dizzy (John Birks Gillespie)
(1917–1993) *American trumpeter, bandleader, and composer*
John Birks "Dizzy" Gillespie grew up in South Carolina, where he received his first music lessons. He began playing TRUMPET in New York City in the 1930s and 1940s. His energy was boundless, and he seemed to be everywhere. After playing his regular gigs with the likes of CAB CALLOWAY, ELLA Fitzgerald, COLEMAN HAWKINS, BENNY CARTER, and others, he could often be found leading impromptu after-hours jam sessions with his buddies. His early work with THELONIOUS MONK and CHARLIE PARKER led to the creation of BEBOP. His bouncy, rapid-fire playing was the impetus behind this jazz style. His record-ing of "Woody n' You" (1944) is considered the first formal musical statement of bebop.[80]

He and Parker formed a quintet in 1945 that laid down some of the trademark tune of bebop, including "SALT PEANUTS." Gillespie then formed his own sextet, tried his hand at running a big band, and recorded regularly.

Gillespie was also one of the earliest African-American jazz artists to embrace Latin rhythms in his music. He added conga player CHANO POZO to his band in 1947 and created the style now known as Latin (or Afro-Cuban) jazz.

Gillespie was not only the leading soloist of bebop but its most articulate spokesperson. For much of the rest of his career, he was recruited by one group or another as a soloist and traveled widely around the world as a leading ambassador of jazz. He toured Europe for the State Department from 1956 to 1958. He was a frequent player with Jazz at the Philharmonic. By the time of his 75th birthday, he was considered the prime spokesperson from the classic era of modern jazz and was heard far and wide in the 1980s during a renaissance of interest in bebop. Gillespie was a joyous performer whose cheeks puffed impossibly large and whose trumpet horn was bent poignantly skyward. His showman-ship was matched by his virtuosity with the trum-pet. His style of playing was so difficult to master that few musicians have been able to re-create it, yet he is one of the most imitated of jazz musicians. Some of his trumpet phrases, such as the CHORUS in "Salt Peanuts," is one of the phrases most often "quoted" in solos by other artists. Gillespie some-times playfully repeated a single note over and over, each time introducing a subtle variation in tone, INFLECTION, volume, or rhythm. As a songwriter, he composed some of the most lasting classics of jazz, including "Salt Peanuts," "con Alma." "Groovin' High," and "A Night in Tunisia." About his style, he once remarked, "It's taken me all my life to learn what not to play."

Gillo, Raúl See MACHITO.

"God Bless the Child" (1941) *recorded performance by Billie Holiday*
BILLIE HOLIDAY wrote the lyrics for this tune by A. Herzog Jr. and recorded it a year later with the Eddie Heywood Orchestra. It is a great example of Holiday's articulate and touching singing style. The tune became one of her most famous. This recording, released by Columbia, features a muted TRUMPET SOLO by ROY ELDRIDGE.

Gonzalez, Ruben (1919–2003) *Cuban piano player*
The extraordinary Afro-Cuban PIANO soloist Ruben Gonzalez began his career in the 1940s playing in Cuban casinos. He became widely known outside Cuba only in the late 1990s as one of the players involved with the Afro-Cuban All-Stars and the movie *Buena Vista Social Club*. His rollicking style, developed early in his career, was a wondrous blend of American jazz and Latin rhythms. His playing had a remarkable punch, the stuff of Argentinian tango, which he picked up while touring there in the 1950s. He was an early player of the cha-cha-cha dance music, which came out of Havana in the 1960s. At age 77, he was persuaded to come out of retirement and record some of his music for posterity. Even though his own piano had long since rotted from age and he was suffering from arthritis, his playing powers had not been diminished. The results were two remarkable albums cut before his death in 2003. *Introducing Ruben Gonzalez* (1997) features his elegantly florid style and nostalgia for Latin music, yet it swings with the surprising jump of THELONIOUS MONK. Gonzalez was also one of the key members of the Buena Vista Social Club, and an inspiration for several generations of Afro-Cuban musicians.

Goodman, Benny (1909–1986) *clarinet player, bandleader, and composer*
As a Jewish boy growing up in Chicago, Goodman learned his first RIFFS while taking CLARINET lessons

at his synagogue. He was a quick study and an imaginative player who, by the time he was 20, had already been playing professionally for several years. He was swept up by SWING music, which was all the rage at the time. He heard the likes of the DUKE ELLINGTON and PAUL WHITEMAN orchestras, and dreamed of creating his own BIG BAND. After several prosperous years as a SESSION musician, he formed his own group in 1934. His band was featured on the radio, and a nationwide tour followed. Most of their concerts on this tour were not well attended, but they forged ahead. By the time the group reached California and the Palomar Ballroom in Los Angeles, their fame had grown and an eager crowd went crazy for the swing sound of Benny Goodman.

Goodman's playing was full of wit and surprise. He was technically very skilled and although the clarinet wasn't normally the leading SOLO sound of a swing band, Benny rocked the house with his magnificent performances. He also shone as a soloist in a QUARTET that he formed during the same period. It featured musicians from his orchestra, Teddy Wilson on PIANO, and legendary artists GENE KRUPA on DRUMS and LIONEL HAMPTON on VIBRAPHONE. Goodman was aware that being white gave him opportunities that evaded many of the best black artists of the time. He was one of the first white bandleaders to add black musicians to his orchestra. Benny used jazz to help break down racial barriers in society.

Gordon, Dexter (1923–1990) *American tenor and soprano saxophone player and composer*
Dexter Gordon grew up in Los Angeles, where he took up the alto saxophone at age 15. He studied music composition and theory, switched to tenor saxophone, but quit school when he was 17 to play with the Harlem Collegians, a Los Angeles band. Soon after, in 1942, he was playing with LIONEL Hampton's band alongside ILLINOIS JACQUET and made his first recording with this ensemble. After playing for a time with the big

Benny Goodman's Orchestra (Goodman, far right)

bands of FLETCHER HENDERSON and LOUIS ARMSTRONG, Gordon was recruited for the extraordinary band of BILLY ECKSTINE and went to New York City. Eckstine's troupe was a cauldron of early BEBOP. It was during the mid-1940s that Gordon established himself as a unique voice of the bebop movement. After splitting from Eckstine, he recorded with CHARLIE PARKER and DIZZY GILLESPIE and then formed the first of many of his own groups. He took a liking to Europe, where jazz was very popular, and in 1962, moved to Copenhagen, where he was in great demand. After returning to the United States in 1977, he was given an acting role in the movie 'Round Midnight (1986). His portrayal of an American jazz artist living in Europe earned him an

Academy Award nomination. Gordon was a pivotal bebop and hard bop player. His style was a blend of the smooth LESTER YOUNG sound and the energetic riffs of Charlie Parker. He was a tall man with an imposing presence, which inspired ZOOT SIMS to remark that "Dexter always had that big sound, from the early days. He's a big man. Stands to reason he's gotta lot of lungs.[81]

Grammy Awards

These annual music awards have been given by the Recording Academy since 1957. Awards are given in many musical categories for artistic achievement, technical proficiency, and overall excellence in the recording industry, without regard to album sales or CHART position. Jazz awards are given in the following categories: CONTEMPORARY JAZZ, Jazz Female Vocal, Jazz Male Vocal, Jazz composition, Jazz FUSION, Latin Jazz, Jazz Instrumental Individual/Small Group, Jazz Instrumental Soloist, Jazz Large ENSEMBLE, Jazz Soloist, Jazz Vocal, Jazz Vocal/Duo/Group. Not every award has been given every year. One of the awards that has been given each year since 1957 is that for best jazz instrumental performance. See Appendix V for a list of winners. Note the absence of many prominent names such as JOHN COLTRANE, MILES DAVIS, and DIZZY GILLESPIE. Although these artists did win some Grammy over the years, the taste of the Recording Academy leans toward safer music, particularly that of PIANO players. For example, John Coltrane only won a single Grammy, and it was after he died (1981, best SOLO performance). Other legends still active after the founding of the Grammy and who garnered awards include LOUIS ARMSTRONG (1), CHARLIE PARKER (1, posthumous), Dizzy Gillespie (2), Miles Davis (8), and DUKE ELLINGTON (11).

See also APPENDIX V: GRAMMY AWARDS FOR JAZZ.

Great Britain   See EUROPEAN JAZZ.

guitar

In early jazz, the role of the acoustic guitar was that of playing CHORDS and keeping a rhythm. It did not emerge as an effective SOLO instrument until the use of guitar amplification in the 1940s and the proliferation of the solid-body electric guitar in the 1950s. Players who greatly influenced the style of jazz guitar playing included EDDIE LANG, CHARLIE CHRISTIAN, and DJANGO REINHARDT.

guitar synthesizer

A type of music SYNTHESIZER, pioneered in the late 1970s, for modifying the output of an electric GUITAR. Modern guitar synthesizers are usually compact and consist of a control unit, a keyboard-less synthesizer in a small box connected to the guitar through an electronic pickup. The guitar player can control the synthesizer to modify the sound of the guitar before it is amplified. A guitar synthesizer can be used to imitate the sound of others instruments (e.g., strings, horns, FLUTES), enhance the normal sound of the guitar, or create special effects (e.g., echo, reverb, loops). They are controlled either by hand or with a foot pedal. JOHN MCLAUGHLIN and PAT METHENY have both explored the use of guitar synthesizers in their music.

Haden, Charlie (b. 1937) *American bass player and composer*

Haden is an innovative BASS player whose major contribution was to bring some rhythmic skeleton to the FREE JAZZ style of radical horn players. As a youngster he played and sang in his family's country music band. He was later schooled in classical bass TECHNIQUE and jazz harmonies but was capable of breaking all the rules when ORNETTE COLEMAN brought him into his now-legendary free jazz QUARTET in 1957.

Haden developed a new style of bass playing that worked within free jazz. Because this style of jazz did not follow the CHORD progressions and meter of TRADITIONAL JAZZ, Haden created a way of playing that was both supportive of the other players and flexible enough to let him perform his own free solos. Coleman's playing would shift spontaneously from one key to another, often free of any detectable rhythm. His playing was free flowing and constantly transforming. A bass player is normally required to lay down a steady pattern of notes as the foundation for the other players. But Coleman had changed the rules. "I had to learn right away how to improvise with Ornette," explained Haden, "which not only meant following him from one key to another and recognizing the different keys, but modulating in a way that the keys flowed in and out of each other and the new harmonies sounded right."[82]

Haden was able to work Coleman's freewheeling style of IMPROVISATION and provide enough rhythm to give the players a point of reference to unify the music. Haden has great instincts for free jazz and set the example for other free jazz bassists that followed him, including DAVE HOLLAND and MALACHI FAVORS.[83]

After working with Coleman, Haden branched out, contributing to the music of KEITH JARRETT and working with CARLA BLEY and the Jazz Composers Orchestra. His own bands have included the Liberation Music Orchestra for which he and Carla Bley wrote music for revolutionary movements that combined BIG BAND with free jazz and Latin folk music. Other fruitful experiments led by Haden include the music produced by Old and New Dreams (with DON CHERRY, Dewey Redman, and ED BLACKWELL, 1976) and Quartet West (1986).

Haden's warm classical sound has lent an unusual freedom to the art of jazz bass playing. His passion for bass playing is equaled by an extraordinary curiosity in the creative process. "As long as there are musicians who have a passion for spontaneity," Haden said, "for creating something that's never been before, the art form of jazz will flourish."[84]

Hall, Jim (b. 1930) *American guitar player, composer, and bandleader*

Hall is one of the masters of the understated jazz GUITAR. His smooth, sophisticated playing was the inspiration for many younger players in the 1960s and 1970s. His mother got Hall his first guitar at age nine while the family was living in Cleveland, Ohio. He was taking lessons while in junior high school and played with a student band. It was about this time that he first heard a recording of CHARLIE

CHRISTIAN playing with BENNY GOODMAN, which inspired him to take up jazz playing. He moved to Los Angeles in 1955, and his first big break came when CHICO HAMILTON hired him to play for his group the same year. Hall was soon making records and playing for various groups in and around Los Angeles. Hall was part of the RHYTHM SECTION that backed singer ELLA FITZGERALD from 1960 to 1961, a GIG that gained him much attention.

Although known as a single-line soloist, he did not sound like the bop guitarist Charlie Christian. Hall's playing is mellow, yet he plays freely and lightly without effort. He is best when interpreting familiar standards, giving them new life with the moving sound of his softly amplified guitar.

Hall has worked with many artists over the years, including Lee Konitz, SONNY ROLLINS, BILL EVANS, ART FARMER, and RON CARTER. Hall recorded some strikingly beautiful duos with bassist Ron Carter in 1972, 1982, and 1984. He has led his own COMBOS off and on since the mid-1960s, has composed works for larger jazz ENSEMBLES, and continues to distinguish himself as the consummate guest artist. He has also recorded some striking duo albums with fellow guitarists PAT METHENY (*Jim Hall & Pat Metheny*, 1999) and BILL FRISELL (*Dialogues*, 1995). Hall has no plans for retiring and continues to tour, play, and record. He has a modest appraisal of his own talent and sound. "I think of myself more as a pretty good musician who happens to play the guitar," said Hall in 1996. ". . . Even though in the last few years I've started fooling around with various effects which changes the sound, I still like a basic, what I think of as a Lester Young sound or a Coleman Hawkins sound, that mellow guitar sound."[85]

Hamilton, Chico (b. 1921) *American drummer*

Born in Los Angeles, Hamilton got his start drumming as a teen with schoolmates CHARLES MINGUS, Illinois Jacquet, and Dexter Gordon. At age 21, Hamilton played on a recording SESSION for ELLA FITZGERALD and LESTER YOUNG. After his army service ended in 1945, he became the house drummer for a Los Angeles club and then toured with LENA HORNE from 1948 to 1955. During this period he also worked at home in Los Angeles doing studio work with GERRY MULLIGAN and others, getting a reputation as a drummer with the cool or West Coast jazz style. In 1952, he played with Mulligan and CHET BAKER in their highly influential PIANO-less QUARTET, setting the standard for COOL JAZZ at the time.

Calling Hamilton's drumming "cool" was more than a little misleading, though. He has a hard-swinging style that blends elements of BOP and HARD BOP, but without overpowering the players around him. He formed his first band in 1955 and has toured regularly since. As a bandleader, he gained a reputation for putting together unusual combinations of instruments such as FLUTE, CLARINET, and cello. Many stellar jazz players got a chance to play early in their careers with Hamilton's bands, including Paul Horn (1956–57), ERIC DOLPHY (1958–59), RON CARTER (1959), Charles Lloyd (1961–63), Gabor Szabo (1961–65), Sadao Watanabe (1965), LARRY CORYELL (1966), and JOHN ABERCROMBIE (1970). Hamilton learned much about composing and orchestration from Lena Horne's husband, Lennie Hayton, and also forged a career as a COMPOSER for MOVIES, television, and advertising jingles in the 1960s and 1970s. He is still active in the studio and continues to tour.

Hammer, Jan (b. 1948) *Czech piano and electronic keyboard player and composer*

Jan Hammer was learning to play classical PIANO music by age six. Beginning to play jazz as a teen, he immigrated to the United States in 1968 and attended the BERKLEE COLLEGE OF MUSIC in Boston. After serving as an accompanist for SARAH VAUGHN, he became a founding member of JOHN MCLAUGHLIN's groundbreaking FUSION group, MAHAVISHNU ORCHESTRA (1971 to 1973). His energetic, BLUES-influenced SYNTHESIZER playing was a showcase of Mahavishnu. The image of Hammer playing a strap-on portable keyboard synthesizer, trading lightning-fast RIFFs with guitarist McLaughlin, was a primordial image of the formative years of fusion. After the breakup of the original Mahavishnu, he collaborated with Mahavishnu's drummer, BILLY COBHAM, led his own group, and released his first SOLO album, *The First Seven Days,* in 1975. He also freelanced his artistry to many other artists, including rock guitarist Jeff Beck, AL DI MEOLA, and Mick Jagger. Hammer began to make music for motion pictures and television in the 1980s, resulting in a popular hit with his theme to the TV show *Miami Vice* (1985). He continues to be active as a soundtrack COMPOSER, SIDEMAN, and bandleader.

Hammond organ See ORGAN.

Hampton, Lionel (1908–2002) *American vibraphone, drum, and piano player, vocalist, and bandleader*

The dynamic Hampton was best known as a wizard on the VIBRAPHONE. He shares the distinction of being one of the most influential vibe players in jazz history with GARY BURTON. Hampton began his career as a drummer but added vibes to his calling card after giving them a try during a recording SESSION with LOUIS ARMSTRONG in 1930. There is much more to the Lionel Hampton story than vibes playing, though. He was one of the first jazz musicians to break the color barrier.

One night in 1936, while leading his own band in a performance at the Paradise Café in Los Angeles, BENNY GOODMAN, GENE KRUPA, and Teddy Wilson came in to hear Hampton. Before Hampton knew it, the three white musicians had joined them for a JAM onstage. This led to Goodman asking Hampton to join his QUARTET and do some recording the next day. Hampton not only made the recording SESSION but joined the Goodman quartet and BIG BAND from 1936 to 1940. The recording and stage appearances made Goodman's outfit one of the first racially integrated in jazz.

After leaving Goodman, Hampton formed his own big band and had great success in the 1940s. He was also responsible for helping the careers of many notable musicians who played with him, including Dexter Gordon, Illinois Jacquet, Fats Navarro, QUINCY JONES, ART FARMER, CLIFFORD BROWN, CHARLES MINGUS, WES MONTGOMERY, CLARK TERRY, and vocalists DINAH WASHINGTON, BETTY CARTER, and Joe Williams. Hampton's big band style was energetic and electrifying, making it one of the most popular SWING bands of the era. Since the 1950s he performed and recorded widely in small COMBO, big band, and duet formats. Hampton perfected his swinging SOLO vibe style while playing with Benny Goodman in the 1930s.

Hampton's contribution to jazz vibes is that he played the instrument like a drummer, using lightning-quick RIFFs and a heavy beat to drive the sound of his orchestra. His signature tune, "Flying Home" (1942) was a best seller for him. Hampton wrote more than 200 works in his six-decade career, including major symphonic works such as "King David Suite" (1953) and "Blues Suite." He was performing into his 90s. He was appointed to the board of the Kennedy Center by President George Bush Sr. and awarded the National Medal of the Arts by President Bill Clinton.

Hancock, Herbie (b. 1940) *American piano and electronic keyboard player, composer, and bandleader*

Hancock is the most influential PIANO and keyboard artist to appear since the emergence of HARD BOP. He is an innovator in the use of music technology, advancing the use of electronic keyboard instruments in jazz throughout his career. He is also one of the most successful jazz artists in terms of record sales and industry accolades. While most jazz artists are fortunate if their record albums sell as many as 20,000 copies, Hancock has two recordings—*Headhunters* (1973) and *Future Shock* (1983)—that have sold more than a million copies. Among his many industry citations, he has won eight GRAMMY

AWARDS and one Academy Award (1987 for the soundtrack to *Round Midnight*). He is also active in jazz education and charitable work. In 1996 he founded the Rhythm of Life Foundation to "help narrow the gap between those technologically empowered and those who are not and to find ways to help technology improve humanity."[86]

He is the Distinguished Artist in Residence at Jazz Aspen, an organization devoted to the preservation and performance of jazz and American music. Hancock is also a board member of the THELONIOUS MONK Institute of Jazz, which sponsors worldwide programs in jazz education.

Hancock was a child piano prodigy and performed with the Chicago Symphony Orchestra at the age of 11. His early jazz influences were OSCAR PETERSON and BILL EVANS. His interest in technology is also evident from his stay at Grinnell College, where he double-majored in music and electrical engineering. He performed jazz GIGs while still in college and was recruited by DONALD BYRD for his group in 1960, bringing Hancock to New York. He was given his first record contract by Blue Note records and released his first recording under his leadership, *Takin' Off* (1963). Working with Hancock on the record were Donald Byrd and Dexter Gordon. The recording was an immediate success, and its signature tune, "WATERMELON MAN" became a hit on both the jazz and rhythm and blues CHARTs. He next worked with the legendary MILES DAVIS from 1963 to 1969 in what was arguably the greatest jazz COMBO of the 1960s.

The group from 1963 to 1964 included Davis, Hancock, RON CARTER (BASS), WAYNE SHORTER (tenor SAXOPHONE), and Tony Williams (DRUMS). Hancock stayed on while other personnel in the QUINTET changed, eventually becoming, in 1969, a largely electric jazz group and a precursor of jazz FUSION. Davis recordings during this period that included Hancock were *E.S.P., Nefertiti, Sorcerer, Miles in the Sky,* and *IN A SILENT WAY.* While working with Davis, Hancock also recorded several albums of his own and began to work on music for television and MOVIES.

Hancock's mastery of modern jazz blends a variety of influences. Hancock left Davis in 1969 to form his own sextet (later septet) and dove headlong into his own exploration of fusion. Four albums with this lineup—*Fat Albert Rotunda* (1969), *Mwandishi* (1970), *Crossings* (1972), and

Herbie Hancock

Sextant (1972)—reveal a rapid evolution of his music from the tight electric jazz style of the Davis quintet to a jazz funk and fusion sound. *Crossings* and *Sextant* represent the most experimental and imaginative work in the Hancock catalogue. It was much closer to the conceptual music of SUN RA than to Miles Davis. The lineup for these two records says volumes: Hancock (electric piano, piano, Melotron, percussion), Billy Hart (drums, percussion), Buster Williams (electric and string bass, percussion), Benny Maupin (soprano saxophone, alto FLUTE, bass CLARINET, piccolo, percussion), Patrick Gleason (Moog SYNTHESIZER), Victor Pontoja (congas), plus voices. The addition of a synthesizer player as a SIDEMAN was a first in jazz and predated the availability of portable, polyphonic versions of the Moog. The synthesizer was used on these records primarily to create atmospheres and effects and to modulate the sounds of other instruments.

Following the mild success of this septet, Hancock launched a new unit and a new jazz-funk sound, resulting in the best-selling *Headhunters* (1973). This style was more in tune with dance rhythms and led to a successful formula that he continued throughout the 1980s. During the 1970s he also began to tinker with synthesizers and microcomputers to embellish his sounds. He was one of the first musicians anywhere to use an early synthesizer controlled by a personal computer—in this case an early Apple II computer outfitted with a synthesizer sound card. By the 1980s he had effectively integrated a variety of innovative electronic sounds into his work. The album *Future Shock* (1983) mixed funky jazz, electronic keyboards, and a DJ performing scratch rhythms on a turntable. This album resulted in another pop hit for Hancock, the song "ROCKIT" and its companion music video, both of which further elevated Hancock's status as a keyboard innovator.

Since that time, he returned to more jazzy projects but often with a blend of musical genres. In a more traditional vein, he produced an album of pop song interpretations, *The New Standard,* in 1996 and a duet album with Wayne Shorter in 1997. His album *Gershwin's World* (1998) was an imaginatively conceived tribute to the work of COMPOSER George Gershwin. It featured jazz players as well as pop and rock stars including Joni Mitchell and Stevie Wonder. As if not to dismiss his most accomplished piano skills, Hancock also arranged and performed a version of Gershwin's Concerto For Piano and Orchestra in G, 2nd movement, on the record. Another recent work is *Future 2 Future* (2001), another hybrid of drum and bass, hip-hop, and WORLD MUSIC on which Hancock is joined by Wayne Shorter, bassists Charnett Moffett and Bill Laswell, and drummer Jack DeJohnette, among others.

One consistent aspect of Hancock's music has been his attempt to broaden otherwise narrow categories of music, fusing elements of jazz with rhythm and blues, funk, pop, and hip-hop. His first work was a synthesis of HARD BOP, r&b, and the funk sound of HORACE SILVER. The influence of Miles Davis is also evident in Hancock's most jazz-oriented work where he always provides a sumptuous spaciousness for solos and melodic development. While it might be fair to say that Hancock never created a unique new style in jazz, he produced the next best thing, a "convincing synthesis of pre-1960 jazz piano styles," particularly those of BUD POWELL, BILL EVANS, and Horace Silver.[87]

Hancock's playing exhibits a lively but carefully thought-out plan for solos and improvisations that always seem to come full circle. With more than 40 years of music making behind him, Hancock's interests these days have broadened to the importance of music to society and culture. Hancock's passion for technology is equaled by his concern that technology can create a new form of social inequality for those who can't afford to work with it. He believes that an appreciation of culture can foster wisdom. "Without wisdom, the future has no meaning, no valuable purpose," says Hancock. "What establishes value is something that is going to move humanity forward. If humanity is not in the equation, it's like the planet without any human beings on it."[88]

Handy, W. C. (1873–1958) *American composer, cornet player, and bandleader*

W. C. (William Christopher) Handy is known as the "father of the BLUES." He published the music for many of the songs that were popular in the early days of NEW ORLEANS JAZZ. He often wrote his songs based on traditional blues themes. His first popular tune was "Memphis Blues" (1912), based on a campaign song that he wrote for E. H. Crump, a mayoral candidate in Memphis. His most popular song was "ST. LOUIS BLUES" (1914). Other familiar jazz and blues songs that he wrote include "Beale Street blues" (1917), "No Name Waltz" (1918), "Long Gone" (1920), "Southside" (1922), "Harlem Blues" (1923), and "Wall Street blues" (1929).

Handy grew up in Alabama. He took a job picking berries so that he could buy his first GUITAR. When he took the instrument home, his father was so mad that he made the young man return the guitar and trade it for a dictionary. As a teenager, though, his musical interest led to his learning to play the CORNET. He began playing blues and working with various local groups. He took a job with Mahara's Minstrels, a traveling minstrel show and eventually became the bandleader. For three years he toured the southern United States. He also took a teaching post at the Huntsville Agricultural and Mechanical College. By 1903, however, he began to lead his own bands and tour the South. It was during this time that he began to publish his songs.

After living in Memphis for several years, he moved to New York in 1917 to make records but also to start his own music publishing company. He is mainly remembered today as a publisher of classic tunes from the South, many of which became jazz standards. He was also an important documentarian of the blues and published the book *Blues: An Anthology* in 1926. After that, he slowly devoted more and more of his composing time to writing spiritual and religious music.

hard bop

A style of jazz that emerged in the 1950s as a simplified form of BEBOP. It contained the rhythmic vitality of bop but freely drew from rhythm and blues to forge a captivating, energetic sound. While solos were a part of hard bop, it downplayed the technically demanding virtuosity required to play a DIZZY GILLESPIE or CHARLIE PARKER bop tune. Representative hard bop artists included ART BLAKEY's Jazz Messengers, MAX ROACH, HORACE SILVER, SONNY ROLLINS, JIMMY SMITH, and STANLEY TURRENTINE.

Hardin, Lil (1898–1971) *American piano player, composer, arranger, and bandleader*

Lil Hardin was already an accomplished PIANO player by age 19 and joined JOSEPH "King" OLIVER's Original Creole Jazz Band in 1917 in Chicago. After leading her own band for a spell in 1920, she toured with Oliver's band until it returned to Chicago in 1924. While she was with King Oliver, she met and married the second cornetist in the band, one LOUIS ARMSTRONG. They split from King Oliver and for a time Armstrong played in Hardin's band. As his fame grew and he began to lead his own groups, she continued to write songs for him and often played and sang with his HOT FIVE AND HOT SEVEN. Although she split from Armstrong in 1931, divorcing him in 1938, she continued her career as a COMPOSER, ARRANGER, bandleader, and house musician for Decca Records.

Hargrove, Roy (b. 1970) *American trumpet player and composer*

Hargrove quickly established himself as a leading TRUMPET whiz during the late 1980s. In his fairly brief career so far, he has led QUARTETS, QUINTETS, and NONETS, played in BIG BANDS, and has recorded over nine albums as a leader. He is also a sought-after SESSION man. His style is classic HARD BOP, and when he plays a smoldering ballad it conjures up the sound of a young MILES DAVIS. In 1996 he recorded the GRAMMY AWARD–winning album *Habana*, a major foray into Afro-Cuban jazz in collaboration with some of Cuba's best-known jazz players. What is perhaps most impressive about Hargrove is his innate talent for bringing together influences from various musical genres into a cohesive jazz experiment. His recent work includes *Hard Groove* (2003), a recording made in collaboration with rhythm and blues, jazz, jam band, rappers, and hip-hop artists, resulting in a fresh take on ACID JAZZ and funk. "I just wanted to open a door that would allow the musicians involved in jazz and the musicians involved in the r&b/hip-hop mainstream to form some music that would have no limit," Hargrove explained. "It's like a merging of those two worlds."[89]

Many attempts to blend hip-hop and jazz do so only superficially, using rigid beats and decorative solos that never seem to mesh. Hargrove's approach is successful because it sounds like a group of musicians playing together, grooving together, to make convincing jazz that swings with hip-hop sensibility.

Harlem

An African-American neighborhood of Manhattan in New York City that was known for its jazz clubs during the 1920s and 1930s. Among the scores of jazz clubs in Harlem, four stood out: the COTTON CLUB, Connie's Inn, Small's Paradise, and Barron Wilkins' Club. Most of the large clubs allowed only white customers. Connie's broke the rules by sometimes allowing African-American patrons to sit in late at night after the white customers had left. During a time of racial segregation in America, the clubs in Harlem allowed many African-American performers to make a name for themselves, including DUKE ELLINGTON, COUNT BASIE, and BILLIE HOLIDAY. Live radio broadcasts from Harlem helped spread the joy of jazz around the nation and the world, and fueled the excitement of the JAZZ AGE. Harlem evolved into the cultural center of the African-American community and the place where jazz exploded in popularity during the years prior to World War II. After the heyday of BIG BAND SWING in the early 1940s, Harlem became the hot spot for the development of BEBOP, most notably because of jam sessions at MINTON'S PLAYHOUSE and Clark Monroe's club.

Harlem Renaissance

Term given to the cultural movement centered in HARLEM in the 1920s featuring the work of African-American artists in music, literature, painting, theater, and dance.

Harley, Rufus (b. 1936) *American bagpipe, flute, and alto saxophone player*

How does one become a jazz legend? The answer for Rufus Harley was to dedicate his 40 years in jazz to playing the bagpipes. That's correct—*jazz bagpipes*. The piper from Philadelphia is known around the world for his unusual specialty and has played and recorded with jazz greats, including SONNY ROLLINS, HERBIE MANN, SONNY STITT, and MAX ROACH. He was a SAXOPHONE player in the HARD BOP style and moved to the bagpipes in the 1960s, inspired by the bagpipe music played at the funeral of John F. Kennedy in 1963, but it hasn't been easy. He was fired on the spot the first time he brought the pipes out for a jazz GIG.

By 1965 he had made a serious enough impression to earn a record contract, releasing *Bagpipe Blues*. Even though he made few recordings in the 1970s and 1980s, he remained a popular performer in Philadelphia and toured the world playing SOLO and with small jazz groups. The range of his playing is remarkable considering the difficulty of sustaining sounds and playing long melodic lines. "The bagpipe is an instrument that does not stand for any unnecessary nonsense," advised Harley in 1970.[90]

The bagpipe consists of a bag that is blown full of air and four reed pipes that sound when the air in the bag is slowly squeezed out. Three of the pipes play sustained tones in different octaves and the fourth pipe is fingered to play a melody. The piper must keep the bag inflated by blowing into it. Being a reed instrument, however, the bagpipe can have a sound reminiscent of the soprano SAXOPHONE. Harley's playing also uses the characteristic drone of the bagpipe with great effect, setting a tone for his solos.

He returned to recording in 1998 with the CD *Brotherly Love* and released the recording *The Pied Piper of Jazz* in 2000. It is safe to say that Rufus Harley is unquestionably the world's greatest jazz bagpipe player.

Harris, Barry (b. 1929) *American piano player, composer, bandleader, and educator*

The BEBOP piano style of Barry Harris owed much to BUD POWELL and THELONIOUS MONK, of whose music he was a noted interpreter. Harris got his start in Detroit playing at clubs such as the Blue Bird and Rouge Lounge, where he backed up such artists as MILES DAVIS, MAX ROACH, LESTER YOUNG, and Lee Konitz. By the end of the 1950s, Harris had established himself as Detroit's premier bebop pianist as well as a teacher of this style of playing. He moved to New York in 1960 and became a regular sideman for COLEMAN HAWKINS and SONNY STITT. He made recordings with CANNONBALL ADDERLEY, DEXTER GORDON, YUSEF LATEEF, ILLINOIS JACQUET, and Hank Mobley and became widely known as the piano player on the superb LEE MORGAN album *The Sidewinder* (1963). By the 1970s, Harris was leading his own combos and devoting more and more time to teaching. He has been active as a teacher and performer for five decades and is highly regarded for his talents as a player and educator. He continues to teach at the Jazz Cultural Center in New York, which he help found in 1982. He is a prolific recording artist. His recording *Barry Harris: Live in New York* (2003) features tributes to DIZZY GILLESPIE and Monk.

Hartman, Johnny (1923–1983) *American singer and piano player*

Hartman was a smooth singer with a deep, charming voice. He was singing and playing PIANO from age eight and studied voice in college. After his military service, his first professional job was singing for the BIG BAND of EARL HINES. Ironically, Hartman was replacing Billy Eckstine, a singer with whom Hartman has always been compared. Eckstine had left the Hines troupe to start his own band. It was a big break for the "boy singer" Hartman, who stayed with Hines for several months until his band broke up. Hartman then sang for the DIZZY GILLESPIE orchestra from 1947 to 1949, an opportunity that secured his place as a unique vocal stylist. After Gillespie, he worked with pianist ERROLL GARNER (1949) and then embarked on a successful solo career as a recording artist and television performer.

Hartman did not sing with the customary bravado of most SWING band vocalists. He had a rich-toned baritone voice and used almost no VIBRATO. His sound was sultry, relaxing, and extraordinarily articulate. It is clear in a Hartman recording that the lyrics meant everything to him. Words slowly formed into melody, syllable by syllable, each embellished with emotion and meaning.

His first record, *Songs From the Heart* (1955) featured a QUARTET led by trumpeter Howard McGhee. Although his career was on the upswing throughout the 1950s, Hartman's biggest boost came with his superb duet album with tenor SAXOPHONE giant JOHN COLTRANE, *John Coltrane and Johnny Hartman* (1963). What seemed like an unlikely pairing to many turned out to be a uniquely jazzy interpretation of ballads by two artistic masters of the genre. From this album came their remarkable interpretations of standards including "My One and Only," "Dedicated to You," and BILLY STRAYHORN's "Lush Life." This recording resulted in much activity for Hartman, including additional jazz albums and a respectable career as a pop singer. His album *Once in Every Life,* recorded in 1980, earned a GRAMMY nomination for the singer. Just two years later, Johnny Hartman died at age 60. His unique voice and understated style have elevated Hartman to something of a cult figure in the jazz world. Interest in Hartman revived in 1995 due to director Clint Eastwood's selection of four Hartman songs for the soundtrack of the movie *The Bridges of Madison County.* John Coltrane, when asked to explain why he had recorded a duet album with Hartman, simply said, "There was something about his voice."[91]

Hawkins, Coleman (1904–1969) *American tenor saxophone player*

Hawkins is the granddaddy of the jazz tenor SAXO-PHONE. Before Hawkins, the tenor saxophone was used little as a SOLO or LEAD instrument. But as soon as he hit the New York scene in the early 1920s with his mellow tone and long, flowing solos, a gang of imitators followed in his footsteps. Yet for nearly 45 years he remained the standard to which all other tenor players were compared. Alto saxophone player Cannonball Adderley saw firsthand the effect that Hawkins had on his rivals. "A young tenor player was complaining to me that Coleman Hawkins made him nervous," explained Adderley. "Man, I told him Hawkins was supposed to make him nervous! Hawkins has been making other sax players nervous for forty years!"

Hawkins's first good GIGS were playing BLUES-influenced jazz in Kansas City with Jesse Stone and his Blues Serenaders (1922) and MAMIE SMITH's Jazz Hounds (1922–23). In 1924 he moved to New York to join the FLETCHER HENDERSON Orchestra, one of the first cauldrons of BIG BAND SWING. He was an instant star and stayed with Henderson for 10 years. It was during this time that Hawkins's love of expensive clothes, cars, and a good time became part of his legend. He was also intolerant of any rival sax player who challenged him and served as the sledgehammer of Henderson's swinging, no-holds-barred style of play. Hawkins was no stranger to CUTTING CONTESTS and took on all rivals during many a late-night JAM during the 1930s.

In 1934 Hawkins moved to Europe. Staying there until 1939, he first played with the Jack Hylton Orchestra and then traveled extensively on the Continent. He sat in with local groups but also formed his own COMBOS. In 1937 he recorded with BENNY CARTER, Stephane Grappelli, and DJANGO REINHARDT in Paris. At the outbreak of war in Europe, Hawkins returned to the States, eager to re-establish himself as the preeminent tenor man around. In 1940 he recorded "BODY AND SOUL," his most popular tune, which forever became associated with his name.

Coleman Hawkins

While some tenor players shrunk at the challenge of playing BEBOP, Hawkins quickly established himself as a force to be reckoned with in this new genre. Although he is not remembered as one of the seminal forces of BOP, he had the force of mind and TECHNIQUE to keep up with the young lions. In 1944 he brought DIZZY GILLESPIE into his QUARTET for an early bop recording SESSION. At one time or another, he also hired rising stars such as THELONIOUS MONK, MILES DAVIS, and MAX ROACH to play for him. During the 1950s and 1960s, he toured and recorded frequently. His staged cutting contests were a popular feature added to the JAZZ AT THE PHILHARMONIC program while he was with it from 1946 to 1951. He also became a familiar participant on the budding jazz festival scene, particularly at the NEWPORT JAZZ FESTIVAL.

Hawkins's influence went beyond his immediate contemporaries during the swing era. Later tenor players, including SONNY ROLLINS and JOHN COLTRANE, freely cited Hawkins's importance to their playing. He had excellent playing technique. His deep, mellow tone was instantly recognizable. What made Hawkins so influential was his innovative reinvention of songs as he played them. This was due not only to his manipulation of melody, like trumpeter LOUIS ARMSTRONG, but also because of his acute awareness of the CHORD structure of a song. He was fascinated by the progression of chords in a song and liked to build harmonic complexity on top of what was given. This often meant twisting the melody in some interesting ways so that a song's harmonies could be embellished. His classic recording of "Body and Soul" (1939) begins with a note-for-note delivery of the familiar melody, which he never completes. Instead, he never looks back, building drama and creating a melodic journey that was unparalleled in the history of jazz saxophone. Despite its unconventional nature, this amazingly complex IMPROVISATION was a hit with record buyers. Hawkins's stature as a jazz legend was secured long before his death in 1969. "Some people say there was no jazz tenor before me," Hawkins explained later in life. "All I know is I just had a way of playing and I didn't think in terms of any other instrument but the tenor. I honestly couldn't characterize my style in words. It seems like whatever comes to me naturally is what I play."

head

When a piece of music consists of an opening theme followed by SOLOS, the opening theme is called the "head." After the solos are complete, the musicians might "take it from the head," returning to the opening theme.

head arrangement

An ARRANGEMENT worked out or improvised by a group of musicians without writing it down. These arrangements are kept in their heads, or memorized.

Head Hunters (1973) *album by Herbie Hancock*

This album features HERBIE HANCOCK (keyboards), Bennie Maupin (tenor SAXOPHONE, soprano saxophone, saxello, BASS CLARINET, alto FLUTE), Paul Jackson (bass), Harvey Mason (DRUMS), and Bill Summers (percussion). Hancock had already showcased his talents as a keyboard player with MILES DAVIS and on his own SOLO albums, but *Head Hunters* was his coming-out party. It is the best-selling jazz record of all time. The reason is the joy of the playing, the dexterity of the musicians, and the wry combination of the old and the new. The sound was heavily electronic in its use of keyboards and bass. Hancock provided the funk and the space onto which Maupin brushed his colorful solos. There is an undeniable rhythm to this recording that owes a lot to the popular music of Sly and the Family Stone, Parliament, and James Brown. Hancock managed to pick up that wonderful funk and lace it with jazz. As if needing to remind the listener of his jazz roots, Hancock also included a new funked-up version of his old song, "WATERMELON MAN."

headliner

The leading act on a concert date.

"Heebie Jeebies" (1926) *recorded performance by Louis Armstrong and his Hot Five*

LOUIS ARMSTRONG's first "hit" record (released by Okeh) featured one VERSE of SCAT SINGING, a playful practice Armstrong had picked up while singing on the streets with his friends in New Orleans. Although it wasn't the first example of scat put on record, Armstrong's style was so breezily unpredictable and jazzy that it has been forever recognized as the first important example of scat ever recorded.

Henderson, Fletcher (1898–1952) *American pianist, composer, arranger, and bandleader*

He is known as a pioneering jazz ARRANGER and for creating the first BIG BAND devoted to playing jazz. Although having had musical training as a child, Fletcher's ambitions originally pointed elsewhere. He graduated from college in Atlanta, where he studied chemistry and math. He then moved to New York to attend graduate school but soon found his musical roots calling him. He took a part-time job playing recording SESSIONS at Black Swan Records for such famous BLUES singers as Ethel Waters and Bessie Smith. In 1922 he formed his own group, the Fletcher Henderson Orchestra, which was primarily a dance band. Orchestras like

Henderson's, consisting of 10 or more players, generally played only dance music. But he was intrigued by the sound of jazz coming from smaller COMBOS in Chicago and New York.

By 1923 Henderson began to shift the music of his orchestra toward jazz, which was all the rage by then. In 1924 Henderson recruited none other than the hottest jazz musician of all, LOUIS ARMSTRONG, to play in his big band. Other musicians working with Henderson at the time included COLEMAN HAWKINS and DON REDMAN. This was the first true big band devoted to jazz. His example led to the era of big band SWING music. One reason for the success of the big band formula was the ability of the bandleader to arrange the music to produce a powerful, unified, musical voice. While some musicians excelled at playing an instrument, Henderson excelled at arranging music and frequently offered his talents to other bandleaders such as TOMMY

Fletcher Henderson

"God Bless the Child" and "Strange Fruit" were two of her best-known songs. She first performed "Strange Fruit" in New York in 1939 to a racially mixed audience. The song was about the darker side of race relations in America, where black men were still being lynched by white mobs in the South. The poetic lyrics delivered with deliberate remorse by the remarkable Lady Day, read in part: "Southern trees bear a strange fruit, Blood on the leaves and blood at the root, Black bodies swaying in the southern breeze, Strange fruit hanging from the poplar trees." Holiday was blessed with talent, but also used her artistry to help further the cause of African Americans.

Holland, Dave (b. 1946) *British bass, bass guitar, and cello player, composer, and educator*
Holland is the dean of British jazz bassists. He started working with the BASS GUITAR as a teen but switched to DOUBLE BASS after being inspired by recordings of the great jazz bassists RAY BROWN and Leroy Vinnegar.[95]

After studying classical bass, he was still playing with orchestras when he began gigging with jazz players on the London jazz scene, 1965 to 1968. Among those he jammed with were Ronnie Scott and JOHN SURMAN.[96]

MILES DAVIS heard him play and recruited Holland for his band. Holland moved to New York and played with Davis on the seminal *IN A SILENT WAY* (1969) and *BITCHES BREW* (1970) albums, two cornerstones of FUSION jazz. While in New York, Holland began working on recordings and performing with many other artists. The next influential group he joined was Circle with CHICK COREA (1970), which disbanded after a year.

The 1970s saw Holland follow several productive paths that have continued throughout his long career. He made his first record as a leader, *CONFERENCE OF THE BIRDS* (1972), continued to explore collaborations and performances with other innovative players, and began to teach both privately and at schools. In latter years he worked

on performances and recordings as a SOLO artist. Most recently, he has turned his attention to directing a BIG BAND while continuing to be a highly visible SESSION player and small group SIDEMAN. Holland is one of the most respected and sought-after bassists in CONTEMPORARY JAZZ. He has been a part of many Grammy-winning projects, including his own Dave Holland big band that won the GRAMMY AWARD for Best Large Jazz Ensemble Album in 2002. His list of collaborators includes HERBIE HANCOCK, Jack DeJohnette, PAT METHENY, ANTHONY BRAXTON, Sam Rivers, and STAN GETZ, among others.

Holland is known for his playing within CHORD structures as well as FREE JAZZ. He has a big, strong sound that flows with a natural spontaneity. He embraces the entire repertoire of jazz, having learned the WALKING BASS, the timekeeping of QUINTET and Big band playing, as well as the unbridled freedom of free IMPROVISATION.

Holmes, Richard "Groove" (1931–1991) *American organ, piano, and bass player*
This self-trained keyboard player was working on the small-club circuit when he was discovered by Les McCann in 1960. This led to a recording contract and a series of successful albums featuring his jazz trio format of HAMMOND ORGAN, DRUMS, and GUITAR. His early recording sessions were in a TRADITIONAL JAZZ vein and featured such players as BEN WEBSTER (tenor SAXOPHONE), Les McCann (PIANO), and PAUL CHAMBERS (BASS). In 1973 he joined forces with Jimmy McGriff to record and perform a series of organ duets. He toured steadily from the mid-1960s through the 1980s, gaining a steady following, especially in Southern California. With his trio he had a hit record with the song "Misty" in 1965.[97]

He said that his playing was inspired by jazz bassists rather than other organ players. This is evident in the exquisite style of his bass pedal playing on the organ. Holmes was a soulful player whose style was emulated by many funk players.

Horn, Shirley (b. 1934) *American singer and piano player*

Shirley Horn is an American classic and one of the great voices of jazz. In more than 50 years she has carved a unique niche for herself as a perennially reliable singer of jazz and pop standards. Accompanying herself on PIANO, and at her best when only joined by a BASS player and drummer, her slow, breathy delivery is one of the most intimate in jazz. She studied music at Howard University. Her influences range from OSCAR PETERSON to Claude Debussy. From the start she was determined to make it on her own, forming her first trio in 1954. Her first recordings were not highly successful, but with the encouragement of MILES DAVIS, she began to rise in popularity after appearing on the same bill with him at the Village Vanguard in New York.[98]

Davis reportedly insisted to the Vanguard staff that he would not perform unless Horn opened for him.[99]

She continued to record sporadically but thrived primarily on performing in jazz clubs around the

Shirley Horn

Washington, D.C., area. Her recording career took a turn for the better in the late 1980s, when she signed a contract with the Verve label. For a singer who came of age during an era of greats including ELLA FITZGERALD, SARAH VAUGHN, BILLIE HOLIDAY, and CARMEN MCRAE, Horn successfully found her own original style. She has the ability to take a familiar song and transform it forever. Her slowly paced delivery and expressiveness give the impression of an intimate conversation. Her most successful record has been "Here's to Life" (1992).

Horne, Lena (b. 1917) *American singer*

Lena Horne is a popular singer with jazz roots who is best known for her elegant demeanor, silky VIBRATO voice, and for breaking the color barrier in Hollywood MOVIES. Horne's mother got the 16-year-old a job as a dancer at HARLEM's COTTON CLUB in 1934. After being immersed in the jazz world of the Cotton Club, she took a job singing with the Noble Sissle Orchestra (1935–36) and then became one of the first African-American singers to front a white BIG BAND when she toured with Charlie Barnet (1940–41). Her successful singing career soon gave way to a movie contract with MGM.

She was the first African American to sign a long-term contract (seven years in this case) with a major Hollywood studio. Built into her contract was a clause that she would not be playing the small parts of housekeepers, maids, or jungle natives usually given to blacks at the time. She made 13 films but only had significant acting roles in the two that were cast with all blacks, *Cabin in the Sky* (1943) and *Stormy Weather* (1943). Her recording of "Stormy Weather" (1943) as the title track of the movie resulted in her biggest musical hit and her most recognized tune.

Horne remained a popular recording artist through the 1960s and frequently toured, playing large and small venues. In 1981, at the age of 64, she starred in a successful one-woman show on Broadway, *The Lady and Her Music*, recounting the music of her career and her battle for the equal rights of African Americans in the entertainment world.

hot

Fast and fierce music. The term was often used to describe the style of play of early jazz artists such as LOUIS ARMSTRONG, JELLY ROLL MORTON, and DJANGO REINHARDT, but applies equally to BOP and other artists such as DIZZY GILLESPIE, JOHN COLTRANE, and ART BLAKEY.

Hot Club de France

During the 1920s many American jazz artists took their music to Europe, where an eager new audience awaited them. The French were especially wowed by jazz, and it was in Paris that the Hot Club was founded in 1932. It was the most famous haunt for American jazz performers. Between 1932 and 1934, FATS WALLER, DUKE ELLINGTON, and LOUIS ARMSTRONG all performed there. The Hot Club was also the home of the first skilled EUROPEAN JAZZ COMBO, the quintette du Hot Club. The group feature violinist Stephane Grappelli and the legendary gypsy guitarist DJANGO REINHARDT. When the Germans occupied France during World War II, Grappelli left for England, but Reinhardt stayed in Paris. The Hot Club itself continued to operate despite German censorship on some kinds of jazz music. During the war the club was even used as a headquarters for secret meetings of the French resistance.

Hot Five and Hot Seven

The Hot Five and Hot Seven were the names given to the first recording session combos led by LOUIS ARMSTRONG. Although many of these players often found themselves sharing the same stage, particularly in LIL HARDIN Armstrong's own band, the Hot Five and Hot Seven did not really exist outside of the recording studio. From 1925 to 1928, Armstrong and these players recorded some of the most brilliant and influential records of the early

jazz era. These records captured for all the world to hear the exciting sound of HOT JAZZ that Armstrong had been developing during the early 1920s. These were the first recordings under Louis Armstrong's own name and marked the beginning of his rise to great popularity. The recordings also trace his development as a trumpeter and his transition from jazz firmly rooted in the New Orleans style to a hot style of his own that changed all of jazz.

The original Hot Five included some of the best instrumentalists of the CHICAGO JAZZ style. In addition to Armstrong on TRUMPET, the COMBO consisted of his wife Lil Hardin Armstrong on PIANO (who also wrote music for the group), JOHNNY DODDS on CLARINET, KID ORY on TROMBONE, and Johnny St. Cyr on BANJO. Armstrong's explosive SOLO on "Cornet Chop Suey" (1926) made it clear that Armstrong had come of age as a jazz soloist without rival. For the Hot Seven recordings in 1927, Armstrong added tuba and DRUMS to the group. EARL "FATHA" HINES also joined on piano and helped push the Armstrong sound further yet from its New Orleans roots. Hines's solo on "Chicago Breakdown" (1927) used his new "trumpet" style of playing piano solos, influenced by Armstrong, and made the piano an equal partner with other group members when it came to IMPROVISATION.

Not every track recorded during these sessions was remarkable, especially on the 1925 discs, which contain several clinkers as the group tried to find its musical identity. But once they were on track, the results were often remarkable. Some of the best Hot Five and Hot Seven tracks included "HEEBIE JEEBIES" (1926), "Big Butter and Egg Man" (1926), "Skit-Dat-De-Dat" (1926), "S.O.L. Blues" (1927), "Potato Head Blues" (1927), "Wild Man Blues" (1927), "Struttin' With Some Barbecue" (1927), "Hotter Than That" (1927), and "West End Blues" (1928).

hot jazz

This style of jazz featuring individual soloists that evolved from NEW ORLEANS JAZZ during the early 1920s was mostly played by transplanted New

Orleans musicians such as Freddie Keppard, King Oliver, Kid Ory, and Louis Armstrong. Armstrong was the most significant influence, developing his freewheeling solo style of playing in the early 1920s. His recordings with the Hot Five and Hot Seven in the mid-1920s provide a document of this exciting new stage in the history of early jazz. By the end of the 1920s, hot jazz had evolved into the larger ensemble music called swing.

house band

A combo, big band, or jazz orchestra that is regularly featured at a particular nightclub or other venue.

Hubbard, Freddie (b. 1938) *American trumpeter, flugelhorn player, composer, and bandleader*

Along with trumpet greats Miles Davis and Clifford Brown, Freddie Hubbard is one of the most influential stylists of modern jazz trumpet. Not only was he talented, but he also had an ear for many styles of jazz and fit in perfectly with musicians as varied as Art Blakey's hard bop sound, Eric Dolphy's free jazz, and Quincy Jones's soothing music. Hubbard formed his own band after leaving the Jazz Messengers in 1964. Miles and Hubbard were the most imitated trumpeters of the 1970s. However, the sounds of these two musicians were quite different. Whereas Davis played solemnly, almost sadly, Hubbard was joyful and loose. Davis often strayed from the beat. Hubbard, on the other hand, not only nailed the beat with force but liked to kick up the pace to double time. Hubbard is, above all else, an imaginative player who takes risks. That's what makes his performances unpredictable, fresh, and lively.

Hunter, Alberta (1895–1984) *American singer*

Hunter was a classic blues singer from the early years of recorded jazz who surrounded herself with some of the best jazz sidemen (see sideman) of the era. After running away from her home in Memphis in 1906, she settled in Chicago and began to work and sing in clubs. Her big break came when she befriended Lil Hardin, a piano player in "King" Oliver's Creole Jazz Band. While singing with Oliver she became a local favorite. But those were harrowing days in Chicago clubs. During one performance, her piano player was shot and killed while they were onstage.[100]

She moved to New York soon.

A popular recording artist in the 1920s, some of the musicians who accompanied her included Louis Armstrong, Sidney Bechet, Fats Waller, Fletcher Henderson, Duke Ellington, and Eubie Blake.[101]

She wrote much of her own material. Her song "Down Hearted Blues" became a hit for Bessie Smith in 1923. Hunter spent much of the 1930s in Europe doing stage productions and performing widely. She returned to America and started singing swing with convincing talent. During World War II she entertained troops and then returned to America, where she first cared for her ailing mother then embarked on a nursing career for 20 years. She returned to music in 1977, age 82, and made three successful records. Although her sweet vibrato was mostly identified with blues singing, Hunter was a jazzy singer whose talent often surpassed the normal ordinary blues format.

Ibrahim, Abdullah (b. 1934) *South African piano, soprano saxophone, and cello player and composer*

Ibrahim was born Adolph Johannes Brand and adopted the stage name of Dollar Brand when he began playing professionally. He changed his name to Abdullah Ibrahim after converting to Islam in 1968. He is one of the most influential jazz artists of the last 50 years. As a member of the famed Jazz Epistles in 1959, he and band mates HUGH MASEKELA (TRUMPET) and Kippi Moeketsi were part of one of the first widely accepted jazz combos in South Africa. Their recording *Jazz in Africa* was the first made by SOUTH AFRICAN JAZZ musicians. He moved to Europe in 1962 to lead his own trio. An encounter with DUKE ELLINGTON led to the album, *Duke Ellington Presents the Dollar Brand Trio* (1963).

Ellington and Ibrahim remained close and with the Duke's help he was booked at the 1965 NEWPORT JAZZ FESTIVAL. Ibrahim also substituted for Ellington during an engagement of the Duke's band in 1966. After that, he toured widely in America and Europe with many leading musicians, including ELVIN JONES, DON CHERRY, and GATO BARBIERI. During the 1970s, Ibrahim continued touring but also explored composing for larger ENSEMBLES and mixed media. One of his most ambitious works, *Kalahari Liberation Opera* (1982) incorporated music, drama, and dance. It was widely performed in Europe and was a vivid call for the civil rights of South African blacks who were still suffering under the white government's apartheid segregationist policies.

He continues to tour as a group leader, soloist, and participant in larger productions of his music for orchestra. His PIANO playing is lyrical and melodic, with a light touch and a rocking rhythm that is reminiscent of Ellington. During the past 20 years, Ibrahim has increasingly incorporated elements of African music, including chants, rhythms, and instrumentation, into his work. In 1997 he began a fruitful collaboration with drummer MAX ROACH. The widely recorded Ibrahim has been dividing his time between many recent projects. The release of *Africa Suite* (1999) and *African Symphony* (2002), which capture Ibrahim playing many of his signature pieces with an orchestral string setting, and *African Magic* (2003) mark a return to trio work.

improvisation

Making up music on the spot during a performance, improvisation may be done by one or more musicians at the same time. It does not rely on written parts or playing music that has been memorized. In traditional improvisation, one is usually trying to invent a new melody that fits the underlying structure of a song. Free improvisation may not begin with an underlying song structure at all, allowing the musician to invent an entire composition at the moment that it is being played. True jazz does not exist without some element of improvisation because jazz is a music of personal expression.

"In a Sentimental Mood" (1962) *recorded performance by Duke Ellington*

Featuring DUKE ELLINGTON (PIANO), JOHN COLTRANE (tenor SAXOPHONE), Aaron Bell (BASS), and ELVIN JONES (DRUMS), released by Impulse!, written by Ellington, this is one of the most hauntingly lovely jazz tunes ever recorded. It fused the talents of two all-time greats, the Duke and 'Trane. Who would have imagined that the artistry of these extremely different talents would have worked so well together? The two of them knew it! The result is a meeting at the crossroads where the basic language of jazz allows even the most diverse of artists to communicate. It begins with a spare piano line by the Duke. Then Coltrane's mellow sax sweeps in like a jet and plays a warm melody supported by the gentle accompaniment of the bass and drums. It is a blend of masters, a classic sound that, in 1962, was reminiscent of the history of jazz while at the same time hinting at its broadening future.

In a Silent Way (1969) *album by Miles Davis*

Some say that FUSION began with this 1969 album, released by Columbia, which captured the first largely electric jazz COMBO led by MILES DAVIS. It featured seven musicians who went on to forge the best fusion music of the 1970s; HERBIE HANCOCK (electric piano); CHICK COREA (electric piano); WAYNE SHORTER (tenor SAXOPHONE); DAVE HOLLAND (BASS); JOE ZAWINUL (electric piano and ORGAN); JOHN McLAUGHLIN (GUITAR); and Tony Williams (DRUMS). Featuring only two extended tracks, the music revolved around themes played and then improvised freely by the musicians. It has the feeling of a collage, a SET of musical impressions. With this record, Davis put an even greater distance between his HARD BOP past and his new music. As a foreshadowing of the future, it represented jazz that slowly unfolded, somewhat instinctively rather than by a master plan, into a music of expanded consciousness. *In a Silent Way* inspired a new style of play that was much imitated in the 1970s.

Incredible Jazz Guitar of Wes Montgomery, The (1960) *album by Wes Montgomery*

Released by Riverside, this album established WES MONTGOMERY as the most interesting jazz guitarist to emerge since the days of BEBOP. His style was well developed by this stage. He picked with his thumb and used very soft chording to give his sound a cushioned attack. His melodies and IMPROVISATIONS were some of the most articulate and well executed in the history of jazz GUITAR.

Inflated Tear, The (1967) *album by Rahsaan Roland Kirk*

Featuring RAHSAAN ROLAND KIRK (tenor SAXOPHONE, FLUTE, manzello, stritch, CLARINET, whistles), Ron Burton (PIANO), Steve Novosel (BASS), Jimmy Hopps (DRUMS). This album was released by Atlantic. Kirk was a gifted instrumentalist and showman. His music was constructed around his amazing talent for playing two horns at once (and sometimes a nose flute to boot!). He was also a master of CIRCULAR BREATHING, the ability to seemingly play a wind instrument without taking a break for a breath. This was perhaps his most satisfying studio album. The music is as incredibly alive and raucous as it is surprising. Kirk ably brought elements of native African music into his compositions, broadening the horizon of TRADITIONAL JAZZ listeners.

inflection

The special expressive sounds that a jazz artist creates with his or her instrument. Listening closely to jazz will reveal many possible inflections. These include the way a note is held, the attack of a sound, the rise or fall of a note, ACCENTs, bending the note, TREMOLO, VIBRATO, and many other TECHNIQUES.

Inner Mounting Flame, The (1972) album by John McLaughlin and the Mahavishnu Orchestra

At the time of its release by Columbia, the first album by the MAHAVISHNU ORCHESTRA seemed like the perfect antidote to the breezy wanderings of MILES DAVIS's FUSION efforts. With striking virtuosity on every instrument in the band, McLaughlin forged a driving sound that fused the wildest grunge and feedback of the late Jimi Hendrix with impressive group interplay. The music had many novel features: the SYNTHESIZER SOLOS of JAN HAMMER, the athletic verve of BILLY COBHAM's drumming, the burning chords of Jerry Goodman's VIOLIN, and the driving pulse of Rick Laird's BASS. Above it all soared JOHN McLAUGHLIN's GUITAR, transmitting lines of notes to which the other players constantly replied. This is fusion bliss; jazz virtuosity with a raucous rock sound.

International Sweethearts of Rhythm

A 16-piece, multiracial, all-female SWING band that toured the United States during World War II, this group of accomplished women was groundbreaking in many ways. It was an all-female band in a male-dominated business. Its racially mixed lineup brought together players who were, wholly or partly, African American, Mexican, Asian, Puerto Rican, Native American, and white.[102]

The word *International* in the name of the group referred to the "visible ethnic and racial variety" that was a natural part of the group's makeup.[103]

It also had a bona fide star in "TINY" DAVIS, an American TRUMPET player and singer who was dubbed the female LOUIS ARMSTRONG.

The band was formed in 1937 as a fund-raiser for the all black Piney Woods Country Life School in Mississippi and played together until 1950. Anna Mae Winburn joined the band as leader and ARRANGER in 1941. The Sweethearts had become popular enough by 1943 to take its show on the road. Its tour hit the black theater circuit, stopping at such time-honored venues as the Apollo in HARLEM, New York, the Royal in Baltimore, and the Howard Theater in Washington, D.C.[104]

During one phenomenal week in 1941, the band set a box office record for the Howard Theater by selling more than 35,000 tickets.[105]

The sound of the Sweethearts was big and brassy and their musicianship unparalleled in the world of all-female swing bands. Those women who came to play with the Sweethearts appreciated their talented company. However, the music of the Sweethearts was not the only message they delivered. Having originated from a school system, they symbolized the importance of an elementary education for underprivileged African Americans across the country. The multiracial membership of the group was also an important eye-opening experience for many whites in a segregated America. One gentleman who saw them perform put it very plainly. "Here I sat in a segregated audience and was witnessing a performance by women who looked like they were from all over the world. This was my first visual experience with integration—my glance into what the civil rights movement would be about approximately two decades later."[106]

A 30-minute documentary film, *International Sweethearts of Rhythm*, was made about the band in 1987 by Greta Schiller and Andrea Weiss.

"It Don't Mean a Thing (If It Ain't Got That Swing)" (1932) recorded performance by Duke Ellington

Featuring DUKE ELLINGTON and His Orchestra, with IVIE ANDERSON (vocal), released by Columbia, this song became the signature tune of the SWING generation. It was the first song to use the word *swing* in its title. It is a great example of the hundreds of tunes written by Ellington for the three-minute format of the 78-rpm record. The muted horns, the jumping rhythms, and the rollicking vocal by Anderson say it all. This was swing!

Jackson, D. D. (b. 1967) *Canadian piano and organ player and composer*

The Canadian-born, New York–based Jackson is one of the rising stars of CONTEMPORARY JAZZ. The classically trained artist received his masters in jazz from the Manhattan School of Music in 1991. He has played PIANO since the age of 6. He credits the late musician and teacher Don Pullen as one of his most creative influences. It was Pullen who helped the young Jackson think more openly about composing. Instead of laboring over an idea, Pullen advised that he just "think of something, you write it down; you try not to judge it, and you proceed from there."[107]

Jackson is an admirer of KEITH JARRETT and possesses many of that artist's characteristics: a flawless TECHNIQUE steeped in classical music, a penchant for playing with small groups, and a writing style that blends classical music with jazz. His first album, *Peace-Song* (1995), showed enormous range and agility in his playing. His Monk-like RIFFS immediately branded him as a post BOP player. There were other facets of his playing on that first album, however, that he has more fully explored in later work. He sometimes uses a "sheets of sound" attack, playing a bruising barrage of atonal chords that CECIL TAYLOR would admire. He has a skilled touch for melody and can also free the piano, much like Jarrett, from the bounds of rhythmic accompaniment to create a vivid soundscape of varied textures and feelings.

Jackson works regularly with his own small COMBO, but is also a commissioned artist and COMPOSER of larger scale works. *Sigame* (2001) was a relaxed romp with an Afro-Latin connection. His most ambitious work, *Suite for New York* (2003), is a sincere and disarming tribute to the tragedy of 9/11. It combines poetry with a large-scale jazz orchestra and strings, and harkens back to the larger works produced by jazz giants of the past, including DUKE ELLINGTON and CHARLES MINGUS. In commenting on *Suite for New York*, critic Harvey Siders aptly described Jackson's style as a "fusion of futuristic jazz, contemporary classical, streetwise funk and Afro-Cuban sensuality."[108]

Jacquet, Illinois (Jean-Baptiste Jacquet) (b. 1922) *American tenor and alto saxophone player and band leader*

A Texas tenor, Illinois Jacquet, is one of those musicians who seems to have played with everybody. He first made his mark with his soulful solo on the tune "Flying Home," recorded with LIONEL HAMPTON's band in 1941. It was a precursor of a soulful style of saxophone playing that would become the bread and butter of CANNONBALL ADDERLEY and a host of soul-jazz players in the 1960s. The list of people with whom he played spans nearly every style of classic jazz, from the territory swing of Milt Larkin to the jumping Kansas City sound of early CHARLIE PARKER, the big bands of CAB CALLOWAY and COUNT BASIE, the JAZZ AT THE PHILHARMONIC showcase led by Norman Granz and the mellower rhythms of LESTER YOUNG, NAT KING COLE, and CHARLES MINGUS. Throughout it all, Jacquet delivered a mellow, bold, horn sound that could attack sharply when needed or soothe the soul with warm tones.

jam
To improvise together.

Jamal, Ahmad (b. 1930) *American piano and keyboard player and composer*
Ahmad Jamal is a gifted, though perhaps underappreciated, jazz innovator. He first gained notice in the early 1950s working with his trio, using sparse piano arrangements that accentuated silence and blocks of sound, along with well-crafted shifts in tempo and dynamics. He was a strong influence on the early work of MILES DAVIS, who credits Jamal with having influenced his development as a composer and player. Remembering what he thought upon first hearing Jamal, Davis said, ". . . he knocked me out with his concept of space, his lightness of touch, his understatement, and the way he phrased notes and chords and passages."[109]

Davis also liked Jamal's tune selections, which seem to embrace the most unlikely of popular songs, transforming them into jazz masterworks. This approach influenced many players of the 1950s, including Davis, CHET BAKER, JOHN COLTRANE, and others whose song selections reflected Jamal's pioneering style. Jamal has continued as a jazz innovator for five decades. In 1994, he received the American Jazz Masters award from the National Endowment for the Arts. The same year, he was named a Duke Ellington Fellow at Yale University, where he performed commissioned works with the Assai String Quartet. On *In Search of Momentum* (2003), Jamal continues to explore the subtle moods of the piano with the touch of a jazz master.

James, Harry (1916–1983) *American trumpet player and bandleader*
Harry started out playing in the circus with his family, eventually leaving to join the local band circuit in the early 1930s. While playing in the Ben Pollack BIG BAND (1935–37), he became known for his showy virtuosity on the TRUMPET. BENNY GOODMAN had the hottest SWING band in 1937 and hired James as part of his dynamic trumpet section. This exposure enabled James to start his own band a couple of years later. James was always the center of his band's universe. His extraordinary SOLOS, thought to be excessively sentimental and ornate by some jazz fans, made him one of the most popular musicians in the country. Fortifying the popularity of his band was his use of singers, including Frank Sinatra. With the decline of the big bands, James dabbled in small group work. During the 1950s he left the realm of popular music and returned to TRADITIONAL JAZZ, touring Europe with his small group. During the 1960s, he explored big band sounds again and became a popular fixture on the nightclub and hotel circuit. At his best, his playing could be sensitive and brooding. His work will be remembered for having lent authentic jazz virtuosity to popular song.

jam session
A group of jazz musicians playing together informally. Historically, jam sessions came about during the 1930s as a way for jazz artists to exercise their licks and have some fun after hours. The idea of "jamming" led to the acceptance of IMPROVISATION as a featured part of formal jazz performances.

Japanese jazz
Tokyo probably has more working jazz musicians than any city other than New York. The ascendancy of jazz in Japan has been astonishing, if not puzzling, to many Westerners. American jazz is so deeply rooted in the social and cultural history of African Americans, that it is hard for some to imagine the universal appeal of jazz, especially to an Asian culture. Yet, if we remember that the essence of jazz is unavoidably a music of *personal expression,* it is easy to understand its appeal to any world culture. Moreover, Japan has a rich heritage of traditional music for instruments such as the koto (a plucked stringed instrument) and shakuhachi (valveless, bamboo FLUTE). Traditional Japanese music is noted for being rhythmically free, a style that was perfected on

the shakuhachi flute during the Tokugawa period (1600–1867) of Japanese history. To play with such freedom of expression, a shakuhachi musician relied on a sense of heightened awareness and intuition about life called satori rather than a set of logical rules for playing music. The parallels to jazz IMPROVISATION are clear and provide a cultural bias toward improvisation at the heart of traditional Japanese music.

In the late 1870s, as Japan became increasingly familiar with Western culture and industry, there was an ambitious educational program throughout the country to modernize its society so that it could compete with the economies of Europe and America. This included exposure to American popular music. By the time that jazz was first heard in Japan, it was a country that was curious and receptive to Western cultural ideas. Contrary to popular belief, jazz did not first reach the shores of Japan during the American occupation following World War II. Jazz actually reached the shores of Japan just before 1920, about the same time that the first jazz recordings were made.[110]

Jazz instruments and recordings were first brought back to Japan in the 1910s and 1920s by Japanese musicians traveling to San Francisco from ports at Yokohama and Kobe. They reportedly traded their VIOLINS for SAXOPHONES and picked up sheet music and recordings of RAGTIME, dance music, and the BLUES.[111]

The first professional jazz band was the Laughing Stars, founded in 1923 in Kobe.

The introduction of jazz into Japanese culture was not without controversy. While modern city dwellers were fascinated by jazz, many Japanese objected to its introduction into their culture, feeling that the importation of music borrowed from another culture watered down their own national identity. From the 1920s through to the end of World War II (1945), jazz continued to be the subject of serious public debate as Japan itself was undergoing unprecedented social upheaval. As Japan became increasingly militarized for war, the government was afraid that jazz encouraged certain aspects of Western culture that they found

objectionable: unfettered freedom of expression and racial and gender equality.

After World War II, Americans brought live jazz to Japan, and it exploded in popularity. The first postwar generation of Japanese jazz artists were largely imitative of American artists. The first important tours of Japan by American artists began in 1953 when LOUIS ARMSTRONG paid his first visit (followed by tours in 1954 and 1956). Then Norman Granz brought the famed JAZZ AT THE PHILHARMONIC program to Japanese shores. Among the players on the Granz tour were ELLA FITZGERALD and OSCAR PETERSON. Peterson became a favorite of the Japanese and has since toured the country more than 20 times. DUKE ELLINGTON toured Japan in 1964, as did BENNY GOODMAN. By the 1970s the adulation for American jazz in Japan encouraged many musicians to take their acts to Asia, including BENNY CARTER, ELVIN JONES, ART BLAKEY, and many more.

It wasn't until the 1960s and 1970s that Japanese jazz artists began to forge a reputation for originality in performance, composition, and improvising. Some artists, such as Yoshiko Akiyoshi, came to America to forge a career in jazz, many after studying at the BERKLEE COLLEGE OF MUSIC. Others have been catalysts for a vital jazz scene throughout their native country. Among these are Japanese jazz greats Sadao Watanabe (alto and soprano saxophones), Hino Terumasa (TRUMPET and FLUGELHORN), Aki Takase (PIANO), Kei Akagi (piano and keyboards), Kazumi Watanabe (GUITAR), Takeshi Watanabe (DRUMS), Tiger Okoshi (trumpet), Junko Onishi (piano), Hidehiko "Sleepy" Matsumoto (tenor saxophone, flute), Ryô Kawasaki (guitar), and Yôsuke Yamashita (piano). Japan currently has a lively jazz community and jazz groups ranging from AVANT-GARDE and HARD BOP to big bands and orchestral jazz. The country also has arguably the best sales of jazz recordings anywhere in the world.

Jarreau, Al (b. 1940) *American singer*

Five-time Grammy Award winner Al Jarreau is known for his funky, gymnastic interpretations of popular song. He has a solid background as a jazz singer having first worked with the George Duke trio in small clubs and then branching out on the club circuit in Los Angeles and New York. His first album, *We Got By* (1975), met with critical acclaim in Germany. After touring Europe, he released his second album, *Look to the Rainbow* (1977), which featured live tracks and won him his first American GRAMMY AWARD. That made him the talk of jazz singing at the time and established him as a daring interpreter of song. Though his career has drifted mostly into popular music, his jazz roots are still evident in much of his work. He combines a BLUES breeziness with a dexterous voice and mellow tone that he can bend with great effect over a wide vocal range. He also uses a variety of percussive sounds to punctuate his singing of upbeat, BOP-influenced tunes.

Jarrett, Keith (b. 1945) *American piano player and composer*

Jarrett's lasting appeal stems from a creative intensity and dedication that has set him apart from most other jazz artists. A PIANO prodigy from Allentown, Pennsylvania, Jarrett was performing piano recitals by age seven. After first playing professionally while still a teen, he attended the BERKLEE COLLEGE OF MUSIC on a scholarship in 1962 at age 17. The allure of public performance was so great that he left Berklee after a year and began playing in local Boston night spots. It was during this time that his immersion in jazz began to take shape. After some promising GIGS in Boston with notables such as Tony Scott and RAHSAAN ROLAND KIRK, Jarrett moved to New York to further his career. He arrived in 1965 without a gig. He was a regular at the Village Vanguard Monday night JAM SESSIONS, hoping for a chance to sit in.

When the chance came, he made the most of it. ART BLAKEY was in the audience and hired Jarrett on the spot to become a member of his Jazz Messengers.[112]

After working with Blakey in 1965 and 1966, Jarrett took a job with Charles Lloyd, touring and

recording extensively. The experience he gained with Lloyd significantly influenced his style of playing. MILES DAVIS was also an admirer of Jarrett's and asked him to play electric piano in his FUSION group from 1969 to 1971. During the same period he was working on his own music and led a group featuring BASS player CHARLIE HADEN, drummer Paul Motian, and reed player Dewey Redman. With the exception of his fusion work with Davis, Jarrett has largely stayed away from electric jazz.

He first explored the possibilities of performing as a SOLO improviser in the early 1970s, a brash move for a young piano player. The encouragement he needed to pursue his solo work came from ECM, a fledgling German jazz record label at the time

Keith Jarrett

with whom Jarrett has been associated ever since. He recorded his first solo album, *Facing You* (1972), for ECM. This successful record led to a solo tour of Europe in 1973 with 18 performances. The best of these performances were released on an ambitious triple-record set, *Solo Concerts* (1973), garnering awards from publications as diverse as *Down Beat,* the *New York Times,* and *Time* magazine.[113]

Jarrett also remained interested in classical music and began to make a name for himself in this field with the release of *In The Light* (1974), also from ECM. The eight works on the record included a fugue for harpsichord, a BRASS QUINTET, a string QUARTET, a work for GUITAR and strings, and an orchestral string section, among others.

By 1975 the 30-year-old Jarrett had established a solid reputation in three areas of performance: as a leader of small groups playing TRADITIONAL JAZZ, as a solo artist performing jazz improvisations, and as a concert pianist and soloist on the classical circuit. These are the three tracks he has followed ever since, and with great success. His outpouring of work has been prodigious but has also taken its toll on his health from time to time. By 1985, after several years of juggling composing and performances of jazz and classical music, he was exhausted. He withdrew temporarily and found renewed energy in a collection of self-produced solo works made on a cassette recorder at home. But instead of using only piano, he built the recordings around folk instruments such as a Pakistani FLUTE, tablas, glockenspiel, GUITAR, and miscellaneous percussion instruments. The experience resulted in 26 tracks (later released as the recording *Spirits*) that marked a personal rejuvenation in his desire to make and perform music.

He has since continued to work with his Standards Trio, playing jazz classics, as a solo pianist, and as an occasional COMPOSER and soloist of classical music. In 1996 Jarrett was again plagued by fatigue and illness, but has steadily come back to continue his work with his Standards Trio, solo concerts, and recordings. His jazz playing is noted for his strong left hand and gospel-like drive and a light right hand that can make melodies float deli-cately. His instincts come from many influences. The virtuosity of ART TATUM and BUD POWELL is found in his improvisations and a touch of Debussy's impressionism appears in his interpretation of standards. As an improviser, he has a long imagination and draws upon an encyclopedic knowledge of RIFFS, phrases, and TECHNIQUES to build spontaneous works of startling clarity. Jarrett's improvisations are like thrilling novels; the story leads up to a terrific plot twist.

JATP   See JAZZ AT THE PHILHARMONIC.

jazz

The origin of the word *jazz* is unknown. It seems to have come from New Orleans slang and had alternative spellings such as *jass* and *jasz* before the spelling *jazz* came into popular use. Prior to that, the music we now call jazz had gone by many names, among them "hot music" and "gut-bucket music."[114]

That the words *jass* and *jazz* imply action and excitement is undeniable. That they were also synonymous with a host of other four-letter words for the sex act is probable. One of the first printed appearances of the word *jazz* was on a 1917 poster in New York announcing performances of the Original Dixieland Jazz Band. The group's name had actually been the Original Dixieland Jass Band. But when it was discovered that kids in the neighborhood were having fun scratching out the *J* in the title, the name was quickly changed to *Jazz.* By 1920 the word *jazz* was the most widely accepted term for this new American music.

Jazz Age, the

A period in American history, during the 1920s, when the rise of jazz music symbolized an excitement and prosperity in American culture. The mystique of the Jazz Age was captured by newspaper writer J. A. Roberts when he wrote in 1925, "The true spirit of jazz is a joyous revolt from convention, custom, authority, boredom, even sorrow, from everything that would confine the soul of man and hinder its riding free on the air."[115]

Jazz at Lincoln Center (JALC)

Jazz at Lincoln Center (JALC), located in New York City, promotes the appreciation of jazz by staging performances, providing classes in jazz playing and listening, and preserving jazz history. Cofounded in 1987 by WYNTON MARSALIS and Stanley Crouch, Marsalis remains the artistic director. The work of JALC is featured widely through live concerts, radio and television performances, publications, and audio recordings.

On October 18, 2004, JALC entered a new era with the opening of a new concert facility at Columbus Circle near Lincoln Center. The Frederick P. Rose Hall, built at a cost of $128 million, is the world's first performing arts center designed especially for jazz concert, education, and broadcasting. It includes three main performing spaces of various size. On September 30, 2004, JALP dedicated its new Ertegun Jazz Hall of Fame with the official induction of its inaugural class of members.

See also APPENDIX VI.

Jazz at the Philharmonic

The fortunes of BIG BANDS were falling after World War II. This was partly because of the introduction of BEBOP as the hot new jazz sensation. Jazz promoter Norman Granz had an idea to help ignite interest in big bands again. He organized a charity concert at the Philharmonic Auditorium in Los Angeles in July 1944. The show was such a success that he took it on the road. Before too long, "Jazz at the Philharmonic" (JATP) was entertaining audiences around the world for seven months each year. Each performance featured set pieces as well as JAM SESSIONS. During its 23 years its rotating showcase of stars included legends from all forms of jazz: ELLA FITZGERALD and COUNT BASIE, OSCAR PETERSON, CHARLIE PARKER, DIZZY GILLESPIE, and BENNY CARTER. Between 1957 and 1966 the JATP tours were confined to Europe. Granz gracefully brought the JATP era to a close with a farewell tour of the United States in 1967. After that, the concept was continued in spirit by tours organized by Granz under the aegis of the JATP.

Jazz Hall of Fame   See APPENDIX VI.

Jazz: Hot and Hybrid (1946) *book by Winthrop Sargeant*

Sargeant's book was one of the first to analyze the technical aspects of jazz. He treated jazz as "serious" music, worthy of the same kind of analysis given classical music. Published by E.P. Dutton.

Jazz Institute of Chicago

The Jazz Institute of Chicago was founded in 1973. It is a not-for-profit organization "dedicated to the preservation and perpetuation of jazz in all its forms." In addition to the annual Jazz Festival and Jazz Tour, the Jazz Institute of Chicago sponsors educational programs for young people, community-based programs and activities, and preserves the rich jazz tradition of Chicago.

jazz-rock fusion   See FUSION.

Jazz Times

Popular American magazine about jazz artists, performances, and recordings, its humble beginnings go back to 1970, when it was a record store newsletter called *Radio Free Jazz*.

Jenkins, Leroy (b. 1932) *American violinist, composer, educator*

Jenkins was teaching VIOLIN in the Chicago school system during the late 1960s, when he joined forces with jazz musicians in the Association for the Advancement of Creative Music. The violin is an uncommon jazz instrument. Jenkins's playing was even more unusual still. He was known for his rhythmic pounding of the strings and driving percussive sounds. Jenkins established himself as a singularly expressive voice in jazz circles. He has collaborated with many AVANT-GARDE jazz musicians, including ANTHONY BRAXTON, CECIL TAYLOR, ALICE COLTRANE, and RAHSAAN ROLAND KIRK.

Jensen, Ingrid (b. 1969) *Canadian trumpet and flugelhorn player*

Ingrid was raised in a musical family. Her mother was a pianist and choral director, her younger sister, Christine, a saxophonist and pianist. After showing great promise on TRUMPET with her high school band, she attended the BERKLEE COLLEGE OF MUSIC in Boston from 1987 to 1989. After that she began rocketing to jazz stardom through several jobs with important big bands, including the MINGUS BIG BAND, the MARIA SCHNEIDER Orchestra, and the all-woman big band Diva. She is currently on the faculty at the Peabody Conservatory of Music in Baltimore. She previously taught in Austria as professor of jazz trumpet at the Bruckner Conservatory of Music and at the Hochshule für Musik in Berlin. Now based in New York, she continues to travel extensively around the world, teaching and playing. She has recorded several CDs as a group leader and her debut CD, *Vernal Fields* (1994), received excellent reviews from critics.

Recalling the smooth trumpet sounds of MILES DAVIS and Woody Shaw, Jensen is a gifted player with exciting IMPROVISATION skills. She is particularly good at playing ballads, which are a good choice for showing off her wonderfully smooth, silky sound. Jensen is held in high regard by other musicians and is definitely a voice of future jazz. Critic Mark Keresman remarked about Jensen's *Higher Ground* CD (1998), "Like [Woody] Shaw, Jensen is mindful of the tradition in that she swings, plays real pretty *and* with fire, but realizes

that you don't live up to 'the tradition' by playing it safe."[116]

Jobim, Antonio Carlos (1927–1994) *Brazilian composer and guitar and piano player*

Jobim and his associate João Gilberto (vocals) began recording BOSSA NOVA songs in the late 1950s, a musical style that combined the feel and instrumentation of COOL JAZZ with Brazilian music. Many American and European listeners first became aware of Jobim's music on the soundtrack of the award-winning 1959 film *Black Orpheus*. Interest in the bossa nova increased dramatically following Jobim's appearance at CARNEGIE HALL in 1962 with STAN GETZ, Gilberto, and DIZZY GILLESPIE in a program featuring Brazilian compositions. Jobim's popularization of the bossa nova brought Brazilian music into the mainstream of jazz and American popular music. By the end of the 1960s, many of Jobim's compositions had entered the jazz repertoire, including "Desafinado" (1957), "Quiet Night of Quiet Stars" (1964), "The Girl from Ipanema" (1963), and "Jazz Samba" (1963).

Johnson, James P. (1891–1955) *American piano player and composer*

Johnson grew up in New Jersey and New York City. His mother taught him to play PIANO, and he developed a unique style of his own known as STRIDE PIANO. He first learned to play RAGTIME and popular songs and soon fused them in his own music with touches of gospel and the BLUES. He is one of the most original and influential of all jazz artists. FATS WALLER was one of his students and COUNT BASIE was greatly influenced by him when he first came to New York. Johnson was there at the beginning of jazz and influenced its transition from ragtime. He was one of the first jazz recording artists ("Carolina Shout," 1921). Johnson was much in demand as an accompanist and recording artist throughout his career. He was also a serious COMPOSER of large ENSEMBLE and orchestra music, including ballets and operettas. His most famous song was

"CHARLESTON." His speed on the keyboard and dexterity are legendary.

Jones, Elvin (1927–2004) *American drummer, composer, and bandleader*

The younger brother of trumpeter THAD and PIANO player HANK, Elvin Jones was known for his dexterous POLYRHYTHMIC drumming technique. His fluid style marked a transition from the athletic BOP and HARD BOP drumming of the 1940s and 1950s to a more interactive style of drumming in the 1960s. In Jones's case, he was working in the classic JOHN COLTRANE QUARTET from 1960 to 1966 and was a partner with Trane in changing the fundamental sound of modern jazz. This was a seminal time for jazz as artists including MILES DAVIS and Coltrane, having previously worked together, were launching their own new styles as an alternative to bop and hard bop. Davis and Coltrane had begun their exploration with MODAL JAZZ.

Jones, having been influenced by the great bop drummer ART BLAKEY, was developing a rhythmic style of his own that complemented the tonal style exemplified by Coltrane and Davis. He was not merely keeping time like most drummers before him. In Jones's playing, the accented beat no longer ruled. He freed himself from being chained to a steady rhythm. This transformed the drummer from being a mere accompanist to being a fully interactive player with the other musicians.[117]

This allowed him to react to the other soloists more while providing a rhythmic tension that held the four players together as a unit. Using mallets and sticks and his feet, he seemed able to carry on two or three musical conversations at the same time. When finding a beat was important to the music, Jones liked to move the ACCENT around the drum kit, never letting it settle for too long on one snare, cymbal, tom-tom, or bass drum.

By 1966 Coltrane was clearly moving toward a more freely improvised sound that was not entirely to Jones's liking. The drummer left Coltrane's group when the saxophonist hired a second drum-

Elvin Jones

mer in 1966. His first outings as a leader after Coltrane were in a hard bop vein. He continued to work with saxophonists, sometimes two at a time. Eventually, while working with reed and FLUTE player Sonny Fortune, the sound of Jones's own group was beginning to approach the outer reaches of FREE JAZZ that the drummer had once tried to escape when he left Trane.

In 1988 Jones led an all-star group of musicians in a worldwide "*A LOVE SUPREME*" tour in honor of John Coltrane. In recent years Jones has worked and toured regularly with his group Jazz Machine. The experience of working with Coltrane clearly was a highlight in his career. Many years later, Jones explained what it was like to be in the eye of the Coltrane hurricane. "Right from the beginning to the last time we played together," he explained, "it was something pure. The most impressive thing was a feeling of steady, collective learning. . . ." "If there is anything like perfect harmony in a human relationship that was as close as you can come," Jones once said.[118]

Jones, Hank (b. 1918) *American piano player*

Hank is the oldest of the "three sons of jazz," his brothers being renowned COMPOSER and ARRANGER THAD JONES and drum innovator ELVIN JONES. Growing up in Pontiac, Michigan, Hank and his brothers got their start in music playing in their uncle's band. In 1944 he took his excellent PIANO skills to New York, where he worked as a SIDEMAN for many of the biggest names in the business. His style was elegant and smart, but unobtrusive, making him an excellent accompanist. He was a part of the BOP scene while playing with Hot Lips Page at the Onyx Club. Once word got around about Jones's playing, he was in great demand and worked with a variety of bandleaders, including COLEMAN HAWKINS, Billy Eckstine, and Andy Kirk. Jones toured with Norman Granz and JAZZ AT THE PHILHARMONIC in 1947 and then became ELLA FITZGERALD's accompanist from 1948 to 1953.

His list of freelance sessions and guest spots is extensive, including GIGS with CHARLIE PARKER, BENNY GOODMAN, and his brothers, Thad and Elvin. He was the original pianist with the Thad Jones–MEL LEWIS Orchestra in 1966. One of his longest jobs was with CBS from 1959 to 1975, when he worked with various studio bands, including the Ray Bloch Orchestra (the band on the Ed Sullivan IV show). He continues to work in his later years as a reliable and affable sideman who always brings an informed sophistication to his work. He is noted for having a personal style based on a simple philosophy. "When you listen to a pianist," he said, "each note should have an identity, each note should have a soul of its own."[119]

Jones has brought this personal style to work with him every day for more than six decades.

Jones, Philly Joe (1923–1985) *American drummer and bandleader*

This Philadelphian began playing DRUMS at age four and also learned PIANO from his mother, a music teacher. He came to prominence working with MILES DAVIS during the 1950s. After that he was a sought-after SESSION man and toured extensively, including Europe, with the likes of SARAH VAUGHN, ERROLL GARNER, KENNY CLARKE, BILL EVANS, and Red Garland. Jones lived, worked, and taught in Europe during the 1970s. He started the FUSION group Le Gran Prix in 1975.

Perhaps the most influential drummer of the 1950s, Jones did not fit the classic mold of the jazz drummer. Most drummers in the 1950s were mostly timekeepers. If they had a moment to show off, it was usually during a drum BREAK that was isolated from the flow of the music. But Jones changed all of that. His bold style was active at all times. He showed that a drummer could add excitement to every moment of the music while still keeping the basic beat. He did this with crisp snare work, tasteful fills, and brilliant work with brushes and cymbals. He used the complete drum set at all times. His playing constantly surprised the listener but did not distract from the other musicians. His work greatly influenced the style of jazz drumming that is still heard today. Along with fellow drummer ELVIN JONES (no relation), Philly Joe set the course for jazz drumming of the future.

Jones, Quincy (b. 1933) *American composer, arranger, producer, and trumpet player*

Jones may be best remembered as the man who produced Michael Jackson's *Thriller* record, but he has a long and solid history in the development of modern jazz. Once a TRUMPET player with the LIONEL HAMPTON band in 1951, he ventured into composing and arranging for others. He led his own BIG BAND and, as musical director, toured Europe with the theater production of *Free and Easy* (1959–60). After working with COUNT BASIE as an ARRANGER in the early 1960s, he took a job as PRODUCER and executive in the record industry.

His talents as an arranger, conductor, and record producer made him uniquely talented in the recording industry. Sympathetic to the needs of the artist, he has a reputation for bringing out some of the finest work. His list of artists reads like a who's who of music history legends: PEGGY LEE, Billy Eckstine, COUNT BASIE, and Frank Sinatra among them. He did a good deal of music writing for television and crossed over to rock production on occasion, especially for Aretha Franklin and Michael Jackson. Although more a stranger to jazz in the last couple of decades, he produced an interesting hybrid of jazz and hip-hop in 1989 called *Back on the Block* featuring snippets of classic artists such as ELLA FITZGERALD, Sarah Vaughan, DIZZY GILLESPIE, MILES DAVIS, and Ray Charles, with a bevy of contemporary artists including rapper Ice-T, Kool Moe Dee, and Big Daddy Kane. It is a loving tribute to African-American musicians from a man whose artistic direction has helped shape the popular music scene for more than 40 years.

Jones, Thad (1923–1986) *American trumpet, cornet, flugelhorn, and valve-trombone player, composer, arranger, and bandleader*

Jones, the older brother of famed drummer ELVIN JONES, was a self-taught player who began playing professionally when he was 16. He became a popular soloist with the COUNT BASIE Orchestra from 1954 to 1963. While with Basie, he showed a talent for composing and arranging. In 1965 he and drummer friend MEL LEWIS formed a BIG BAND composed of the best studio musicians in New York. Dubbed the Thad Jones–Mel Lewis Orchestra, it had a weekly GIG at the Village Vanguard in New York for 10 years. The orchestra was an outlet for Jones's writing and arranging

and set high standards for other big bands to follow. Jones unexpectedly left the group, and the country, in 1978 to live in Denmark. In Europe he formed his own big band and continued to work, often for a jazz radio orchestra. While in Denmark, he studied composition and took up the valve TROMBONE.

His talent as a player has always been overshadowed by his reputation as a COMPOSER and ARRANGER. He improvised with the imagination of a serious composer who was always a few steps ahead of those he was playing with. His boisterous playing, excellent ear for arranging, and ability to drive home a heartfelt composition made him much loved by jazz musicians and fans. One tribute from another musician came in the form of a quip from MILES DAVIS, who said, "I'd rather hear Thad Jones miss a note than hear Freddie Hubbard make twelve."[120]

Joplin, Scott (1868–1917) *American composer and piano player*

Raised in Texas and originally self-taught as a musician, Joplin began to take classical PIANO lessons at age 11 and developed a penchant for composition. Known as the father of RAGTIME music, he wrote some of the most popular tunes of the 1890s that widely influenced early jazz pianists such as JELLY ROLL MORTON. Joplin's most famous tunes include the "MAPLE LEAF RAG" (1899), "The Entertainer" (1902), and the "Wall Street Rag" (1909). Joplin was an astute businessman. He sold the rights to "Maple Leaf Rag," his most famous piano rag, to music publisher John Stark & Son in exchange for receiving a penny royalty for every copy of the music that was sold, plus 10 free copies for his own use. In six months, the sheet music had sold 75,000 copies. This one song alone provided Joplin with a modest royalty every year for the rest of his life.[121]

Joplin was one of the most celebrated composers of the ragtime era. Among his longer, extended compositions is the opera *Treemonisha* (1911).

Kansas City jazz

Early jazz migrated first from New Orleans to Chicago and New York. Then it put roots down in Kansas City, where several big names made their mark during the late 1920s and 1930s. Among them were COUNT BASIE, LESTER YOUNG, MARY LOU WILLIAMS, and Bennie Moten. Back then in Kansas City, the working musician was kept busy at all times. CHARLIE PARKER once recalled, "I came up in Kansas City when the joints were running full blast from 9 p.m. to 5 a.m. Usual pay was a $1.25 a night, although somebody special, like Count Basie, could command $1.50." They weren't making a lot of money, so there had to be something about the music that attracted them. Kansas City jazz differed from music being played elsewhere. It didn't use the simultaneous IMPROVISATION of the New Orleans style. Nor did it feature the sophisticated arrangements of New York jazz. Instead, it was based on short phrases, or RIFFS, that were repeated over the CHORD CHANGES. Some songs got away without a formal written tune at all. The players kept playing variations on the riffs, making decisions on the fly. It was an easygoing, relaxed style of jazz. This new style of jumping jazz was also called Kansas City SWING, which led to the rollicking BIG BAND dance music of the late 1930s.

Kenton, Stan (1911–1979) *American bandleader, composer, arranger, piano player, and educator*

Kenton was an influential bandleader whose experiments with orchestration and flair for packaging the sound he called "PROGRESSIVE JAZZ" has been called innovative by some and pretentious by others. The truth probably lies somewhere in between. Beginning with his first BIG BAND in 1940, Kenton worked to create a unique sound based on unusual instrumentation and compositions that verged on the AVANT-GARDE. His first band had a rapid-fire reed sound that he dubbed "Artistry in Rhythm." By 1948 he had completely changed his approach, adding to the SAXOPHONES a heavy BRASS contingent including five TRUMPETS and five TROMBONES. This assemblage was called his "progressive jazz" experiment and became extremely popular as a West Coast big band alternative to BEBOP. Kenton was selling out large venues for a jazz orchestra, including the 15,000-seat capacity Hollywood Bowl.

He had less success in 1950–52 with his largest unit ever, the 44-piece Innovations in Modern Music Orchestra, which added a string section, FRENCH HORNS, bassoons, and oboes to his established big band. The music of this outfit was more strictly composed and experimental, dabbling in contrasting meters and the fascinating sound textures that Kenton was able to produce with such a broad collection of instruments. However, his fans did not like the new Kenton, partly because the music was not suited to dancing. He returned to a more palatable swing band format in the mid-1950s, but continued to work strings, French horns, and other classical instruments into his arrangements. His "Mellophonium Orchestra" (1960–63) was an even more extreme experiment in horns, having 14 brass players.

Some of the many accomplished alumni of Kenton's orchestras include Shelly Manne, Art Pepper, MAYNARD FERGUSON, Lee Konitz, and Zoot Sims. Kenton's trademark was the creation of an adventurous sound that could bridge a gap between contemporary classical music and jazz. He was an early experimenter with up-TEMPO and often unusual meters, Latin and Afro-Cuban rhythms, and the development of sound textures unique to jazz instrumentation. Over his long career he was able to showcase the work of many third stream jazz composers who strove to combine elements of classical music with jazz. Among his most popular recordings were "Artistry in Rhythm," "Eager Beaver" and "Intermission Riff," from his 1940s era. He toured extensively during the 1950s and 1960s, was a frequent guest on television, and over time earned the respect of jazz critics and fans alike who were interested in the bravado sound of his ambitious projects.

Kenton was also a committed educator. His earliest efforts consisted of the Stan Kenton Clinics (1959 to 1963), whose annual gatherings brought together working musicians with students of jazz. By the 1970s he was a regular speaker at universities and toured with his band for campus clinics. This effort became nearly a full-time occupation by the mid-1970s. Kenton himself certainly understood the artistic and commercial risks he had taken with this experimental approach to jazz. "I've lunged too far ahead!" he once admitted. . . . "If I had stayed with Artistry in Rhythm and not moved so quickly into another phase, progressive jazz, we would have had the biggest commercial success of any band the country had ever known and I probably would have been a millionaire many times over. I also would have been bored out of my skull and no doubt ended up on some 'pillow farm' somewhere high atop the Hollywood Hills."[122]

Keppard, Freddie (1890–1933) *American cornet player*

In the earliest years of NEW ORLEANS JAZZ, Keppard succeeded BUDDY BOLDEN as the king of the CORNET after Bolden's institutionalization in 1907. He was a bold, brash player who could perform for hours. He would cover his fingers with a handkerchief to keep his fingerings secret from the watchful eyes of rival players.[123]

With Bill Johnson, he formed the Original Creole Orchestra (1911–18),[124] one the first authentic black New Orleans jazz bands to tour outside the South. Keppard had the opportunity to become the first New Orleans jazz artist to make a record, but refused an offer from Victor Records in 1916 because he was afraid of giving away his licks.

The excitement caused by the Original Creole Orchestra in Chicago was a big reason why the

Freddie Keppard

greatest players of New Orleans jazz began moving there. Keppard himself lived in Chicago beginning in 1918. The young LOUIS ARMSTRONG soon came to Chicago as well and became the latest sensation in cornet playing. While Armstrong went on to great fame and fortune, Keppard's career slowly fell apart because of his alcoholism. His continued to play in the 1920s, usually as a SIDEMAN. His best recordings were made in 1926 and 1927, including the songs "Stock Yard Strut" and "Salty Dog." Even though his playing was in sharp decline by this time, these recordings provide a small glimpse at his powers as an early master of jazz cornet.

Kind of Blue (1959) *album by Miles Davis*

Featuring MILES DAVIS (TRUMPET), Cannonball Adderley (alto SAXOPHONE), JOHN COLTRANE (tenor SAXOPHONE), BILL EVANS and Wynton Kelly (PIANO), PAUL CHAMBERS (BASS), and Jimmy Cobb (DRUMS), this is the most celebrated album of the modern jazz age. It features true giants of their era. Hearing Davis and Coltrane pair off on solos was itself a treat. With *Kind of Blue,* Davis brought the idea of MODAL JAZZ to the forefront.

In modal jazz, improvisations are based on the notes available in a given musical SCALE instead of the changing chords of a song. For example, the black keys or the white keys on a piano each represent a different scale. In modal jazz, players improvise using all of the available notes in a predetermined scale rather than only the notes available in a series of chords. The sound is freer and less bound to the ground.

The solos on *Kind of Blue* depart from a solid footing laid down by swinging drums and bass. Bill Evans, one of the piano players on the album, described the piece "So What" as a "simple figure based on 16 measures of one scale, 8 of another and 8 more of the first, following a piano and bass introduction in free rhythmic style." Like much of Davis's most influential work, this music is challenging for the musicians to make but easy for the listener to enjoy. *Kind of Blue* sounds so mainstream today because its influence has been felt by every player since its release. Its lessons remain at the heart of the artistic choices that jazz players continue to make today.

Kirk, Rahsaan Roland (1935–1977) *American tenor saxophone, flute, manzello, clarinet, stritch, and trumpet player, composer, and bandleader*

Kirk was a spirited and innovative instrumentalist who, inspired by vivid dreams, learned to play two and three wind instruments at the same time. Blind from the age of two due to a nurse's accident with his eye medication, he took up music in grade school, playing bugle and TRUMPET by age nine.[125]

Rahsaan Roland Kirk

Except for a short stint with CHARLES MINGUS and tours with Dexter Gordon and Johnny Griffin in the early 1960s, Kirk primarily worked on his own, sometimes backed by a small RHYTHM SECTION.

"Stritch" and "manzello" were his names for the alto and soprano SAXOPHONEs that he bought in a pawnshop and modified for his own playing purposes. He could simultaneously play the tenor saxophone, the stritch, and the manzello, creating three-part harmony by himself. By the early 1960s he had also mastered the TECHNIQUE of CIRCULAR BREATHING, which allowed him to play notes indefinitely without pausing for a breath. He was also a tremendous jazz FLUTE player and often used the technique of singing or humming notes at the same time that he was blowing them, again creating chords and harmonies with himself. His musical style was rooted in BEBOP and HARD BOP but later included elements of African music and percussion.

Although it was his bevy of novel playing techniques that often enticed people to first listen to Kirk, they were soon won over by his sheer musicality and imagination as a COMPOSER and improviser. His most celebrated album was *THE INFLATED TEAR* (1968), although some of his later albums, including *Volunteered Slavery* (1969), are a better showcase for his improvisatory style. *Natural Black Inventions* (1971) is a SOLO album featuring the multi-instrumentalist practicing his most amazing one-man jazz COMBO stunts. Kirk was an activist for the rights of African-American jazz musicians and was a participant in several protests on television talk shows to gain more exposure for black artists.[126]

He was slowed by a stroke in 1975, then was on the way back to playing in 1977, when a second stroke ended his life.

Krall, Diana (b. 1964) *Canadian singer and piano player*

Krall follows in the tradition of past PIANO-playing singers who have had success in both jazz and popular music. She notes with awareness the accomplishments of greats such as NAT KING COLE, SARAH VAUGHN, SHIRLEY HORN, and one of her favorites, CARMEN MCRAE. A piano player since age four, and performing regularly since the 10th grade, Krall attended the BERKLEE COLLEGE OF MUSIC in 1982 and 1983 and is well schooled in the history and styles of jazz. Her first gigs were playing piano only, until a job in Los Angeles required her to try her hand at singing. She made her first record under her own name in 1993 and has garnered steady critical acclaim and commercial success ever since.

Krall is essentially an acoustic musician, usually backed by a TRADITIONAL JAZZ RHYTHM SECTION composed of BASS, DRUMS, and GUITAR. Her repertoire includes classic pop tunes made famous by other jazz greats as well as songs penned by her contemporaries, not the least of whom is her husband, Elvis Costello. She specializes in torch songs and romantic ballads. Her gentle, studied phrasing is reminiscent of ELLA FITZGERALD and Carmen McRae. Some critics have argued that her fame as a jazz singer is due more to clever marketing by her record company than any deeply rooted jazz instincts. Veteran jazz critic Nat Hentoff questions whether she is a jazz singer at all. "Jazz singing is much more than a craft," he argues. . . . "but to merit being called a jazz singer you have to have something to say—your own story—as it moves you then and there. Arrangements tailored just for you—and, in Krall's case, a carefully constructed aura of taking yourself seriously—won't help if you don't know when and how to let yourself go."[127]

Others defend her as a singer capable of drawing great emotion out of other people's music, all supported by her excellent skills at working the piano.

Krupa, Gene (1909–1973) *American drummer and bandleader*

His parents wanted Gene to go into the priesthood. Instead, he picked up the drum sticks and became the high priest of BIG BAND drummers. He earned his reputation as a hard-driving player while with the BENNY GOODMAN Orchestra from

1934 to 1938. Until Krupa, drummers literally took a back seat and stayed out of the spotlight. He made the DRUMS into a SOLO instrument. Krupa's infectious style and athletic talent led to a generation of high-profile drummers, including BUDDY RICH and MAX ROACH.

Krupa experienced enormous success in the late 1930s and early 1940s with various bands of his own, including one that featured 40 members and a string section. Drummers became a featured attraction of SWING bands because of Krupa's influential public profile. He wrote a book about drumming and sponsored drum contests that attracted much publicity. With the growing popularity of BEBOP by the mid-1940s, interest in big bands diminished. Krupa adapted and formed a trio that became a regular attraction with Norman Granz's JAZZ AT THE PHILHARMONIC concerts.

Drum battles, including a monumental duel with BUDDY RICH in 1952, became a featured event of the Philharmonic dates. Krupa's health was not the best throughout the last 20 years of his life, but he continue to tour and play when possible, including an occasional reunion with Goodman. Bop drumming icon MAX ROACH recalled one of those famous drum battles. "It was Buddy, Gene Krupa, and Louie Bellison. Me, Dizzy [Gillespie], and Bird [CHARLIE PARKER] were the talk of the town, and I felt good, really strong. But I knew who I was up against. Buddy was strong that day, but the guy who took out everybody was Gene. He razzle-dazzled the **** out of us. Buddy and I were competing with each other, and we learned a real lesson from Gene that day. Play to the audience. He had them rolling in the aisles. Ha! It was a lesson in show biz that Buddy never forgot."

JAZZ FIRSTS

1890–1907	BUDDY BOLDEN led one of the first acknowledged jazz bands.
1911	Possibly the earliest recorded example of SCAT SINGING was made by Gene Greene, singing a popular RAGTIME tune "The King of the Bungaloos."
1911–1918	FREDDIE KEPPARD's Original Creole Orchestra became one of the first authentic, black NEW ORLEANS JAZZ bands to tour outside of the South.
1914	JAMES REESE EUROPE and his Society Orchestra became the first African-American ensemble to make commercial recordings.
1914	James Reese Europe conducted the first all-black ENSEMBLE to appear at CARNEGIE HALL.
1917	"LIVERY STABLE BLUES," by the all-white Original Dixieland Jazz Band, became the first example of New Orleans style jazz put on record.
1917	One of the first printed appearances of the word *jazz* appeared on a poster in New York City announcing performances of the Original Dixieland Jazz Band.
1920	MAMIE SMITH made the first BLUES record.
1921	Harry Herbert Pace founded the first black-owned record company, Black Swan.
1921	JAMES P. JOHNSON becomes one of the first African-American artists to cut a jazz record. Among the songs he recorded were "Carolina Shout," "The Harlem Strut," and "Keep Off the Grass."
1922	KID ORY's Creole Orchestra became the first African-American band to make an authentic recording of New Orleans jazz.
1923	Japan's first professional jazz band, The Laughing Stars, was founded.
1924	FLETCHER HENDERSON created the first BIG BAND devoted to jazz, laying the groundwork for the SWING era.
1926	LOUIS ARMSTRONG popularized scat singing with the recording of "HEEBIE JEEBIES." Although it wasn't the first example of scat put on record, it was undoubtedly the most influential.
1931	DUKE ELLINGTON became the first jazz artist to record a long piece requiring more than one side of a 78 rpm disc ("Creole Rhapsody").
1932	Duke Ellington recorded the song "IT DON'T MEAN A THING (IF IT AIN'T GOT THAT SWING)," the first song with the word *swing* in its song title.
1936	BENNY GOODMAN became the first noted white bandleader to add African-American musicians to his ensemble, breaking the color barrier that had separated jazz artists.

1937   Benny Carter organized the first internationally based, interracial band to make a recording.

1938   Benny Goodman played Carnegie Hall, the first such concert at the famous venue. The concert helped put authentic jazz in the headlines and featured black and white musicians playing together on the same stage, an uncommon sight in an America that was still racially divided.

1940   Lena Horne became the first African-American singer to front a white big band, that of Charlie Barnet.

1946   The book *Jazz: Hot and Hybrid* was published, the first to analyze the technical aspects of jazz.

1947   The first successful Afro-Cuban jazz was created by Chano Pozo and Dizzy Gillespie and showcased at a Carnegie Hall concert.

1954   The Newport Jazz Festival became the first large-scale outdoor music festival devoted to jazz.

1957   João Gilberto made the first bossa nova record ("Desafinado").

1959   *Kind of Blue* by Miles Davis was released. Over the years it has become the top-selling jazz album of all time.

1959   *Jazz in Africa* by the Jazz Epistles was the first recording made by South African jazz musicians.

1959   Ornette Coleman introduced free jazz.

1959   *Time Out* by Dave Brubeck became the first jazz recording to sell over a million copies.

1969   Miles Davis recorded *In a Silent Way* with the first widely acknowledged, largely electric jazz combo, ushering in the beginning of fusion jazz.

1972   Herbie Hancock added Moog synthesizer player Patrick Gleason to the lineup of his group for the recording of the album *Crossings*. This was one of the first instances of a synthesizer player being used as a sideman in a jazz group, and predated the availability of portable synthesizers.

1978   Herbie Hancock became the first noted jazz musician to use a computer-controlled synthesizer, the Alpha-Syntauri, based on an Apple II computer.

1992   The album *Doo-Bop* by Miles Davis and hip-hop producer Eazy Mo Bee is released following Davis's death. Although only partially completed by Davis himself, the album ushers in a new style of jazz blending elements of hip-hop, funk, rap, and jazz. It becomes a seminal example of early acid jazz.

Lacy, Steve (1934–2004) *American soprano saxophone player and composer*

Steve (Steven Lacritz) Lacy, was well schooled in the visual arts and music when he turned from classical music to jazz in the late 1950s. He was one of the soprano SAXOPHONE's most accomplished players and always approached his music with the spirit of an explorer. Throughout his career, he never ceased to experiment and grow as an artist. His first interest was NEW ORLEANS JAZZ, a style that allowed him to make a connection with the work of SIDNEY BECHET, the first great soprano saxophone player in jazz. For six years (1953 to 1959), AVANT-GARDE pianist CECIL TAYLOR took Lacy under his wing and introduced him to his free-form style of composing and improvising. Lacy next worked with GIL EVANS and THELONIOUS MONK and admitted later that he "was constantly" out of his depth, pushing the upper limits of his ability both as a player and as a conceiver of music.[128]

He survived these experiences with a greater sense of self and the directions that jazz was capable of taking. He collaborated with COMPOSER CARLA BLEY and FREE JAZZ trumpeter DON CHERRY in the 1960s. Moving to Europe in 1967, Lacy worked with various groups including an experimental band, Musica Electronica Viva, which combines electronic music with jazz IMPROVISATION. He moved to Paris in 1970. During the 1970s and 1980s he began to work with his own groups and compositions, touring extensively, and began to integrate elements of other world cultures in his music. He has also performed extensively as a SOLO artist. When Lacy picked up the soprano saxophone in the 1950s, it was no longer in widespread use in jazz.

His style evolved from that of New Orleans melodies to the austere and sometimes lightning-fast and jagged lines of notes required to play Monk, Taylor, and free jazz styles. He had tremendous upper range on his instrument, an approach that Lacy compared to playing only with the right hand of the PIANO. His own composition style evolved from the whole of his experience, from the straight-up playing of New Orleans jazz or the avant-garde work of Monk. Lacy's goal in composing was "finding the appropriate structures to contain the type of improvisational material that we had discovered."[129]

As a result, his work was a blend of free jazz and composed parts. Throughout his career, Lacy pushed the limits of jazz in ways that always kept him on the leading edge of music innovation. He was a noted interpreter of Monk's music, especially some of the pianist's lesser known tunes, as showcased on the Lacy album *Reflections—Plays Thelonious* (1958), *Monk's Dream* (2000), and *Monk's Moods* (2002) with the Asian American Orchestra. *The Rent* (1999) is a fine example of Lacy's recent compositions that include space for improvisation.

Laine, Cleo (b. 1927) *British singer*

Laine is the only singer to have received Grammy nominations in the Female Jazz, Popular, and Classical performance categories. She is an astute

do more for a song by a mere rolling of her eyes or with a quick, crooked smile than most pop singers can with all the vocal diction training possible and years of dramatic tutelage."[130]

Lewis, George (b. 1952) *American trombone and tuba player, electronic musician, composer, and educator*

While still in high school, Lewis taught himself to copy LESTER YOUNG tenor SAXOPHONE solos on the TROMBONE. He joined the ASSOCIATION FOR THE ADVANCEMENT OF CREATIVE MUSICIANS (AACM) in 1971 and studied music theory with MUHAL RICHARD ABRAMS. Lewis kept up his jazz playing while studying philosophy at Yale University (1972–74), working GIGS with AVANT-GARDE notables including ROSCOE MITCHELL and ANTHONY BRAXTON. Lewis became interested in computer music and electronic media during the late 1970s, extending his reach into electronic and experimental music mixing live IMPROVISATION with interactive computer-based music systems. As an educator, he has been associated with a number of colleges, including Mills College, Simon Fraser University, the School of the Art Institute of Chicago, and the University of California at San Diego. Although many of his key musical influences remain jazz musicians, such as JOHN COLTRANE, CHARLIE PARKER, and Anthony Braxton, calling Lewis a jazz musician at this stage is something that even he might question. He has taken jazz to another place, a zone where all forms of sound experimentation become a part of his medium of expression. At the heart of his work remains a sensibility for improvisation that he mastered while practicing the art of jazz.

Lewis, Mel (1929–1990) *American drummer, arranger, and bandleader*

Mel Lewis was a workmanlike drummer who got his start playing in BIG BANDs, including that of STAN KENTON (1954–56). During the early 1960s the respected drummer was frequently called upon to accompany some of the biggest names in the business, including BENNY GOODMAN, DIZZY GILLESPIE, and GERRY MULLIGAN. In 1965, while making a living as a prominent studio musician in New York, he and buddy THAD JONES formed a band composed of the best studio players around. The band was originally conceived as a weekly practice unit to polish their skills and have some fun. But it became so popular that the duo christened it the Thad Jones–Mel Lewis Jazz Orchestra and took the show on the road. Between 1965 and 1978 the orchestra played often at the Village Vanguard in New York but also went overseas and even to the Soviet Union. Jones left the venture in 1978, leaving Lewis to continue the orchestra as sole leader. As a drummer, Lewis was valued for his ability to hold complicated arrangements together, leading the band ahead with sure-footed SWING.

lick

A part played by one musician, often as a melodic SOLO.

Lincoln, Abbey (b. 1930) *American singer composer*

Born Anna Marie Woolridge in Chicago, her stage name changed several times until her promoter convinced her to settle on Abbey Lincoln in 1956. She is a multitalented master of several fields, including singing, songwriting, painting, acting, and social activism. Her career as a noted jazz singer spans 40 years. Growing up in Michigan, she turned to singing while still in high school. She made her first album in 1956, backed by another jazz great, BENNY CARTER. Her career as a movie actress also began to take shape about this time when she appeared in the film *The Girl Can't Help It* in 1957. This was a pivotal experience for the young singer. The film starred sexpot Jayne Mansfield and featured a title song sung by Little Richard. She was not happy with her first movie experience. "They wanted to make me a glamour type when I first got to Hollywood. . . . I sang something called Spread the Word. No, nothing happened with that. They weren't interested in what I was singing. They were just interested in me wearing that Marilyn Monroe dress. The one she wore in *Gentleman Prefer Blondes*."[131]

She credits innovative BOP drummer MAX ROACH for rescuing her from the clutches of moviedom. She began to hang out with Roach and other bop superstars in New York, writing songs and broadening her singing style. She was married to Roach from 1962 to 1970. They collaborated on several projects, often produced to increase public awareness of civil rights issues. Most notable was her performance on *We Insist! Freedom Now Suite*, Roach's socially conscious opus (1960).

During the 1960s she continued to develop two parallel careers, one as an actress and one as a singer. As her fame as a movie and television actress grew, her singing took a backseat. In 1989, however, she signed a record contract with Verve that has resulted in more than a half dozen startling albums of Lincoln's jazz singing. She has been compared to BILLIE HOLIDAY with good reason. Like Holiday, Lincoln has a remarkable sense of phrasing and articulation that makes her singing poignant, yet always touched by the BLUES. Lincoln loves to break up a lyric into shorter fragments that come bursting out one thought at a time. She changes the emphasis on syllables to give her delivery a conversational feel. Her tones are mellow and commanding. She uses VIBRATO sparingly and turns every song into a deep personal statement.

Her interest in social affairs has taken her far and wide, including a 1975 trip to Africa, where African leaders gave her the new name of Aminata Moseka. Her philosophy of life as an artist is clear. "When everything is finished in a world," she said, "the people go to look for what the artists leave. It's the only thing that we have really in this world—is an ability to express ourselves and say, I was here."[132]

Liston, Melba (1926–1999) *American composer, arranger, and trombone player*

Liston was a pioneer jazz-playing woman who played with several successful bands led by men before leading her own COMBOS and orchestras. However, her greatest impact might be found in her superb arranging. After playing and touring in a small group led by Dexter Gordon in 1947, she joined DIZZY GILLESPIE's BIG BAND in 1950 for a year and then toured internationally with Gillespie with another one of his lineups in 1956 and 1957. After playing with her own QUINTET in the late 1950s, she then traveled with QUINCY JONES in 1959 and 1960 with the musical theater show *Free and Easy*. During the 1960s she played with several groups but focused most of her energy on writing songs for others, including Tony Bennett, DUKE ELLINGTON, Milt Jackson, and Diana Ross. During the 1970s Liston turned her attention to teaching jazz through a six-year assignment at the Jamaica School of Music. When she returned to the United States in 1979, she formed her own group, Melba Liston and Company. A stroke slowed her considerably in 1985, but by the 1990s she was once again able to resume some composing work.

She was a trailblazer in jazz during a time when most doors were firmly closed to women. Along with MARY LOU WILLIAMS, she was one of the only successful female jazz artists to share the stage with men during the 1940s and the growth of BEBOP. Though her TROMBONE playing is overshadowed by her accomplishments as a COMPOSER and ARRANGER, two excellent examples of her playing exist on record. One is with the Dexter Gordon group's recording of "Mischievous Lady" (1947) and another is her SOLO on the Dizzy Gillespie big band arrangement of "Cool Breeze," recorded at the NEWPORT JAZZ FESTIVAL in 1957. She was one of the most brilliant trombonists of the 1940s and 1950s, man or woman.

"Livery Stable Blues" (1917) *recorded performance by the Original Dixieland Jazz Band*
The first example of NEW ORLEANS JAZZ put on record. The group was white, not black, but they were able players. The popularity of this record released by Victor created great interest in jazz around the country, paving the way for many artists, most of them African American, to make additional records and benefit from the many years of work that had gone into the development of jazz in New Orleans, Chicago, and New York.

Lloyd, Charles (b. 1938) *American tenor saxophone and flute player, composer, and bandleader*
As a bandleader Lloyd helped launch the careers of KEITH JARRETT, Jack DeJohnette, and MICHEL PETRUCCIANI. During the 1960s the FLUTE-and sax-playing bandleader was one of the few jazz musicians who could appeal to an audience of rock musicians. Such was the spirit in San Francisco when Lloyd performed sold-out jazz GIGS at the famous Fillmore West rock venue (1967) and then repeated the feat at the Fillmore East in New York. He took his group to an arts festival in the Soviet Union to become the first American jazz musicians to play behind the Iron Curtain. He and MILES DAVIS both succeeded in breathing life into the business of jazz at a time when rock music dominated American culture. After those glorious years of touring, Lloyd gradually dropped out of public view. In 1989 he was back recording and since then has produced an intriguing collection of thoughtful, well-conceived music. Particularly striking is his collaboration with guitarist JOHN ABERCROMBIE and BASS player DAVE HOLLAND, *Voice in the Night* (1998), a moody but immensely interesting work.

Lovano, Joe (b. 1952) *American tenor, alto, and soprano saxophone and alto and bass clarinet player*
Joe Lovano is a popular saxophonist whose versatile style has been compared to the sound of JOHN COLTRANE, the offbeat rhythms of THELONIOUS MONK, and the soul of COLEMAN HAWKINS. He learned his early LICKS from his father, who taught him to play Ralph Burns's composition "Early Autumn" as an exercise in changing keys. One of Lovano's early GIGS was with the WOODY HERMAN Orchestra from 1976 to 1979. After that he earned a reputation as a popular SIDEMAN and collaborator. His big break came when he was signed to a record contract with Blue Note in 1990. He has recorded more than 22 albums as a bandleader, including 16 with Blue Note. He has recorded his Grammy-winning album *52nd Street Themes* (2000) and a popular follow-up, *On This Day . . . At The Vanguard* (2003) with his BEBOP-influenced NONET. His collaborators have included MEL LEWIS, GONZALO RUBACALBA, Paul Motian, CHARLIE HADEN, BILL FRISELL, and others. Lovano is known as a skilled player with heart and a wealth of influences that he draws upon with the ease of a jazz master.

Love Supreme, A (1964) *album recorded by the John Coltrane Quartet*
Featuring JOHN COLTRANE (tenor SAXOPHONE), McCOY TYNER (PIANO), JIMMY GARRISON (BASS), and ELVIN JONES (DRUMS), it was Coltrane's intensity that made him the most influential jazz artist of the 1960s. *A Love Supreme* (released by Impulse!) was recorded just three years before his death in 1967. Yet its power and drive provides no clue that its maker was suffering from severe alcoholism and drug addiction. Coltrane called this music a statement in spirituality. His playing on this record is precise and often lyrical but at times also transforms into wild sheets of sound that defy description. In fact, the entire work defies categorization, as the work of a true master sometimes does. This album-length jazz suite captures the John Coltrane Quartet at the height of their skill and power. *A Love Supreme* is one of the most popular jazz recordings of all time.

Machito (Raúl Grillo) (1912–1984) *Cuban-American singer and percussionist*
Machito, born Raúl Grillo, in Florida, was raised in Cuba and moved to New York in 1937. Machito grew up around many of the leading musicians in Cuba. He first played with bands in Cuba, playing mostly popular dance music. He continued in this vein when he first came to New York, performing with bands led by Xavier Cugat, Noro Morales, and others. He started his own band with brother-in-law MARIO BAUZÁ and directed the music toward jazzier arrangements, combining Cuban melodies and rhythms with SWING. He continued to lead this group for 40 years. He helped popularize the New York MAMBO style of music and dance in the late 1940s and was an important influence in the integration of Latin music with American jazz. Notable fans of his music included STAN KENTON and DIZZY GILLESPIE, who both in turn introduced Afro-Cuban elements into their music. At the suggestion of PRODUCER Norman Granz, Machito also recorded with CHARLIE PARKER. At the time of his death he was reaching a new audience with a BIG BAND playing salsa music.

Maghostut, Malachi Favors See FAVORS, MALACHI.

Mahavishnu Orchestra, The See FUSION, JOHN.

mambo
Name given to a dance style and its accompanying music, which is of Cuban origin, dating from the 1930s.

Mangione, Chuck (b. 1940) *American flugelhorn and keyboard player, composer, arranger, and bandleader*
If SMOOTH JAZZ needed a father, then it might as well be CHUCK MANGIONE. Mangione is probably the most widely known player of jazz FLUGELHORN. He began playing HARD BOP in the early 1960s, including a GIG with ART BLAKEY and the Jazz Messengers from 1965 to 1967. In the 1970s he divided his time between playing, teaching at the Eastman School of Music in Rochester, and guest conducting with the Rochester Philharmonic. In 1977 the unexpected success of his recording "Feels So Good" propelled him into the status of jazz pop star. This song was arguably the catalyst for the radio format known as smooth jazz. After that, his music became decidedly tame, more like easy-listening than pure jazz.

Although continuing to work on music for television and touring, Mangione largely disappeared from the public eye during the 1980s and 1990s. More recently, he released the albums *The Feeling's Back* (1999) and *Everything for Love* (2000) as part of his comeback as a recording artist. His current music is a welcomed throwback to the COOL JAZZ of the 1950s, with a sound that is strangely reminiscent of MILES DAVIS from that period, another player who was no stranger to the flugelhorn. A unique distinction for Mangione is that he is caricatured on the Fox network animated television show *King of the Hill,* where he acts as celebrity spokesperson for Mega-Lo-Mart stores.

Manhattan Transfer

Manhattan Transfer is a four-member vocal group specializing in jazz tunes and VOCALESE. Founded in 1969 by doo-wop singer Tim Hauser, the first successful lineup of the group took shape by 1972 and included Hauser, Janis Siegel, Laurel Masse, and Alan Paul. At first, the group's selections ranged from doo-wop to campy interpretations of pop songs and old standards. Their first minor hit was "Operator" (1975), a gospel tune from the 1950s. By 1979 the group had begun to showcase their taste for jazz with some extraordinary vocalese productions, including "Four Brothers" (1978) and their rendition of the JOE ZAWINUL/WEATHER REPORT tune "BIRDLAND" (recorded in 1979). "Birdland" earned them their first GRAMMY AWARD and was the most played jazz recording of 1979.[133]

Although their repertoire continues to include a wide range of music from show tunes to pop, BLUES, and jazz, the Manhattan Transfer is steeped in jazz know-how and has dedicated many of their most interesting recordings to this genre. Some of their most successful jazz-flavored releases include *Mecca for Moderns* (1981), *Vocalese* (1985, with 12 Grammy nominations), *Swing* (1997), and *Couldn't Be Hotter* (2003).

Mann, Herbie (1930–2003) *American flute, tenor saxophone, and clarinet player, composer, and bandleader*

Mann is the most recognized jazz flutist of the last 50 years. He is also a jazz artist most difficult to categorize because of his many influences and tendency to work outside of the jazz mainstream. He traveled extensively during the 1950s, first as part of

an army band in Europe (1950–53), and then when he took his Afro Jazz sextet on a long tour of Africa sponsored by the U.S. State Department (1959–60). He was primarily a tenor SAXOPHONE player until a colleague invited him to play FLUTE on a CARMEN MCRAE record in 1955. He took quickly to mastering the flute so that by 1958 it was his primary instrument. By this time he was already an experienced studio musician and PRODUCER of music for television dramas.

He spent much of the 1960s abroad, visiting Brazil and Japan. By the mid-1960s his music was fusing elements of Latin jazz, BOSSA NOVA, Middle Eastern music, and Japanese folk music. His sound was unique, and he became a regular club performer on the New York jazz scene, particularly at the Village Gate. He is largely credited today as an originator of the concept of WORLD MUSIC and having helped popularize Latin jazz. As a flute player, he was a perennial favorite of the annual *Down Beat* poll and became a regular at many jazz festivals at home and abroad. He briefly tried to cash in on the disco craze of the 1970s, but when that was over he returned to his unique blend of COMBO jazz flavored by Brazilian elements.

His recording career slowed down due to ill health in the late 1990s, but he completed an album in 2002, *Eastern European Roots,* exploring European folk music and jazz. Among his dozens of albums, those of his live performances of the 1960s, including *Live at the Village Gate* (1961) and *Live at Newport* (1963), provide the best proof of his unflinching style and rhythmic touch as a major jazz flutist.

Mantler, Michael (b. 1943) *Austrian trumpet player, composer, and arranger*

In 1962 the classically trained Mantler came to the United States, where he attended the BERKLEE COLLEGE OF MUSIC. His early work in America included a stint with CECIL TAYLOR. Mantler met CARLA BLEY, whom he later married, in the mid-1960s. Bley and he were both interested in creating large scale works for jazz orchestra, but after some failed attempts they went on tour in Europe as part of the QUINTET Jazz Realities in 1965 and 1966. Back in the United States, Mantler and Bley formed the Jazz Composer's Orchestra Association (JCOA), a nonprofit foundation to commission and perform new compositions for jazz orchestra. The crowning achievement of the JCOA was the recording of Bley's monumental work *Escalator Over the Hill* (1968–71), but difficulty distributing the experimental work precluded its commercial success. Mantler formed New Music Distribution Service in 1972 to help remedy the problem of distributing independently produced music. By the mid-1970s he and Bley were operating out of a recording studio they built in Woodstock.

Mantler has thrived on composing ambitious, AVANT-GARDE jazz works, often on commissions from American and European orchestras. He returned to live in Europe in 1991. His music is strongly avant-garde and blends elements of contemporary classical orchestration with jazz. In 1993 he formed the ENSEMBLE Chamber Music and Songs, which features his TRUMPET, a vocalist, guitarist, keyboard player, and string QUARTET. His recent compositions include jazz influenced operas, symphonies, and songs for chamber orchestra.

"Maple Leaf Rag" (1899) *song by Scott Joplin*

If there is one song that typifies RAGTIME music more than any other, it is "Maple Leaf Rag," named after the Maple Leaf Club in Sedalia, Missouri, where SCOTT JOPLIN was a pianist. It is by far the most popular ragtime piece ever. It is a happy song with syncopated PIANO playing and figuring that sometimes imitate the rhythmic plucking of BANJO strings. The song made a comeback 15 years after Joplin's death. It was a hit in 1932, when SIDNEY BECHET's New Orleans Feetwarmers recorded it.

Maria Schneider Jazz Orchestra See SCHNEIDER, MARIA.

Marsalis, Branford (b. 1960) *American tenor and soprano saxophone player, composer, and bandleader*

Branford is the older brother of WYNTON MARSALIS. His taste in music is as eclectic as his brother's, but decidedly different. As a tenor player, he emulates SONNY ROLLINS and JOHN COLTRANE. Branford's soprano SAXOPHONE borrows much of its lyricism from WAYNE SHORTER. His own groups display a penchant for the AVANT-GARDE fused with elements of rock and BOP. He has been an eager collaborator with a variety of artists, most notably Sting on the album *Dream of the Blue Turtles* (1985) and Bruce Hornsby as COCOMPOSER of the work "Barcelona Mona" (1994) for the Barcelona Olympics in Spain. He has been nominated for and won several GRAMMY AWARDS. He is also no stranger to working in television and films. He worked on music for the documentary *Baseball* by Ken Burns and was the musical director of *Jay Leno's Tonight Show* in 1992. He recently joined the faculty of Michigan State University and is active as a record PRODUCER.

Marsalis, Wynton (b. 1961) *American trumpet player, composer, arranger, bandleader, and educator*

"Jazz is exactly like modern American life. If we work things out, we have a good time. In jazz, we call that swinging."[134]

These are the words of today's leading spokesperson of jazz, Wynton Marsalis. Born in New Orleans and the son of pianist and educator Ellis Marsalis, Wynton showed an aptitude for the TRUMPET at a young age. By 14, he was a promising player of both classic jazz and symphonic trumpet music. Upon moving to New York in 1978 to attend the Juilliard School, he picked up jazz GIGS around the city and began to make a reputation for himself. He joined the legendary ART BLAKEY and his Jazz Messengers in 1980 and began to understand the nuance of jazz ENSEMBLE playing. This led to the founding of his own band and guest spots with

Wynton Marsalis

some jazz greats, including SARAH VAUGHN, DIZZY GILLESPIE, and SONNY ROLLINS. His first SOLO record, *Wynton Marsalis* (1983), was followed by two more albums the same year.

In 1987 he cofounded JAZZ AT LINCOLN CENTER and serves as the educational program's artistic director. In the 1990s he began to focus more on composing, dividing his efforts between music for dance, concert hall, and BIG BAND productions. He wrote music for the Garth Fagan Dance Company, the New York City Ballet, Twyla Tharp and the American Ballet Theater, and for the Alvin Ailey American Dance Theater. One of his most ambitious works, *All Rise* (1999), combines his many musical interests into an ambitious

production for big band, gospel choir, and symphony orchestra. In 2004, his work at Jazz at Lincoln Center resulted in the completion of a new multimillion-dollar center for the performance, education, and broadcasting of jazz. As a jazz artist, his TECHNIQUE is highly polished and informed of the traditions of the genre, but there is noticeable remoteness to his style that diminishes its emotional impact.

Regardless of this impression, Marsalis is greatly admired as a player and spokesman for jazz. He devotes much of his time to educational activities. Marsalis is, without question, the most eloquent ambassador that jazz has ever had. He reminds us that jazz is not merely a form of music;

it is a history of social movement in America and symbolizes not only the strife, but the harmony that can take place when people work together. "Jazz enables us to understand and enjoy the individuality of each person. It encourages us to listen to one another with empathy. And listening is a most important skill to teach in this age of global communication."[135]

Martino, Pat (b. 1944) *American guitar player, composer, and bandleader*

As a young GUITAR player, Martino paid his dues as a SIDEMAN for several jazz and rhythm and blues organists, including Richard Groove Holmes. Martino heard JOHN COLTRANE play and jammed with the great WES MONTGOMERY. He emerged as a leader of his own COMBOS in the late 1960s and forged a TRADITIONAL JAZZ sound that was an extension of HARD BOP without drifting into rock FUSION, which was also emerging at the time. His earliest albums as a leader, including *El Hombre* (1967) and *Baiyina* (1968), display his breezy, articulate style. The album *Consciousness* (1974), one of his most ambitious, finds Martino immersed in the same kinds of modal explorations that had occupied Coltrane. This edgy, experimental side of Martino was produced at a time when other expert electric guitarists might have tried to capitalize on the fusion jazz movement that was so popular then.

In 1976 Martino suffered a brain aneurysm that required surgery. Although successful, the operation resulted in serious memory loss. Martino had no memory of playing guitar or his career. He made a dramatic comeback, spending much time reacquainting himself with his own recorded music, eventually reversing the memory loss. After making his first comeback appearance in 1987, Martino continues to tour and record. His 1997 CD *All Sides Now* features duets with other guitar players including Les Paul, Michael Hedges, Joe Satriani, Kevin Eubanks, and others, many of whom were inspired by Martino's playing.

Mary Lou Williams Women in Jazz Festival

This annual jazz festival founded in 1997 is held each spring at the Kennedy Center in Washington, D.C. It highlights the contributions of women in jazz and is named for the great jazz pianist MARY LOU WILLIAMS. The festival features the jazz artistry of women from all over the world, playing every style imaginable, including BIG BAND, ballads, red-hot funk, icy cool BLUES, and TRADITIONAL and PROGRESSIVE JAZZ.

Masekela, Hugh (b. 1939) *South African trumpet and flugelhorn player, singer, composer, and bandleader*

Masekela is one of the leading figures of SOUTH AFRICAN JAZZ. He became popular in the United States with a hit called "Grazing in the Grass" in 1968. The high-spirited sound of Masekela and other South African musicians brought a new energy to jazz and fused it with native African music. In his 30-year career Maskela has performed with artists ranging from Paul Simon to LOUIS ARMSTRONG. His legacy as a spokesperson for the civil rights of blacks in South Africa has made him an unofficial ambassador for oppressed people wherever he performs. His playing has always been marked by an energetic blend of funk and jazz backed by an African beat. His latest work, exemplified by *Time* (2002), has moved away from pure jazz to a more popular blend of world sounds, including touches of gospel, funk, jazz, Afro beat, and Latin music.

McClure, Kit (b. 1951) *American trombone, flute, clarinet, and saxophone player, composer, and bandleader*

McClure was educated at Yale University, where she played TROMBONE in a jazz-rock ENSEMBLE during her days as a medical student. After graduating from college, she moved to New York City and took up music full-time as a teacher and SIDEMAN. After several years of freelance work and tours, she formed the all-female Kit McClure BIG BAND in 1982. The 16-piece band has since had a steady following and has toured widely in America and Europe. McClure focuses on classic big band music. One of the group's recent recording projects was a re-creation of the music of the famed all-women big band from the 1940s, the INTERNATIONAL SWEETHEARTS OF RHYTHM. For this 2004 project McClure researched, transcribed, and arranged accurate renditions of numbers made famous 50 years ago by the famous multiracial, all-female band.

McConnell, Rob (b. 1935) *Canadian valve trombone player, composer, arranger, and bandleader*

McConnell is best known for his innovative BIG BAND arrangements and reviving an interest in big band composing in the late 1960s. He founded the 16-piece Boss Brass band in 1968 and established a style of ARRANGEMENT that favored the BRASS instruments. In fact, his group didn't include any SAXOPHONES or other reed instruments until 1971. The signature sound of Boss Brass includes tight harmonies punctuated by long, sometimes, unaccompanied passages. McConnell and the Boss Brass has been much lauded over the years and won one of its several GRAMMY AWARDS in 1984 for *All in Good Time* as Best Big Band Album of the Year. McConnell also produced two successful albums for singer MEL TORME in the late 1980s. After taking a break to teach, McConnell reformed the Boss Brass in 1991 and continues to record and tour. Their release in 2004 of *Even Canadians Get the Blues* marked the Boss Brass's first extended exploration of the BLUES.

McFerrin, Bobby (b. 1950) *American singer, composer, and educator*

McFerrin is a stylish and playful singer who uses his four-octave range to create inventive vocal IMPROVISATIONS. Not content to sing only lyrics, he often embellishes his tunes with percussive vocalizations to create a complex accompaniment for himself. He has collaborated with other artists in many musical genres, including pop, folk, jazz, choral, and classical. He has worked with jazz artists WYNTON MARSALIS, WAYNE SHORTER, CHICK COREA, and HERBIE HANCOCK, and has worked with classical music organizations such as the Vienna Philharmonic as a conductor and guest performer. His best-selling popular song was "Don't Worry, Be Happy" (1989), from his best-selling album *Simple Pleasures*. The song and album earned him several GRAMMY AWARDS. In the 1990s he continued to explore his singing skills in multiple genres, including tours with the 12-voice acapella chorus Voicestra, a tour with CHICK COREA, and recordings with cellist Yo Yo Ma. McFerrin's distinctive voice is unique in all of jazz, and he is certainly one of the singing wonders of modern music.

McLaughlin, John (b. 1942) *British guitar and guitar synthesizer player, composer, bandleader*

McLaughlin is one of the most scintillating and influential electric guitarists in modern jazz. The self-taught musician grew up in England listening to the BLUES and playing for popular rock groups such as Georgie Fame's Blues Flames, the Graham Bond organization, and Brian Auger's Trinity. An admirer of jazz, he paid close attention to the many new sounds coming from America in the mid- to late 1960s. The spirited IMPROVISATIONS of JOHN COLTRANE and the funky electric jazz of MILES DAVIS both attracted him. He calls his first hearing of Coltrane's *A LOVE SUPREME* in 1965 a milestone in his life. At the time, he admitted later, he could not "understand at all what Coltrane is doing musically on this record."[136]

As the music of Coltrane and Davis sunk in, however, McLaughlin began to see a new path for his own playing and composing. He formed his first QUARTET in 1969, including DAVE HOLLAND (BASS), JOHN SURMAN (reeds), and Tony Oxley (DRUMS), that resulted in the album *Extrapolation* (1968, with Brian Odges replacing Holland on bass). It was an early no-frills experiment in blending rock and jazz and showcased some excellent compositions by the guitarist. In 1969 McLaughlin came to America and, with the help of Dave Holland, began to make important musical connections. He jammed with Jimi Hendrix, was introduced to Tony Williams and Miles Davis, and began a lifelong spiritual quest as a disciple of Indian guru Sri Chimnoy.

These were heady times for the young Brit. The fruits of these newly made friendships resulted in several associations with groups and recordings. In 1969 he joined drummer Tony Williams's Lifetime, an innovative early FUSION group growing out of Williams's work with Miles Davis. Playing with Williams and McLaughlin were Jack Bruce of Cream on bass and the phenomenal LARRY YOUNG on ORGAN. The two records cut by this short-lived team hinted at the burning, distorted GUITAR sound that McLaughlin would soon perfect. Miles Davis also became a fan of McLaughlin's playing and hired him for four landmark fusion sessions: *IN A SILENT WAY* (1969), *BITCHES BREW* (1970), *A Tribute to Jack Johnson* (1970), and *Live Evil* (1970). McLaughlin is probably more responsible for the rock feel of these recordings than any other participant. It was during these sessions that McLaughlin's fully formed, electronically contorted sound was unleashed.

During the same period, as if to prove that he wasn't only about electric guitar and feedback, he also released the exquisitely quiet acoustic guitar masterpiece *My Goal's Beyond* (1970). Significantly, this album showcased his delicate, quasi-Flamenco touch on the strings in a number of tunes that blended folk, classical, Indian, and Spanish guitar traditions.

In 1971 McLaughlin's fame was assured once and for all with the formation of his fusion group, the MAHAVISHNU ORCHESTRA. The lineup included McLaughlin playing a double-neck electric guitar (one 12-string, one six-string), JAN HAMMER on electronic keyboards, Rick Laird on bass, Jerry Goodman on electric VIOLIN, and the incomparable BILLY COBHAM on drums. The first earth-shaking CHORD of their debut self-titled album clearly announced that they were taking fusion where Miles refused to go; into a hard-rocking style of instrumental songwriting as a setup for highly

John McLaughlin

charged improvisation and group interaction. McLaughlin's group played tight, loud music with intense cohesion. The communication among group members was so startling that they seemed all to be of one mind. The group toured on the rock music circuit, sometimes playing second bill to acts like the Grateful Dead's Jerry Garcia. By the time of their second album, however, in 1973, they were HEADLINERS. Though never achieving the commercial success of WEATHER REPORT, the Mahavishnu Orchestra remains, to many, the crowning example of a successful FUSION of the energy and emotion of rock with the virtuosity of jazz.

After the break up of the Mahavishnu Orchestra in 1975, McLaughlin continued to work on many fronts as a leader, guest artist, and SOLO artist. He has always nurtured outlets for his many different styles of playing. Since 1976 he has led his small acoustic COMBO Shakti, which creates a fusion of Western and Indian music. His sidemen in this case include classically trained musicians L. Shankar (violin), Zakir Hussain (tabla), and T.H. Vinayakaram (ghatam). In the early 1980s he devoted much time to a loving collaboration with fellow acoustic guitar players AL DI MEOLA and Paco de Lucia that resulted in some extraordinary trio recordings and tours. He has composed and recorded symphonic suites for guitar and orchestra, resulting in *The Mediterranean Concerto* (1990) and *Thieves and Poets* (2003). As a solo and combo player he has also been a key innovator in the use of electronic technology, including SYNTHESIZERs such as the Synclavier and the Photon guitar synthesizer.

No matter which guitar he picks up, the John McLaughlin style is widely recognized as a unique voice in jazz. His solos are often long and sinuous, consisting of rapid-fire flights of 16th notes punctuated by ACCENTed pauses and sustained distortion. He has also brought a master's sense of interplay to any group in which he plays, proving that the hallmark of jazz playing is often the ability to listen to others and react in kind. He is a quiet, composed family man whose approach to music might shock anyone who doesn't know his work. "I need provocation in music, I need to be provoked," said McLaughlin. "And I want to provoke too. Hopefully, I do. And I think deep inside we all need this, to get out of our lethargy and indolence."[137]

McPartland, Marian (b. 1918) *British piano player, composer, bandleader, and educator*

Marian McPartland was a classically trained PIANO player who had a knack for jazz. After moving to the United States with her new husband, Jimmy McPartland, in 1945, she began a productive career playing clubs as a soloist and with a trio. During the 1960s, after the breakup of her marriage, her musical activities branched out in several directions. She played for a spell with BENNY GOODMAN's QUINTET, had a jazz radio program in New York, and began to reach out as a teacher of jazz to underprivileged children and teenagers. In the 1970s she toured widely, played at international jazz festivals, and occasionally collaborated with symphony orchestras. Her lively playing, wise historical perspective, and articulate voice have made her a treasure of the jazz world.

McRae, Carmen (1920–1994) *American singer and piano player*

McRae's career was mostly overshadowed by those of SARAH VAUGHN and ELLA FITZGERALD, but she was a remarkably stylish singer in her own right. Her relaxed and carefree approach to phrasing gave her singing an intimate, conversational quality, not unlike BILLIE HOLIDAY. McRae was, in fact, connected to Holiday in an interesting way. When she was only 18, McRae wrote the song "Dream of Life," which Holiday recorded.

McRae's own career started slowly, but she was in good company. She had steady work as a singer with BENNY CARTER in 1944 and the Mercer Ellington band from 1946 to 1947. But it was not until she first led her own trio in 1954 that her career took off. She recorded steadily over the years and remained popular with jazz fans. She collaborated with DAVE BRUBECK on several occasions, recorded live duets with BETTY CARTER, and recorded astounding tributes to THELONIOUS MONK and Sarah Vaughn in the closing years of her career.

Medeski, John (b. 1965) *American piano, organ, and electronic keyboard player and composer*

John Medeski is the unofficial leader of the innovative groove band Medeski, Martin, and Wood (MMW). The groove band phenomenon grew out of the success of rock jam bands such as the Grateful

Carmen McRae

Metheny, Pat (b. 1954) *American guitar and guitar synthesizer player, composer, and bandleader*

Metheny is one of the most popular and versatile modern jazz guitarists. He is a highly absorbent student of GUITAR whose music is a hybrid of TRADITIONAL JAZZ guitar, easy listening, Latin, and rock. One of his guitar idols was WES MONTGOMERY, whose gentle, flowing style is evident in Metheny's work. Metheny, originally a TRUMPET player, also admires the soft, lyrical playing of CLIFFORD BROWN. Metheny studied at the BERKLEE COLLEGE OF MUSIC and first toured with instructor GARY BURTON in 1974. After making his record debut in 1974, Metheny embarked on his own career as leader and COMPOSER.

Pat Metheny

Dead and Phish. MMW brought that freewheeling form of performing to the jazz scene in the early 1990s. The signature sound of the group is Medeski's funky Hammond B3 ORGAN. He plays in a style that fuses funky pop music, exotica, and jazz into danceable grooves. Backed by drummer Billy Martin and bassist Chris Wood, Medeski's repertoire ranges from DUKE ELLINGTON classics to movie music and soul music. With the CD *Combustication* (1998), they added a hip-hop twist with the appearance of guest DJ Logic. Their influence on the jazz music scene has been substantial, even inspiring some old-line players such as guitarist JOHN SCOFIELD to recruit new players and take a more jam band approach in their shows.

His distinctive sound embraces electronic effects to broaden the audio palette and provide atmosphere. He is equally at home SOLOing on guitar as he is on guitar SYNTHESIZER, an extension of the guitar, which gives him other instrumental sounds to command. Despite a tendency to produce softly flowing and melodic music, there is no doubting Metheny's musical aptitude. He often surprises his regular listeners with a sharp left turn into the AVANT-GARDE, such as his earnest 1986 collaboration with FREE JAZZ pioneer ORNETTE COLEMAN (*Pat Metheny/Ornette Coleman*).

He started the Pat Metheny Group in 1977 with keyboard player Lyle Mays. With the exception of Metheny and Mays, the makeup of this group has changed several times over the years. Among the best-known sidemen (see SIDEMAN) have been Jack DeJohnette, Dewey Redman, MICHAEL BRECKER, and CHARLIE HADEN. Despite these changes, the Pat Metheny Group has remained its founder's most prominent showcase. The resulting music is always branded by Metheny's light and introspective melodies played over a lush atmosphere of perky rhythms and supportive keyboards. One distinctive quality of the music, as exemplified on *STILL LIFE TALKING* (1987), is a chanting CHORUS of harmonizing voices that accompany many of the pieces. He is the recipient of 16 GRAMMY AWARDS for achievements, including composing, performing, and recordings. They include a Grammy in 2002 for the Best Contemporary Jazz Album, *Speaking of Now.*

MIDI

Musical Instrument Digital Interface, or MIDI, is an interface technology that links computer software to hardware. It is the standard interface employed by all commercial makers of music technology. MIDI permits electronic music instruments made by different companies to be linked electronically for control purposes during performance. It allows a single performer using a single keyboard or other controller (e.g., software) to play more than one instrument at a time, regardless of the make and manufacturer of the gear. The control signals from the single keyboard are transmitted through MIDI interface communications to the other synthesizers that are linked to it. It permits the orchestration of music using a variety of MIDI-compatible instruments.

Miller, Glenn (1904–1944) *American bandleader, composer, and trombone player*

Miller was a modest TROMBONE player with a knack for arrangements and a mind for business. In his short career, ended tragically by the disappearance of his small plane while en route from England to France during World War II, his BIG BAND was the most commercially successful of its day. He got his start with TERRITORY BANDS in the mid-1920s before becoming a successful ARRANGER and SIDEMAN for TOMMY and JIMMY DORSEY and BENNY GOODMAN, among others. Miller's first successful venture as a bandleader came in 1938. During the early 1940s his band achieved astounding success playing mildly swinging ballads and popular tunes, including "Moonlight Serenade," "American Patrol," "String of Pearls," and "In the Mood." Miller's band was the epitome of popular dance bands of the time. If there had been MTV, they would have had the top music video. Upon entering the service during World War II, he led a big band in the military and entertained the Allied troops in England. The Miller sound was unmistakable. It depended on a unique device: a swinging CLARINET over a bed of four SAXOPHONES. After his death the band continued under the guidance of Jerry Gray and Ray McKinley, and the Miller sound became widely imitated.

Miller, Marcus (b. 1959) *American electric bass, keyboard, and percussion player, composer, arranger, and producer*

Miller is part of a new generation of multi-instrumentalist players who also know how to work the tools of recording technology to produce excellent recordings. He was raised on Long Island and followed in the musical footsteps of his father, a talented jazz pianist and church organist. He was playing CLARINET, PIANO, and BASS professionally by the age of 15. After playing with flutist Bobbi Humphrey and keyboard artist Lonnie Liston Smith, Miller found a niche as a successful studio musician. He won acclaim for his work with Aretha Franklin, Roberta Flack, and DAVID SANBORN. His next challenge was playing backup on the road to one of his idols, MILES DAVIS, between 1980 and 1982. This was a period of maturity for Miller. "I learned from him," explains Miller, "that you have to be honest about who you are and what you do. If you follow that, you won't have problems."[138]

After touring with Davis, Miller took a turn at producing a record for David Sanborn in 1982 and released the first record under his own name, *Suddenly* (1983). In 1986 he produced the extraordinary *Tutu* for Miles Davis. The trumpeter seemed to be content to sit back and let Miller do his magic. The instrumental credit for the album simply reads: "Miles Davis, trumpet all other instruments Marcus Miller except indicated." It was a tour de force of bass playing, electronic keyboards, drum machines, and the signature imprint of Davis's plaintive trumpet, a FUSION of jazz and pop with a funky drive.

Miller has continued to expand his reach in the music business, winning a GRAMMY AWARD for Best R&B Song in 1991 for "Power of Love/Love Power." In 1994 he composed and produced *Tales,* an intriguing mix of documentary snippets from conversations with jazz greats and Miller's contemporary interpretation of the music they perfected. "I was trying to get the album to sound like a conversation that I've been hearing all my life," he explains. "A conversation between me and mostly older musicians." He continues to compose, front his own group, and perform with other players as diverse as Luther Vandross, Eric Clapton, David Sanborn, and Joe Sample.

Mingus, Charles (1922–1979) *American bass player, composer, arranger, and bandleader*

First and foremost a COMPOSER, jazz legend Charles Mingus was a tireless practitioner whose personal approach to jazz created fiery and often controversial work. He was an outspoken opponent of the commercialization of jazz, especially to the detriment of African-American artists who originated it. His music was often inseparable from his message, and he demanded that his players feel the message in order to play it properly. A recurring theme throughout his work was racial prejudice, hate, and persecution. His autobiography, *Beneath the Underdog* (1971), not only succeeds in underscoring his own myth as an angry artist, but also is an anguished look at the passions and events that obsessed him.

As a young man he was mostly exposed to classical music. He first studied TROMBONE and then cello, finally taking up the acoustic BASS at age 16. He studied classical music composition and began playing professionally as a jazz SIDEMAN while still in his teens. He worked early on with LOUIS ARMSTRONG (1941–43) and others, including KID ORY and LIONEL HAMPTON. Mingus was an extraordinary bass player by this time. He played with RED NORVO from 1950 to 1951 and then settled in New York to establish his career as a bandleader and composer.

If there was a hot GIG in town, Mingus was usually a part of it. During his initial years in New York he worked with everyone from CHARLIE PARKER, MILES DAVIS, and BUD POWELL to ART TATUM, STAN GETZ, and DUKE ELLINGTON. Mingus had a terrific grasp of both BIG BAND SWING and COMBO BOP, both of which greatly influenced his own composing. He established his own group, the Charles Mingus Workshop, in 1955. It was indeed a laboratory for his compositions and included many changing players over the years. Many extraordinary soloists did time with the Mingus group, including THAD JONES, RAHSAAN ROLAND KIRK, and ERIC DOLPHY. He was co-musical director with MAX ROACH of a jazz festival on Cliff Walk at Newport in protest of the practices of the NEWPORT JAZZ FESTIVAL in 1960. During the 1960s he began working and writing for larger bands and ensembles, although he kept his QUINTET active until about 1975.

Mingus's music is a rich combination of modern jazz idioms including bop, HARD BOP, and cool. It also reveals a tenderness for the BLUES and gospel music that often underscores the emotional power of his work. As a bassist he was agile and played with a full tone. His classical training was evident in the TECHNIQUE that he employed in his compositions. He used COUNTERPOINT, quickly shifting TEMPOS, and intriguing combinations of instruments. All of these techniques helped to tell the story of his compositions. To preserve the spontaneity of composing in real time, he sometimes sang or played parts to his sidemen rather then writing them down using musical notation. His arrangements could be bright and jumping or moody and introspective.

Charles Mingus

Each of his works, long or short, unfolds with an originality that is often surprising. Along with Ellington, he is one of the most accomplished jazz composers of all time. Some of his most noted works include "Goodbye Pork Pie Hat" (1959), "Wednesday Night Prayer Meeting" (1959), "Duke Ellington's Sound of Love" (1974), "Fables of Faubus" (1960), and the "Black Saint and the Sinner Lady" (1963). His most fertile recording period was from 1959 to 1960, when he released four milestone albums: *BLUES AND ROOTS* (1959), *MINGUS AH UM* (1959), *Mingus Dynasty* (1959), and *Mingus Presents Mingus* (1960). The legacy of Mingus is kept alive by the MINGUS BIG BAND, a rotating ENSEMBLE of New York–based players who perform big band arrangements of Mingus's compositions every week.

Mingus Ah Um (1959) *album by Charles Mingus*

CHARLES MINGUS remains relevant to today's jazz players because of his serious SWING, versatility as a BASS player, and uncompromising creativity as a COMPOSER. He recorded *Mingus Ah Um* during the peak of his powers during a short stay with Columbia Records, which released the album. With MILES DAVIS, JOHN COLTRANE, ORNETTE COLEMAN, and DAVE BRUBECK breaking into new jazz styles at the time, Mingus's work on this album is surprisingly classic. He calls forth the powers of the African-American jazz tradition with works that summon up the BLUES, BIG BAND swing, BOP, and sensitive balladeering. His classic tune "Goodbye Pork Pie Hat" is from this album.

Mingus Big Band

The legacy of CHARLES MINGUS, who died in 1979, includes several assemblages of performers who regularly perform the COMPOSER's music. Of these, the Mingus Big Band is the most visible and certainly the most influential as one of the premier big bands currently performing. It is a 14-piece band under the artistic direction of the composer's wife, Sue Mingus. It has performed weekly gigs in New York since 1991. Sometimes taking its spot is the larger Charles Mingus Orchestra. Players are made up from an impressive pool of leading New York sidemen (see SIDEMAN). The Big Band tours frequently, and three of its six recordings have been nominated for GRAMMY AWARDS.

Minton's Playhouse

A HARLEM jazz club that became the crucible of BEBOP during the 1940s. Founded in 1938 by saxophonist Henry Minton, the club was located on 118th Street in a former dining room of the Hotel Cecil. It was acquired by bandleader Teddy Hill in 1940. One of the weekly features of the club was a Monday night JAM SESSION. Working musicians would congregate to JAM and experiment at Minton's on Monday nights and after hours following their regular performances. Regular "guests" at Minton's included DIZZY GILLESPIE, CHARLIE PARKER, CHARLIE CHRISTIAN, KENNY CLARKE, JIMMY BLANTON, and ROY ELDRIDGE. THELONIOUS MONK was a house musician and encouraged a freewheeling spirit of experimentation with new sounds and rhythms. He helped kick-start BUD POWELL's career by encouraging him to sit in at the jam sessions. Dizzy himself described the workshop nature of his days at Minton's this way, "What we were doing at Minton's was playing, seriously, creating a new dialogue among ourselves, blending our ideas into a new style of music. You only have so many notes, and what makes a style is how you get from one note to another. . . . We invented our own way of getting from one place to the next."[139]

Mitchell, Roscoe (b. 1940) *American soprano, alto, tenor, and bass saxophone, flute, piccolo, oboe, clarinet, and percussion player, composer, and bandleader*

Mitchell took part in the formation of the ASSOCIATION FOR THE ADVANCEMENT OF CREATIVE MUSICIANS (AACM) in 1965 and formed a sextet about that time to play FREE JAZZ. *Sound* (1966) was a bold statement in the face of all of the JOHN COLTRANE wannabes of the time, and set a new outer limit for free jazz. Mitchell and his group created textures of sound. They played in a zone where any sound could be considered musical. The use of miscellaneous bells and percussion as a backdrop for some of the work was much imitated by later artists. Mitchell cofounded the ART ENSEMBLE OF CHICAGO in 1969, one of the most long-lived and groundbreaking experimental jazz groups.

Throughout his career, Mitchell has consistently shaken up established ideas, and expectations, about jazz and reconfigured them into something new. His compositions range from works for his own SOLO instruments to jazz COMBOS, pieces for string ensembles, trios, percussion groups, orchestras, a recorder ENSEMBLE, and toy instruments. He pioneered the concept of "scored improvisations" that gave his players cues and ideas that led to IMPROVISATION. "You have to know composition," explains Mitchell, "to be a good improviser. If you don't know how to think like a composer, you'll never be able to construct long pieces."[140]

Mitchell's specialty is playing high-pitched WOODWINDS such as the soprano SAXOPHONE, piccolo, CLARINET, and FLUTE, a sonic realm that he broke open with his innovative playing beginning in the 1960s. His recent compositions include "The Bells of Fifty Ninth Street" for alto saxophone and Gamelan Orchestra (2000), and "59A" for solo soprano saxophone (2000).

Moanin' (1958) *album by Art Blakey and the Jazz Messengers*

This is the definitive HARD BOP recording. This was one of the swingingest Jazz Messenger lineups with ART BLAKEY (DRUMS), LEE MORGAN (TRUMPET), Benny Golson (tenor SAXOPHONE), Bobby Timmons (PIANO), and Jymie Merritt (BASS). "Along Came Betty," "Moanin'," and "Blues March" are among the Blakey classics. The solos are measured, Blakey plays brilliantly, and Morgan's soft trumpet plays well against Golson's saxophone.

modal jazz

A style of jazz pioneered at the end of the 1950s, based on theories published by COMPOSER and theorist GEORGE RUSSELL in his book *The Lydian Chromatic Concept of Tonal Organization* (1953). In modal jazz, improvisations are based on different scales, or modes, rather than CHORD CHANGES and songlike harmony. A SCALE is a predefined set of notes. The most familiar Western scale is the chromatic scale, which has 12 notes per octave. Jazz musicians playing modal jazz often draw upon scales other than those associated with the chromatic scale. The term *modal jazz* was created by composer George Russell. MILES DAVIS introduced the style in a big way with the release of the record *KIND OF BLUE* in 1959.

Modern Jazz Quartet, The

As jazz COMBOS go, most do not stay together for more than a few months or years. The American Modern Jazz Quartet (MJQ) is an exception to the rule. Founded in 1952 by PIANO player John Lewis, vibraphonist Milt Jackson, BASS player Percy Heath, and drummer KENNY CLARKE, this group remained a vital performing and recording unit for more than 20 years before they disbanded in 1974. Except for the departure of Clarke in 1954 and the arrival of drummer Connie Kay, the members of the QUARTET remained intact throughout its long and successful career. All four original members had come up playing with the stars of BEBOP in New York. The creation of the MJQ was an attempt on their part to create a brand of serious jazz that combined the discipline of classical music with the vibrancy of bop. The MJQ was essentially a RHYTHM SECTION using the piano and vibes as the melodic voices. Piano player John Lewis was classically trained and had already mastered a sparse style of playing while accompanying such heavyweight SOLO artists as

DIZZY GILLESPIE and LESTER YOUNG. Lewis's playing was decidedly classical in nature but with a jazz SWING. The more colorful melodic voice of the group was provided on the vibes by Milt Jackson. His fluid runs and precision harmonies contrasted nicely with Lewis's staid style, forming the creative tension that made the quartet's music bounce with excitement. The music of the MJQ might be viewed as conservative and dressy when compared to the shenanigans happening on other jazz fronts during the 1950s, 1960s, and 1970s. But they remained true to their musical values and created a body of impressive recorded works that demonstrate what virtuosity in jazz playing is all about.

Monk, Thelonious (1917–1982) *American piano player, composer, and bandleader*

In 1992, while making a campaign appearance on MTV, Bill Clinton told interviewer Tabitha Soren that when he was young, his dream had been to play SAXOPHONE with THELONIOUS MONK. To this comment, Soren replied quite seriously, "Who is the loneliest monk?" How quickly legends are forgotten! Funny as this is, Thelonious Monk was an iconoclastic COMPOSER of BEBOP whose lack of public charm was a turnoff to many people. His music was equally at odds with mainstream jazz. He was fortunate to be acknowledged as a jazz master during the peak of his career, but because he retired so early from the business (at age 58), the importance of his work seems to have prematurely faded from public memory. Fortunately, critics and jazz fans alike have kept his legend and influence alive so that every few years there seems to be a resurgence of interest in the loneliest monk's work.

He was born Thelonious Sphere Monk in Rocky Mount, North Carolina. His style is impossible to define. Although he is often thrown into the category of bebop, this is mainly because he was there in New York during the formative years of this style in the early 1940s. He was actually responsible for launching the career of the first truly great bop PIANO player, BUD POWELL, but could not quite be put into this category himself. This was due to his unorthodox compositions. He had a sharp, often blunt, attack on the keys. He used CHORDS that seemed out of tune to most people, a TECHNIQUE AVANT-GARDE composers call DISSONANCE. Although he used some techniques borrowed from STRIDE PIANO, his playing was not traditional.

He was the house piano player at MINTON'S PLAYHOUSE, the birthplace of bebop. Along with DIZZY GILLESPIE, BUD POWELL, and CHARLIE PARKER, Monk was instrumental in changing the rhythms, harmonies, and structures of jazz that transformed SWING into bop. He mostly worked as a leader of small COMBOS, although a few of his partnerships are legendary. When he and MILES DAVIS recorded together in 1954 (*Miles Davis and the Modern Jazz Giants*), the two almost came to blows over their musical differences. Even so, Davis later acknowledged Monk as one of his most important influences. Although not nearly so popular as other bop stars during the 1940s, Monk began to receive critical acclaim by the mid-1950s. He recorded with JOHN COLTRANE, led a 10-piece band in 1959, and toured widely with other jazz luminaries during the 1960s. He retired in 1975 due in part to illness.

Some of Monk's compositions are jazz classics, including "Round Midnight," "Straight No Chaser," "EPISTROPHY," "Blue Monk," and "Off Minor." As a truly experimental artist, he was always seeking new ways of working with chords, fresh approaches to SYNCOPATION, and surprisingly abstract melodic and SOLO development. Although a man of few words, and a challenge to anyone who tried to interview him, he is responsible for some of the wittiest lines ever uttered about jazz. Supposedly he once quipped that writing about jazz was like "dancing about architecture," an obvious barb aimed at those who tried to analyze his music on paper. Through it all, he had a demanding sense of perfection and a clear sense of what he was trying to accomplish. "You know, anybody can play a composition and use far-out chords and make it sound wrong," he once remarked. "It's making it sound right that's not easy."[141]

Monterey Jazz Festival

An annual jazz festival established in 1958 in Monterey, California, it is the major annual jazz festival on the West Coast of the United States. Founded by Jimmy Lyons, the first festival featured greats DIZZY GILLESPIE, LOUIS ARMSTRONG, John Lewis, Shelly Manne, GERRY MULLIGAN, ART FARMER, Ernestine Anderson, HARRY JAMES, MAX ROACH, and BILLIE HOLIDAY. Every year since then, the festival takes place on the third weekend in September.

Montgomery, Wes (1925–1968) *American electric guitarist*

Montgomery had a melodic, self-taught style that was influenced by CHARLIE CHRISTIAN. Montgomery's early professional gigs were with the LIONEL HAMPTON band in 1948–50. He toughed out the 1950s, working a day job and playing GIGS at night. Work opened up for him in the early 1960s after playing a SET with the JOHN COLTRANE sextet at the MONTEREY JAZZ FESTIVAL. Although he could play the bop style associated with Christian, in later years he developed a mellower sound. Unlike most guitarists, who use a finger or pick to pluck the strings, Montgomery only used his thumb. This gave his playing a softer quality. He combined playing solos on single strings with softly strummed chords and octave changes to create a mellow tone. This style earned him a spot on the pop charts in 1968 with a sleepy version of the Beatles song "A Day in the Life." He died suddenly of a heart attack the same year. His quietly dazzling sound influenced a generation of guitarists who were leaving rock and roll and trying to find a voice for themselves in jazz.

Montreux Jazz Festival

Europe's most important annual jazz festival, it takes place in the Swiss town of Montreux each summer. Founded in 1967, it has always featured a mix of jazz greats, up-and-coming European artists, and rock and pop acts.

Morgan, Lee (1938–1972) *American trumpet player*

Morgan hailed from Philadelphia and developed a smooth HARD BOP style of playing while working with DIZZY GILLESPIE (1956–58) and ART BLAKEY (1958–61). He led his own group in the early 1960s but withdrew from the jazz scene for part of 1962 and 1963 because of health problems resulting from drug abuse. Thinking he was dead, one radio announcer even programmed a memorial service for him! After regaining his health, Morgan came back with a roar, recording his most popular album, *The Sidewinder* (1963). It also featured tenor saxophonist JOE HENDERSON. *The Sidewinder* revealed a hip, Latin-tinged funk style that had crossover appeal to those less familiar with jazz. Morgan began as a practitioner of CLIFFORD BROWN's smooth, round TRUMPET sound. To this he added his own punchy attack to melodies and a surging tone that was often spun around long, sustained phrases. His end came unceremoniously in 1972, when he was shot to death in a nightclub by a female acquaintance.

Jelly Roll Morton

Morton, Jelly Roll (Ferdinand Joseph La Menthe) (1890–1941) *American piano player, arranger, composer, and bandleader*

Ferdinand Joseph La Menthe "Jelly Roll" Morton was one of the first jazz composers and a colorful influence in the shaping of early jazz history. He hailed from New Orleans, the cauldron of jazz, where he divided his time as a young man between playing PIANO, hustling, billiards, and entertaining in minstrel shows. He developed a style of music that blended the many influences in his experience: classical music, RAGTIME, BLUES, spirituals, marches, and popular song. He took the essential SYNCOPATION of ragtime music and gave it a lighter, more rhythmically dynamic feeling.

He blended diverse forms of music and also established the piano player as the central figure in jazz composition. His TECHNIQUE was superb, and it suited his flashy personality. He could play two melodies at the same time, as if he were composing parts for other players. He was one of the first to distribute jazz compositions by sheet music. He was also instrumental in taking early jazz outside of New Orleans and teaching others how to play it. He did not gain fame until the age of recordings. His most celebrated records were made in Chicago and New York with his group the Red Hot Peppers between 1926 and 1930. These were his most successful years. Among his best-known recordings are "The Pearls" (1923), "Wolverine Blues" (1923), "BLACK BOTTOM STOMP" (1926), "King Porter Stomp" (1926), and "Jelly Roll Blues" (1924). His popularity dimmed when the era of BIG BAND SWING took over during the 1930s.

He spent the last years of his life often embroiled in controversy, largely due to his published claims in 1938 that he, and he alone, had created jazz in

1902. Historians have consistently debunked this myth. Jazz was not so much an invention by any one individual as it was the result of many cultural influences that materialized bit by bit from the hands of many. Morton's understanding of what makes jazz different from other music is indisputable. He said that, "Jazz music is a style, not compositions; any kind of music may be played in jazz, if one has the knowledge."[142]

Moseka, Aninata See ABBEY LINCOLN.

Moten, Bennie (1894–1935) *American piano player, composer, and bandleader*
Moten hailed from Kansas City and was one of the originators of the hard-driving KANSAS CITY JAZZ style made famous later by COUNT BASIE. Moten started out playing RAGTIME and NEW ORLEANS JAZZ in Kansas City. By the late 1920s he had built his trio into a BIG BAND that was a popular dance orchestra. Many well-known players got their start playing with Moten, including Count Basie and BEN WEBSTER. Moten toured constantly and was at the peak of his powers as a bandleader and performer when he died prematurely at age 41 during a tonsillectomy. Basie took over the band when Moten died, forming the core of the Count Basie Orchestra that followed.

movies See APPENDIX IV: JAZZ IN THE MOVIES.

Mulligan, Gerry (1927–1996) *American baritone, soprano, clarinet, and piano player, composer, arranger, and bandleader*
Mulligan is the most important and influential baritone SAXOPHONE player in jazz history. He was also a gifted ARRANGER and COMPOSER. His first work was writing arrangements for radio orchestras. This led to his job as a SIDEMAN in GENE KRUPA's band, for which he also composed and wrote arrangements. He received wide acclaim at the time for his com-

position "Disc Jockey Jump" (1947) and his ARRANGEMENT of the bop standard "How High the Moon" (1940), both recorded with Krupa in 1946–47. Along with GIL EVANS and MILES DAVIS, Mulligan was a key composer, arranger, and player in the *BIRTH OF THE COOL* sessions in the late 1940s. Taking advantage of the critical acclaim won by the *Cool* sessions, Mulligan was able to strike out on his own as an arranger and bandleader.

The baritone saxophone is not the most used horn in jazz, but Mulligan was proving that this large, awkward instrument could have a leading role. As if to drive this point home, his first QUARTET

Gerry Mulligan

1954 by pianist George Wein. Jazz greats including LOUIS ARMSTRONG, DUKE ELLINGTON, and DAVE BRUBECK performed at the festival in its early years. The program continues to draw the biggest names in jazz to its annual weekend event. Now known as the JVC International Jazz Festival since 1984, the annual event takes place in Newport, Rhode Island. It is the major annual jazz festival on the East Coast of the United States.

New York

New York City may not be the birthplace of jazz, but any early jazz musician who was destined for success usually found it after making it in New York. The JAZZ AGE was all about the music of New York. That's where the record companies were. That's where jazz got on the radio. Musicians migrated to New York from New Orleans and Chicago, but many were local musicians as well. What made New York jazz different was its sophistication. Composers such as DUKE ELLINGTON and JAMES P. JOHNSON combined elements of European music with jazz from the South. The ARRANGEMENTs were elegant. The larger jazz orchestras did not use IMPROVISATION as much as New Orleans and Chicago groups. Instead, they played sweeping horn arrangements and clever combinations of instruments. In time, New York jazz would be characterized as fast and HOT JAZZ, open to experimentation, and willing to mix with the rhythm of other cultures, particularly Cuba and Latin America. It is doubtful that the hectic pace and rapid-fire solos of BEBOP could have originated anywhere but in New York.

See also CARNEGIE HALL; COTTON CLUB; HARLEM; HARLEM RENAISSANCE; JAZZ AT LINCOLN CENTER.

nonet

A COMBO consisting of nine musicians, bigger than a combo but not quite a BIG BAND, the nonet offers the bandleader a unique sound that can be both big and small. No instrument dominates the sound of a nonet because there are usually no more than two of any one kind of instrument. The ARRANGER must rely on clever combinations of different instruments to define the mood and soul of music played by a nonet. While SOLOS are important to a nonet, they tend to blend more with the overall texture and direction of the music rather than breaking free as they do in a smaller or larger band.

Norvo, Red (1908–1999) *American vibraphone and xylophone player*

Red Norvo was born Kenneth Norville in Beardstown, Illinois. He first learned PIANO but switched to xylophone while in high school. He was the first musician to bring a mallet instrument into mainstream jazz playing. At first a novelty in jazz, the man with the mallets began a promising career first as a radio studio musician for NBC before he joined the PAUL WHITEMAN Orchestra around 1930.

Norvo was an astonishingly creative musician who did for the xylophone what SIDNEY BECHET did for the SAXOPHONE. Norvo provided the style, the TECHNIQUE, and the imagination needed to make a mallet instrument a SOLO instrument in jazz. His first recordings in 1932 revealed a mature player with a sensibility for SWING. He played two- and four-mallet styles and delighted in unusual arrangements that would highlight the wide, mellow range of the xylophone. One of his most influential and beautiful recordings was "BIX" BEIDERBECKE's "In a Mist," made in 1933. He took the trumpeter's tune and scored it for five-octave "instrument" that combined the xylophone and marimba, Bass CLARINET (played by BENNY GOODMAN), BASS, and GUITAR.[144]

This piano-less jazz QUARTET blended the bass clarinet and mallet instruments in a moving rendition of this ballad that some think is an improvement on its COMPOSER's rendition.

Norvo made several attempts to maintain his own larger swing bands, but the public never quite warmed-up to his quiet swing. In 1943 he switched from xylophone to vibes, which provided a richer sound that could be sustained longer. Norvo also concentrated on working with small groups at this time, which was a more popular showcase for his talents. He was in great demand around this time, touring off and on with Benny Goodman and using both DIZZY GILLESPIE and CHARLIE PARKER as sidemen (see SIDEMAN). In the 1950s, working in a trio format, featuring CHARLES MINGUS for a time on bass, Norvo helped usher in the era of COOL JAZZ with its gently percolating rhythmic interplay. He worked steadily after 1960 as a featured artist in Las Vegas until a stroke in 1986 made it difficult for him to play anymore.

Norway   See EUROPEAN JAZZ.

O'Farrill, Chico (1921–2001) *Cuban composer, arranger, and trumpet player*

O'Farrill was a leading COMPOSER of the Afro-Cuban jazz movement. He first came to New York in 1948 and joined the Latin jazz experiments already underway by DIZZY GILLESPIE and CHANO POZO. O'Farrill's specialty was extended jazz pieces. His work was performed by many of the great SWING and BOP artists, including BENNY GOODMAN and STAN KENTON, and his "Afro-Cuban Jazz Suite" was recorded in 1950, featuring CHARLIE PARKER and BUDDY RICH. Other noted works that blended his sophisticated composition methods with the purifying energy of Latin jazz included "The Aztec Suite" (1959), written for trumpeter ART FARMER, and "Six Jazz Moods" (1962). After spending much of the 1970s and 1980s making a living writing commercial jingles, there was a resurgence of interest in O'Farrill's music around 1993. In the last years of his life, he led a BIG BAND in weekly performances at BIRDLAND in New York, took part in newly minted recordings of his works, and wrote new orchestral works, including *Trumpet Fantasy* (1995) for WYNTON MARSALIS.

Although his style could be called brash and over the top at times, there is no doubt that O'Farrill's enthusiastic blend of Latin and American jazz has had a lasting influence on a new generation of jazz composers. He took the excitement of Latin rhythms and instrumental arrangements and skillfully integrated them with elements of serious classical music. The idea that this was even possible first occurred to him when he came to New York in 1948. "That's when I saw the possibilities," O'Farrill

remembered. "You didn't need to sacrifice the richness of jazz to keep that drive going. You didn't have to be simplistic to be rhythmic."[145]

Oliver, Joseph "King" (1885–1938) *American cornetist and bandleader*

Early jazz had its roots in the music of African Americans living on plantations just after the Civil War. King Oliver personally witnessed this transition. He was probably born on a plantation and later raised in New Orleans. He gained early fame playing for KID ORY's band and then moved to Chicago, where he formed the Creole Jazz Band. The band included several of the best musicians playing New Orleans– and Chicago-style jazz: Oliver and Armstrong on cornets, Honore Dutrey on trombone, Bill Johnson on string bass, JOHNNY DODDS on clarinet, BABY DODDS on drums, and LIL HARDIN (who married Armstrong in 1924) on piano. This extraordinary talented group went into the recording studio in 1923 and laid down some classic tracks of New Orleans jazz, including "Riverside Blues," "Chimes Blues," and "Dipper Mouth Blues." These recordings captured the art of New Orleans jazz in its finest form, featured inspired duets by Armstrong and Oliver, and the King's famous solo on "Dipper Mouth Blues." Oliver was a disciplined player with excellent TECHNIQUE. He often used mutes, cups, and glasses to change the sound of the horn, sometimes creating a wah wah effect. The music of this group was intense and punchy. The Creole Jazz Band offered probably

Joseph "King" Oliver (top center) and band

the truest rendition of the early NEW ORLEANS JAZZ style to be heard in other parts of the United States. Oliver's skill was greatly admired among other trumpeters, including Armstrong, who acknowledged him as his most important influence.

organ

The electric organ is a keyboard instrument that has its roots in church music. It became a popular jazz instrument during the 1940s and 1950s and continues to be the instrument of choice for some jazz keyboard players. The HAMMOND ORGAN is the most popular organ among jazz players. Its warm, undulating tones are created by an analog process employing 91 spinning tone wheels. The various voices of the organ are controlled by "draw bars" that can change the sound of the instrument in varying degrees. The models B-3 and B3000 and

their cousins are the instruments of choice for most devoted jazz organ players. The B-3 has two 61-note keyboards, special effects including VIBRATO, and a full complement of BASS pedals. It was first used in the 1950s and is still highly prized. The electric organ may also be used to play bass notes in the absence of a string bass or bass GUITAR player. This can be done using either foot pedals or the left hand. Influential organ players of jazz include JIMMY SMITH, RICHARD "GROOVE" HOLMES, SHIRLEY SCOTT, and LARRY YOUNG.

Original Dixieland Jazz Band

Many times in the history of jazz, white musicians have found commercial success at making jazz before their African-American forebears. This is a tale often repeated in the course of jazz history. The first such instance of note was that of the

Original Dixieland Jazz Band (ODJB). Founded by Nick La Rocca in 1916, the group played their version of the New Orleans–style jazz made by black combos such as those led by FREDDIE KEPPARD and JOSEPH "KING" OLIVER. The five young white players were no mere amateurs, however. Hailing from New Orleans, they had frequented jazz clubs for many years. La Rocca himself had played in more than a dozen groups prior to forming the ODJB. They turned out to be good students of African-American music.

The ODJB got their first big GIG in Chicago and soon caught the attention of record PRODUCERS eager to capture the sound of NEW ORLEANS JAZZ on record for the first time. But they may not have been the first choice to make the historic record. The legend goes that CORNET player FREDDIE KEPPARD, of the Original Creole Band, was first asked to make a record. This prominent African-American jazz musician might have been the first to record a jazz record except that he refused because he didn't want anyone to copy his LICKS! A record company next

Original Dixieland Jazz Band

turned to the ODJB, and they obliged. In 1917 they recorded the first piece of jazz music, entering the history books with a lively novelty piece called the "LIVERY STABLE BLUES." It became an instant hit. It was a watered-down version of New Orleans jazz, featuring the players doing imitations of barnyard animals, but it put the sound of jazz in the homes of many American who otherwise would not have heard it. It was the beginning of the growing explosion of interest in jazz. Whatever happened to Freddie Keppard? He didn't make any records until he was past his best playing days, so no one will ever hear what kinds of licks he was jealously protecting. The ODJB disbanded in 1925.

Ory, Kid (1886–1973) *American trombone player, composer, and bandleader*

Ory was a product of the melting pot of turn-of-the-century New Orleans culture. He was Creole of African-American, French, Spanish, and Native American ancestry. Originally a BANJO player during the formative years of jazz in New Orleans, Edward "Kid" Ory switched to TROMBONE and by 1917 was leading his own band. At one time or another his sidemen (see SIDEMAN) included KING OLIVER, LOUIS ARMSTRONG, SIDNEY BECHET, and others, some of the seminal names of early jazz. He moved to California in 1919 and established Kid Ory's Creole Orchestra with some transplanted New Orleans musicians. In 1922 Ory and his group became the first African-American players to make an authentic recording of NEW ORLEANS JAZZ. He played with Louis Armstrong, JELLY ROLL MORTON, and King Oliver in the mid- to late 1920s, before retiring in the 1930s to run a chicken farm. He made a comeback in the 1940s and 1950s, when New Orleans style jazz enjoyed a resurgence in popularity. He was the first great trombone player in jazz. He played what is called a "tailgate" style,

using the trombone to create a rhythm underneath the lead horn players, and providing sweeping slides and embellishments to ACCENT a tune.

Out There (1960) *album by Eric Dolphy*

While his more popular recording, *Out to Lunch*, might be more accessible, *Out There*, released by Prestige, is a clear example of what made ERIC DOLPHY so admired by his peers. His technical virtuosity and quickly shifting IMPROVISATION are simply startling. The opening track, "Out There" begins with a SOLO by RON CARTER on cello, after which Dolphy explodes into a double-time alto SAXOPHONE solo that hardly breathes for three minutes. Avoiding any recognizable CHORD progression, he simply flies through a line of notes that walks the scales, is embellished by twisty VIBRATO, and somehow all makes sense as if it were all preconceived. There are some clear MONK and MINGUS influences here, with a BLUES undercurrent on some of the tamer tracks.

overdubbing

A recording technique in which two or more audio tracks are combined to create the final version of a recorded piece of music. Prior to the availability of the tape recorder about 1950, all music was recorded live in one take, with all of the musicians, including vocalists, performing at the same time as if they were in concert. With the advent of the tape recorder, it became possible to construct a piece of music using multiple tracks. Musicians' parts could be recorded individually, at different times, or even in different locations. Then the best "takes" for each were selected and combined (mixed) to create the final product. Overdubs are also used to create novel effects, such as adding multiple vocal tracks by the same musician or making a few singers sound like a chorus.

Parker, Charlie (1920–1955) *alto saxophone player*

Charlie "Bird" Parker grew up in Kansas City, the home of a vibrant jazz movement in the 1920s and 1930s. Bird was one of the most original and influential jazz soloists of all time. His distinctively powerful sound and rapid-fire delivery set new standards for jazz SAXOPHONE. He was the most original player on this instrument since SIDNEY BECHET first dazzled audiences in the 1920s.

After taking several jobs playing mainstream band music, Parker's personal breakthrough came when he joined Billy Eckstine's band in New York. One of Parker's band mates was trumpeter DIZZY GILLESPIE. While in New York, Parker also heard the extraordinarily new sounds of drummer KENNY CLARKE and jazz PIANO innovator THELONIOUS MONK, both of whom inspired him to experiment more freely by pushing the limits of his own style of play. Together, Parker and Gillespie shaped the exciting jazz style called BEBOP.

Bebop pushed the skill of the artist to the extreme with its lightning-fast melodies, harmonic shifts, and dazzling rhythms. In the creation of bebop, Parker and Gillespie also succeeded in reclaiming a piece of jazz for black artists, many of whom had been shoved aside during the 1940s as white mainstream bands took over the popular jazz music scene. Bebop was in many ways too difficult for most other players to copy, regardless of race.

Many of Parker's brightest moments in music were captured on record. He played with many of the most noted jazz artists of his time. Other musicians were awed and humbled by his talent. CHARLES MINGUS, who was not normally generous with his praise, noted that "Most of the soloists at Birdland had to wait for Parker's next record in order to find out what to play next."[146]

Charlie Parker

In addition to Gillespie, his list of collaborators included pianist Monk, bassist Charles Mingus, drummers BUDDY RICH and MAX ROACH, and trumpeter MILES DAVIS. Notable songs featuring Parker on record include "Night in Tunisia," "SALT PEANUTS," "Embraceable You," and "Parker's Mood."

Unfortunately, Parker was troubled by drug abuse that eventually brought an end to his life at the young age of 35. His original playing, extraordinary skill, and innovation made Parker one of the greatest of all jazz legends. Bandleader Jay "Hootie" McShann once remarked, "They said Bird played bebop, but Bird could still swing. I've heard a lot of guys play bebop, but they wasn't swinging."

Pastorius, Jaco (1951–1987) *American bass guitar player and composer*

Guitarist PAT METHENY called Pastorius ". . . the last jazz musician of the 20th century to have made a major impact on the musical world at large."[147]

This praise can be justified, explains Metheny, by the number of times a day you hear someone copying the LICKS of the innovative BASS player.

Pastorius came of age in Fort Lauderdale, Florida. At first a drummer, he settled on playing bass GUITAR by default. He was 16 at the time and playing DRUMS with a local group, Los Olas Brass. He lost his drumming job to the more accomplished Rich Franks. When the bass player for the group quit during a rehearsal, Pastorius said he would play bass for them. They gave him a week to learn his parts, and he quickly mastered them.[148]

He played backup to rock and soul artists and even took a GIG on a Caribbean cruise ship where his exposure to reggae became an influence on his fluid, worldly style. His start in jazz came in 1969, when he wrote arrangements and played bass for a bop-style BIG BAND led by Ira Sullivan in Florida. Still only a teen, the young musician was on his way to early stardom.

His big break came in 1975, when his playing impressed Bobby Colomby when he visited Florida with his jazz-rock band Blood, Sweat, and Tears.

Colomby brought Pastorius to New York and produced his first album with the help of HERBIE HANCOCK, WAYNE SHORTER, and others. Released in 1976 Pastorius's fluent and lyrical bass playing made an immediate impact. In 1976 he was hired by WEATHER REPORT as their new bass player and stayed with them during five of the group's most fruitful years. By 1981 his unique voice on bass had become as recognizable to Weather Report fans as those of keyboard player JOE ZAWINUL and saxophonist Shorter. Pastorius's style of playing had broad appeal and resulted in several collaborations with rock artists, including Blood, Sweat, and Tears and Joni Mitchell.

After leaving Weather Report, he formed his own group, Word of Mouth. Using a lineup that included bass, steel drums, and horns, the music relied heavily on the bass to voice the melodies. Although his career was skyrocketing at the time, Pastorius was unable to overcome mental problems caused by drug and alcohol abuse. His career slowly declined in the mid-1980s after his increasingly erratic and unreliable behavior. He died as the result of a beating by a bouncer outside a Florida nightclub in 1987. STANLEY CLARKE and Pastorius were the most influential electric bass players of the 1970s.

Pastorius was a pioneer of the fretless electric bass, an instrument that gave his CHORD and note fingering a fluid, distinctive sound. As a jazz player, he was accomplished at various styles of playing that were demanded of him in Weather Report. But he most excelled at playing solos where his dazzling command of his instrument and extraordinary ear for melody were best showcased. He had fluid style and could switch from funk to reggae to FREE JAZZ styles of playing with uncanny flair. His sound was full and honey-toned, and rich with expression. He made innovative use of special effects such as delay and reverb, accompanying himself by playing suspended to which he could add melodies and RIFFS. The legacy of his musical imagination lives on in the playing of many of today's best bassists, including MARCUS MILLER, RICHARD BONA, and STEVE SWALLOW.

Peterson, Oscar (b. 1925) *Canadian piano player, composer, and bandleader*

One of the best-loved and accomplished pianists in jazz history, Oscar Peterson has been playing professionally for more than 50 years. His strong-willed father, an amateur musician, insisted that all five of his children learn to play the PIANO and various BRASS instruments. Peterson was a quick learner and while still a teenager took classical piano lessons from an accomplished Hungarian pianist, Paul de Marky. At age 14, Peterson won a national amateur contest sponsored by the Canadian Broadcasting Corporation and garnered the chance to play on the radio each week during a program called Fifteen Minutes' Piano Rambling.[149]

Before too long, he was beginning to play with other musicians in and around Montreal, including high school chum MAYNARD FERGUSON.

Peterson's first important professional GIG was with the Johnny Holmes Orchestra (1942 to 1947), a dance band that also included Maynard Ferguson and his brother Percy. Peterson was the only black member of the band. Soon word of his immense talent made it to the United States, and in 1949 jazz PRODUCER Norman Granz brought the pianist to New York as a performing guest at his JAZZ AT THE PHILHARMONIC series backed by BASS player RAY BROWN and drummer BUDDY RICH. Peterson was a hit and joined the Philharmonic tour for several years. For the first two years of the tour, Peterson was teamed only with Brown. In the third year Granz suggested that he bring on a third player.

Peterson first added a drummer but soon decided that a trio consisting of piano, bass, and GUITAR would be more to his liking. This trio format had already become popular in the hands of NAT KING COLE, and it was emulated by many others including ART TATUM and Peterson. After a year working with two other guitarists, Peterson found in Herb Ellis the perfect guitar player to complement his sophisticated, modern style of SWING. The Oscar Peterson Trio, including Ray Brown and Herb Ellis, was one of the hardest-working and most admired

Oscar Peterson

trios in all of jazz. So enamored of Nat King Cole was Peterson that he took a turn at vocals during this period as well. But it was always his sophisticated, yet classic, piano playing that garnered the most praise.

After 1958 the makeup of the trio changed from time to time, and Peterson began to explore his role as a collaborator with many of the greatest names in jazz, including DIZZY GILLESPIE, LESTER YOUNG, LOUIS ARMSTRONG, Stephane Grappelli, COUNT BASIE, ELLA FITZGERALD, and LIONEL HAMPTON. His fame spread to Europe, where he was a frequent visitor and participant in concerts and festivals. By the 1970s, continuing under the production guidance of Granz, Peterson successfully explored a career as a SOLO artist. It was in these recordings that best illustrated his tremendous TECHNIQUE and knowledge of music. In the 1980s, with the onset of arthritis, Peterson did less

thing called creativity but from different sides of the bank. So what would I call it? Basically it's just Now Jazz, it's just New Jazz, there's no other way. It's not something that could have been done in the 50s or the 60s. It's now."[153]

pocket trumpet

A compact version of the standard three-valve TRUMPET. It is preferred for its high, clear tones by some jazz musicians including DON CHERRY.

polyrhythm

The playing of two or more independent rhythms to create contrast in a piece of music. An example in jazz might be having the string bass player using a different beat than the drummer or having two contrasting drummers.

Ponty, Jean-Luc (b. 1942) *French violin player*

Ponty was the leading proponent of jazz VIOLIN coming out of the early 1970s FUSION jazz movement. A classically trained musician, he left the world of symphonic music, plugged in his violin, and went after a career in rock and jazz. He developed a bouncy BEBOP style of playing that emulated horn players rather than past greats of jazz violin. He recorded his first SOLO album in 1964 at age 22 and soon found himself in great demand as a guest artist and SIDEMAN. In 1967, in his first American concert appearance, he played with John Lewis of the MODERN JAZZ QUARTET at the MONTEREY JAZZ FESTIVAL, the same festival that featured rock stars such as Jimi Hendrix. This led to more recordings and a fruitful working relationship with progressive rocker Frank Zappa (1969–73). He joined the MAHAVISHNU ORCHESTRA for recordings and tours from 1973 to 1975, then moved to America and began to lead his own groups.

He has continued in the fusion jazz vein both as a guest artist and a leader. Ponty's virtuosity on the violin is without peer. Perhaps more important, he

took the violin to the next stage of its evolution as a jazz instrument by plugging it into an amplifier and working with effects and synthesizers to embellish the sound. Ponty did for the violin what MILES DAVIS did for the TRUMPET—he used electronics to broaden its reach as an instrument. More than that, he modernized violin playing so that it could coexist in even the most electrified of jazz COMBOS.

Powell, Bud (1924–1966) *American piano player and composer*

Bud Powell was the first great BEBOP PIANO player. He was a gifted student of music who by age 10, his father recalled, could already play "everything he'd heard by Fats Waller and Art Tatum."[154]

While working alongside rising bop stars DIZZY GILLESPIE and CHARLIE PARKER in the mid-1940s, he developed a liberating keyboard style that could match the energy and pace of the horn players who most defined bebop. Before Powell, jazz piano clung to either a heavily CHORD-based structure for supporting other players or the delicate and bouncy rhythm of stride playing (see STRIDE PIANO). Powell unleashed the piano, focusing on long, extended solos using his amazingly gifted TECHNIQUE.

Some of his ideas were derived from ART TATUM and THELONIOUS MONK, whom he greatly admired. His patented sound used the left hand sparingly while the right hand danced acrobatically over the keys with remarkable pace and touch. No one disputes that Bud Powell was the first to synthesize the chemistry of bop horn playing with the piano, making it an equal partner. Monk was well aware of the genius of Powell's playing. Following Powell's death, Monk remarked, "No one could play like Bud; too difficult, too quick, incredible!"[155]

With Monk's help, he first appeared at MINTON'S PLAYHOUSE in New York during the genesis of bebop. He was a member of Cootie Williams's group with whom he made his first records in 1943 and 1944. After that he was a well-known face on the bop scene and played with CHARLIE CHRISTIAN,

Bud Powell

Parker, Gillespie, SID CATLETT, Dexter Gordon, and many others.

Unfortunately, Powell was a tortured soul who, beginning with a hospital stay in 1945, suffered from recurring bouts of mental illness mixed with substance abuse for the rest of his short life. This did not prevent him from influencing others, and he was admired by nearly every great player in jazz. He wrote and recorded several classics of bebop including "Tempus Fugit," "Dance of the Infidels," "Un Poco Loco," "Hallucinations," and "Glass Enclosure," the titles of the latter three poking fun at his own mental illness. His recording with

Charlie Parker, *Jazz at Massey Hall* (1953) is an undeniable classic. Although he was institutionalized much of the time in the 1950s, things were looking up when he moved to Paris with his wife and son in 1959.

He played on the Paris scene, formed his own trio, and seemed to be recuperating. However, he contracted tuberculosis in 1962. Although he could still perform, upon returning to the United States to play BIRDLAND in 1964, his health began to fail again. He died in Brooklyn after two years of inactivity and illness. Fortunately, he left behind a legacy of music that influenced an entire generation of new players. Keyboard player HERBIE HANCOCK has said about Powell, "Every jazz pianist since Bud either came through him or is deliberately attempting to get away from playing like him."[156]

Pozo, Chano (1915–1948) *Cuban percussionist and singer*

Pozo was a major influence in the development of Afro-Cuban jazz in America. He was essentially a folk musician who was schooled in Cuban and West African melodies and rhythms. After coming to America, he was teamed with the DIZZY GILLESPIE BIG BAND for a performance at CARNEGIE HALL in 1947. The result was the first widely acknowledged success at combining Afro-Cuban folk music with jazz, especially BEBOP. Some of the songs made famous by Pozo's association with Gillespie were "Cubana Be, Cubana Bop" (1947), and "Tin Tin Deo." His career in America was short-lived; Pozo was killed in a bar fight in New York in 1948. His contributions to the origins of Afro-Cuban jazz and his penetrating style of drumming have had a lasting effect on this popular jazz style.

Preservation Hall, New Orleans

Dedicated to the playing of traditional NEW ORLEANS JAZZ, founded in 1961, located on St. Peter Street in the heart of the French Quarter of New Orleans, the club features nightly performances in a small, rustic hall reminiscent of the early days of jazz. The "house" band generally includes a seven-piece COMBO playing PIANO, TRUMPET, TROMBONE, CLARINET, string BASS, BANJO, and DRUMS, a format not unlike that used in the old days by "KING" OLIVER and LOUIS ARMSTRONG.

producer

The producer is the person in charge of a recording SESSION or concert performance. Producers work with musicians to select the music, ARRANGEMENTS, and instrumental combinations that will best spotlight an artist's talents. Producers often develop a long-term working relationship with a musician. Several well-known jazz producers include Teo Macero (Columbia Records), Francis Wolff (Blue Note), Orrin Keepnews (Riverside/Fantasy), George Avakian (Columbia), Bob Thiele (Impulse), John Hammond (Columbia), and LEONARD FEATHER.

progressive jazz

A composed form of jazz made popular by STAN KENTON and GIL EVANS during the 1940s and 1950s. It combined jazz elements and instruments with those of classical music. It could also be called symphonic jazz.

Puente, Tito (1925–2000) *American vibraphone, timbales, and percussion player and bandleader*

Tito (Ernestito Antonio) Puente was born of Puerto Rican parents in New York City. Known fondly as the MAMBO King, Puente was instrumental in fusing the sounds of Latin popular music and jazz. He was playing professionally by age 16 in local Latin groups. He became interested in BIG BAND music in the 1940s and studied for two years at the Juilliard School. He led his own Latin-influenced groups in the 1950s, when he became known for his energetic performances and mambo dance hits. His signature instrument was the timbale, a set of high-pitched DRUMS that are struck with a drum stick.

He was a great showman with a jubilant smile and energy that never seemed to quit. He collaborated with many jazz artists over the years, including Cal Tjader and WOODY HERMAN, and was a familiar face on television for many years. In the 1980s he formed the Latin Percussion Jazz Ensemble and toured widely. He continued to work all his life, but it wasn't until the late 1980s and 1990s, with a resurgence in the popularity of Latin music in North America, that he once again attained the level of name recognition that he once knew in the 1950s. His jazz work influenced many others who continue to make a unique blend of American and Latin jazz.

quartet

A COMBO consisting of four musicians. A TRADITIONAL JAZZ quartet consists of PIANO, BASS, DRUMS, and a melody instrument such as a SAXOPHONE or TRUMPET. A quartet is the most common size for a jazz combo because it includes a complete RHYTHM SECTION plus at least one soloist.

quintet

A COMBO consisting of five musicians. A quintet usually has a three-person rhythm section and two soloists.

race music

Term once given to music created by African-American artists, including folk, BLUES, and early jazz. Recordings of this music were called *race records,* a term that did not fade from use until about 1950, when the record industry adopted the term *rhythm and blues.* This was about the same time that the worlds of jazz and rhythm and blues were becoming widely multiracial.

See also RECORDINGS OF EARLY JAZZ.

race records

Popular recordings made before 1950 were given this name because they featured African-American musicians and were sold mainly to black audiences. As the popularity of jazz and BLUES crossed racial barriers, "race records" became known by the more enlightened name of "rhythm and blues."

See also RACE MUSIC; RECORDINGS OF EARLY JAZZ.

ragtime

A kick-up-your-heels style of music that was a precursor to jazz. Ragtime emerged during the 1890s and became wildly popular in the years following 1900. Combining elements of European classical music with African-American influences, it used SYNCOPATION to create a "ragged" bounce in the music. Ragtime was most often associated with PIANO playing COMPOSERs, including SCOTT JOPLIN and JELLY ROLL MORTON.

Rainey, Ma (Gertrude Malissa Nix Pridgett)
(1886–1939) *American singer*

Gertrude Pridgett, also known as Ma Rainey, first performed with her family in minstrel shows in the southern United States. She was 16 when she married Will "Pa" Rainey, another entertainer. Together, they put together their own road show and began a tour featuring popular songs and the blues. Ma befriended Bessie Smith (no relation) in 1912, and gave the young woman lessons in the blues and her first important public performances. The "Mother of the Blues" forged a successful career of performing and recording the blues throughout the 1920s. She had her own band but had also been accompanied by such jazz greats as LOUIS ARMSTRONG, FLETCHER HENDERSON, Tampa Red, and TOMMY DORSEY. She was widely recorded, having laid down over a hundred songs. Rainey is one of the earliest historical links to the southern blues tradition of the 19th century.

recordings of early jazz

Jazz grew up about the same time that music was first being recorded. Record releases prior to 1915 were mainly of popular songs and classical music. The most successful record companies, including Victor and Columbia, were at first reluctant to record jazz. They considered it RACE MUSIC since it was mostly played by African Americans. They did not believe that recordings made by black musicians would appeal to white buyers. An early exception to this belief were the wonderful records made for Victor by the talented COMPOSER and bandleader JAMES REESE EUROPE and his Society Orchestra. In 1914 he became the first African-American bandleader to record with an ENSEMBLE consisting of all black musicians. The style of music they recorded was RAGTIME rather than jazz, but it was nonetheless a significant breakthrough for African-American artists.

By about 1915 jazz was spreading from New Orleans to other regions of the country, most notably Chicago and New York. Record companies took note. They began snooping around for artists to record. FREDDIE KEPPARD, of the Original Creole Orchestra, was one of the best African-American jazz artists around. A record company approached him in 1917 to make the first recording of genuine NEW ORLEANS JAZZ. Afraid that others would copy his LICKS, Keppard reportedly refused the offer. As fate would have it, then, Victor signed the all-white ORIGINAL DIXIELAND JAZZ BAND in 1917 and jazz history was made. Their recording of the funny "LIVERY STABLE BLUES" became an instant hit. With the success of this record, the race was on to issue more recordings of jazz.

The first recording by an African-American COMBO playing in the New Orleans style was the band of trombonist KID ORY in 1922. PIANO players, including FATS WALLER and COUNT BASIE, also made their first recordings in that same year. KING OLIVER's band, featuring LOUIS ARMSTRONG, made its first records in 1923. Armstrong himself, after having left Oliver's band, made perhaps the most famous and influential jazz recordings of all time in 1926 and 1927. He recorded a number of songs, including "HEEBIE JEEBIES," with his Hot Five QUINTET in 1926. This song featured the first important example of recorded SCAT SINGING, which Armstrong later claimed was actually due to his forgetting the lyrics. In 1927 he formed a combo of seven players (the Hot Seven) and laid down some of the baddest tracks ever to be recorded. Armstrong's music and the performances of his group departed for the first time from the traditional style of New Orleans jazz. Rather than every

musician playing melodies at the same time and none taking the LEAD, Armstrong and his players took turns on SOLOS. Thus, with his HOT FIVE AND HOT SEVEN recordings, Louis Armstrong established jazz as the soloist's art.

By about 1920 several record companies began producing a line of recordings that they called "RACE RECORDS" because they were aimed at the African-American audience and featured black performers. The most successful of these companies were Okeh Records, Vocalion, Paramount, Columbia, and Victor. Harry Herbert Pace founded the first black-owned record company, Black Swan, in 1921. The struggling company met with many obstacles put in their way by white-owned record companies but managed to produce some important recordings. FLETCHER HENDERSON, who would pioneer the concept of BIG BAND SWING music, was the house piano player at Black Swan. Thanks to two big hits recorded by Ethel Waters in 1921, "Down Home Blues" and "Oh Daddy," Pace's company was able to survive its bumpy first year.

After two more years of relative success for Black Swan, white-owned companies wanted a piece of the action and began to compete for the right to record major Black artists. Pace's small company was not able to match their offers, began to lose his most important recording stars, and by 1923 had to declare bankruptcy. In its brief three-year history, however, Black Swan had demonstrated that recordings by African-American artists had wide commercial appeal, a significant development for jazz and popular music.

Redman, Don (1900–1964) *American alto and soprano saxophone player, composer, arranger, and bandleader*

Redman was a solid jazz figure in the era preceding World War II. He came from a musical family and earned a degree in music from Storer College in 1920.[157]

He was a classically trained COMPOSER and could play many orchestra instruments, a talent that enabled him to take a new approach to arranging BIG BAND jazz. He took a job as an ARRANGER and lead saxophonist for FLETCHER HENDERSON in 1923. During the mid-1920s he was a featured accompanist on recordings by BLUES singers Bessie Smith and Ethel Waters. In 1927 he left Henderson's band to take a job as musical director of McKinney's Cotton Pickers. Why he did this was a matter of debate because his accomplishments with the Henderson outfit were certainly more impressive than those with the Cotton Pickers. But this seemed to set a pattern of unfulfilled promise that followed him throughout his career.[158]

When given the chance, Redman seemed to take jobs that paid the bills over those that offered greater creative opportunity or that may have been noteworthy from an historical point of view.

There is no doubting, however, that he was one of the most sought-after arrangers for both small ensembles and big band orchestras. He arranged or composed music for LOUIS ARMSTRONG and His Savoy Ballroom Five, PAUL WHITEMAN, Ben Pollock, JIMMY DORSEY, COUNT BASIE, and many others. One of his early and most notable contributions to jazz arrangements came when he was working for Henderson. Louis Armstrong, already a famous SOLO artist, joined the band. The challenge for Redman was to find a way to integrate the brassy style of Armstrong's solos into the big band context. The result was a more up-TEMPO and energetic big band sound, making Redman one of the first arrangers to create the sound of SWING for a large ENSEMBLE.

Reeves, Diane (b. 1956) *American singer and composer*

Diane Reeves is a CONTEMPORARY JAZZ singer whose vocal style is often compared to the powerful intimacy of SARAH VAUGHN and the scat stylings of ELLA FITZGERALD. Reeves was discovered by CLARK TERRY while she was performing with her high school BIG BAND at a National Association of Jazz Educators Conference in Chicago. She began singing with Terry's jazz COMBO while she attended college. Her musical interests extended beyond jazz, however. She did SESSION work in Los Angeles on pop records, toured with the Brazilian group led by Sergio Mendez in 1981, and dabbled with the music of the West Indies while working with singer Harry Belafonte (1984).

Beginning in 1987, upon signing a record contract with Blue Note Records, she returned to jazz in a big way. It took several years for Reeves to win back jazz fans who had watched her drift into pop, Latin, and Caribbean music. She did so partly by working on her records with some of the biggest names in jazz: HERBIE HANCOCK, FREDDIE HUBBARD, McCOY TYNER, Tony Williams, and STANLEY CLARKE to name a few. She performed with BENNY CARTER at CARNEGIE HALL (1996). Her 2003 CD, *A Little Moonlight* (2003), was a focused, straight-up jazz recording that recalls everything from Sarah Vaughn and BETTY CARTER to ASTRUD GILBERTO. Her singing is warm, articulate, and knowledgeable of the rich history of jazz vocalists.

Reinhardt, Django (Jean-Baptiste Reinhardt) (1910–1953) *Belgian guitar player and composer*

Jean-Baptiste "Django" Reinhardt is a unique jazz legend and probably the most influential jazz artist from outside the United States. He was born in a Gypsy caravan and learned VIOLIN and acoustic GUITAR as a teen, first playing local folk songs. His left hand was so badly injured in a fire in 1928 that he lost the use of two of his fingers. Working around this disability, he developed a new method for fingering CHORDS and played a style that began to emphasize melodies over chords. He admired the playing of American EDDIE LANG and fused the folk sound of Gypsy music with American HOT JAZZ.

Prior to Reinhardt, most jazz guitarists only played brief solos consisting of chords. Reinhardt had a flamboyant and virtuosic style that could not be contained by chords. His work is lush with melodies and IMPROVISATIONS that run lines of notes all up and down the scale. His improvisations were ornate and worthy of any top-notch COMPOSER of modern music. He was marvelous at playing ballads but could make the guitar SWING. He could play lightning fast and, unlike CHARLIE CHRISTIAN, often embellished his notes with rich VIBRATO.

Reinhardt met French violinist Stephane Grappelli in 1934 and formed the QUINTET of the HOT CLUB DE FRANCE, a prolific COMBO that cut more than 200 tracks before the onset of World War II.[159]

While Grappelli left France during the German occupation, Reinhardt risked his life by staying behind. He survived the war by wandering with his fellow Gypsies but also by the aid of German officers who admired his work. His most-loved recordings include "Djangology" (1937, with Grappelli), "Swing Guitars" (1937), "Minor Swing" (1937, with Grappelli), and "Nuages" (1940, with brother Joseph also on guitar).

After the war, he made his one trip to America on the invitation of DUKE ELLINGTON. His first remark upon stepping off the boat was reportedly, "Where's Dizzy playing?"[160]

His visit was not long, but he played with Ellington a few times, immersed himself in BOP but did not like it much, and tried playing electrically amplified guitar for the first time. Back in Europe, he teamed up with Grappelli again for another series of astounding recordings. He continued his wandering ways for several years, picking up performances with a variety of combos. He lived life fully like a candle burning from both ends. He died suddenly of a stroke at age 43, at the top of his game. He was the first EUROPEAN JAZZ musician to have a significant influence on American players.

rhythm and blues

A rhythmic dance version of the BLUES that led to the development of rock and roll. Rhythm and blues was originally performed and associated with African-American artists and was called RACE MUSIC until about 1950.

rhythm section

The rhythm section of an ENSEMBLE consists of instruments that provide accompaniment to other musicians. A rhythm section includes instruments that play notes, chords (e.g., PIANO, GUITAR, vibes, and BASS), and beats (e.g., DRUMS, and congas). A typical rhythm section in a jazz COMBO includes a drummer, bass player, and piano player.

Rich, Buddy (1917–1987) *American drummer*

The dynamic Buddy (Bernard) Rich was a child star in his parents' vaudeville act, took up DRUMS, and was leading his own band by age 11. A lover of BIG BAND music, by age 21 he was already making a name for himself as one of the most swinging drummers around. His brash, no-holds-barred style was both athletic and dazzling. Drum SOLOS were a feature of his shows, and he loved to compete with fellow drummers for the bragging rights of being the world's greatest. His supersonic drumming style was the driving force behind the brash sound of the TOMMY DORSEY Orchestra. Rich seemed to bang on the snares so hard that they competed with the blaring horn section for attention.

After the decline of the big bands in the 1940s, Rich took up singing and worked in smaller groups. Then, in the 1960s, when Elvis and the Beatles were ruling the airwaves, he formed another big band that gained surprising popularity with a new generation. He was seen widely on television and often appeared as a drummer for singer Frank Sinatra. Rich toured the world and played to millions. He was arguably having the best time of his career when he died from heart failure in 1987. Even legendary drummer GENE KRUPA called Rich "The greatest drummer ever to have drawn breath."

ride cymbal

A suspended cymbal used by jazz drummers. It has a melodic "tinging" sound and is often used to keep time. The sound of a ride cymbal resonates for a long time unless the drummer mutes it with a hand.

ride rhythm

The CHING-chick-a-CHING-chick-a rhythm pattern played by a drummer on the ride cymbal to keep time.

riff

A riff is a short musical phrase or melody that is repeated during a song. It is usually used as background for a soloist and provides a common point of reference as the music develops.

Roach, Max (b. 1924) *American drummer, composer, bandleader, and record producer*

Roach is one of jazz's most respected and interesting drummers. He started playing DRUMS at age 12 and then studied classical music in New York. From college he started working in jazz clubs with greats such as COLEMAN HAWKINS and DIZZY GILLESPIE. While playing with CHARLIE PARKER in the late 1940s, he became known for his blazing style that was a perfect complement to Parker's supersonic speed on the SAXOPHONE.

Considered a drummer from the BOP era, he helped expand the language of the drum kit in jazz. In playing bop, the drummer was not only a time-keeper. Roach used his drum kit to add ACCENTS to the melody and prod the music ahead. Rather than kicking hard on the bass drum to make a loud rhythm, he "feathered" it lightly for a softer beat and used his hands to accent time on the snares and cymbals.

Roach also formed his own QUINTET and, like ART BLAKEY, was responsible for showcasing many rising stars of jazz over the years. The message of his own compositions was often political, raising social awareness of racism in America. He has collaborated widely with artists in dance and film, and takes time now and then to teach music as well.

"Rockit" (1983) *recording by Herbie Hancock*

Featuring HERBIE HANCOCK (keyboards), Michael Beinhorn (keyboards), Bill Laswell (BASS), Grandmixer DST (turntables), Daniel Ponce (bata). After a period in the 1970s when Hancock's music seemed to be all about electronic gadgetry, he put some funk in his sound and produced the hit album *Future Shock*. "Rockit" was the most frequently played piece from that album. It also inspired an award-winning video starring various robotic figures dancing to the music. It had punchy keyboard, a catchy melody, and the new percussive sound of scratching turntables. Hancock's electronic blend was part jazz, part hip-hop, and part rhythm and blues. It was Hancock's most successful record since HEAD HUNTERS 10 years earlier.

Rollins, Sonny (b. 1930) *American tenor and soprano saxophone player*

Rollins has been called the world's greatest living SAXOPHONE player and soloist. He calls himself a perfectionist. He took a break from the public eye for a couple of years beginning in 1959 to perfect his TECHNIQUE. Rollins was spotted practicing on the Williamsburg Bridge in Manhattan, a ritual he apparently kept up for a couple of years. When asked why, he simply said, "We have to make ourselves as perfect as we can." Practicing into the wind apparently enabled him to perfect an even louder, robust sound.

Rollins took up the tenor saxophone with a fury when he was only 17. He was schooled in BEBOP and worked with greats THELONIOUS MONK, BUD POWELL, and ART BLAKEY before joining MILES DAVIS in 1951. Rollins admired the big sound of COLEMAN HAWKINS and brought a sense of urgency and excitement to his playing. He joined the HARD BOP COMBO led by MAX ROACH and CLIFFORD BROWN in 1955. When Brown died unexpectedly, Rollins helped Roach run the group and stayed with him until 1957, when he began to lead his own group.

Rollins made a remarkable series of records in the late 1950s, including six alone in one year. Each added to the growing legend of his extraordinary playing, the powers of which are most evident on *Work Time* (1955), *SAXOPHONE COLOSSUS* (1956), *A Night at the Village Vanguard* (1957), and *The Freedom Suite* (1958). He plays with a full sound and a restless sense of IMPROVISATION. His SOLOS can be so long at times as to seem painful as he irons out every wrinkle of possibility from a given tune. His association with great drummers, including Max Roach and ELVIN JONES, demonstrates a rhythmic confidence that allows him to lead the beat with his sax.

By the late 1960s Rollins, like JOHN COLTRANE, developed a liking for long, solo improvisations. His own compositions are rooted in the frantic pace of bop but he also enjoys writing songs with a West Indian calypso flair. His performances are usually marked by an extended improvisational battle with other band members. Although the pace of his life has slowed in recent years, he practices continually and still thrives on public performances. Though Rollins was never in the spotlight as much as his contemporaries, those who know jazz well know that Rollins has been an inspiration to countless players.

Rova Saxophone Quartet

A San Francisco–based SAXOPHONE group featuring Jon Raskin, Larry Ochs, Andrew Voight (replaced by Steve Adams in 1988), and Bruce Ackley, founded in 1977, the group specializes in AVANT-GARDE and FREE JAZZ, but not without a sense of humor. Their work ranges into the experimental, and they have collaborated with noted composers Alvin Curran, Terry Riley, and ANTHONY BRAXTON. On occasion they take on additional members for special projects, such as four additional reed players for the record *Pipe Dreams* (1994). Individual members are also active in SOLO projects and other collaborations.

Rubalcaba, Gonzalo (b. 1963) *Cuban pianist and composer*

Rubalcaba studied classical PIANO and has stunning TECHNIQUE. He started playing jazz as a teenager, jamming regularly with Cuban jazz combos. His speed, touch, and lyrical playing brought him to the attention of American bassist CHARLIE HADEN. Rubalcaba recorded with Haden in Cuba. After appearances at the Montreal and MONTREUX international jazz festivals in 1989, the secret was out. His music is sophisticated and dazzling. It has the excitement and power of Latin jazz but also uses the delicacy of classic American jazz. He has recorded in styles ranging from BEBOP and HARD BOP to jazz that is heavily flavored with native Cuban percussion. His music and his extraordinary talent make Rubalcaba a unique star of Latin jazz.

Russell, George (b. 1923) *American composer, bandleader, educator, and piano player*

Russell is the father of MODAL JAZZ, an idea that he described in writing in 1953. This led to the modal jazz experiments of MILES DAVIS, JOHN COLTRANE, and others beginning in the late 1950s. In modal jazz IMPROVISATIONS are based on different scales, or modes, rather than CHORD CHANGES and songlike harmony. Russell's roots in jazz go back to his days as a drummer and ARRANGER for the BENNY CARTER BIG BAND in the mid-1940s.

After being replaced on DRUMS by MAX ROACH, he concentrated on composing and arranging. He has always had a voracious appetite for different styles of music, absorbing influences and synthesizing them into something new. His early arrangements combined BEBOP and Afro-Cuban jazz, resulting in such works as "Cubana Be, Cubano Bop" (1947), recorded by DIZZY GILLESPIE's band. During the early 1950s, while working as a freelance arranger, he wrote his famous self-published pamphlet on modal jazz, *The Lydian Chromatic Concept of Tonal Organization* (1953).

Russell has since led his own COMBOS and big bands in the United States and Europe and has been on the faculty of the New England Conservatory of Music off and on since 1969. His own compositions have embraced everything from FREE JAZZ to rock and roll, and he is widely regarded as one of the pioneering spirits of new jazz theory. Players who have worked with Russell include John Coltrane, BILL EVANS, Dizzy Gillespie, Max Roach, ERIC DOLPHY, RAHSAAN ROLAND KIRK, and JAN GARBAREK. Russell has been twice awarded Guggenheim fellowships and was a MacArthur Foundation grant recipient. He published an updated version of his modal jazz theory in 2001 entitled *The Art and Science of Tonal Gravity.*

"Salt Peanuts" (1945) *recorded performance by Dizzy Gillespie and his All Star Quintet*
Featuring DIZZY GILLESPIE (TRUMPET, vocal), CHARLIE PARKER (alto SAXOPHONE), Al Haig (PIANO), Curly Russell (BASS), SID CATLETT (DRUMS), this is one of the classic hits of jazz and documents the birth of BEBOP. Both Gillespie and Parker are in top form. It is fast and furious and funny, with Gillespie providing a short vocal CHORUS exclaiming "salt peanuts, salt peanuts" between breathtaking stints on the trumpet. The melody is but a PHRASE. The players hit some VERSEs together, ride the octaves up and down, throw in a few well-chiseled SOLOS, then bring it all home again in only about three minutes. Gillespie and Parker succeeded in defining a new sound for jazz COMBOs with "Salt Peanuts."

Sanborn, David (b. 1945) *American alto and soprano saxophone player*
Sanborn is a popular SAXOPHONE stylist who straddles the fence between jazz and rock. After college he got his professional start playing with BLUES bands and recorded with the Paul Butterfield Blues Band from 1967 to 1972. During the early 1970s he was in demand as a SIDEMAN for rock acts, including the Rolling Stones, Stevie Wonder, David Bowie, James Brown, the Eagles, and Bruce Springsteen.[161]

During the mid-1970s Sanborn switched to jazz as a result of working with GIL EVANS and the Brecker Brothers. He began to lead his own bands in the mid-1970s and released his first album as a leader, *Taking Off*, in 1975. He has since continued to record as a leader and has plentiful work as a sideman on records and television. His playing is strongly blues influenced and has a powerful, emotional impact. He is a smooth interpreter of jazz and rock and creates a palatable, if soft-edged, blend of accessible jazz.

Sanders, Pharoah (b. 1940) *American tenor saxophone player and composer*
SUN RA convinced Sanders to change his first name from Farrell to Pharoah. After starting out in the 1950s as a rhythm and blues player, Sanders went to California, where he took up jazz under the tutelage of Dewey Redman and PHILLY JOE JONES. Upon moving to New York in 1962 Sanders became immersed in the AVANT-GARDE and found himself playing with several experimental musicians. These included FREE JAZZ specialist DON CHERRY and the incomparable Sun Ra. After playing in Sun Ra's Arkestra until 1965, he moved on to stand beside JOHN COLTRANE in the legend's last group.

His sensibilities were akin to Coltrane's, and he felt entirely at home in the eye of the storm while playing with Trane. Coltrane's work at that time had reached a spiritual pinnacle that stripped the music of most of its structure. There are times when the playing of the two sax men was stripped down so far as to consist only of IMPROVISATIONS around one or two CHORDS. But Sanders thrived on the challenge of making this music breathe with life, and breathe it did. After Coltrane's death,

Sanders continued to work with his wife, ALICE COLTRANE, who took over the group.

From there, Sanders began a long and successful career as a leader and SESSION man. His first group (1969–70) engaged the spirituality of Coltrane and rocked with a FREE JAZZ sense of euphoria. Playing with Sanders was the singer and free yodeler Leon Thomas, who brought a taste of avant-garde poetry to the COMBO. Sanders worked with Michael Mantler and CARLA BLEY as part of the Jazz Composer's Orchestra and embraced FUSION jazz as part of his GIG. Since then, he has successfully experimented with various formulas, always finding a niche to showcase his stellar TECHNIQUE and mellow sound. From jazz funk to fusion to free jazz and more traditional combo jazz, Sanders career is marked by one satisfying exploration after another. Most recently, his work is reminiscent of the musical meditations conducted with Leon Thomas, but now with a decidedly world beat influence. The album *With a Heartbeat* (2003) features a laid-back but jazzy mix of WORLD MUSIC and a heavy RHYTHM SECTION led by the BASS of Bill Laswell.

Sandoval, Arturo (b. 1949) *Cuban trumpet, flugelhorn, piano, and percussion player and singer*

Sandoval's highly influential sound is best described as supercharged. He has been playing TRUMPET since age 12, received his musical education in Cuba, and was soon leading his own groups. He was one of the founding members of the group Irakere in 1973, which fused Afro-Cuban music with rock. DIZZY GILLESPIE heard Sandoval and Irakere play in 1977, cementing a long-lasting friendship. Through Gillespie, Sandoval also found a playing partner and perfected his BEBOP CHOPS. Sandoval defected from Cuba in 1990 with his wife and son and has been based in Florida ever since. His playing is spirited and blends classical, bop, and Afro-Cuban traditions. He is able to play in many styles, including NEW ORLEANS JAZZ, Spanish

flamenco, bebop, COOL JAZZ, and HARD BOP. He might be at his glorious best in recapturing the swinging sound of Cuban-influenced BIG BAND jazz ala Dizzy Gillespie.

Santamaria, Mongo (1922–2003) *Cuban conga player, percussionist, and composer*

Santamaria got his start playing with local Afro-Cuban bands until he left the country in 1948 and traveled to the United States. Working there with artists as diverse as George Shearing and TITO PUENTE, Santamaria was one of the chief proponents of Afro-Cuban jazz, which became popular during this period. He recorded with DIZZY GILLESPIE in 1954, an American counterpart who was also popularizing Latin rhythms and instrumentation in his music.

Based on the West Coast in the late 1950s, he began to lead his own groups. He wrote the song "Afro Blue" (1959), which became a popular Latin jazz work that was later recorded by JOHN COLTRANE and others. His interpretation of HERBIE HANCOCK's song "WATERMELON MAN" became a top 10 hit in 1963. Santamaria worked with many styles of music during the 1960s, but remained a leader of the Afro-Cuban tradition for the balance of his career. *Mambo Mongo* (1992) is a particularly strong recording featuring a solid BIG BAND Afro-Cuban sound. The Latin rhythms and ENSEMBLE ARRANGEMENTS of Santamaria have greatly influenced the incorporation of Cuban rhythms into jazz, rock, and rhythm and blues music.

Savoy Ballroom

This HARLEM jazz spot and dance club operated from 1926 to 1958 and occupied the whole block of 140th Street on Lenox Avenue. The Savoy was one of the best-known ballrooms in Harlem, a historically black neighborhood of New York City, and its audiences were predominantly African American. It held up to 4,000 customers. Dance music was the focus of the Savoy. The famous Lindy Hop dance originated there, and the club sponsored regularly scheduled dance contests and battles of the bands. CHICK WEBB's band was a regular at the Savoy and competed in most of the battles. Famous bands that played the Savoy included those of DUKE ELLINGTON, COUNT BASIE, FLETCHER HENDERSON, and BENNY GOODMAN. Several vocalists also made names for themselves by fronting these bands, including BILLIE HOLIDAY (with Count Basie) and ELLA FITZGERALD (with Chick Webb).

saxophone

The wonderful jazz soloist SIDNEY BECHET introduced the soprano saxophone as a SOLO instrument to jazz in 1921. Following Bechet, BIG BANDS relied on multiple saxophones to provide a big, booming sound. The saxophone in all of its variations has since become the most popular and widely recognized reed instrument of jazz. The saxophone comes in various sizes, each with a different pitch range. The soprano, alto, tenor, and baritone saxes are the most commonly used, in order from highest to lowest pitch range. Players who have greatly influenced jazz sax playing include Sidney Bechet (soprano), COLEMAN HAWKINS (tenor), LESTER YOUNG (tenor), BENNY CARTER (alto), CHARLIE PARKER (alto), ERIC DOLPHY (alto), JOHN COLTRANE (tenor), and WAYNE SHORTER (soprano).

Saxophone Colossus (1956) album by Sonny Rollins

SONNY ROLLINS was playing in the shadows of JOHN COLTRANE and MILES DAVIS at the time he recorded this, one of seven albums he made in a single year. Considered his best collection, Rollins's steady and sensuous sax represents the best straight-up reed playing of the post-bop era. "St. Thomas" is the result of his fling with Caribbean beats and melodies. It also includes his lilting rendition of "Moritat," better known as "Mack the Knife." Released by Prestige.

scale

An arranged set of musical pitches in ascending or descending order. Also called a mode.

See also MODAL JAZZ.

scat singing

Bim, bop, bam, and dwee dooda ya. A vocal style in which the singer uses nonsense syllables to improvise on a melody. In this way the vocalist becomes like another instrument of a jazz ENSEMBLE. Famous "scatters" include ELLA FITZGERALD and LOUIS ARMSTRONG.

Schneider, Maria (b. 1960) American composer, arranger, and piano player

Schneider has established herself as one of the most gifted of the new composers and arrangers of large BIG BAND ensembles. After graduating from the Eastman Music School, she worked with jazz legend GIL EVANS, contributing to such projects as the musical arrangements for the soundtrack of the movie *The Color of Money* (1986) and playing in the touring ENSEMBLE for Sting's 1987 European tour. She became a widely commissioned COMPOSER during the 1990s, particularly in Europe. Her reputation as a big band leader, composer, and ARRANGER was firmly established by leading a Monday night GIG with the Maria Schneider Jazz Orchestra at the Visiones club in New York from 1993 to 1998. She has been nominated for GRAMMY AWARDS and has been a perennial favorite in *Down Beat* and *Jazz Times* critic's and reader's polls since the early 1990s. In 1996 she received the Critic's Choice award for best composer at the Jazz Awards at Lincoln Center. Schneider's sound incorporates a blend of jazz tradition from DUKE ELLINGTON to GEORGE RUSSELL and THAD JONES.

Schuller, Gunther (b. 1925) American composer, French horn player, conductor, author

Schuller has led three successful parallel lives in music. His first was as a FRENCH HORN player who advocated the FUSION of elements of classical music with jazz. He invented the term THIRD STREAM JAZZ in 1957 to describe this style. His second career has been as the author of two important texts on jazz history, *Early Jazz* (1968) and *The Swing Era* (1989). His third career has been as a COMPOSER and conductor of classical music, particularly of an AVANT-GARDE nature. As french horn player, he took part in the historic BIRTH OF THE COOL sessions with MILES DAVIS, GIL EVANS, and GERRY MULLIGAN from 1948 to 1950. He advocated third stream jazz in the late 1950s and was encouraged by several noted jazz composers who worked with him on this idea, including GEORGE RUSSELL and CHARLES MINGUS. Although many of Schuller's own compositions are written for classical music orchestras, they often include elements borrowed from jazz. Some of his works were written in collaboration with specific jazz artists. "Conversation" (1959) and "Concertino for Jazz Quartet and Orchestra" (1959) were first performed by the MODERN JAZZ QUARTET. He wrote the jazz ballet *Variants* (1961) for the George Balanchine ballet company. While president of the New England Conservatory of Music from 1967 to 1977, Schuller revived an interest in works of composer SCOTT JOPLIN. Schuller's arrangements of Joplin's music were subsequently used for the soundtrack of the popular movie *The Sting* in 1974. More recently, Schuller reconstructed and conducted the posthumous 1989 performance of a work by the late Charles Mingus. Schuller continues to compose, conduct, and teach. He is reportedly working on the much-anticipated third volume of his scholarly jazz history, which will document the development of jazz since 1945.

Schuur, Diane (b. 1953) *American singer and piano player*

Schuur, who is blind from birth, is promoted as a jazz singer but has gained widespread popularity with lovers of easy listening music. Her musical roots are solid, and her early support from jazz greats DIZZY GILLESPIE and STAN GETZ clearly denote her obvious talent in the field of jazz. After playing at the White House in the 1980s, she got a record contract and has been producing a steady stream of glossy ballads with BIG BAND ARRANGEMENTs ever since. Jazz critic LEONARD FEATHER may have explained the enigma of Diane Schuur early on when he wrote that she was "a singer who has all the right qualities: technique, range, adaptability to various pop, gospel, jazz and blues concepts."[162]

The GRAMMY AWARD–winning artist continues to be a perennial favorite on the popular music charts. She is an accomplished singer who, in crossing over from jazz to pop, deserves the same recognition afforded past jazz singers who did the same. Schuur is often compared to ELLA FITZGERALD and SARAH VAUGHN, although she does not command the respect of TRADITIONAL JAZZ artists afforded to those timeless voices from the golden years of big bands.

Scofield, John (b. 1951) *American guitar player and composer*

Scofield is one of the most absorbing and skilled CONTEMPORARY JAZZ guitarists. Like so many other players, he got his start playing in rock and roll bands. By age 15 he was learning jazz and eventually took up studies at the BERKLEE SCHOOL OF MUSIC. One of his first important public GIGs was playing backup to GERRY MULLIGAN and CHET BAKER at CARNEGIE HALL in 1974. This led to an extended stay with the exceptional jazz FUSION band led by BILLY COBHAM and George Duke, recording sessions with CHARLES MINGUS, and a gig with GARY BURTON. Scofield began leading his own groups in the late 1970s but also took a job with MILES DAVIS in 1982 that lasted until 1985 and resulted in his appearance on three Davis albums.

Since that time, he has led his own combos, made recordings of his own, and is a frequent contributor to the recordings of others. His playing is part traditional and part AVANT-GARDE. He has a superb touch and explores lines of notes with grace, direction, and objectivity. At his most experimental, he dabbles with clusters of notes, electronics, and FREE IMPROVISATION. His most accessible music is always just a step away from a BLUES-influenced orientation. He plays with an icy sense of funk. His album *Loud Jazz* (1987) was a breakthrough effort with such pleasant lyricism that it became the soundtrack for the Weather Channel for the better part of a year.

Although his playing can be compared to PAT METHENY's, Scofield has a decidedly scientific approach to his improvisations that strays further from the soft sound of "new age" jazz than does Metheny's. His reputation as a guitarist now extends far beyond the borders of North America, and Scofield is a frequent visitor to Europe, where his work is also highly regarded. In 1996 he played in the London premier of *Blood on the Floor,* a contemporary classical work with jazz elements composed by Mark-Anthony Turnage. By the late 1990s Scofield was looking for a new direction in his music. He found it in the kind of JAM band music

John Scofield

being performed by younger groups such as Medeski, Martin, and Wood. In response to this impulse, he put together one of his best ensembles ever, a group consisting of much younger players: Avi Bortnick (GUITAR), Jess Murphy (BASS), and drummer Adam Deitch. The result was the CD *Uberjam* (2002) and Scofield's first Grammy nomination in his 30-year career.

Scott, Jimmy (b. 1925) *American singer*

"Little" Jimmy Scott was stricken with a hormone disorder when he was young, preventing his normal growth as an adolescent. This left him with small stature and an unusually high-pitched voice. He first came to prominence singing with the LIONEL HAMPTON band beginning in 1948. This partnership resulted in his first hit record, "Everybody's Somebody's Fool" (1950). He had a successful solo career in the 1950s but more or less dropped from sight in the 1960s and 1970s due to a contractual dispute with his record company.[163]

He made a successful comeback in the 1980s and 1990s, offering his interpretations of tunes by songwriters as diverse as Prince, Bryan Ferry, John Lennon, and Elton John. Scott's polished style of delivery, so perfect for ballads, has the ability to transport the listener to another place. He is widely admired by other singers though few can hope to achieve the spellbinding effect that Scott achieves through a combination of his unusual voice, practiced delivery, and emotional strength. Guitarist and songwriter Lou Reed has said of his friend, "He has the voice of an angel and can break your heart."[164]

Scott, Shirley (1934–2002) *American organ and piano player, composer, and bandleader*

Another remarkable organist from the Philadelphia area, Scott was a contemporary of JIMMY SMITH. She studied PIANO and TRUMPET as a teen. She was so enamored with playing music that she ran away for a week while in high school to play GIGS with a band that passed through the area. Running away may have been a mistake, but her love for jazz was not. She began playing gigs in the vital Philadelphia club scene in the mid-1950s. She switched to playing ORGAN one night at the request of a club owner whose regular organist had not shown up.[165] She played with Eddie "Lockjaw" Davis from 1956 to 1960 and was featured on more than a half dozen recordings with his group.

After being in demand as a SESSION player in the late 1950s, she formed her own trio and recorded several albums. She began touring with saxophonist STANLEY TURRENTINE in 1960, and then married him. She played with his group for about 10 years until they divorced. Her career as a bandleader took off again in the 1970s. She toured with her own group and began a long and fruitful career of making records that lasted until the mid-1990s.

The Queen of the organ played everything from pop standards and BLUES to her own mellow compositions. During the short-lived run of Bill Cosby's game show, *You Bet Your Life* in 1992, Scott led the studio band that played during the show. In 1996 she recorded a haunting SOLO album at the Cathedral of Bayonne in France, which was to be one of her last completed projects.

Like other Philadelphia organists, Scott had a special feel for the blues and a full, expressive sound that made the organ wail. What distinguished Scott's playing was its marvelous SWING and her ability to blend with other instruments in an ENSEMBLE setting. She interacted well with other soloists and often inspired them to shine. The work of Scott and Turrentine in the 1960s was a key influence on the development of soulful jazz that made its way into popular music and rock like that created by Booker T. She also taught jazz at Cheyney University in 1991.

Segundo, Compay (1907–2003) *Cuban guitar player and bandleader*
After first learning to play the "tres," a Cuban GUITAR with three pairs of metal strings, Segundo invented his own guitar, which he called the "armonico." The

armonico had seven strings instead of the customary six found on most guitars. He wrote his first song at age 15 and became a popular musician during the 1940s playing both CLARINET and guitar. During the 1950s he sang at the Buena Vista Social Club, a music club in Havana where many Afro-Cuban folk and jazz musicians performed. With the coming of revolution and Fidel Castro in the 1960s, the club and many cultural outlets for music were closed down. It wasn't until the mid-1990s that Segundo and many of his musical colleagues were rounded up for renewed performances by the guitarist Ry Cooder. The result was a 1999 documentary, *The Buena Vista Social Club*, which led to new recordings for Segundo and other Cuban artists such as RUBEN GONZALEZ. The music of Segundo and his generation of Cuban musicians was a powerful influence on the development of Afro-Cuban jazz in the United States in the 1940s.

session
A date to play music, such as a recording session or JAM SESSION.

set
Part of a performance. A set is usually the first or second half of a performance. Sets are generally divided by an intermission.

Shape of Jazz to Come, The (1959) *album by Ornette Coleman*
This album features ORNETTE COLEMAN (alto and tenor sax), DON CHERRY (POCKET TRUMPET), CHARLIE HADEN (BASS), Billy Higgins (DRUMS). Coleman is the godfather of FREE JAZZ. Among his first record albums, *The Shape of Jazz to Come, Free Jazz,* and *Double Quartet* split the world of jazz wide open with their wildly free expression. This was a new dialect using the language of jazz. Free jazz made the wailings of JOHN COLTRANE seem almost tame by comparison. It's next to impossible to find a CHORD

in this music. Coleman is a skilled player who freely runs with one fantastic idea after another. Yet it hangs together somehow. This represents the quartet's first major statement on record.

Sharrock, Sonny (1940–1994) *American guitar player, composer, and bandleader*

Imagine a style of GUITAR work that blends the feedback of Jimi Hendrix, the finger work of a horn player, and the "sheets of sound" of JOHN COLTRANE, and it might approximate the sound of Sonny Sharrock. Born in upstate New York, Sharrock probably would have become a SAXOPHONE player had he not suffered from asthma. Instead, he took up guitar and taught himself the basics. After a year at the BERKLEE COLLEGE OF MUSIC in 1965, he moved to New York and began gigging with jazz players including PHAROAH SANDERS, HERBIE MANN, and DON CHERRY, with whom he toured Berlin in 1968. He was briefly a part of the MILES DAVIS group in 1969, long enough to sit in on some of the trumpeter's most biting FUSION sessions. One of these was the *Jack Johnson* sessions, for which Sharrock's contribution alongside fellow guitarist JOHN McLAUGHLIN went uncredited until the reissue of the recordings almost 30 years later.

Sharrock was one of the early FREE JAZZ guitarists. His sound was seismic and hot. Bassist Bill Laswell invited him to join his group Last Exit in 1986, which brought the guitarist some well-deserved attention and led to a longtime working relationship with Laswell, who produced several Sharrock recordings. His trademark sound was the screeching sliding chord. He played unimaginable clusters of notes as chords, lending a free jazz feeling to even the most ordinary tunes. Another familiar Sharrock sound was that of the chorused melody in which the same tune is played in two octaves at once, a TECHNIQUE that he handled by himself using pedal effects or with another soloist playing along with him. Sharrock was a student of IMPROVISATION and took pride in his original approach. "For better or worse," he once said, "you are your own truth."[166]

Although poorly represented on record, there are some great examples of his work to be found. His most well-rounded recording was *Ask the Ages* (1991), which included saxophonist Pharoah Sanders, ELVIN JONES (DRUMS), and Charnett Moffett (BASS). The compilation *Into Another Light* (1996), produced by Bill Laswell after the guitarist's death, is a revealing collection of tracks that traces Sharrock's versatile and innovative sound over the years. His first album as a leader, *Black Woman* (1969), was recently reissued on CD (2001). In the early 1990s Sharrock finally began to get some critical notice, largely due to his manic soundtrack for a late-night animated parody of talk shows, *Space Ghost Coast to Coast*. Sadly, just when popularity was knocking on his door, he died of a heart attack.

Shaw, Artie (1910–2004) *American clarinet and saxophone player, composer, and bandleader*

Artie Shaw was born Arthur Jacob Arshawsky in New York City. He learned to play SAXOPHONE and CLARINET when he was 14, favoring the alto saxophone during his formative years. He left home at age 15 to become a SIDEMAN in various dance bands. When he was 16, he remained with the Cleveland-based band led by Austin Wylie, for whom Shaw not only played but also assumed responsibilities for running rehearsals and arranging some songs.

Shaw was immensely curious about jazz and closely studied the work of LOUIS ARMSTRONG and "BIX" BEIDERBECKE. He listened to their records and even made a trip to Chicago in 1927 to hear Armstrong in person. In 1929 Shaw joined a dance band of Irving Aaronson, based in Hollywood. While staying in Chicago, Shaw became interested in contemporary classical music, listening to recordings of symphonic works by Stravinsky, Bartók, and Debussy, among others. In the young musician's mind, he was beginning to imagine a style of jazz that combined both classical and jazz instrumentation.

Shaw remained in New York in 1930 and became a sought-after studio musician, specializing mostly

Artie Shaw

in alto saxophone. But the music business was a struggle, and he was unhappy simply playing the music of others. At the tender age of 22 Shaw actually "retired" from music for two years. He spent his time in upstate New York, chopping wood for a living and trying to improve his skills as a writer of books.[167]

However, music was always on his mind. After returning to New York in 1934 to complete his formal education, he resumed GIG work to pay the bills.

His fortunes turned dramatically in 1936 during one of the first concerts of SWING bands held at Broadway's Imperial Theater in New York. By this time Shaw had begun to compose music that combined elements of classical and jazz music. To the surprise of the audience, he led an octet consisting of a string QUARTET plus a jazz RHYTHM SECTION and

Shaw playing lead clarinet as soloist. He composed a work for the occasion called "Interlude in B-flat," and the audience loved it. With that performance Shaw not only jump-started his music career again but invented what has now been called THIRD STREAM JAZZ. Shaw then formed his own BIG BAND and for the next few years was a true superstar of swing.

His trademark sound was nearly unique in the business. It used strings and elements of modern classical music to bring energizing new ideas to jazz. His clarinet playing soared. He was one of the first white bandleaders to bring African-American artists into his band, including singers BILLIE HOLIDAY and LENA HORNE. His biggest hit was "Begin the Beguine" (1938). By this time, the Artie Shaw Orchestra was earning about $60,000 a week for its performances, a staggering figure in those days.[168]

His personal life sometimes overshadowed his musical accomplishments. He was married eight times, including two highly publicized betrothals to Hollywood stars Lana Turner and Ava Gardner.[169]

Shaw left the business briefly in 1939, only to return with a retooled and larger big band featuring a full string section, WOODWINDS, and FRENCH HORNS. This ENSEMBLE had a hit record with the song "Frenesi" (1940). From this large ensemble came his new touring band and a smaller COMBO he called the Gramercy Five. The hits kept coming as Shaw produced classic versions of "Star Dust," "Moonglow," and "Dancing in the Dark." During World War II Shaw joined the navy and led a navy big band on tours to entertain troops in the Pacific.

By the early 1950s, with BOP and HARD BOP replacing big band swing as the jazz music of choice, Shaw withdrew from the business once again. He put down his clarinet for good in 1954 after one final concert with his beloved Gramercy Five. During the 1950s he took up short story writing and penned his lengthy autobiography, *The Trouble with Cinderella.* He returned to music once again as a bandleader in 1983. He is acknowledged as one of the greatest jazz clarinetists of all time and an innovative COMPOSER and leader who continually introduced new ideas to jazz.

Shepp, Archie (b. 1937) *American tenor, alto, and soprano saxophone player, pianist, singer, composer, and educator*

Shepp is a gifted jazz musician with roots in the FREE JAZZ movement of the 1960s. After learning to play tenor SAXOPHONE in high school, he studied at Goddard College. In the early 1960s he played with AVANT-GARDE PIANO player CECIL TAYLOR in New York. Shepp coled the group New York Contemporary Five with John Tchicai and DON CHERRY (1963–64). He worked occasionally with JOHN COLTRANE in the late 1960s.

Shepp pioneered the use of jazz to present political messages using poems and dramatic readings as part of his performances. He is also a playwright and an actor. His music swung from sentimental BEN WEBSTER–style ballads to wild free jazz romps. He worked in the 1970s with trumpeter Cal Massey and others, embarking on regular tours of Europe and other continents. His first college-level teaching post was at SUNY-Buffalo from 1969 to 1974. His early playing style began as an earnest version of Ben Webster but evolved into one of the most distinctive, and eclectic, sounds in modern jazz. He is probably most outstanding as a player of TRADITIONAL JAZZ styles.

Shepp has devoted much of the last 20 years to teaching both in the classroom, where he is a professor at the University of Massachusetts at Amherst, but also in the revival of traditional jazz as a performer with his various COMBOs. He is a popular artist in Europe, particularly in Paris. In speaking about past innovations in jazz, particularly by African-American artists, Shepp is clearly concerned that new generations of musicians will become increasingly less aware of past achievements. He explains, "After a decade, a musical idea, no matter how innovative, is threatened. Just look at what's happened since Parker and Coltrane. The reason is that black music thrives on change. We've got to keep trying new things just to stay around. It's hurt us in a way because we haven't been able to develop retrospective, re-creational institutions that would preserve our culture the way others have."[170]

When he was last seen by the author, Archie Shepp was playing to a packed house in Paris in 2005 where he wowed the crowd with traditional jazz, free jazz, and even some blues numbers.

Sheppard, Andy (b. 1957) *British tenor and soprano saxophone player, composer, arranger, and bandleader*

Reportedly Sheppard did not pick up the tenor SAXOPHONE until inspired to do so at age 19 by JOHN COLTRANE records. This derailed his plans to attend art school and led him on a journey that has made him one of the most adventurous jazz reed players on the British jazz scene. After playing with other groups, he formed his own COMBO in the early 1980s and recorded his first album as a leader in 1987 (*Andy Sheppard*). Sheppard is also at home in a BIG BAND setting and has worked with three particularly innovative COMPOSERS, GIL EVANS, GEORGE RUSSELL, and CARLA BLEY. He formed his own BIG BAND, the Soft on the Inside Big Band, in 1990, composed of European players. After success with this format he turned to a FUSION and FREE JAZZ format with his group Co-Motion (1991), eventually expanded to a larger unit called Big Co-Motion (1993). He continues to work with various ENSEMBLE formats and has become a popular composer for other bands. Like jazz artists RANDY BRECKER, STANLEY CLARKE, and HERBIE HANCOCK, Sheppard is frequently found crossing over to rock and hip-hop styles.

Shorter, Wayne (b. 1933) *American tenor and soprano saxophone player, composer, and bandleader*

Shorter is perhaps best known as the most recognizable SAXOPHONE player of the jazz FUSION genre of the 1970s. He studied music for four years at New York University, then went into the army from 1956 to 1958. HARD BOP pianist HORACE SILVER, who had a keen eye for new talent, already had his eye on Shorter and convinced the soldier's company commander to let Shorter take extended leave now and then to play some GIGS. During his last month in the army, dressed in his army uniform, he went with Silver to see MILES DAVIS play in Washington, D.C. It was an eye opener. JOHN COLTRANE was playing with Davis, and singer ABBEY LINCOLN sat in for some songs.[171]

After playing with Silver a few times, Shorter was in great demand when he left the army. John Coltrane met up with him and confided that he was about to leave Davis's group. He wanted to know if Shorter wanted his spot in the band. At the same time, ART BLAKEY expressed interest in Shorter but the gig he took for several months was with MAYNARD FERGUSON. This led to Blakey offering him a post as SIDEMAN and musical director, a spot Shorter filled until 1964 when he joined Miles Davis for a run of six groundbreaking years for both musicians.

Shorter recorded his first record under his own name in 1959 and continued to lead his own groups in recording sessions on and off throughout the 1960s. While with Davis, Shorter added soprano saxophone to his repertoire and honed a unique voice that blended perfectly with the funky, amplified sound of Davis's TRUMPET. Working with Davis, Shorter was one of the key architects of jazz rock fusion. His style had by that time also branched away from that of John Coltrane, with whom he had been constantly compared until then. Davis also asked Shorter to write songs for his group. Many of these, including "Footprints," "Paraphernalia," "E.S.P.," and "Nefertiti" were key components of the evolving Davis sound. Shorter truly bloomed as a performer and COMPOSER while with Davis. Miles would later remark, "When he came into the band it started to grow a lot more and a whole lot faster, because Wayne is a real composer. . . . Wayne also brought in a kind of curiosity about working with musical rules. . . . He understood that freedom in music was the ability to know the rules in order to bend them to your satisfaction and taste."[172]

Shorter played on the BITCHES BREW sessions, then left Davis in 1970. The same year he released

his own experiment in fusion, *Odyssey of Iska* (1970), a collection of organically branching, plaintive works that hinted at a new, more fluid sound. The five works on *Iska,* each possessing simple but emblematic titles such as "Wind," "Storm," "Calm," "After Love/Emptiness," and "Joy," ebbed and flowed freely around these various moods. As a composer Shorter was providing spaces for FREE IMPROVISATION while at the same time allowing the music to seamlessly coalesce into a tight rhythmic statement. Later in 1970 Shorter teamed with keyboard player JOE ZAWINUL, also a veteran of Miles Davis's *Bitches Brew* sessions, to form the most lauded fusion group of the time, WEATHER REPORT. He stayed with Weather Report until 1985, when it disbanded.

Since then, Shorter has continued to lead his own groups and take part in recording sessions for others. He has also been a favorite guest artist of several rock stars, including Carlos Santana and Joni Mitchell. Although he started out emulating the tenor saxophone playing of John Coltrane and SONNY ROLLINS, Shorter developed a style that was more subtle and tuneful. His TECHNIQUE is superb. One reason that his sound is so distinctive is that he does not depend on the most obvious expressive techniques of VIBRATO and volume that most players depend on so heavily.[173]

Instead, he carefully shapes the attack and decay of his sound, slowly bends notes, and contrasts dreamy hypnotic playing with notes that dance rapidly like stones skipping across a lake.

In the course of his career, Shorter has evolved from the SOLO-based jazz of the 1950s and 1960s to the ENSEMBLE playing and IMPROVISATION that made fusion unique. His playing under other bandleaders (e.g., Blakey, Davis, Weather Report) seems to have been freer and less structured than his approach with his own groups. His playing since Weather Report recalls the acoustic jazz of the mid-1960s. His recorded output has slowed considerably during the past 10 years, not for lack of interest, but for a renewed spirituality that informs his life. "There is so much more to living and life," says Shorter, "than

Wayne Shorter

doing music. It is working on . . . the areas of life that can be left unattended. . . . Music is a drop in the ocean of life."[174]

His recent performances feature works by himself and others, including a mix of folk, Latin, and American pop standards. He has won eight GRAMMY AWARDS over the years, including the 2003 Grammy for Best Jazz Instrumental Album, Individual or Group for his album *Alegria*. Shorter is a stellar talent who has defined his own space in a domain with many masters. Davis described him well when he said, "Wayne was always out there on his own plane, orbiting around his own planet. Everybody else in the band was walking down here on earth."[175]

shuffle rhythm

A rhythm style common to the BLUES and often found in jazz, particularly SWING music. In a shuffle rhythm, the main beat is subdivided by smaller beats. In a typical 4/4 shuffle rhythm, each beat is subdivided into three eighth-note triplets. The shuffle feel is achieved by accenting the first and third eighth notes of each triplet, often using a high-hat or ride cymbal. The shuffle is reinforced by the kick drum on the first beat of the bar and the snare drum on the two and four beat.

sideman

Any player in a jazz band other than the bandleader.

Silver, Horace (b. 1928) *American piano player, composer, and bandleader*

The exuberant Horace Silver came of age as a PIANO player in the early 1950s. His lively, gospel-influenced RIFFS and harmonies became the driving force behind HARD BOP. Now known as the "Grandpop of hard bop," Silver was only doing what he felt was natural at the time. HARD BOP, he has said, is just "a term that the critics put out on the music, but I would say that it's bop with a little more energy to it. There was polite bop and then there was hard bop. The polite bop was more sophisticated. . . . The hard bop is real slam, bang, kicking ass kind of music."[176]

His style was a predecessor of funk and was emulated and copied by keyboard and horn players alike. Silver also made bop more accessible by trading the long, exhausting solos made famous by CHARLIE PARKER and DIZZY GILLESPIE with simpler, easier to follow melodies, change-ups, and melodic development. In a word, he added SWING to bop and brought it closer to the mainstream of jazz musicianship.

Silver got his big break playing with STAN GETZ in 1950 and 1951. After moving to New York City (he hailed from Connecticut), he lent his services to notables such as ART BLAKEY, COLEMAN HAWKINS,

Horace Silver

and MILES DAVIS in the early 1950s. The PRODUCERS at Blue Note Records were so impressed with his versatility and style that they hired him in 1952 to make records for them, an arrangement that stood for nearly 30 years. In 1954 Silver was instrumental in assembling a COMBO for a recording SESSION consisting of himself on piano, Art Blakey (DRUMS), Kenny Dorham (TRUMPET), Hank Mobley (tenor SAXOPHONE), and Doug Watkins (BASS).

This was the first recording of what came to be known as the Jazz Messengers. All but Blakey would depart by 1956, and the Jazz Messengers became the brand name of his rotating ENSEMBLE of players for many years. Silver also nurtured many sidemen (see SIDEMAN) into fame, such as DONALD BYRD, ART FARMER, WAYNE SHORTER, JOE HENDERSON, and RANDY and MICHAEL BRECKER. Silver is a prolific COMPOSER, having recorded mostly his own works with his own QUINTET since the mid-1950s. "I wake up in the morning with music in my head a lot of times," he explains. . . . "I hear it in my head and I just go check it out on the piano and put it on my tape recorder and develop it."[177]

His playing represents the essence of the hard bop style.

Simone, Nina (1933–2003) *American singer, composer, and piano player*

Simone was a temperamental but astonishing jazz diva with classical music training whose keen social consciousness made her a spokesperson for African-American civil rights. Born Eunice Waymon in North Carolina, one of eight children, she started PIANO lessons at age six. In 1943 she gave her first piano recital. It was a bittersweet affair that would influence the course of her life. It was sweet because it was her first public performance, but bitter because her parents were forced to move from the first row to make room for some white patrons.

She studied classical music at the Juilliard School in New York and was a promising pianist. In 1954 she took a job playing piano at a bar in Atlantic City, New Jersey. Apparently the owner of the bar had expected her to play *and* sing. Not having ever sung in public before, the 20-year-old musician was taken aback but forged ahead. The rest is legend. She was soon a popular attraction at the club and changed her given name to the stage name of Nina Simone.

She was both a prolific songwriter and a generous interpreter of music from various genres. Simone was equally at home singing jazz, BLUES, gospel, folk, popular, or show tunes. Her biggest hits as a singer included "I Loves You Porgy" (1959) from the musical *Porgy* and *Bess,* "I Put a Spell on You" (1964), and "To Be Young, Gifted and Black" (1966). During the 1960s she was a highly visible and outspoken member of the Civil Rights movement and wrote many songs to express the plight of African Americans.

The most vivid and powerful of these was "Mississippi Goddam!" (1963), one of her first protest songs. It was written after the murders of civil rights leader Medgar Evers in Mississippi and four black schoolchildren in Alabama in 1963. "Picket lines, School boycotts," she sang, "They try to say it's a communist plot. All I want is equality, for my sister my brother my people and me." It was a passionate call for justice sung with anger and defiance. It almost cost Simone and her band their lives as they toured the South, trailed at times by the Ku Klux Klan and often kicked out of towns where whites did not want them to perform. Simone eventually left the United States by 1972 and took up residence in Europe.

After fading from the radar during much of the 1970s, Simone made a comeback from Europe with the song "My Baby Just Cares for Me" (1987). This success revived her career and made her once again welcome not only in the many less developed countries that she championed, but in the United States

Nina Simone

as well. Her excellent piano playing and formidable vocal range were as unique as her songs. Her delivery was melodramatic and spellbinding. She could sing bluesy and sultry or pick it up for a bright pop tune. There was always anticipation in her work, moments of practiced delivery to drive home the meaning of the lyrics. She was known as a perfectionist, practicing many hours per day throughout much of her career. Her selection of songs ranged from rock and roll to Beatles and Bee Gees tunes, including a much-imitated rendition of the Gibb Brothers' "To Love Somebody."

Her contribution to jazz was in forging a unique blend of classical, folk, and blues while exercising her tremendous vocal range and TECHNIQUE as a jazz vocal "instrumentalist." She could sometimes be finicky with an audience, but only because she wanted to give them the best performance possible. Her number one rule when on stage? "I have to be composed, I have to be poised," she explained in 1999. "I have to remember what my first piano teacher told me: 'You do not touch that piano until you are ready and until they are ready to listen to you. You just make them wait.'"[178]

Nina Simone died in France at age 70 at the height of her interpretive talents.

Sims, Zoot (John Haley Sims) (1925–1985)
American tenor, alto, and soprano saxophone and clarinet player

Zoot Sims was one of the purest swing saxophonists. His style blended the bombast of LESTER YOUNG with the creativity of CHARLIE PARKER. After having first learned drums and clarinet as a boy, he switched to tenor saxophone at age 13. He was a consummate musician even at a young age, landing at age 17 a professional gig with the Benny Goodman orchestra, with whom he continued to play off and on for most of his career. He was part of Woody Herman's "Four Brothers" saxophone section from 1947 to 1949.[179]

After additional stints with the bands of Stan Kenton, Buddy Rich, and Artie Shaw, and others, Sims settled into a satisfying career as a freelance

session man, although he sometimes coled a combo with his friend Al Cohn. Sims was also known for his wisecracking behavior. He once toured Russia with the Benny Goodman band in 1962, a trip that was beset by mishaps and difficulties brought about by authoritarian Soviet officials. When asked what it was like playing Russia with the Goodman band, Sims answered, "Every gig with Benny is like playing in Russia."[180]

"Singin' the Blues" (1927) *recorded performance by Frankie Trumbauer and his orchestra*

This song featured FRANKIE TRUMBAUER (c-melody SAXOPHONE) and "BIX" BEIDERBECKE (CORNET). After LOUIS ARMSTRONG, the solos of Trumbauer and Beiderbecke were probably the most imitated by younger musicians. Beiderbecke in particular was an innovator on the cornet. That his work was noticed at all is a miracle due to the long shadow cast by Louis Armstrong and Beiderbecke's own tragically short life. Yet at the time, Beiderbecke reacted to Armstrong's creative genius with innovations of his own. He got inside melody and harmony like nobody before him, and his contributions are clearly evident on this recording, released by Columbia. This, combined with Trumbauer's light and melodic playing, add up to one of the most influential recordings in early jazz history. At the time of its release, this recording was second only to the work of Armstrong in its impact on the evolving style of jazz.

Smith, Bessie (1894–1937) *American singer*

Bessie Smith was a remarkable BLUES singer, "The Empress of the Blues," whose warmth and style made her the most magnetic of the classic female blues singers. Raised in poverty, she took a job in 1912 singing with a small group of traveling entertainers that included MA RAINEY. It was Rainey who taught Smith the style of blues singing. Smith left the group in 1915 and joined TOBA (Theatre Owners Booking Association), which sent her on singing tours of the vaudeville circuit. By the early

1920s she had developed a solid following of her own. She signed a record deal with Columbia in 1923 and released "Downhearted Blues," which became an enormous hit. It sold 750,000 copies, rivaling the record of then–Blues queen MAMIE SMITH (who was not related to Bessie).[181]

She quickly became the top TOBA act and the highest-paid black entertainer of the time, earning as much as $2,000 per week.[182]

Smith was a prolific recording artist and frequently sang vocals backed by some of the best musicians of the day, including LOUIS ARMSTRONG, FLETCHER HENDERSON, and JAMES P. JOHNSON. Her appeal also crossed racial barriers, and the blues became popular with mainstream audiences all over America. By about 1930, however, the popularity of the blues was dwindling, as was the career of Bessie Smith. She died tragically in an automobile accident in 1937, just at a time when she was poised to make a comeback as a swing band singer.[183]

Bessie Smith was a spirited woman who took charge of her career. Her dark side sometimes showed occasional crude behavior, and she had a difficult streak that made her hard to manage. Once, while preparing for a week of performances in 1936 at the famed Apollo Theater in Harlem, the manager of the theater refused to give Smith an advance payment for her work. "She stormed out of his office and into the crowded lobby of the theater, threw her two hundred pounds on the floor, and treated the startled patrons to a performance they had not paid for." At which point, Smith proceeded to lie on her back, beat her fists and heels wildly into the floor and shout at the top of her lungs, "I'm the star of the show, I'm Bessie Smith, and these ****** bastards won't let me have my money!" At which point, the manager gave her an advance.[184]

Smith, Jimmy (1925–2005) *American organ and piano player and vocalist*

Jimmy Smith is at the top of the list of a select few jazz ORGAN players. He grew up near Philadelphia, a region with a rich tradition of jazz organists. He wasn't the first famous jazz organist, but he catapulted the instrument to prominence with his punchy Hammond sound and smooth BOP style. He originally learned to play PIANO and BASS, studying at both the Hamilton and the Ornstein schools of music. He played piano professionally with Don Gardner's Sonotones from 1951 to 1954. By 1955 he had switched to playing organ and formed his own trio consisting of organ, DRUMS, and GUITAR.

After recording for Blue Note in 1955, his unique sound brought him much acclaim. He became a sought-after musician and played on a series of successful Blue Note albums with his own group and other artists. His credits include SESSIONS with everyone from ART BLAKEY, Lou Donaldson, STANLEY TURRENTINE, and Kenny Burrell to providing a SOLO on Michael Jackson's album *Bad*. He has toured widely around the world, including recent GIGs in the mid-1990s in Japan and Europe.

Smith is the model upon which most modern organists in jazz and rock have fashioned themselves. His style is astonishingly bright and pulsing. He makes great use of the varied tones, or stops, of the Hammond. Smith's solos are dazzling, and he is quick with both his hands and his feet, where the bass pedals are played. His style has a flair for BOP with a deep-rooted touch of rhythm and blues. At age 75 he released the CD *Dot Com Blues*, featuring a royal gathering of blues legends, including BB King, Etta James, Taj Majal, and Dr. John. When they made up the term *pulling out all the stops,* they must have been talking about the incredible Jimmy Smith.

Smith, Mamie (1883–1946) *American singer*

Smith was a versatile singer who is mainly credited with having been the first singer to record the BLUES. Smith was not the first African-American singer to make a recording. There are discs and cylinders recorded as early at 1895 by artists such as singer George W. Johnson, but she had the distinction of being one of the earliest black recording artists with great success.

She moved to New York in 1913, when she was 30 years old. She worked on the vaudeville scene in New York, appearing in various musical reviews and singing at clubs in HARLEM. In 1920, while appearing in the show *Maid of Harlem* at the Lincoln Theater, she was approach by PRODUCER Perry Bradford to make a record for the OKeh label. Her first recording, including the song "That Thing Called Love," was a moderate success and marked one of the first popular recordings by a black singer. In August of the same year she went back into the studio and recorded the blues classic "Crazy Blues" from *Maid of Harlem*.

The record sold an amazing million copies in six months and launched nationwide interest in blues recordings.[185]

This recording alone was responsible for jump-starting the careers of many other black singers and performers as America developed a seemingly unquenchable thirst for the blues. It was also the first so-called RACE RECORD, leading to the establishment of rhythm and blues records as a popular and influential American musical genre.

Smith's singing reached beyond pure blues. She toured with her own group, the Jazz Hounds, during the 1920s, working with such notables as Willie "The Lion" Smith, COLEMAN HAWKINS, and Bubber Miley. She amassed a fortune and lived extravagantly, packing clubs and wearing expensive feathered gowns. Smith also appeared in several films, including *Paradise in Harlem* (1939). Unfortunately, interest in the blues that she was famous for declined in the 1930s, as did her health due to a severe arthritic condition. With her money spent, and no one to look after her, she died penniless in a New York boardinghouse in 1946.[186]

Smith, Stuff (1909–1967) *American violin player, singer, and composer*

Stuff (Hezekiah Leroy Gordon) Smith was the most original jazz violinist of the SWING era. He was also known for his temperamental behavior and quick temper, both of which were played out in his wild, aggressive assault on the electric VIOLIN. He played hard and rhythmic music, giving new verve to the otherwise staid reputation of the violin in early jazz.

He first learned violin from his father. In 1924, at age 15, he heard LOUIS ARMSTRONG for the first time while attending Johnson C. Smith University on a classical music scholarship. He was influenced so strongly by Armstrong that he left college to pursue a career in jazz. By 1926 he was working full time with Alphonso Trent's TERRITORY BAND in Dallas. He then played with JELLY ROLL MORTON and later formed his own band in Buffalo in 1930, which eventually led to a sextet that he led in New York at the Onyx Club in 1935. Smith and his COMBO, the Onyx Club Boys, were fixtures at the 52nd Street club for several years.

In 1936 Smith recorded his first record and signature tune, a novelty called "I'se a Muggin." It was a comedy song sung by drummer Ben Thigpen, partly in scat (see SCAT SINGING). It contained perhaps the first recorded use of the word BEBOP.[187]

Many other records followed. He said that his one and only influence was Louis Armstrong, and his style of "hot" violin playing certainly showed it. Along with JOE VENUTI and Stephane Grappelli, he was one of the most influential pre–World War II jazz violinists.

His career eclipsed during the 1940s but reemerged in the late 1950s, particularly as a SIDEMAN on some terrific DIZZY GILLESPIE sessions. In 1957 Smith teamed with fellow violinist Stephane Grappelli on the record *Violins No End*. He toured extensively in the 1960s and relocated to Europe until his death in Germany at age 58. He was plagued by ulcers and other health problems, particularly from alcohol abuse. His playing became the stuff of legend in the 1960s on the EUROPEAN JAZZ scene, where he influenced a new generation of rising players, including JEAN-LUC PONTY.

Smith, Tommy (b. 1967) *Scottish tenor saxophone player and composer*

Smith is one of the young lions of the current EUROPEAN JAZZ scene. Having been inspired by COLEMAN HAWKINS and JOHN COLTRANE recordings, he first picked up the SAXOPHONE at age 12. He was a quick learner, performing by age 15. He attended the BERKLEE COLLEGE OF MUSIC in Boston from 1984 to 1986. After graduating, he began touring first with CHICK COREA and then with his former teacher, GARY BURTON. Smith has a genius for listening and assimilating various jazz styles and always seems to be one step ahead of anyone who tries to categorize his sound.

During the late 1980s, this boy wonder recorded a series of jazz radio programs for the BBC that featured Chick Corea, Tommy Flanagan, Arild Andersen, Bobby Watson, Gary Burton, and the BBC Scottish Symphony Orchestra. He made various early recording appearances, including some under his own name with a reluctant Blue Note Records, but came fully into his own on the Scottish label Linn. *Reminiscence* (1993), his first recording for Linn, found him at home in a small COMBO format.

His musical vision continued to span various styles of ideas and playing. He also began to work on longer works with a classical slant. In 1993 Smith was awarded the post of COMPOSER in Residence at the Glasgow International Jazz Festival. For the festival, he wrote a suite of compositions for the Strathclyde Youth Jazz Orchestra and "Sonata No. 1" for PIANO and saxophone. He accomplished all of this by age 26.

His work and recordings have continued to explore TRADITIONAL JAZZ formats as well as large ENSEMBLE writing. In 1996 he opened Scotland's first National Jazz Institute as director of music and included coursework written by him. He collaborated with poet Edwin Morgan in 1996 to produce a suite of music entitled *Beasts of Scotland* for the Glasgow International Jazz Festival. He recorded a reunion album with Gary Burton. In 1997 he received commissions for new works from the Royal Scottish National Orchestra, the Paragon Ensemble, and the Traverse Theatre. In 1998 he released an album of DUKE ELLINGTON/BILLY STRAYHORN ballads, *The Sound of Love*. In 1999 he released an album of classical music called *Gymnopedie*, including his arrangements of works by Satie, Grieg, and Bartok, as well as the world premiere recording of his own "Sonatas for Saxophone & Piano." His work in jazz continues with the Tommy Smith American Quartet featuring Smith (tenor saxophone) and Americans Dave Kikoski (piano), James Genus (BASS), and Greg Hutchinson (DRUMS). Smith has now found an original voice and sound that should be interesting to follow in years to come.

smooth jazz

Smooth jazz is not a style, but a radio format. It features TRADITIONAL JAZZ playing and singing in the form of popular song and other works of melody that have wide appeal. It is sometimes called "new age jazz" and is quiet and laid back, lacking the interplay and IMPROVISATION of traditional jazz.

solo

One player in a group improvises while others provide accompaniment, usually in the middle of a song structure. In some jazz styles, more than one musician might take a solo at the same time or the accompaniment might be improvised to follow the soloist. The term *solo* may also refer to a musician who plays unaccompanied.

Song for My Father (1964) *album by Horace Silver*

The opening PIANO RIFF of the title track of this record is easily recognizable as the riff that Steely Dan copied for their song "Rikki Don't Lose That Number." They were not the first rock musicians to imitate HORACE SILVER's funky PIANO. This album refines the blend of rhythm and BLUES, gospel, and

HARD BOP that Silver invented in the 1950s and is a hallmark of the Horace Silver sound.

soundies

Soundies were an early precursor to music videos. They were three-minute, black-and-white films made by the Soundies Distributing Corporation of America, Inc. Designed to be played in coin-operated viewing machines, soundies could be seen in public places such as restaurants and nightclubs. More than 1,800 soundies were distributed in the United States and Canada from 1941 to 1947, but fewer than 100 of these were of jazz artists. See Appendix IV: Jazz in the Movies.

South African jazz

Of the more than 50 nations that make up the continent of Africa, the country of South Africa is the most industrialized. Strong ties to Europe and America brought jazz to South Africa, where it began to thrive in the hands of local musicians as early as the 1940s. The first recording by a black South African jazz group was *Verse I.* It was made by the Jazz Epistles, a sextet that played an extraordinary blend of American jazz and African *kwela* music, which they called "township bop." Members of the group included PIANO player Dollar Brand (later known as ABDULLAH IBRAHIM) and the legendary HUGH MASEKELA on TRUMPET. Another popular group of the same era was the Blue Notes, led by piano player Chris McGregor and featuring both white and black musicians such as Dudu Pukwana (alto and soprano SAXOPHONES).

If the essence of jazz is about freedom and self-determination, then it found a perfect stage on which to express itself in South Africa. South Africa has a long history of racial division. The history of jazz in South Africa is inseparable from the country's history of social inequality. The white government's policy of racial segregation, called apartheid, did not allow whites and blacks to assemble or perform together. This forced many South African jazz

ENSEMBLES to leave the country during the 1960s. Groups such as the Jazz Epistles and the Blue Notes went into self-exile and spread their special brand of jazz around the globe. These artists were also influential in drawing the world's attention to the suffering of South African blacks under apartheid. Partly because of the attention given the subject by such musicians, nations around the world eventually condemned the policies of apartheid. Moral and political victory was realized in 1994, when apartheid ended and Nelson Mandela became South Africa's first black president.

Throughout the long struggle, the jazz of South Africans could be heard all around the world. Interest in American jazz grew in South Africa during the 1930s and 1940s. Those who lived in a big city like Cape Town could buy 78 rpm recordings of DUKE ELLINGTON and other SWING artists. Ships that occasionally docked there brought along BIG BANDS for the locals to hear. But the explosion in jazz interest in South Africa came with the BOP sounds of THELONIOUS MONK, DIZZY GILLESPIE, and CHARLIE PARKER. Recordings of their music were a great inspiration to budding South African jazz artists. It is ironic that jazz has had such a strong influence on South African music since the roots of jazz itself lie in the music of Africa. Perhaps this is one reason why South African musicians were so ready to embrace jazz as a vital music of their own.

South African jazz evolved into several FUSIONs of jazz and African pop music. Earliest among these styles was *marabi,* which dates from the 1920s. *Marabi* blended the sounds of RAGTIME and NEW ORLEANS JAZZ with a haunting rhythm that repeats in a trancelike fashion. A singer improvised over this rhythm and a simple three-CHORD structure. Those who played *marabi* were among South Africa's first professional black musicians. They included groups such as the Jazz Maniacs, the Merry Blackbirds, and the Jazz Revellers.

Following the popularity of *marabi* came a style called *kwela.* This music was all the rage in the 1940s and 1950s. The term *kwela* itself was used with double meaning. It is from the Zulu word for "get up." In the slang of the poor black township neighborhoods, "kwela-kela" referred to the police vans that would come to haul protesting blacks away. But as a musical term, it cried out for all to get up and dance. *Kwela* usually featured a tin whistle as the lead SOLO instrument and reminded many of American swing jazz. Popular *kwela* artists included Lemmy Mabaso, Willard Cele, Elias Lerole and His Zig-Zag Flutes, and Spokes Mashiyane and His All Star Flutes.

Another South African style that was influenced by American jazz was *mbaganga,* which is sometimes called "township jive." *Mbaganga* is an Africanized jazz that became the popular music of South Africa. It featured lead singers backed by GUITAR, BASS, and BRASS instruments over a strong rhythm PHRASE that was repeated jubilantly. Popular *mbaganga* artists from the 1960s and 1970s included the singers Miriam Makeba, Dolly Rathebe, and Letta Mbulu. Popular groups included the Skylarks, Dark City Sisters, Flying Jazz Queens, the Manhattan Brothers, Kippie Moeketsi, and Malathini and the Mahotella Queens. Masekela himself became popular in the United States with a hit called "Grazing in the Grass" in the 1970s.

The high-spirited sound of Masekela and other South African musicians brought a new energy to jazz and fused it with native African music. Before too long American artists, including the ART ENSEMBLE OF CHICAGO, RAHSAAN ROLAND KIRK, and groups led by MILES DAVIS and HERBIE HANCOCK, were bringing the rhythms and melodies of African music into their new jazz. Abdullah Ibrahim has forged a remarkable career as a piano COMPOSER, performing with his small group or to the accompaniment of orchestra. Other influential South African groups included the Brotherhood of Breath (led by Chris McGregor), Pukwana, and Moholo. Zim Ngqawana (saxophone) plays jazz with a folk music twist. Moses Molelekwa revives the classic sound of *marabi* piano RIFFs accented by electronica touches. Cape Town–based guitarist Jimmy Dludlu combines African-style electric guitar with a big-band format. A new generation of singers includes Bayete, Gloria Bosman, Max Mntambo, and Busi Mhlongo.

Still Life Talking (1987) *album by Pat Metheny*

A leading FUSION player and GUITAR virtuoso, PAT METHENY brought his skillful production abilities to the forefront with this album. It combines his softly ebbing jazz harmonies with a persistent choral accompaniment and Brazilian accents. The importance of Metheny collaborator Lyle Mays is also evident through his PIANO and quietly undulating electronic keyboard sounds that shadow the other players. Stylistically, this album created one of the most copied sounds in contemporary music. Despite its leanings toward the SMOOTH JAZZ format, there is a virtuosity and interplay among the players on this record that clearly marks it as a keynote of modern jazz.

Stitt, Sonny (1924–1982) *American alto, tenor, and baritone saxophone player*

Edward "Sonny" Stitt was second only to CHARLIE PARKER as the most influential alto sax player of the BEBOP era. Coming of age as a player with the THAD JONES band in Michigan in the early 1940s, Stitt claimed that he had developed his own bop style prior to his first meeting with Parker in 1943. Like Parker and DIZZY GILLESPIE, Stitt joined the innovative BIG BAND of Billy Eckstine in 1943 for a time as he fine-tuned his style of playing. By 1945 Stitt was known as one of the most exciting voices of bop, recording with Gillespie and many others. He became a reliable fixture on the New York bop scene. He had a fruitful recording career as a SIDEMAN and could always be counted on to raise the quality of musicianship of those playing around him.

Although Stitt's style is sometimes hard to distinguish from Parker, his consistent and thoughtful solos were often easily imitated by others more than Parker's more dazzling technical feats. It can be said with fairness that Parker originated the basic style of bop alto SAXOPHONE playing, while Stitt mastered the TECHNIQUE and made it accessible to others. He played with precision and consistency and worked with a patterned form of IMPROVISATION that was logical and easy to follow. Some of his best recorded solos can be heard on "Eternal Triangle," recorded with Gillespie, "Blues Up and Down" recorded with Gene Ammons, and "Afternoon in Paris," recorded in 1950 with BUD POWELL. All of these examples, and the more than 100 recordings that Stitt made under his own name, show a master of the bop style in full command of his powers.

"St. Louis Blues" (1929) *recorded performance by Louis Armstrong and his orchestra*

Featuring LOUIS ARMSTRONG (TRUMPET) and his orchestra, Armstrong's updating of the classic W. C. HANDY tune is more upbeat. This was definitely not the BLUES anymore. It is a great example of the energy that Armstrong injected into NEW ORLEANS JAZZ, making it the art of the SOLO. It was one of the recordings that set the stage for the SWING era. Released by Columbia.

"Stompin' at the Savoy" (1941) *recorded performance by Charlie Christian*

This record featured CHARLIE CHRISTIAN (electric GUITAR), Joe Guy (TRUMPET), THELONIOUS MONK (PIANO), and KENNY CLARKE (DRUMS). Christian was guitarist for the BENNY GOODMAN sextet, which had a regular weekly GIG in Meadowbrook, New York. When they took Mondays off, Christian would head to HARLEM to JAM with other players. A recording of "Stompin' at the Savoy" was made by a fan during the formative years of BEBOP and later released by Esoteric. Christian's jamming was spectacular. This recording reveals how he alternated traditional BLUES passages with extended SOLOS that left many jaws dropping. His quick-witted changes and long solos influenced many players in the years that followed. This recording is important because

Christian died young of pneumonia and left very few recordings of his work with small ensembles.

Storyville

Storyville was the "red light" district of old New Orleans where jazz got its start in clubs and bars. When it was shut down by authorities in 1917, many jazz musicians were suddenly out of work and migrated to Chicago.

"Straight, No Chaser" (1951) *recorded performance by Thelonious Monk*

THELONIOUS MONK was a BEBOP COMPOSER in a world of bebop improvisers. "Straight, No Chaser," along with his "Round Midnight," "EPISTROPHY," and "Well, You Needn't" have become jazz standards. He used some of the most challenging CHORD CHANGES in jazz, which became a constant bane to improvisers.[188]

But he learned from listening to DUKE ELLINGTON that the BLUES were at the heart of jazz. Monk's compositions almost never strayed too far from African-American roots. "Straight, No Chaser" is based on a single PHRASE that Monk repeats numerous times on the PIANO, each time starting at a different point on the measure. Moving the phrase as he does places ACCENTs on different notes with each pass through the up-TEMPO rhythm. Vibraphonist Milt Jackson does a commendable job following Monk's lead.

Strayhorn, Billy (1915–1967) *American composer, lyricist, arranger, and piano player*

Billy "Swee' Pea" Strayhorn was one of the most talented songwriters of the JAZZ AGE. His long collaboration with DUKE ELLINGTON produced some of the most beloved songs of the era. As a young man growing up in North Carolina and then Pittsburgh, Pennsylvania, Strayhorn was first interested in classical music. He was an accomplished pianist by the time he graduated from high school and played a PIANO concerto at the convocation.[189]

He became interested in jazz after high school and met Duke Ellington in 1939, when the bandleader brought his show to Pittsburgh.

Impressed with some of the 24-year-old's songs, he hired him primarily as a lyric writer. One of the song's that the Duke acquired was the sophisticated "Lush Life," a work that Strayhorn reportedly wrote while he was a soda jerk at age 16.[190]

Strayhorn was soon a part of the Duke's entourage and traveled with the band. It took him a couple of years to fully embrace the style of the orchestra and how best to write songs for it. About this time he wrote one of his most recognizable tunes, "TAKE THE A TRAIN," which soon became the theme song for the Ellington band.

Strayhorn worked almost exclusively for Ellington during most of his career, writing lyrics, songs, and arrangements for the orchestra and small groups associated with it. He occasionally played PIANO, but his contributions were mainly as the creative songwriting partner of Ellington. Their symbiotic working relationship was so successful that it is difficult to hear differences in their respective works. Strayhorn touches included the use of the brighter and higher-pitched sounds of the orchestra, ARRANGEMENTs of instruments that were less dense than Ellington's, and the clear influence of classical music.[191]

Among the hundreds of works Strayhorn wrote for the orchestra were such famous songs and instrumentals as "Day Dream," "Satin Doll," "Chelsea Bridge," "After All," "Passion Flower," and "Johnny Come Lately." Strayhorn was also there when Ellington began writing his extended, more classically oriented works, such as *The Perfume Suite.* He rarely appeared at concerts with Ellington, but did play piano duets with the Duke at private affairs.

Strayhorn was diagnosed with cancer while he was in his 40s, but continued to work closely with the band. His last piece, "Blood Count," was composed while in the hospital. The Duke was devastated by the loss of Strayhorn, whom he once described as, "my right arm, my left arm, all the eyes

in the back of my head, my brain waves in his head, and his in mine."[192]

In his darkest times Ellington often found that the best form of expressing his feelings was through his music. Just three months after the death of his longtime collaborator, the Duke recorded the touching and brilliant AND HIS MOTHER CALLED HIM BILL as a personal tribute. In years to follow, other jazz greats, including ART FARMER, acknowledged their appreciation of Strayhorn's work by recording tribute albums of their own for the extraordinary Swee' Pea.

stride piano

A rhythmic style of jazz PIANO playing developed during the 1920s and 1930s. The left hand of the musician "walks" or strides over the lower keys to play rhythm and harmony at the same time. The right hand plays melodies or improvises. Notable stride artists included JAMES P. JOHNSON and FATS WALLER.

string bass   See DOUBLE BASS.

Sun Ra (1914–1993) *American piano, organ, synthesizer, and keyboard player, composer, and bandleader*

Sun Ra liked to claim that he was from the planet Saturn, but he was actually born Herman Poole "Sonny" Blount in Birmingham, Alabama. He grew up listening to and playing the BLUES and had a commanding ear for melody. He began playing with groups as a teenager and studied music in college. His roots were in BIG BAND jazz. He played PIANO and arranged music in the FLETCHER HENDERSON Orchestra in Chicago from 1946 to 1947. A flamboyant and charismatic character, he formed his own group in the mid-1950s to explore his brand of blues and jazz mixed with free form playing.

His group, known as the Solar Arkestra, made a name for itself in AVANT-GARDE jazz by the mid-

1950s. The size of the group varied widely over its 35 years of existence, sometimes reaching as many as 50 players. But its core members stayed with Sun Ra for life, including saxophonists Pat Patrick, Marshall Allen, and John Gilmore. The group began to make a long series of mostly self-produced records in the early 1960s and moved from Chicago to New York and then finally to Philadelphia, its home base for many productive years.

Sun Ra's music began in the 1950s as a blend of HARD BOP and Ellington SWING. His interest in POLYRHYTHM and sound textures edged his music into the avant-garde. He was one of the first jazz musicians to make effective use of electronic keyboards, including the electric piano as early as 1955. His brand of avant-garde jazz predated ORNETTE COLEMAN by several years.

Sun Ra organized his performances around free form explorations of basic themes, often blues based, that evolved into elaborate SOLO and group improvisations. Every performance was something of a workshop. His shows were also something of a mystical journey, with the group singing and playing songs about space travel, living on Jupiter, and orbiting the sun. By the time of the Arkestra's greatest success in the 1970s, his road show had taken on the atmosphere of a circus, with costumed dancers,

multimedia presentations, and the bandleader himself bedecked in a wizard's cape or other strange adornments. It was an extravaganza unlike any other in jazz, but success is often fleeting in this field, and the group struggled financially, playing numerous long GIGS and selling their own cheaply produced recordings to make ends meet.

The Arkestra experienced their most success touring colleges and also Europe during the 1970s. In the 1980s interest waned and Sun Ra brought his otherworldy themes back down to earth, showcasing TRADITIONAL JAZZ and swing with his space-age twist. One of Sun Ra's accomplishments was to explore the huge diversity of effects and sounds that can happen when you have a big band. His arrangements were often more textural than harmonic. His imaginative and rollicking piano playing is sometimes compared to DUKE ELLINGTON. As a stylist, the structure of his music changed over the years. In the early 1950s it was closely aligned with hard bop and swing. There is a touch of MODAL JAZZ in some of his works. He also worked in textures of electronic music associated with the European avant-garde of the 1960s. One can also hear Third World chant and African drumming in his music. His works in the 1960s were largely based on concepts rather than individual songs. Extended works might unravel slowly through the pulsing sound of an ORGAN or other electronic keyboard.

Sun Ra was a great bandleader, able to manage a wide range of sounds and players into an absorbing and unique jazz experience. He should be discussed in the same light as equally provocative and accomplished avant-garde jazz legends JOHN COLTRANE, CECIL TAYLOR, and Ornette Coleman, but he is more often neglected than taken seriously. There are more than 100 recordings of Sun Ra's music out there somewhere, most produced on his tiny Saturn label, and most not available on compact disc. But a wise jazz collector should scoop up these old vinyl gems now because the Arkestra of the past will surely become music of the future.

Sun Ra

What was his music all about? Sun Ra was mindful of the predicament of working people, and particularly the history of underprivileged African-American people in America. His music was a door to the imagination, a way to enlighten one toward a better view of the self. He said, "I wanna calm people down, put 'em in a sort of dream state, between myth and reality. They just gotta learn to use their intuition. . . . You got to learn to *understand* rather than *overstand* your position regarding so-called reality."[193]

Surman, John (b. 1944) *British baritone and soprano saxophone, bass clarinet, and synthesizer player, composer, arranger, and bandleader*
John Surman, one of Europe's most durable and talented jazz players, emerged on the London scene in the 1960s. Born in Tavistock, Devon, England, Surman first played baritone SAXOPHONE and attended the London College of Music (1962–65) and the London University Institute of Education (1965–66). During this period he also worked with Mike Westbrook as a SIDEMAN and ARRANGER for his small, experimental COMBOs. He was honored as best SOLO player at the 1968 MONTREUX JAZZ FESTIVAL, where he appeared with Westbrook, thus catapulting him into the spotlight. His work on the baritone saxophone during this period greatly extended the use of that instrument in jazz.

Surman was one of the first instrumentalists to play in the extreme higher pitch ranges of this instrument.[194]

He played on the important JOHN MCLAUGHLIN album *Extrapolation* (1969), an early exploration of jazz and rock FUSION. From 1969 to 1972 he toured exhaustively in Europe with his group The Trio, which included Barre Phillips on BASS and Stu Martin on DRUMS. The Trio specialized in unfettered FREE JAZZ IMPROVISATION and was a sensation wherever it played. After a period of rest he took some new directions with the sax trio SOS in 1973 and also began to compose music for dance companies such as Carolyn Carlson Dance Co. at the Paris Opera (1974 to 1979). During that time he began to include the SYNTHESIZER in his arsenal

of instruments, tinkering with ways to accompany himself with electronic harmonies and rhythms without escaping from the essence of his jazz sound.

By the late 1970s Surman was well established as an adventurous and thoughtful performer and COMPOSER. He continued to collaborate with other players during the 1980s but also explored the possibilities of solo work on an important series of eight albums with ECM Records. Some of these were solo efforts, others collaborations with the likes of drummer JACK DEJOHNETTE, Karin Krog, and Paul Bley. This period from 1979 to 1992 allowed Surman to explore composing more fully and integrating of AVANT-GARDE musical ideas and folk music into his sound. Surman has also been commissioned on occasion to write church music. One of his most noted recordings of the 1990s, *Proverbs and Songs* (1996), includes parts for pipe ORGAN and church choir. Surman continues his steady output of superbly conceived records and performances. The spiritual core of his recent music is evidenced again by his collaboration with DeJohnette, *Invisible Nature* (2000), on which the pair combines a sublime spirituality with free jazz improvisation. Surman's trademark sound is the sonorous baritone saxophone played with a backdrop of electronic harmonies and ambient rhythms. His interplay with other musicians is equally superb in a live performance setting. He is one of England's most enduring voices in modern jazz.

Swallow, Steve (b. 1940) *American bass player*
Swallow discovered jazz and BASS playing while in high school and studied music at Yale University until he left to work with Paul and CARLA BLEY in New York in 1960. He found himself in the eye of the AVANT-GARDE jazz storm, working with a variety of leaders and styles. He played with ERIC DOLPHY and THAD JONES as part of the GEORGE RUSSELL sextet, and toured or recorded with many artists as diverse as João Gilberto, BENNY GOODMAN, CHICO

HAMILTON, Zoot Sims, CLARK TERRY, and CHICK COREA. Swallow began writing music as part of the ART FARMER QUARTET (1964) and toured with STAN GETZ from 1965 to 1967.

In 1968 Swallow began a long association with vibe player, bandleader, and educator GARY BURTON. In 1978 he added electric bass to his portfolio and dove headlong into various FUSION projects. He was a member of the JOHN SCOFIELD group (1980 to 1984) and has been a frequent collaborator with Carla Bley, ANDY SHEPPARD, and Steve Kuhn. His compositions were featured in a concert at the London Jazz Festival in 1994, and he frequently works and tours in Europe.

The new millennium found him playing and touring internationally with John Scofield and Carla Bley, with whom he lives in upstate New York. He is a perennial favorite electric BASS player of jazz critics and is known for his fluid, lyrical style that is much like an electric GUITAR. His playing is as distinctive as contemporaries STANLEY CLARKE, JACO PASTORIUS, and DAVE HOLLAND. Using a five-string rather than a four-string electric bass, he has great touch with higher notes not generally associated with the bass. The five-string instrument also allows Swallow to embellish his playing with chords, another domain usually left for electric guitars.

swing

A style of jazz that dominated an era from the early 1930s to the late 1940s. The swing sound was defined by BIG BANDS and became America's most popular music at the time. What makes a song swing? It is more than a steady beat. It is a kicking ARRANGEMENT of harmony, rhythm, and melody that propels the music forward at all times. The use of SHUFFLE RHYTHMS, SYNCOPATION, and melodic IMPROVISATION

were important parts of the swing sound. Big bands used multiple reed instruments to create a full-bodied swinging sound. But swing was not just big band music. It was the essential drive behind small group jazz before and after the big band era. Representative swing artists include COUNT BASIE, DUKE ELLINGTON, the MODERN JAZZ QUARTET, the BENNY GOODMAN QUARTET, GLENN MILLER, and the MILES DAVIS QUINTET.

Switzerland   See EUROPEAN JAZZ.

syncopation

A rhythmic element of jazz derived from African-American slave songs, minstrel music, and a group dance called the cakewalk. It calls for playing unexpected ACCENTs on top of a steady rhythmic pulse or weak part of a beat. SYNCOPATION is an essential part of the feeling of jazz music. It was important to RAGTIME in which the left hand played the steady pulse and the right hand played the accented notes.

synthesizer

A self-contained electronic music instrument for the generation, modification, and playing of electronically produced sounds. Early synthesizers, such as the Moog and Buchla systems from the mid-1960s, were bulky and mostly limited to studio use. The Minimoog and other portable synthesizers with keyboards became available in the early 1970s, adding another unique instrumental voice to jazz, rock, and other music. Early players of synthesizers in jazz included SUN RA, HERBIE HANCOCK, and JAN HAMMER.

See also GUITAR SYNTHESIZER.

take
One recorded performance during a recording SESSION. Multiple takes are frequently done, from which the best performance, or parts of performances, may be selected for the final mix of the music.

"Take Five" See *TIME OUT.*

"Take the 'A' Train" (1941) *recorded performance by Duke Ellington*
Featuring DUKE ELLINGTON and his orchestra, the Duke always managing to produce hit records without diluting the quality of his group's music, "Take the 'A' Train" is one of those amazingly complex arrangements that also makes the audience hum and dance. The piece was written by BILLY STRAYHORN. Duke's PIANO begins gently and is followed by a full-bodied sax VERSE led by BEN WEBSTER. Muted TRUMPETs and other horns weave in and out. The confident BASS of JIMMY BLANTON moves the song ahead with glee. Then the whole thing is decorated by two great SOLOs by trumpeter Ray Nance. The song was so popular that it became yet another theme song for the Duke's band, even though he already had two others!

Tatum, Art (1910–1956) *American piano player*
Tatum, almost blind from birth, overcame his disadvantage to develop extraordinary PIANO TECHNIQUE.

After first learning the GUITAR and VIOLIN, he mostly taught himself by listening to recordings and radio broadcasts. He was awed by FATS WALLER, another piano player with whom he later would become friends.

Tatum is one of the most revered pianists in jazz history. He mastered every style he heard and became a master of IMPROVISATION. In fact, he was a reluctant COMPOSER and mostly enjoyed making familiar tunes his own. There was no doubt that improvisation was serious business with Tatum. "You have to practice improvisation," he once remarked, "Let no one kid you about it!" He was able to come up with endlessly varying improvisations on any tune. He did this not only by changing the melody of a song but also the CHORDS, harmonies, and rhythm. Legend has it that he practiced such variations as a kind of game, taking a popular melody and changing it spontaneously over and over again by gradually changing the chord pattern.

His ability to continually modify the rhythm of a song was a preview of BEBOP. Some of his piano RIFFS were even borrowed by bebop horn and piano players who were influenced by Tatum's high-energy, high-velocity style. He always had an ear for classical music, which drew him to RAGTIME and STRIDE PIANO early on. After igniting his career in Canada, he came to New York in 1932 to play piano at Adelaide Hall. It was during this period that his most influential recordings were made. In 1933 his recording of the familiar "TIGER RAG" set the jazz world on its ear. It was played at a dazzling pace "with the right hand flying along in eighth notes most of the time."[195]

It was an amazing performance for any player. Tatum's career took him on tour around the country and the world, playing clubs and concerts. He formed his own trio in 1943 with guitarist Tiny Grimes and BASS player Slam Stewart, with whom Tatum played off and on until his death in 1956 at age 47.

For the most part, Tatum was an artistic maverick and loner. His style stood apart from others and never quite followed whatever style was hot at the time. Tatum stuck to his own personal vision, making him almost impossible to categorize. His playing was so technically superior to his peers that he was seldom imitated. But there is one thing about which all critics agree; Tatum had the most awesome CHOPS of any jazz pianist. His technique was spectacularly fast with his crossing hands, lightning-fast arpeggios, and oddball harmonies. One legitimate criticism of Tatum is that his musical ideas didn't expand as fully as his technique. He was content to razzle-dazzle with his playing, but his music sometimes seemed out of touch and dated. This is probably one reason that he had so few disciples.[196]

The other side of this coin was expressed by author James Lester when he wrote of Tatum, "Listening to a really good pianist one might say, 'I could never do that.' But confronted with Tatum most musicians have said to themselves, 'Nobody can do that!'"[197]

Taylor, Cecil (b. 1930) American piano player, composer, bandleader, and educator

Like many other anxious young jazz musicians in the 1950s, Cecil Taylor thought it was time for a change. He was one of the few artists capable of pulling it off. At a time when BOP was cooling down and COOL JAZZ was making conservative jazz mainstream, Taylor unleashed an original style of modern jazz that has stood the test of time. He unleashed his alternative style in stages beginning

with his first record, *Jazz Advance* (1956). While playing with a conventional HARD BOP RHYTHM SECTION, his PIANO playing was beginning to take off in a style even more eccentric than THELONIOUS MONK's. Taylor was an alumnus of two music schools and was well versed in the abstract experimental classical music coming out of Europe at the time. He began to use TONE CLUSTERS and DISSONANCE while still holding onto the CHORD structure of hard bop.

By the time his quartet appeared at the NEWPORT JAZZ FESTIVAL in 1957, Taylor had already been branded as an experimenter. Pieces like "African Violets" from his second album, *Looking Ahead!* (1958), ably demonstrate his continued evolution into an extraordinary AVANT-GARDE jazz COMPOSER. The piano on this album is further detached from the rhythm section, creating a disembodied voice that is beautifully, and abstractly, isolated. It is clear that Taylor was not trying to SWING. His musical content was focused on textures and impressions, almost like the visual impressions given by a painting by Matisse.

By the onset of the 1960s, he was playing without an established chord structure or a constant TEMPO. The music was about clusters of sound, explosive moments of realization, and it was very rewarding for listeners who hang on every next, unexpected turn. Taylor's use of atonality was measured and pervasive, as with any serious composer of classical music. His IMPROVISATIONS were not as free-form or squawking as those of ORNETTE COLEMAN, but often latched onto SCALES and interesting clusters of notes as their tonal center. His work became more adventurous so that by the 1970s he was producing his own ENSEMBLE-brand free improvisation.

It could be said that Taylor's composing style is orchestra-like, not COMBO-like. When his group improvises, it focuses on creating interesting cluster of tones and textures. Rhythm is often secondary or merely anticipated because of the lack of a traditional time-keeping rhythm section. Taylor paints huge canvases with his imaginative sound. While

Cecil Taylor

equally important pioneers Ornette Coleman, MILES DAVIS, and JOHN COLTRANE received most of the credit for changing the nature of jazz in the early 1960s, Taylor was an inspiration to them all but seldom received the recognition.

He is still active today, writing ensemble works and seeing some of his works produced for classical ensembles as well. The album *Momentum Space* (1999) teams him with two other jazz legends, tenor saxophonist Dewey Redman and drummer ELVIN JONES. It is an opportunity for these veterans to spotlight their equally influential styles. Taylor is explosive and powerful, pounding out the tone clusters on tracks such as "Nine," but also playful and pondering on his duet with Jones called "It." The album is but one in a collection of many recorded during the 1980s and 1990s that seal the case making Cecil Taylor one of the greatest jazz composers and innovators of all time.

Not everyone dug Cecil Taylor's music. Like Ornette Coleman, Taylor was often criticized by fellow musicians who disagreed with his approach. In 1969, after listening to the Cecil Taylor recording *Unit Structures,* piano player Les McCann exclaimed, "It's different, it's just not my groove, but what gets me is that there are so many other guys

copying, and call it some name like avant-garde which has nothing to do with feeling, as far as I'm concerned. In my opinion that's what jazz is all about; swing and feeling!"[198]

Some say that jazz is still catching up with Cecil Taylor.

Teagarden, Jack (1905–1964) *American trombone player, vocalist, and bandleader*

Raised in Texas in a musical family, Teagarden took up TROMBONE at age 10. Originally influenced by spirituals and BLUES, he first made a name for himself in Kansas City in the early 1920s. Following the example of Jimmy Harrison, he transformed the trombone into a virtuosic SOLO jazz instrument, much as LOUIS ARMSTRONG had done for the TRUMPET. Teagarden was best known for his work with the PAUL WHITEMAN Orchestra in the late 1920s and early 1930s and was often showcased on the bandleader's radio broadcasts.

Teagarden was known for making difficult playing sound easy. His tone was smooth and full, and the impression he gave was one of relaxation, despite the challenging nature of his favorite RIFFS. He was also a good vocalist with a bluesy style. His most popular vocal performance was "Basin Street Blues" with lyrics that he and GLENN MILLER wrote. He recorded the song, singing and playing trombone, in 1929 with BENNY GOODMAN. His long and distinguished career also featured historic work with Louis Armstrong, COLEMAN HAWKINS, and the FLETCHER HENDERSON band. After trying his best to lead his own BIG BAND in the late 1940s, he found solace and steady work as part of Armstrong's All Stars, various small combos that he led, and tours around the world.

technique

The way in which an instrument is played or a singer uses their voice. *Expressive* techniques are special ways in which a player can accentuate or change their sound (see ACCENT).

tempo

The pace, or speed, of a piece of music. An "up-tempo" song is fast paced.

territory bands

Local bands that prospered during the early years of jazz by playing in their region of the country. Territory bands were most popular from about 1915 to 1930 until their music was eclipsed by the popularity of major recording artists and radio broadcasts from big cities.

Terry, Clark (b. 1920) *American trumpet and flugelhorn player*

Terry was born in St. Louis into a family that included several musicians. He learned to play bugle by age 15, and then the valve TROMBONE, and finally the TRUMPET. One of his first GIGS was playing on a riverboat in St. Louis, an experience that immersed him in TRADITIONAL JAZZ playing and IMPROVISATION. He came into his own as a trumpeter while playing for an accomplished navy BIG BAND during World War II. After the service, he was a valued member of several big name bands, including those of Charlie Barnet, COUNT BASIE, and then DUKE ELLINGTON.

His nine-year stint with the Ellington orchestra from 1951 to 1959 and then QUINCY JONES from 1959 to 1960 brought him great notices. In 1960 he became one of the first African-American musicians to become a member of a television studio band, having been hired by NBC to play in the Tonight Show Orchestra led by Doc Severinsen. During this time he also occasionally led his own big band. He became known for his mumbling style of SCAT SINGING and a recording called "Mumbles" which he made with the OSCAR PETERSON Trio in 1964.

After his Tonight Show gig ended in 1972, he divided his time between leading his own combos and touring with other artists, including ELLA FITZGERALD and OSCAR PETERSON. Terry began playing the FLUGELHORN in earnest in the 1970s, and it has become an increasingly important part of his repertoire. He also began to devote more time to teaching others about jazz and has become well known as a clinician. The University of New Hampshire holds an annual jazz festival in his honor. Still active as a teacher, recording artist, and performer, his bouncing, joyous style conveys the pleasures of a life fulfilled by jazz.

Terry is in some ways the living tradition of jazz trumpet. While some of those he mentored have now passed away, including DIZZY GILLESPIE and MILES DAVIS, he continues to thrive as a living link to the days of big bands and BOP. Terry is known for having a wide palette of tones and shapes to his sound. He plays with a vocal quality that Miles Davis emulated. One of the highlights of his performances is when he spars with himself, trading improvisations on the trumpet and flugelhorn. More than a mere gimmick, Terry demonstrates his exquisite mastery of BRASS TECHNIQUE and his unfailing ability to blend traditional jazz, bop, and modern song. He is director of Clark Terry's Big Band Summer Jazz Camp, and an adviser to the International Association of Jazz Educators. Terry has found something affirming in jazz that can bring joy and fulfillment to one's life. He once remarked: "I believe that regardless of how many people you've listened to or emulated over the years, your sound is you and what you really feel inside."

third stream jazz

Third stream jazz is the name given to a recipe for a new kind of musical main course; the kind that results when IMPROVISATIONal jazz is poured through the same funnel as European classical music. What ends up in the bowl may blend well if stirred with an aggressive mixer, but, if entrusted to an inexperienced chef, is likely to separate into two dissimilar elements, like oil and water. The early inspiration for this concoction can be traced to the early years of jazz when white conductors were anxious to filch hot and spicy African-American ingredients for their own overly sweet confections masquerading as jazz. COMPOSERs who have tried to perfect a recipe for this kind of music throughout the decades of jazz history include PAUL Whiteman, ARTIE SHAW, DUKE ELLINGTON, STAN KENTON, GUNTHER SCHULLER, CHARLES MINGUS, and GEORGE RUSSELL.

It was FRENCH HORN player Schuller who invented the term *third stream* in 1957 to describe this style of jazz. In his own work with the MODERN JAZZ QUARTET, Schuller cooked up some of the tastiest examples of this musical delicacy. Still more satisfying recipes for third stream jazz arose from the AVANT-GARDE jazz movement of the 1960s as musicians schooled in the cuisine of European music devoted their talent to experiments in jazz. Among these, MUHAL RICHARD ABRAMS, ANTHONY BRAXTON, and CECIL TAYLOR stand out.

Third stream jazz continues to cook on the back burner today, and is often the product of academic bake-offs where classically trained students try to jazz up their classical music recipes with touches of improvisational jazz. Otherwise, third stream jazz is largely a musical cuisine requiring somewhat scarce ingredients and having too few chefs trained to prepare it properly.

Thompson, Sir Charles (b. 1918) *American piano and organ player, composer and arranger*

As an aspiring young PIANO player, Thomson left home at age 15 to begin a long and fruitful career. He began playing with TERRITORY BANDS in the Midwest in the early 1930s, eventually landing an important GIG with LIONEL HAMPTON in 1940. After playing on a recording with Hampton, he worked with LESTER YOUNG and then ROY ELDRIDGE in New York, then went to California with COLEMAN HAWKINS from 1944 to 1945. Back in New York he played with CHARLIE PARKER and began to freelance with many other leaders. He was also a sought-after ARRANGER and did work for COUNT BASIE and FLETCHER HENDERSON, among others.

Thompson wrote the jazz standard "Robbin's Nest" during his stint with Illinois Jacquet in the late 1940s. During the 1950s he took up ORGAN and also became a leading SESSION man in mainstream jazz. During the 1960s he toured Europe with Coleman Hawkins and others and frequently played clubs in New York. After recovering from a serious illness in the 1970s, he resumed his career. In the 1990s he moved to Japan where he played and recorded frequently. Sir Charles came to prominence during a time of transition from SWING to BOP. He was one of the first accomplished bop piano players. His classy style and ear for other players made him an invaluable ENSEMBLE member.

"Tiger Rag" (1933) *recorded performance by Art Tatum*

ART TATUM's undeniable virtuosity on the PIANO was showcased early on in this recording of a familiar old RAGTIME tune. His SOLO performance was both dazzling and disorienting for those who hadn't heard his playing. After a brief introduction he launches into an assault of eighth notes with the right hand that sweeps up and down the keys while the left hand judiciously blocks out chords in the lower register. The pace of his playing was so fast that it sounded mechanically reproduced or sped up through recording magic. Tatum's "Tiger Rag" set the jazz world on its ear and helped established the artist as a legend in the making.

Time Out (1959) *album by the Dave Brubeck Quartet*

Coming at the end of the COOL JAZZ era, *Time Out* was the first jazz record to sell a million copies. The centerpiece is "TAKE FIVE" written by alto SAXOPHONE player Paul Desmond, whose smoky, laid-back performance simmers on top of a blocky rhythm accompaniment that might otherwise sound jarring. This album well represents the quartet's use of uncommon TIME SIGNATUREs and song structures borrowed from classical music, all of which have had a long-lasting influence on modern jazz. Released by Columbia.

time signature

On sheet music, the two numbers, one appearing over the other, placed at the beginning of the musical staff to indicate the metrical division of a piece. The time signature denotes the number of beats per measure and the note value of each beat. 6/8 and 3/4 are examples of time signatures.

tone cluster

A CHORD made up of notes that are only half a step or whole step apart in a musical scale. On the PIANO, a tone cluster might include white keys that are next to each other or black and white keys that are next to each other. A tone cluster might sound out of tune when compared to the normal chords played in a conventional song. BEBOP PIANO players BUD POWELL and THELONIOUS MONK often used tone clusters in their music.

Tormé, Mel (1925–1999) *American singer, piano player, drummer, and composer*

Known as the "Velvet Fog" because of his smooth vocalizations, Tormé was a devoted jazz singer who also mastered popular song throughout his long and successful career. While only a youngster, he began singing on stage and acting on radio. By age 16 he had written his first song, which was picked up by the popular BIG BAND led by HARRY JAMES. After leading his own group, and a stint in the army during World War II, he emerged as a capable lead singer. He fronted several big bands including those of ARTIE SHAW and BUDDY RICH.

A multitalented musician, he was also gifted as a COMPOSER and ARRANGER. His most popular song is the perennial holiday favorite, "The Christmas Song." Tormé's vocal powers were versatile and surprisingly limber. Tormé was able to make any song his own through his unique phrasing, pitch range, and SCAT SINGING. He was one of those singers with roots in jazz who became a popular singer on the pop charts. Tormé was frequently on television during the 1960s and 1970s, and sustained a long and fruitful career as an entertainer on the nightclub circuit. Throughout it all, jazz always influenced his interpretation of pop songs. He successfully used popular music as a vehicle for introducing the public to the higher calling of jazz.

traditional jazz (classic jazz)

The name given to the stylings of early jazz associated mostly with New Orleans and Chicago. In addition to small COMBOS playing horns, BANJOS, and reed instruments, early jazz had a remarkable variety of PIANO styles, including RAGTIME, stride, and BOOGIE-WOOGIE. Representative artists in this tradition include LOUIS ARMSTRONG, "BIX" BEIDERBECKE, JOSEPH "KING" OLIVER, JELLY ROLL MORTON, FATS WALLER, and FREDDIE KEPPARD.

tremolo

A slight fluctuation in a sound's volume used by singers and instrumentalists as an expressive TECHNIQUE.

Tristano, Lennie (1919–1978) *American piano player, composer, and educator*

Tristano, who began playing PIANO at age four and was permanently blinded by childhood disease at age nine, was an original thinking COMPOSER and performer who experimented with new jazz forms beginning in the 1940s. He was educated at the American Conservatory of Music in Chicago. Although the piano was his main instrument, he could play the tenor SAXOPHONE, CLARINET, and cello. In 1946 he moved to New York, where he began playing with various trios and other combos under his own tutelage.

He created a new stylistic approach to composing jazz that differed sharply from the energetic sound of BEBOP, which was hugely popular at the time. Instead of the short boisterous phrases that DIZZY GILLESPIE and CHARLIE PARKER relied upon, Tristano favored SOLO parts and IMPROVISATIONS featuring long strings of notes that carried the music forward gradually but without too much drama. There is a lack of space or ACCENTs in his phrasing, and an almost mechanical rhythm to the persistent length of his notes. As a young player, Tristano listened to ART TATUM records and copied his solos note for note. As a teacher, he had his students mimic the solos of saxophonist LESTER YOUNG, one of the reigning masters of improvisation at the time.

Tristano surrounded himself with like-minded musicians, including saxophonists Lee Konitz and Warne Marsh. Under Tristano's guidance, they formed the heart of a jazz cult that applied his theories to performance. Tristano was the first jazz artist to seriously explore FREE IMPROVISATION in jazz, some early examples of which include his COMBO recordings of "Intuition" and "Digression" in 1949. After establishing his own studio in 1951, Tristano spent most of his remaining years teaching, rarely performing in public. His composition "Requiem" (1955) includes an impassioned solo that was reportedly a big influence on the developing BILL EVANS. Otherwise, there is generally a sharp contrast between the emotional playing of Evans and the emotionally stripped style of Tristano. Lee Konitz and his soft, dry alto saxophone sound went on to be one of the leading players in cool jazz, a style whose calm and collected nature contrasted sharply with that of BOP.

trombone

The trombone is one of the earliest instruments of jazz. It was borrowed from marching band music and became an important part of such pioneering NEW ORLEANS JAZZ COMBOS as the Peerless Orchestra and the BUDDY BOLDEN Orchestra. Trombones would share in the playing of melodies and also played lower harmony to other instruments such as the CORNET and CLARINET. This BRASS wind instrument is found in two basic types; the valve trombones, with notes played by keys like a TRUMPET, and the slide trombone, which played notes selected by moving a variable slide.

Trumbauer, Frankie (1901–1956) *American c-melody saxophone player, vocalist, and bandleader*

"Tram" has been called the best white saxophonist of the 1920s. His pairing with CORNET player "BIX" BEIDERBECKE resulted in some of the most exciting small COMBO jazz recordings of the 1920s. It was a formative time for jazz. After working with Beiderbecke, the two of them joined PAUL WHITEMAN's Orchestra in 1927. Tram was a favorite player with Whiteman, lending his sparkling light sound to the pop orchestrations of the time. After leaving the Whiteman Orchestra, he led his own group from 1937 to 1939. During World War II he withdrew from music and became a test pilot. Trumbauer favored the c-melody SAXOPHONE, an unusual saxophone with a pitch range between alto and tenor. His 1927 recordings, with Beiderbecke, of "SINGIN' THE BLUES" and other songs showcased their relaxed, effortless sound. Tram's playing was buoyant and precise. He was known for playing slow VIBRATO on the saxophone, a style that was uncommon at the time. LESTER YOUNG, among others, was influenced by this unique tone and approach.

trumpet

Older cousin of the CORNET, the trumpet became one of the preferred SOLO instruments of jazz during the 1920s. This was largely due to the influence of LOUIS ARMSTRONG, who preferred the trumpet's brighter, brassier sound over that of the cornet. Trumpets are available in a wide range of pitch classes and sizes, but the 3-valve B-flat trumpet is most widely used. The trumpet with the highest pitch is the piccolo trumpet. Many players can use the trumpet adequately, but few can master the difficult TECHNIQUE needed to make it stand out. It is played by blowing and vibrating the lips on the mouthpiece and then using combinations of three finger valves to play notes. Blowing harder or softer can change the octave. It can be played loud and full, or soft and warm. Few masters, including LOUIS ARMSTRONG, DIZZY GILLESPIE, and MILES

DAVIS, have fully exploited the full range of this instrument.

Turrentine, Stanley (1934–2000) *American tenor and soprano saxophone player and composer*

Turrentine was a SAXOPHONE player whose BLUES style of soul jazz was popular in the 1960s. He grew up in Pittsburgh, where he learned to play from his father, an amateur saxophone player. His early work in rhythm and blues bands included a stint with Ray Charles in 1952. In the late fifties he concentrated on jazz while playing with MAX ROACH. He was one of the early sax players to work in a small COMBO with a featured organist such as JIMMY SMITH. He formed his own group in 1960 and married organist and singer SHIRLEY SCOTT, who played with him throughout the 1960s. They were divorced in 1971. His work in the 1970s drifted from jazz into the area of heavily produced recordings of pop standards. In the 1980s, returning to jazz, he regained his credibility as a solid sax man by leading small groups and playing clubs again. He recorded widely with many of the big names of jazz, including Roach, Kenny Burrell, DONALD BYRD, JIMMY SMITH, ABBEY LINCOLN, and DIANA KRALL.

12-bar structure

Classic BLUES uses a standard musical form of 12 bars, and an AAB structure of the VERSES.

Tyner, McCoy (b. 1938) *American piano player and composer*

Born and raised in Philadelphia, Tyner is also known by the Muslim name of Sulaimon Saud. Tyner is a unique PIANO stylist and one of the most influential players in modern jazz. As a teen he studied music at the West Philadelphia Music School and later the Granoff School of Music in Philadelphia. By age 17 he was gigging with his own jazz group. Players who influenced his style of piano playing music were ART TATUM and THELONIOUS MONK, but it was really neighbors Richie and BUD POWELL who fired him up about the excitement of jazz. Much jazz piano playing before him relied on block chords and a straight-ahead CHORD progression to move the music along. Tyner was hearing something different in the air.

Call it luck or jazz providence, but being in Philadelphia made a big difference in Tyner's career. It was there, in 1959, that he met the powerhouse SAXOPHONE player JOHN COLTRANE, who happened to be hanging around town between GIGS with MILES DAVIS. Tyner and Coltrane hit it off and began playing informally. When Coltrane decided to split from Davis soon thereafter, he immediately thought of Tyner as the rockbed of his RHYTHM SECTION. Together they developed an extension of Davis's MODAL JAZZ style that took them to stellar regions.

Tyner's chief innovation was to replace the use of familiar chords with unconventional combinations of keys. While most piano players use chords that are spaced using intervals in thirds, Tyner began using fourths and fifths to build his sound. Coltrane sometimes called Tyner's chords "clusters," and they formed a powerful foundation for Coltrane's saxophone explorations. Tyner played hard and loud and perfected several TECHNIQUES that allowed him to be the center of gravity around which other members of the Coltrane QUARTET revolved. He often held a loud note or chord with his left hand while his right hand rhythmically repeated another chord. The sound of his piano, always perceptible to other members of the group, held the music together even as the players freely improvised.

Tyner's work with the Coltrane quartet from 1960 to 1965 was immensely influential. He introduced a new style of playing that the next generation copied, and the old generation tried to adopt. Tyner left Coltrane in 1965 to form his own group, and he has been active in trio and quartet work ever since. His album *The Real McCoy* (1967) is a remarkable extension of his work with Coltrane. It is perfectly crafted to reach the brink of tonal and rhythmic chaos without actually going there. The composing mind of Tyner actively at work, making real-time adjustments to keep the music under his control, is apparent in the music. After a short down period in the late 1960s, he established himself once again as a key voice of jazz piano with an album called *Sahara* in 1972. While around him the sounds of jazz FUSION and Cecil Taylor's high-energy playing were making waves, Tyner confidently laid down the most amazing tracks of controlled, disciplined jazz ecstasy.

Over the years he has experimented with a BIG BAND format, has toured internationally, and has been openly influenced by rich textures and harmonies found in Asian and African music. He continues to compose and perform in various group and SOLO settings to this day and has added many important recordings to his catalog, including solo efforts and sessions with other well-known musicians. He seems most at home doing what he does best, laying down the grand style that has made him a legend.

unison
Two or more musicians playing the same melody at
the same time, sometimes in different octaves.

Vaughn, Sarah (1924–1990) *American jazz singer*

In the pantheon of great jazz vocalists, Sarah Vaughn was one of the most original. She followed in the footsteps of BILLIE HOLIDAY, LOUIS ARMSTRONG, and the only slightly younger ELLA FITZGERALD by establishing an influential style that has often been imitated. Hailing from Newark, New Jersey, Vaughn won a singing contest when she was just 19 at HARLEM's famed Apollo Theater. Also a PIANO player, she was hired by Earl Hines for his band and debuted with him in 1943. Suddenly she was sharing the stage with some of her idols, including DIZZY GILLESPIE and CHARLIE PARKER, who both played with Hines. Still only in her early 20s, she transformed the bop sound of Parker and Gillespie into a unique singing style.

After a stint with Billy Eckstine from 1944 to 1945, her SOLO career went into orbit. Vaughn's performances were dominated during the 1950s and 1960s by her work as a singer of slickly produced love songs. One of her most famous hits was "Tenderly," recorded in 1947, the tune that put her on the pop charts. However, she never forgot her jazz roots and continued to nurture her extraordinary talent in this style of singing throughout her life.

Vaughn impressed other jazz musicians with her knowledge of music and grasp of trends in jazz. Her vocal powers were extraordinary. Vaughn's lowest singing register was nearly the same as that of a male baritone, her highest was that of a soprano. Her sound was lush and smooth, totally unlike the quirky vocalizations of Billie Holiday and Louis Armstrong. She was also pitch perfect with a rich tone and perfect control of VIBRATO. She was unafraid of testing her powers by improvising with the likes of Parker and Gillespie. She was the perfect vocal counterpart to the athletic stylings of BOP's leading soloists. Her brash voice and attitude gave her the nickname of "Sassy" during the SWING and bop eras. This gave way

Sarah Vaughn

to an acknowledgment over the years of Vaughn's prowess as a ballad singer with warm expression and a serious attitude about her work.

By the latter half of her career, she was simply known as "The Divine One." She attributed her unique phrasing to the way she learned piano as a teenager. "While I was playing piano in the school band," she once told an interviewer at *Down Beat*, "I learned to take music apart and analyze the notes and put it back together again. By doing this, I learned how to sing differently from all the other singers."[199]

She said that she was influenced more by horn players than by other singers. Vaughn had a long and successful career. When the fortunes of most jazz players hit rock bottom during the 1960s, she was able to focus her attention on her pop singing career. She toured the world during the 1960s, 1970s, and 1980s, visiting more than 60 countries.[200]

Her catalogue of recordings is full of classics that will remain in print as long as there is jazz in the world.

Venuti, Joe (1903–1978) *Italian-American violin player*

Venuti was a legendary prankster of the JAZZ AGE and the first accomplished jazz violinist. The facts surrounding his birth are disputed. Although raised in Philadelphia, he sometimes claimed that he was born on a ship when his parents emigrated from Italy. He got his start playing with boyhood friend guitarist EDDIE LANG in Atlantic City (1919). The two then went to New York, where they teamed up with a variety of orchestras including those of Red Nichols and Jean Goldkette. Lang and Venuti were a potent influence on the work of later guitarists and violinists, including DJANGO REINHARDT and Stephane Grappelli. Venuti formed Joe Venuti's Blue Four in 1926 and recorded several influential chamber jazz records that brought the style of classical music to the small jazz COMBO.

For the next several years he worked in various well-known jazz and popular music orchestras,

including that of PAUL WHITEMAN. He was a band mate of "BIX" BEIDERBECKE and one time filled the young TRUMPET player's bath with Jell-O. Jazz violinists are few and far between, and Venuti established himself as a popular SIDEMAN. He toured America and the world with his own groups during the 1930s and 1940s, taking time out for World War II. In the 1950s he played regularly with singer Bing Crosby and others. Ill health sidelined him for a period in the 1960s, but he made a comeback in 1968 at the NEWPORT JAZZ FESTIVAL, which renewed interest in his music and the jazz VIOLIN. He inspired a new generation of jazz violinists led by Frenchman JEAN-LUC PONTY. He continued to play in the 1970s, bringing back the sound of SWING, until his death from cancer in 1978.

verse

The first part of a popular song, as distinguished from the CHORUS.

verse-chorus song form

The familiar structure of popular songs in which VERSEs tell the story of the song and the CHORUS is repeated after each verse. This song form is often used in jazz, with players adding improvised phrases during breaks.

vibraphone

The vibraphone is a percussion instrument that can also be used to play CHORDs and melodies. In contrast to its cousin the xylophone, which has wooden slabs, the playing surface of the vibraphone consists of tuned metal bars. These, in turn, have tubular metal resonators that hang below the metal bars and which can be made to resonate with a distinct VIBRATO. The vibraphone was invented in the 1920s and first came into prominence as a jazz SOLO instrument in the skilled hands of LIONEL HAMPTON or GARY BURTON, two influential vibe players.

vibrato

A slight, often rapid, fluctuation in a note's pitch used by singers and instrumentalists as an expressive TECHNIQUE.

violin

A classical music instrument that has often been adapted by innovative jazz players. Its wide pitch range made it ideal both for SOLO parts and for playing harmony to other instruments. Around 1900, when jazz was taking off, the violin was a well-established instrument in popular music. It was used in some early jazz groups, most notably JAMES REESE EUROPE's Society Orchestra around 1913. But because it was difficult to hear the violin over the roar of louder BRASS instruments and percussion, it did not quickly find a place in most jazz combos.

The violin made a comeback in jazz during the SWING era because of the energetic playing of JOE VENUTI, an innovative soloist with the PAUL WHITEMAN Orchestra. Other notable American fiddlers included Eddie South and STUFF SMITH, both African Americans who could hold their own when trading RIFFs with horn players. Another group of early jazz violinists came from Europe. The Frenchman Stephane Grappelli was the most influential of these. He, along with Venuti and Smith, invented the TECHNIQUE for using the violin in jazz. The age of FUSION jazz, amplification, and special effects brought the violin back into prominence in the 1970s as a familiar jazz instrument. Modern jazz violin players include JEAN-LUC PONTY and LEROY JENKINS.

Vitous, Miroslav (b. 1947) *Czech bass and guitar player and composer*

Growing up in Prague, he first learned VIOLIN and then PIANO. By age 14 he switched to BASS, which would become his signature instrument. He is one of Europe's greatest bass virtuosos. While in Czechoslovakia, he studied at the Prague Conservatory of Music and then teamed with

Miroslav Vitous

keyboard player JAN HAMMER and brother Alan Vitous to explore trio playing. After winning a competition in Vienna, he came to the United States to study at the BERKLEE COLLEGE OF MUSIC in Boston from 1966 to 1967. From there he went to New York and began playing GIGS with ART FARMER, FREDDIE HUBBARD, and others, including a brief stint with MILES DAVIS in 1971.[201]

In 1969 the young Czech led a recording SESSION of his own works, which has since become a classic of the pre-FUSION era. The album *Infinite Search* (1969) featured a stellar lineup of Vitous admirers, including HERBIE HANCOCK, JOHN MCLAUGHLIN, and drummer JACK DEJOHNETTE. But it was his work as the founding bass player of the fusion group WEATHER REPORT from 1971 to 1973 that launched his career in a big way. After that, he dropped out for a year to master a newly made custom instrument, a double-neck electric bass and GUITAR. After leading in his own group for a time, he joined the faculty of the New England Conservatory of Music in 1979.

During the 1980s he worked with a variety of groups, including one that he led featuring all-European players including JOHN SURMAN, Jon Christensen, and John Taylor. Vitous was one of the first recording artists featured by ECM records and greatly defined the sophisticated jazz sound exemplified by this European label. By the late 1980s Vitous returned to Europe to live and continued his musical partnerships with fellow Europeans, most notably JAN GARBAREK. One of his pet projects was the creation of a digital library of orchestral sounds, a serious venture that occupied the better part of eight years during the 1990s. In 2003 he revived his recording career with a brilliant new album featuring old friends John McLaughlin, Jack DeJohnette, CHICK COREA, and Jan Garbarek. *Universal Syncopation* (2003) is a whimsical jazz trip that captures the folksy mood of Vitous's playing and compositions.

As a bassist, Vitous is known for his excellent TECHNIQUE and a classical jazz sound that is flavored with the rhythms and bounce of European folk music. He is not a typical "walking" bass player. Instead, he decorates the melody with phrases of his own, uses bowed sustained tones, and provides sumptuous colors to his overall COMBO sound. While with Weather Report, he created a textural sound that has been copied by many other bass players. As a group, Weather Report did not feature solos as much as it did tone poems and textures. Within this context, Vitous excelled at providing color, rhythm, and mood in ways that were not normally expected of bass players.

vocalese

Adding lyrics to a recorded jazz instrumental is often done to the melodies of famous jazz improvisations. An example of vocalese applied to many of the instrumental parts of a song is the Manhattan Transfer's rendition of the WEATHER REPORT instrumental "BIRDLAND." A version of vocalese that applies lyrics to an instrumental SOLO is "Shorty Indigo" by lyricist Jon Hendricks (b. 1921), who put words to each note of a famous Shorty Baker TRUMPET solo for the song "Mood Indigo". Hendricks is acknowledged as one of the masters of vocalese, and wrote music for the Manhattan Transfer record *Vocalese* (1985), which won seven GRAMMY AWARDS. A variation on vocalese finds SCAT SINGING used instead of words, in which case a singer uses nonsense syllables in place of an instrumental part.

wah-wah pedal

A special effect pedal originally used by rock guitarists such as Jimi Hendrix as an expressive tool. It is used by rocking the foot back and forth on a pedal that mutes the sound when the heel is down and adds treble when the toe is down. When rocked rapidly it makes a "wocka wocka" sound, something like the cry of a baby. MILES DAVIS was impressed with Hendrix's use of the wah-wah and began using it with his amplified TRUMPET in 1969. This opened the door for the use of the wah-wah pedal, and other GUITAR effects, with jazz instruments other than the guitar.

walking bass

A BASS part that is played using short notes (quarter and eighth notes). It repeats a pattern of notes from the accompanying chords. This kind of bass playing is derived from the left-hand piano part of BOOGIE-WOOGIE music.

Waller, Fats (1904–1943) *American piano and organ player, singer, and composer*

Thomas "Fats" Waller was a master of the STRIDE PIANO and a prolific songwriter. He grew up in HARLEM. His father was a Baptist preacher and his mother a pianist and organist. They encouraged Thomas to play pump ORGAN at a young age because he seemed to be the most musically inclined of their 12 children. He also took an interest in the PIANO and by age 15 was good enough to

begin playing local shows at cabarets and theaters. His first steady GIG was playing pipe organ at the Lincoln Theater in 1919. This was Harlem's most famous movie house and a great showcase for the flamboyant style of the young musician. He was known to make wisecracks during the silent movies and became as popular a fixture of the theater as the movies themselves.

Although his father wanted him to stick with church music, Waller was also interested in the sound of RAGTIME and jazz that was springing up all around. None other than JAMES P. JOHNSON, the father of stride piano, took an interest in young Waller and gave him private lessons. Stride piano is known for the strong beat produced by the left hand while the right hand plays the melody or improvises. Johnson helped the young man polish his style. "I taught him how to groove, how to make it sweet" remarked Johnson in later years. "The strong bass he had dates from that time. He stuck pretty well to my pattern, developed a lovely singing tone, a large melodic expression, and being the son of a preacher, he had fervor."[202]

Waller began recording piano rolls in the early 1920s. He also became popular as an accompanist, particularly to BLUES singers including Bessie Smith and ALBERTA HUNTER. It was during the 1920s that Waller's talent for writing snappy songs began to bloom. Some of his early songs, including "Wild Cat Blues" (1923) and "Squeeze Me" (1923), were picked up by some well-known bands of the time, including those of FLETCHER HENDERSON and Clarence Williams. Waller began to broadcast on radio by the mid-1920s, and this, coupled with his continued recording and performing around New York, made him a bright star on the rise in the world of jazz.

His career took an even larger leap forward beginning in 1927, when he hooked up with lyricist Andy Razaf to pen some of the era's most memorable songs. Many of these began as numbers for African-American musical revues that were popular on Broadway at the time. Waller and Razaf collaborated on *Keep Shufflin'* (1928) and the spectacularly popular show *Hot Chocolates* (1929). *Hot Chocolates* featured the song "Ain't Misbehavin," which not only became a springboard for the career of Waller, but also for those who performed it onstage, including CAB CALLOWAY and LOUIS ARMSTRONG.[203]

Another popular standard written by the pair was "Honeysuckle Rose."

By this time, Waller aspired to write and perform more serious music as well. One important step toward this goal was his role as piano soloist during a 1929 CARNEGIE HALL performance of James P. Johnson's *Yamekraw* for piano and orchestra. In 1929 he made a series of landmark recordings of stride piano for Victor that included the classics "Smashing Thirds," "My Fate Is in Your Hands," "Handful of Keys," "Numb Fumblin," and "Valentine Stomp." During the 1930s Waller was everywhere. He formed his own group, Fats Waller and His Rhythm, which played original numbers as well as other popular tunes of the time. After seeing Louis Armstrong's success as a singer, despite Satchmo's gravelly voice, Waller also took to being a vocalist with great success.

Waller made many recordings, appeared in at least three movies as a performer, toured Europe, and even broadcast a regular radio program from 1933 to 1934 in Cincinnati. His 1939 trip to London was cut short by the outbreak of World War II, but not before he could compose and record his extended instrumental work, "London Suite" (1939). It was a series of six related SOLO piano pieces and represented his most ambitious attempt at more serious composing. Waller earned the nickname "Fats" because of his 300-pound presence and jovial disposition. He was a party-loving man who could also eat anyone under the table. Legend has it that he could eat almost two dozen eggs and bacon for breakfast and an equal amount of hamburgers at lunch.[204]

On one occasion while working in Atlantic City, he reportedly single-handedly ate a meal consisting of "three chickens, three steaks, hot rolls, potatoes, salad." The waitress who brought out the spread to his table innocently asked, "Where are the rest of the people?" Fats cheerfully replied, to her great surprise: "Nobody but me out here," and ate all of the food.[205]

Unfortunately, after many grueling years of traveling, composing, partying, and performing, he unexpectedly became ill with pneumonia and died in 1943. While James P. Johnson is known as the father of stride piano, Waller added a melodious delicacy to the style that was all his own. He was known for his swinging rhythm and joyful music. Waller's playing was admired by many and copied by most. During the 1970s interest in Waller's music was revived by the Broadway production of *Ain't Misbehavin'*, a musical revue featuring many of Waller's best-loved tunes.

Waltz for Debby (1961) *album by Bill Evans*

After leaving MILES DAVIS, BILL EVANS began to record with his trio format, an approach that would define most of his remaining work. *Waltz for Debby*, recorded live at the Village Vanguard in 1961 and released by Riverside, captures the quietly conversational rapport that was the essence of his music. Accompanied by Scott LaFaro (BASS) and Paul Motian (DRUMS), Evans's delicate touch and penchant for occasionally odd chordings are evident on this memorable time capsule of a record. The modal element of this music makes for some imaginative interplay among the three musicians. *Waltz for Debby* is a classic example of musical communication among players.

Washington, Dinah (1924–1963) *American singer and piano player*

Born Ruth Jones in Tuscaloosa, Alabama, Dinah Washington was the most popular African-American female singer of the 1950s. She was influential in bringing gospel stylings to jazz and popular song. Washington was raised in Chicago, where she got her start singing in gospel choirs as a teenager. In the 1940s she sang in nightclubs around Chicago, where bandleader LIONEL HAMPTON noticed her. She worked with Hampton's band from 1943 to 1946, establishing herself as a unique talent in the field of jazz singing.

Her singing was influenced by both gospel and rhythm and blues, and she was uncommonly comfortable in the more wide-open format of a jazz COMBO. She was notably popular in three musical genres: rhythm and blues, popular song, and jazz. Her work in the 1940s and 1950s was mainly in the jazz and rhythm and blues idioms. She worked with some of the best sidemen (see SIDEMAN) in the business, including trumpeters CLIFFORD BROWN, CLARK TERRY, and MAYNARD FERGUSON, and pianists Wynton Kelly and a very young JOE ZAWINUL.

After having several chart-topping rhythm and blues hits in the 1950s, Washington finally struck it rich on the popular music charts with "What a Difference a Day Makes" in 1959. This song vaulted her to stardom, and most of her later recordings were in the field of popular song. Her urbanization of popular song gave a startling new freshness to the genre, an achievement that actually put off some white music critics of the time. Those who knew better knew that listening to Dinah Washington was like tuning into the sound of the future.

Sadly, she died of an accidental overdose of diet pills and alcohol in 1963 at age 39. Washington's distinctive voice was high-pitched and penetrating. She could sing the sassiest BLUES or charm you with a highly orchestrated ballad. Listening to the way in which she added gospel INFLECTION to her phrasing reminds one of Aretha Franklin, and her jazz numbers have a polished SWING that influenced ELLA FITZGERALD and Nancy Wilson.

"Watermelon Man" (1962) *recorded performance by Herbie Hancock*

Featuring HERBIE HANCOCK (PIANO), FREDDIE HUBBARD (TRUMPET, FLUGELHORN), Dexter Gordon (tenor SAXOPHONE), Butch Warren (BASS), Billy Higgins (DRUMS), it is rare that a jazz tune crosses over and becomes a popular hit, but that is exactly what Herbie Hancock did with this upbeat ode to his days growing up in Chicago. It has a fun, gospel feel, but it is not the piano that steals the show; it's the warm, bouncing soloing of Hubbard. "Watermelon Man" has been recorded by more than 200 artists. It is from Hancock's first SOLO album, *Takin' Off*.

Waters, Ethel (1896–1977) *American singer*

Ethel Waters was a popular African-American singer who began to perform at the age of five in a church choir and came full circle in the latter years of her life as she turned once again to religious music. In between, she was a superb interpreter of BLUES and popular song and a successful actress. She moved to New York in 1917 and began recording for the Black Swan record label in 1921, working with FLETCHER HENDERSON.[206]

Although she is not as well known for singing the blues, her first hits with Black Swan were "Down Home Blues" and "Oh Daddy."[207]

By the mid-1920s, she had crossed over from blues to popular music, finding great success with Columbia Records. Her talents took her to Broadway during the 1930s and also into motion pictures. She appeared in the movie *Cabin in the Sky* (1943), also featuring LOUIS ARMSTRONG, DUKE ELLINGTON, and LENA HORNE. For the film *Pinky* (1949) she earned an Oscar nomination for best supporting actress. From the late 1950s until her death, Waters devoted her life to religious music. She was a skilled singer with great articulation and expression. She influenced a new generation of jazz-pop singers who included Lena Horne and Mildred Bailey, among others.

Weather Report   See FUSION; SHORTER, WAYNE; ZAWINUL, JOE.

Webb, Chick (1909–1939) *American drummer and bandleader*

Webb was the first in a distinguished line of drummers who brought their instrument to the forefront and led their own groups. Though his life ended early, he set the standard for jazz drumming that was continued in later years by GENE KRUPA, BUDDY RICH, MAX ROACH, and ART BLAKEY. Hailing from Baltimore, Webb suffered a childhood ailment that left him with a deformed spine and hunchback. His doctors encouraged him to play DRUMS to exercise his weak legs. He first made his mark in the 1920s as a drummer for groups including the Jazzola Orchestra (1924) before starting his own COMBOS.

After experimenting with a variety of BIG BAND formats and sidemen (see SIDEMAN), he settled into his legendary GIG as leader of the HOUSE BAND at the famed SAVOY BALLROOM in HARLEM (beginning 1927). His players included several musicians destined to become legends in their own right, including Johnny Hodges and BENNY CARTER. Having a drummer as the bandleader was novel at the time. Webb chose his material carefully and created a hard-driving SWING that brought dancers to the Savoy in droves. By 1935 Webb toned down his sound to showcase his new young singer, ELLA FITZGERALD. Together, they had a hit in 1938 with the song "A-TISKET, A-TASKET."

His drumming style was strong and dominating. Unlike other well-established big bands such as DUKE ELLINGTON's, Webb's drumming did more than add color to the sound; it was the driving force behind the dance rhythms. He established the basic rhythm played by all swing bands, that of four beats to the bar played on a BASS drum. While most swing drummers used only the cymbals for occasional emphasis, Webb used them liberally to add texture and excitement to his sound. His imagination and broad use of the entire drum set laid down a colorful foundation for his players. Though

he played in pain much of the time, he was the drummer to beat.

During his tenure at the Savoy, Webb's band was often challenged in CUTTING CONTEST. Other bands dreaded playing against them. Player Benny Payne recalled those days at the Savoy, "It was reputed that Chicklet [Webb] had three different books, or types of musical program. The third was mild stuff, number two was hot stuff, and number one would blow you away. Chick used his number three book on Benny Goodman; he and his band didn't even work up a sweat. But if Earl Hines was in town playing with Chick, then Chick would have to dig into that number one book and bring out the hot numbers. Earl was the only one who could put any pressure on Chick for sheer showmanship, musicianship, excitement, and energy."[208]

That's what Chick Webb was all about. His health worsened in 1939, and although he continued to play with his band as long as possible, he was eventually hospitalized in Baltimore, where he died.

Webster, Ben (1909–1973) *American tenor saxophone player and bandleader*

Webster may not have been a jazz innovator like his mentor COLEMAN HAWKINS, but he is one of the most moving and captivating players in all of jazz history. As a young man, Webster first played PIANO and got a job playing during silent movies in Amarillo, Texas. SAXOPHONE player Budd Johnson showed the young Webster how to play a SCALE on the saxophone, and Webster took to it naturally. He soon found himself playing alongside LESTER YOUNG in the Young Family Band. Although the same age as Webster, Young had a head start on the tenor saxophone and taught his new friend a thing or two about playing. Along with Coleman Hawkins, Webster and Young went on to become the most dynamic and influential tenor saxophone stylists of the SWING era.

Webster became the featured soloist with the BENNIE MOTEN Orchestra in the early 1930s, appearing on such popular numbers as "Lafayette" and

"Moten Swing." He also worked with Andy Kirk, FLETCHER HENDERSON, BENNY CARTER, CAB CALLOWAY, and Teddy Wilson before joining the DUKE ELLINGTON Orchestra in 1940. He was the first important tenor player to work in the Ellington Orchestra, and his robust sound was a kick in the pants for the band. Baritone saxophonist Harry Carney, also with the Ellington band, admitted "Ben brought a new life to a section that had been together a long time, he was inspired and he inspired us so that we worked together."[209]

Webster became well known during his three-year stay with Ellington. He was featured on such numbers as "All Too Soon" and "Cotton Tail" (including a saxophone ENSEMBLE that Webster arranged). After leaving Ellington in 1943 over a dispute, Webster worked with several other bands in the 1940s and was a big draw on the 52nd Street New York jazz scene with his own COMBOS. After rejoining Ellington for a year (1948–49), Webster

became a regular on the JAZZ AT THE PHILHARMONIC tours produced by Norman Granz in the 1950s. He was a popular SESSION man during this period and recorded a classic SET with ART TATUM in 1956. Webster's SOLO on "All the Things You Are" from this session was called "one of the great solos in the history of recorded jazz" by critic Nat Hentoff.

In 1964 Webster moved to Copenhagen, where he continued to played from time to time. Webster had a wide range of styles at his command. His aggressive swing playing was punctuated by his characteristic growls and raspy tone. His touch on ballads had the warmth of firelight. He appeared on many recordings and was known for his ability to play perfectly with whatever ARRANGEMENT was presented to him. Over his long career, Webster always stuck with what he knew best. Although he was knocked during the 1960s for playing an out-of-date style, he retorted by saying, "If you try all different styles that are in vogue, I think you con yourself. Me, I just stick by my guns; I don't want to play out of another man's bag."

Ben Webster

Whiteman, Paul (1890–1967) *American bandleader*

Even though Whiteman's publicist had dubbed him the "King of Jazz," true jazz artists bristled at the suggestion. Whiteman was primarily a skilled showman whose talent lay in producing large-scale orchestra productions featuring some of the best jazz players of the day. He was also white and, like the ORIGINAL DIXIELAND JAZZ BAND, was sometimes accused of stealing the thunder of jazz from its African-American originators. Even so, Whiteman was responsible for exposing elements of jazz music to a wider audience and was beloved as a fair-minded employer who recognized great talent when he heard it.

In 1924 he staged the premiere of George Gershwin's "Rhapsody in Blue" at Aeolian Hall in New York. While "Rhapsody" was not exactly a pure jazz work, its instrumentation and rhythms were inspired by the HOT JAZZ of LOUIS ARMSTRONG

Paul Whiteman Orchestra (Whiteman is second from right.)

and others. Whiteman was known for his extravagant stage shows and spread the sound of his orchestral jazz via the radio and motion pictures. Some of the important players who came to prominence while playing for Whiteman included "BIX" BEIDERBECKE, RED NORVO, JOE VENUTI, TOMMY and JIMMY DORSEY, JACK TEAGARDEN, and FRANKIE TRUMBAUER. The sound of Whiteman's orchestra was smooth as silk, due in part to the large size of his outfit. But it rarely ventured into hot IMPROVISATION and the riskier elements that made true jazz jump with excitement.

Although his orchestra was primarily a white band at the peak of its popularity in the 1920s, Whiteman had as early as 1923 offered jobs to black musicians. He also employed black arrangers and was fully aware of the debt owed to those African Americans who pioneered jazz. The Whiteman orchestra played pleasant pop music with jazz overtones.

Whiteman's popularity with musicians stemmed partly from his being a good sport. On one occasion, his violinist Joe Venuti staged a practical joke onstage that was certainly calculated to make the bandleader lose his cool. They were playing at the Roxy in New York in 1930, an occasion that combined Whiteman's band with the Roxy Symphony to form a unit consisting of a startling 130 musicians. On the bill was none other than Gershwin's "Rhapsody in Blue" with the COMPOSER himself playing PIANO. The concert was to open with the orchestra playing while the stage rose from the pit. Whiteman would then follow them onto the stage. All of this would be signaled by a loud note played on a tuba. Venuti thought this was a bit over the top. He filled the tuba with five pounds of flour. "We had blue full-dress suits," he explained, "and all of a sudden as the curtain went up, the tuba player blew that note and they became white full-dress suits! We looked like snowmen." With great composure, Whiteman came out onstage and simply said, "Pardon me, where are we?" They closed the curtain, dusted themselves off, then started all over again.[210]

Williams, Mary Lou (1910–1981) *American piano player, composer, and arranger*

Williams is a towering figure in the history of jazz. Her composing skills were as sophisticated as DUKE ELLINGTON's, her PIANO playing as gifted as some of the best SWING and STRIDE players, and her curiosity and intellect guided her through a lifelong adventure of experiment and mastery of many jazz styles. She wrote more than 350 songs. That she was a woman in a field dominated by men made her accomplishments all that more remarkable.

Born Mary Elfrieda Scruggs in Atlanta, she was raised in Pittsburgh, where her ear for music was evident at a young age. As a teen she appeared in a traveling vaudeville show called Hits and Bits. When she was only 16, she married John Williams and joined his band. She began doing arrangements for Terrence Holder's band in 1929, which had settled in Kansas City. Williams became a full-time member of the band when the group was taken over by Andy Kirk in 1930. This was her big break. She remained with Kirk until 1942, playing and arranging and greatly influencing the sound of KANSAS CITY JAZZ. Hits that she wrote and played while with Kirk included "Walkin' and Swingin'," "Froggy Bottom," "Steppin' Pretty," and "Cloudy." This was an inspired time in her career. About playing with Kirk, Williams recalled, "I remember not eating for practically a month several times. But we were very, very happy because the music was so interesting, and you forgot to eat, anyway."[211]

She gained a reputation as a great swing piano player and ARRANGER. Her BIG BAND arrangements were so good that she freelanced music and arrangements for other bands, including BENNY GOODMAN, TOMMY DORSEY, and LOUIS ARMSTRONG, among others. After her long stay with Kirk, she coled a sextet with her second husband, Shorty

Baker. She also led her own group, which included none other than ART BLAKEY. After a short time as an Ellington COMPOSER and arranger, she was well enough known as a composer to work under her own name. She composed the *Zodiac Suite*, a colorful orchestral/jazz work, part of which was performed by the New York Philharmonic at CARNEGIE HALL in 1946.

Throughout the 1950s, 1960s, and 1970s, she divided her time between composing, playing in small clubs, touring Europe, and teaching jazz. She touched the lives of many people in the jazz world, particularly women who wanted to make their mark as composers and performers. It has often been said that Williams's music and playing were ahead of their time. She had a keen ear for jazz styles and was a student of the history of her art

Mary Lou Williams

form. She anticipated trends in jazz and moved with determination into the battleground of new sounds. As the swing era drew to a close, she turned her attention to the frenetic rhythms of BEBOP. So influential was she as a bop stylist that THELONIOUS MONK borrowed a RIFF from her song "Walkin' and Swingin'" as the germ of his own "Rhythm-A-Ning."

She was great friends with GILLESPIE, Monk, and BUD POWELL, all of whom considered her the queen of bop. Many of her musician friends would gather at her apartment during the 1940s to trade quips and test their bebop ideas. JAM SESSIONS at her apartment often followed a full night of performing in clubs. "We'd come uptown around four or four thirty in the morning and stay up all day, playing," she recalled. "I had a white rug on the floor and we'd sit on the floor and each one would take turns playing."[212]

In the 1950s and 1960s she moved from bop and HARD BOP to AVANT-GARDE jazz, retiring briefly to pursue religious interests. Her composing began to embrace larger works for orchestra and CHORUS about this time. In 1967, 1969, and 1970 she composed a major religious work titled *Music for Peace*, which was commissioned by the Pontifical Commission on Justice and Peace at the Vatican. An early advocate of teaching jazz history, she recorded *The History of Jazz* for Folkways (now Smithsonian) Records in 1970. On this recording, she narrated a history of jazz music and demonstrated various styles of playing to illustrate her points. She was passionate about teaching the origins of jazz to young musicians. "They've got to know about the older music," she said, "in order to play avant-garde."[213]

Her third mass, *Mary Lou's Mass* (1970), was choreographed by Alvin Ailey. Mary Lou Williams was a giant of jazz whose contributions figured importantly in the very evolution of the music she loved most. Duke Ellington may have summed up Mary Lou the best when he wrote, "Mary Lou Williams is perpetually contemporary. Her writing and performing are and have always been just a lit-

tle ahead throughout her career . . . her music retains and maintains a standard of quality that is timeless. She is like soul on soul."[214]

Williams, Tony (1945–1997) *American drummer and bandleader*

Tony Williams was a hard-hitting and innovative drummer who formed one of the first jazz FUSION bands. He studied composition at the Juilliard School of Music and the University of California at Berkeley. After moving to New York in 1962, he was heard by MILES DAVIS, who asked him to play in his quintet in 1963. Williams was comfortable with rock, jazz, and free-form rhythm playing. He created a unique blend of time keeping and free-form playing that appealed to Davis and helped to channel a new rhythmic direction for jazz. In addition to working with Davis, Williams appeared on the classic ERIC DOLPHY recording *Out to Lunch* (1964). In 1969, Williams struck out on his own to create a fusion of rock and jazz with a trio called Lifetime. The group consisted of Williams, LARRY YOUNG on Hammond organ, and a little-known electric guitarist from England named JOHN MCLAUGHLIN. The resulting recordings of this short-lived venture created some of the most inventive and charged fusion tracks ever made. In the 1970s, William bounced back and forth between various fusion projects and more traditional jazz with such musicians as GIL EVANS, HERBIE HANCOCK, WAYNE SHORTER, RON CARTER, and others. He was leading his own groups from the early 1980s until his death from a heart attack in 1997. One of his last completed projects was *Wilderness* (1996), a piece for orchestra and jazz players, for which he recruited old friends PAT METHENY, MICHAEL BRECKER, and STANLEY CLARKE.

Williamson, Steve (b. 1964) *British tenor, soprano, and alto saxophone player*

Williamson was raised in England by West Indian parents. Williamson's status as a cult figure on the new London jazz scene was earned not so much by what he did but by what he didn't do. Rather than leaping into the recording studio the first chance he got, he honed his skills, mastering the TECHNIQUES of JOHN COLTRANE and others, then worked hard on the local scene to polish his playing. He slowly gained attention by gigging with others, including his fiery work in COURTNEY PINE's late-1980s British BIG BAND, the Jazz Warriors. He also worked at various times with jazz luminaries including ART BLAKEY, ARCHIE SHEPP, Chris McGregor, and Maceo Parker. All along, he listened intently to the vibrant new jazz scene around him, witnessing the emergence of ACID JAZZ, FUSION, and WORLD MUSIC as major influences.

Finally, at age 26, he released his first record under his own name, "A Waltz for Grace" (1990). His was a grandiose mix of FREE IMPROVISATION, funk, and Caribbean reggae, a fashionable sound at the time. After making three records by 1995, he dropped out of the scene to regain his sense of direction in music. When asked about where he had been for several years, he replied, "I didn't go away, but I'd found out that the music industry really looks for the next commercial opportunity rather than looking at you for what you are. . . . But I'd never wanted to be a pop artist, or a major star or anything. I just wanted to write music and play the SAXOPHONE using influences that had been important to me."[215]

Although recording only a few records under his own name since that time, he remains a sought-after SESSION man. Williamson has absorbed the styles of TRADITIONAL JAZZ and plays with a fury that is a cross between the FREE JAZZ of ORNETTE COLEMAN, the soaring solos of John Coltrane, and the technique of ERIC DOLPHY. Williamson is a well-rounded player with a sense for the future. He divides his playing time between two groups. The Steve Williamson Group is a jazz/acid fusion COMBO featuring saxophone, GUITAR, keyboards, BASS, DRUMS, turntables, and vocals. His Future Now QUARTET is more of a straight-up hard-bop, free jazz group. He is one of the brightest stars in the future of new jazz.

Wilson, Cassandra (b. 1955) *American vocalist, guitar player, and composer*

"Smoky" is the adjective often used to describe the soft but declarative voice of Cassandra Wilson. She is one of the leading jazz singers of the day in the tradition of ELLA FITZGERALD, SARAH VAUGHN, and BETTY CARTER. Wilson grew up in and around Jackson, Mississippi, where her father, a musician, encouraged her to sing from a young age. She took PIANO lessons as a youngster and by high school had ambitions of being a famous singer/songwriter like Joni Mitchell. In college she majored in mass communications and seemed destined for a career in broadcasting. All the time, however, she continued to sing with folk and then jazz groups.

Success as a club singer around Jackson encouraged Wilson to learn BLUES, folk, pop, and jazz idioms, all being a rich influence on the local culture of her hometown. Her work with jazz players led to her interest in straight-up jazz singers such as Betty Carter and Ella Fitzgerald. In the 1980s Wilson moved to New York City and began working as a singer in various groups, including New Air and M-Base. She began to make records in the mid-1980s, each of which further established her as a rising star of jazz. Her singing style features a low, sultry voice with amazing range. She is an excellent scat singer (see SCAT SINGING) and likes to improvise with her voice in the great tradition of Ella Fitzgerald. A gifted lyricist and songwriter as well, she is really a jazz singer for a new generation. Outstanding albums include *Blue Light 'Til Dawn* (1993), *Blue Moon Rendezvous* (1998), and *Traveling Miles* (1999) a tribute to MILES DAVIS for which she wrote lyrics. She worked with WYNTON MARSALIS's concert piece about slavery, "Blood on the Fields" in 1997.

Wilson blends what she has heard in rock, jazz, blues, folk, Afro-Cuban, and pop music into a uniquely American mix of new music. One of her trademarks is taking songs from other idioms and interpreting them using jazz style. She loves the challenge that this brings her as an artist. She was talking about this when she said, "I'm always looking for ways to develop as an artist, especially as a jazz artist, to find different ways of testing my voice. New material always pushes you. You have to look for some way to express new material with a jazz sensibility. It's one thing to go to the standards you know because it's very familiar. Once you step outside of that canon and you try material that has never had a treatment like that, then it pushes you, it challenges you."[216]

Cassandra Wilson bends the rules of TRADITIONAL JAZZ and is unafraid to take chances with material that critics might not deem jazz worthy. She astounds and surprises in the greatest of jazz traditions.

Wilson, Nancy (b. 1937) *American singer*

Wilson, like TONY BENNETT, is a gifted singer with jazz leanings who happened to become a successful pop singer. Her early recordings with Cannonball Adderley (1961) established her identity as a warm ballad singer with a BLUES touch. She was a popular recording and television star in the 1960s. Her best-selling album was *Yesterday's Love Songs/Today's Blues* (1964). After 20 years riding the pop charts, she returned to a jazz setting in the 1980s while working with HANK JONES, ART FARMER, and Ramsey Lewis. In the 1990s she became the host of the nationally syndicated *Jazz Profiles,* a weekly documentary radio program about jazz that airs on National Public Radio.

Wilson, Rossiere "Shadow" (1919–1959) *American drummer*

The booming sound of Rossiere "Shadow" Wilson was the thundering force behind many of the best BIG BANDs of the 1940s. He began his career with the Frankie Fairfax band in 1938. He worked with a string of important bandleaders in the 1940s, including BENNY CARTER, LIONEL HAMPTON, EARL HINES, COUNT BASIE, WOODY HERMAN, and others. He was also comfortable playing in small COMBOs. During the 1950s he worked with PIANO player ERROLL GARNER, singer ELLA FITZGERALD, and the master of bop piano, THELONIOUS MONK, and JOHN COLTRANE. Widely recorded and widely recognized as a unique talent, Wilson's loud, driving big band sound was the prototype for many drummers who followed. Wilson was known for his quick footwork on the BASS drum. He was also one of the few drummers—ART BLAKEY being another—who understood how to play with Monk, the result being some marvelous recordings, such as "EPISTROPHY" (1948).

The Wire magazine

Modern music of all types, including jazz, makes its way into the colorful and challenging pages of this British magazine. For information about what's new and most experimental in music and jazz, *The Wire* is a good place to start. The Web site address of *The Wire* is http://www.thewire.co.uk.

woodwinds

A family of instruments including those with reeds in their mouthpieces (SAXOPHONE, CLARINET, oboe, bassoons) and FLUTEs.

world music

Music originating in other cultures, particularly in non-Western cultures where native instruments, musical scales, and approaches to performance vary widely from the music of Europe and America. Music of other cultures has often found a firm footing in jazz. Examples include the integration of South American, Cuban, and African musical elements into American jazz.

Young, Larry (1940–1978) *American organ, piano, and electronic keyboard player*

Young was an influential ORGAN player who died well before the impact of his work was fully accepted. Raised in Newark, New Jersey, he studied PIANO as a boy but learned the organ by hanging out with his father, a nightclub owner who played the organ. By age 17 he was already playing professionally with the likes of Lou Donaldson, Hank Mobley, and some rhythm and blues bands. In 1960 he formed his own trio (organ, GUITAR, DRUMS) and made his first record, *Groove Street,* under his own name. His CHOPS were great, and he was soon in demand as a SIDEMAN.

During the mid-1960s his work on records with drummer ELVIN JONES and tours of Europe with Woody Shaw and DONALD BYRD opened his mind to new ideas in jazz. He was an adventurous player and began to move in the direction of MODAL JAZZ and IMPROVISATION as heard in the work of MILES DAVIS and JOHN COLTRANE. He was one of the first players to embrace the idea of jazz rock FUSION, working not only with Davis in 1969 but also with guitarist JOHN MCLAUGHLIN and drummer Tony Williams. He jammed with Jimi Hendrix and played on Davis's *BITCHES BREW* (1970). In the 1970s he worked as a popular sideman on jazz records with PHAROAH SANDERS, among others. Unfortunately, he died of pneumonia while hospitalized for a stomach infection in 1978.

Among jazz organ players, Young was the closest thing to a FREE JAZZ or AVANT-GARDE organist, an approach now continued by BARBARA DENNERLEIN.

He played with wit and bite, teaming with drummers to create a pulsing undercurrent beneath the lead players. His sound was enormously rich, his improvisations surprising and adventurous.

Young, Lester (1909–1959) *American tenor saxophone and clarinet player and composer*

Lester Young was one of the most influential and innovative tenor SAXOPHONE players in the history of jazz. He was as influential on saxophone as LOUIS ARMSTRONG was on TRUMPET. Young was born in Mississippi into a musical family. They lived not far from New Orleans. His father led a family band including Young and his sister and brother. After playing various instruments for the family band, Young switched to alto saxophone at age 13. He left the family band in 1927 at age 18 to strike out on his own. While playing with Art Bronson's Bostonians, he made the switch to tenor saxophone, his signature instrument.

Young fought convention by developing a style of playing that contrasted sharply with that of COLEMAN HAWKINS, the most popular player of the time. Hawkins had a vibrant, muscular style. He used rapid VIBRATO and fast CHORD CHANGES to color his sound. Young was a quiet, thoughtful man who disavowed the brash show-off style of Hawkins and other players of the day.

In contrast to the style of Coleman Hawkins, Young developed a more personal and melodic alternative. His sound was short on bombast and big on slowly unraveling solos and lighter tones. He stretched out songs by adding new chords as stepping-stones to develop his complex solos. His phrasing, tone color, and stunning use of slow vibrato were greatly influential. He could also develop a SOLO using a minimum of notes. He might begin a solo with a few carefully placed notes and then explore them further in subsequent bars. One of his recordings of the song "Lady Be Good" begins with only 10 notes played over a four-bar section of the piece. It was his placement of the notes, not the number of notes that he played, that made his style so remarkable. His style was so different from Hawkins that it made it difficult for him to keep working when he first started out. Fortunately, he found a sympathetic supporter in the great bandleader COUNT BASIE.

Young joined the Basie band in 1936 for a four-year stint that would be some of the most productive of his career. In the context of Basie's BIG BAND, his playing soared head and shoulders above that of the typical soloist. He loved to jostle with the beat, sometimes playing a little behind it to create exciting interplay between the melody and the rhythm. His colorful IMPROVISATIONS soared above the band yet guided it along with the confidence that only the greatest of improvisers can do. Not only did he record with Basie but also with a QUINTET of Basie musicians and with BILLIE HOLIDAY, who became one of his closest friends. His work with Holiday is remarkably laid-back and perfectly complemented the singer's BLUES style. During this time, Holiday nicknamed him the "President" or "Prez" after Young had given her the name "Lady Day." By calling him "Prez," Holiday was acknowledging Young's prowess as the leading sax player of his day.

In the early 1940s he dabbled with his own groups between stints with Basie and others. During this time, the cool Lester Young style had become well established and was beginning to have imitators. His long, thoughtful improvisations inspired the work of many players who followed, not all of them tenor players, including JOHN COLTRANE, ERIC DOLPHY, Dexter Gordon, GERRY MULLIGAN, and SONNY ROLLINS. Young's solos were so memorable that other players continue to quote them, note for note, to this day. Holiday described his sound this way, "When Lester plays, he almost seems to be singing; one can almost hear the words."

Unfortunately, the story of Lester Young began to take a downturn around 1944, when, at age 35, he was inducted into the army. This proved to be a disaster for the sensitive musician. Lester Young and the army did not mix. Soon after his induction, he was accused of drug possession and imprisoned. Reportedly suffering abuses at the hands of his racist keepers, he was discharged after 15 months, a dispirited man. His later years were less happy and productive, although he continued to perform and record. He was a featured player with the JAZZ AT THE PHILHARMONIC series, often dueling onstage with other greats such as Coleman Hawkins.

Lester Young

Lester Young was a true original and a jazz great. He clearly believed that much jazz lacked originality. He once said, "The trouble with most musicians today is that they are copycats. Of course you have to start out playing like someone else. You have a model, or a teacher, and you learn all that he can show you. But then you start playing for yourself. Show them that you're an individual. And I can count those who are doing that today on the fingers of one hand."

Youngblood Brass Band

This Wisconsin-based band founded in 1994 consists of former high school buddies who play only BRASS and percussion instruments. The result, however, is a far cry from marching band music. Combining their interests in soul, funk, Dixieland, rap, and rock, the Youngblood Brass Band builds an infectious sound using unconventional arrangements of brass. They released their first recording in 1997 under the name of One Lard Biskit Brass Band. They received excellent critical notice for their second album, *Word on the Street* (1998), which featured a NEW ORLEANS JAZZ style sound and their own compositions. Group leader Nat McIntosh is particularly creative in arranging music for his instrument, the tuba, which he can play in a six- to seven-octave range. Recent efforts of the group has broadened to embrace the sounds of hip-hop, Afro-Cuban, Brazilian, and dance music.

Zawinul, Joe (b. 1932) *Austrian piano and synthesizer player and composer*

Zawinul played accordion as a youngster, learning to play European folk songs by ear. He studied classical PIANO at the Vienna Conservatory of Music prior to World War II. After the war, he became interested in jazz and honed his skills with other European players. His first steady jazz GIG was with Viennese SAXOPHONE player Hans Koller in 1952. Zawinul came to the United States in 1959 to study at the BERKLEE COLLEGE OF MUSIC in Boston. It was during this time that he landed his first important gigs as piano player for bandleader MAYNARD FERGUSON, rhythm and blues singer DINAH WASHINGTON, and finally Cannonball Adderley.

It was under Adderley's wing that Zawinul's talent for composing was first put to great use. He wrote many pieces for the pop-jazz Adderley band and won a GRAMMY AWARD for "Mercy, Mercy, Mercy" in 1967. By this time, he had made the electric piano his featured instrument. He became part of the MILES DAVIS group just when the famed trumpeter was beginning to experiment with FUSION jazz. Zawinul and CHICK COREA both played electric piano on *IN A SILENT WAY* (1969). The title song of the album was written by Zawinul. Next came the landmark *BITCHES BREW* (1970) and *Live-Evil* (1970) for Davis.

In 1970 Zawinul and fellow Davis band mate WAYNE SHORTER split to form their own band, WEATHER REPORT. This eclectic group mixed jazz, rock, and WORLD MUSIC in a successful formula that kept them together, with several personnel changes,

for 15 years. It was by far the most commercially successful fusion group, eclipsing in record sales and longevity both the MAHAVISHNU ORCHESTRA and Return to Forever. The most original and accomplished albums of Weather Report were the exceptional *Black Market* and *Heavy Weather*. During this period Zawinul mastered the SYNTHESIZER. With HERBIE HANCOCK, Zawinul was one of the pioneers of using electronic keyboards of all types in a jazz setting, mastering both the technical challenges of using them effectively as well as playing them convincingly as SOLO instruments.

Since the disbanding of Weather Report in 1985, Zawinul has led a variety of lineups, the most recent of which is the Zawinul Syndicate, whose members in 2004 included Amit Chatterjee (GUITAR and vocals), Linley Marthe (BASS), Stephane Galland (DRUMS), Sabine Kabongo (vocals), and Manolo Badrena (percussion and vocals). Zawinul's musical interests have broadened greatly over the years. His work with Weather Report sparked an interest in world music that continues to this day. In 1991 he produced an album for West African singer Salif Keita. In 1993 he worked with classical pianist Friedrich Gulda on "Stories of the Danube." In 2000 he completed an ambitious solo project, "Mauthausen" a memorial for the victims of the Holocaust named for the Austrian concentration camp of the same name.

Zawinul was one of the most accomplished composers and keyboard players of the fusion era. Unlike Miles Davis, whose group efforts often consisted more of IMPROVISATION than written parts,

Zawinul stuck to his COMPOSER's instinct and penned dozens of memorable works for Weather Report. His use of the synthesizer as a serious instrument and not merely a gimmick gave his playing a depth and maturity lacking in much fusion. As a composer, he is apt to explore many different styles. Some of his works rock with funk, others tip their hat to the TRADITIONAL JAZZ writing of DUKE ELLINGTON, and still others materialize as atmospheric sonic experiments. It was probably Zawinul's overwhelming presence on the keyboard that eventually brought an end to Weather Report, a group that sounded more and more like his personal workshop as the years wore on. However, he continues to follow his muse, composing exceptionally beautiful works that resonate with many jazz fans.

Zoller, Attilla (1927–1998) *Hungarian guitar player and educator*

Zoller was one of the first great AVANT-GARDE guitarists. Born in Hungary, he first learned VIOLIN and TRUMPET and performed with his high school symphony orchestra. He picked up the GUITAR after World War II and made a name for himself as a bop guitarist in Budapest clubs. Since 1959 he made his home in either New York or Vermont: In 1959 he studied music at the School of Jazz in Lenox, Massachusetts, where he encountered the FREE JAZZ of ORNETTE COLEMAN. The boppin' and rollicking style of Zoller is often compared to that of JIM HALL, his friend of 40 years. Zoller had his mellow side, playing ballads and COOL JAZZ with such bandleaders as HERBIE MANN (1962–65), BENNY GOODMAN (1967), and ASTRUD GILBERTO (1970). He also played with his own QUARTETs or teamed up with some of the more experimental musicians of the 1960s and 1970s, including RED NORVO, Paul Bley, HERBIE HANCOCK, and Don Friedman. Zoller's style was personal and difficult to categorize, but swinging and inspiring.

Zoller also taught jazz, and he was said to always have time to help out young musicians. He took guitarist PAT METHENY under his wing when the young musician was but 14. He frequented clubs, listening to new players and offering advice to those who appreciated it. Apparently, many did, for he is remembered as a gem of a guitar player and a big-hearted man. "He was always going to check out all the musicians playing around," remembers JOHN ABERCROMBIE, "and inspiring them with words of encouragement, words of laughter and a great joy of being alive that could be catching if you let it."[217]

Zorn, John (b. 1953) *American alto saxophone and clarinet player and composer*

Many critics like to call John Zorn "eclectic" because they don't know what else to call him. This New Yorker's blend of campy mood music, FREE JAZZ, and gamelike compositions is bound to delight even the most serious skeptic of AVANT-GARDE jazz. Zorn has a solid musical background with training in classical music. His exposure to the work of avant-garde COMPOSER John Cage led him to introduce so-called chance operations into his own music. His bag of instrumental tricks sometimes includes partially assembled SAXO-PHONES and bird calls. His music ranges from extremely FREE IMPROVISATION (*The Parachute Years, 1977–1980,* 1997) to ENSEMBLE works (*Locus Solus,* 1983), to colorful renditions of movie and television theme music (*Naked City,* 1990).

In between is a whole spectrum of Zorn music that may never use a saxophone or sound like jazz at all, relying instead on a cadre of well-known New York improvisers to realize his distinctive compositions using voice, percussion, electronic sounds, and other instruments. One of his ongoing projects is a klezmer band called Masada, which might best be described as a combination of ORNETTE COLEMAN and Yiddish SWING. In 1998 he produced a SET of his most often heard Masada tunes for chamber trio and percussion, adding yet another style to his eccentric and always stimulating repertoire (*The Circle Maker,* 1998). Zorn has been a tireless performer and composer on the avant-garde jazz scene for more than two decades. His record label, Tzadik, is responsible for releasing some of the most unusual jazz and experimental music heard anywhere. Nobody explains the spirit and purpose of his music better than Zorn. "It's not just running changes the way Sonny Stitt or Bird did; there's no point in copying that, you can take out the record and play if that's what you want to hear. It's tunes and changes and a certain tradition that needs to be updated to keep it alive. I think music is great today, and I'm trying to play it today."[218]

Appendixes

Appendix I: A Century of Jazz Recordings

Appendix II: Geographical History of Early Jazz (1900 to 1950)

Appendix III: Evolution of Jazz Styles

Appendix IV: Jazz in the Movies

Appendix V: Grammy Awards for Jazz

Appendix VI: Jazz at Lincoln Center Inaugural Hall of Fame Inductees

1900

"An Ethiopian Mardi Gras," by Vess L. Ossman (RAGTIME BANJO).

"Sounds from Africa," by Vess L. Ossman (ragtime banjo).

"Whistling Rufus," by Vess L. Ossman (ragtime banjo).

"You're Talking Rag-Time," by Arthur Collins (ragtime vocal).

1901

"Creole Belles," by Charles Booth (RAGTIME).

"A Hot Time in the Old Town Tonight," by Sousa's Band (military march/ragtime).

"Hu-la Hu-la Cake Walk," by Sousa's Band (military march/ragtime).

"I Couldn't Stand to See My Baby Lose," by Silas Leachman.

"Ragtime Skidaddle," by George Schweinfest (piccolo).

1902

"Bill Bailey Won't You Please Come Home," by Arthur Collins (popular song).

"Creole Belles," by Vess L. Ossman (RAGTIME BANJO).

"The Cake-Walk," by the Victor Minstrels (vaudeville song).

"The Stars and Stripes Forever March," by Ruby Brooks (military march/ragtime).

1903

"Dixie Girl," by Charles Prince's Orchestra (RAGTIME).

"Harmony Moze," by Vess L. Ossman (ragtime BANJO).

"Mr. Black Man," by Arthur Pryor's Band (ragtime).

"The Passing of Ragtime," by Sousa's Band (military march/ragtime).

1904

"By the Sycamore Tree," Vess L. Ossman and Parke Hunter (RAGTIME BANJO).

"Hot Time March," by the Edison Military Band (military march).

"Smoky Mokes," by the Peerless Orchestra (ragtime).

1905

"The St. Louis Rag," by Arthur Pryor's Band (RAGTIME).

1906

"The Dixie Rube," by the Edison Military Band (military march).

"MAPLE LEAF RAG," by the United States Marine Band (RAGTIME piece by SCOTT JOPLIN).

"The Motor March," by Vess L. Ossman (ragtime BANJO).

"St. Louis Tickle," "Koontown Koffee Klatsch," and "The Cannon Ball Rag," by Vess L. Ossman (ragtime banjo).

1907

"Chicken Chowder" and "MAPLE LEAF RAG," by Vess L. Ossman (RAGTIME BANJO).

"The King of Rags," by Arthur Pryor's Band (ragtime).

1908

"Artful Artie," "Southern Beauties Rag," and "Mr. Black Man," by Arthur Pryor's Band (RAGTIME).

"Persian Lamb Rag" and "A Bunch of Rags," by Vess L. Ossman (ragtime BANJO).

1909

"Black and White Rag," by Prince's Band (RAGTIME).

"Black and White Rag," by Victor Dance Orchestra (ragtime).

"Dill Pickles Rag," by Arthur Pryor's Band (ragtime).

"Moose March," by Vess L. Ossman (ragtime BANJO).

1910

"Chatterbox Rag," by Fred Van Eps (RAGTIME).

"The Smiler Rag," by Vess L. Ossman (ragtime BANJO).

"Temptation Rag" and "I'm Alabama Bound," by Prince's Military Band (military vaudeville/ragtime).

"Wild Cherries Rag," by Victor Dance Orchestra (ragtime).

1911

"Alexander's Ragtime Band," by Arthur Collins and Byron Harlan (RAGTIME).

"Canhanibalmo Rag," by Arthur Pryor's Band (ragtime).

"High Society," by Prince's Band (ragtime).

"Rag Pickings" and "A Ragtime Episode," by Fred Van Eps (BANJO ragtime).

"Slippery Place Rag," by the Victor Military Band (military march/ragtime).

"The King of the Bungaloos," by Gene Greene (vocal, ragtime, with perhaps the first recorded example of SCAT SINGING).

1912

"Black Diamond Rag," by Prince's Band (RAGTIME).

"Florida Rag," by Fred Van Eps (BANJO ragtime).

"Grizzly Bear Turkey Trot," by Arthur Pryor's Band (ragtime).

"Hear That Orchestra Rag," by the Peerless Orchestra (ragtime).

"In Ragtime Land," by Arthur Collins (ragtime).

"Stomp Dance," by the Victor Military Orchestra (military march/ragtime).

1913

"Down Home Rag," by the Victor Military Band (military march/RAGTIME).

"Too Much Mustard," by Prince's Band (ragtime).

1914

"Castle Walk" and "You're Here and I'm Here," by the Jim Europe Society Orchestra (first African-American RAGTIME ENSEMBLE to record).

"Down Home Rag," "Florida Rag," "My Hindoo Man," and "Too Much Ginger," by the Van Eps Banjo Orchestra (ragtime).

"Memphis Blues," by the Victor Military Band (military march/ragtime).

"That Moaning Saxophone Rag," by the Six Brown Brothers (African-American SAXOPHONE ENSEMBLE playing ragtime).

1915

"Booster Fox Trot," by the Victor Military Band (military march/RAGTIME).

"Down Home Rag," by Six Brown Brothers (ragtime).

1916

"Hill and Dale," by the Fred Van Eps Trio (RAGTIME).

"My Hawaiian Sunshine," by Wilbur Sweatman (ragtime).

"Pearl of the Harem" and "The Motor March," by Fred Van Eps (BANJO ragtime).

1917

"Boogie Rag" and "Dancing an American Rag," by Wilbur Sweatman and His Jass Band (BLUES/RAGTIME/jazz).

"Fuzzy Wuzzy Rag," "That Jazz Dance," and "Those Draftin's Blues," by W. C. Handy's Orchestra of Memphis (blues and ragtime).

"LIVERY STABLE BLUES," "TIGER RAG," and "Dixie Jass Band One-Step," by the ORIGINAL DIXIELAND JAZZ BAND.

"My Fox Trot Girl," by the Six Brown Brothers (African-American SAXOPHONE ENSEMBLE playing ragtime).

"Pork and Beans," by Earl Fuller's Rector Novelty Orchestra (ragtime).

"Sarah from Sahara" and "Hungarian Rag," by Eubie Blake (ragtime).

1918

"At the Jazz Band Ball" and "Ostrich Walk," by the ORIGINAL DIXIELAND JAZZ BAND.

"Ev'rybody's Crazy 'Bout the Doggone Blues, But I'm Happy," by Wilbur Sweatman's Original Jazz Band (jazz).

"Heart Sickness Blues," by the Louisiana Five (BLUES).

"Key to Key Rag," by Fred Van Eps (BANJO RAGTIME).

"Regretful Blues," by Wilbur Sweatman's Original Jazz Band (blues).

1919

"Beale Street Blues," "Joe Turner Blues," "Yellow Dog Blues," and "Hesitating Blues," by W. C. Handy's Memphis Blues Band (BLUES).

"Broadway Hit Medley," "ST. LOUIS BLUES," "Darktown Strutters Ball," "That Moaning Trombone," by Jim Europe's 369th Infantry Band (military march/RAGTIME).

1920

"Crazy Blues," by MAMIE SMITH (BLUES).

"Irene-Medley," by Eddie Edwards' Jazz Orchestra.

"My Baby's Arms" and "I've Lost My Heart in Dixieland," by the ORIGINAL DIXIELAND JAZZ BAND.

1921

"Carolina Shout," "The Harlem Strut," and "Keep off the Grass," by JAMES P. JOHNSON.

"The Dance They Call the Georgia Hunch," by Clarence Williams.

"Home Again Blues" and "Crazy Blues," by the ORIGINAL DIXIELAND JAZZ BAND.

"How Many Times?" by Bailey's Lucky Seven.

1922

"Eccentric" and "Farewell Blues," by the New Orleans Rhythm Kings.

"Muscle Shoals Blues" and "Birmingham Blues," by FATS WALLER.

"My Mammy Knows" and "On the Gin, Gin, Ginny Shore" by Bailey's Lucky Seven.

"Ory's Creole Trombone" and "Society Blues," by KID ORY's Sunshine Orchestra.

"Put and Take" and "Moanful Blues," by Johnny Dunn and his Original Jazz Hounds.

1923

"Farewell Blues," "Wet Yo' Thumb," "Beale Street Mama," and "Shake Your Feet," by the FLETCHER HENDERSON Orchestra.

"Hallelujah Blues" and "Spanish Dreams," by Johnny Dunn and his Original Jazz Hounds.

"Just Gone," "Dippermouth Blues," "Canal Street Blues," "New Orleans Stomp," and "Where Did You Stay Last Night?" by King Oliver's Creole Jazz Band.

"Weeping Blues" and "Toddlin'," by JAMES P. JOHNSON.

"The Pearls" and "Wolverine Blues," by JELLY ROLL MORTON.

1924

"Choo-Choo" and "Rainy Nights," by DUKE ELLINGTON and his Washingtonians.

"Jelly Roll Blues," by JELLY ROLL MORTON.

"King Porter" and "Tom Cat," by KING OLIVER and Jelly Roll Morton.

"Oh Sister, Ain't That Hot?" and "Steppin' Out," by the FLETCHER HENDERSON Orchestra.

"Riverboat Shuffle," "Fidgety Feet," and "Jazz Me Blues," by the Wolverines (with "BIX" BEIDERBECKE).

"Steppin' on the Blues" and "Traveling Blues," by LOVIE AUSTIN and her Blues Serenaders.

1925

"CHARLESTON," by JAMES P. JOHNSON.

"Charleston Mad" and "Don't Shake It No More," by LOVIE AUSTIN and her Blues Serenaders.

"I'll See You in My Dreams" and "When You Do What You Do," by the FLETCHER HENDERSON Orchestra.

"I'm Gonna Hang Around My Sugar" and "Trombone Blues," by DUKE ELLINGTON and His Washingtonians.

"My Heart" and "Gut Bucket Blues" by LOUIS ARMSTRONG and his HOT FIVE.

1926

"After I Say I'm Sorry" and "Georgia Bo-Bo," by LIL ARMSTRONG's Serenaders (with LOUIS ARMSTRONG).

"BLACK BOTTOM STOMP" and "King Porter Stomp," by JELLY ROLL MORTON.

"East St. Louis Toodle-o" and "Birmingham Breakdown," by DUKE ELLINGTON's Kentucky Club Orchestra.

"Georgia Grind" and "Parlor Social Stomp," by Duke Ellington and His Washingtonians.

"HEEBIE JEEBIES," "Cornet Chop Suey," "Big Butter and Egg Man," and "Skit-Dat-De-Dat," by Louis Armstrong and his HOT FIVE.

"Stock Yards Strut" and "Salty Dog," by FREDDIE KEPPARD's Jazz Cardinals.

"Stringing the Blues," by JOE VENUTI.

"Too Bad" and "Snag It," by "KING" OLIVER and his Dixie Syncopators.

1927

"BLACK AND TAN FANTASY," by DUKE ELLINGTON and Bubber Miley.

"Friar's Point Shuffle," by the Jungle Kings.

"Jazz Me Blues," by "BIX" BEIDERBECKE and His Gang.

"SINGIN' THE BLUES," by FRANKIE TRUMBAUER and His Orchestra, featuring "Bix" Beiderbecke.

"S.O.L. Blues," "Chicago Breakdown," "Potato Head Blues," "Wild Man Blues," "Struttin' with Some Barbecue," and "Hotter Than That," by LOUIS ARMSTRONG and his HOT FIVE AND HOT SEVEN.

"Washboard Blues," by PAUL WHITEMAN and his orchestra.

1928

"Add a Little Wiggle," by EDDIE LANG.

"Crying and Sighing," by McKinney's Cotton Pickers.

"Down by the Levee" and "Parkway Stomp," by Albert Wynn's Creole Jazz Band.

"South," by BENNIE MOTEN.

"Weatherbird," a duet by LOUIS ARMSTRONG and EARL HINES.

"West End Blues," by Louis Armstrong and his HOT FIVE.

1929

"Blue Devil Blues" and "Squabblin'," by Walter Page's Blue Devils.

"Dog Bottom," by CHICK WEBB.

"Smashing Thirds," "My Fate Is in Your Hands," "Handful of Keys," and "The Joint Is Jumpin'," by FATS WALLER.

"ST. LOUIS BLUES," by LOUIS ARMSTRONG and his orchestra.

1930

"BODY AND SOUL," "I'm a Ding Dong Daddy," and "I'm in the Market for You," by LOUIS ARMSTRONG and the New Cotton Club Orchestra.

"Cloudy Skies" and "Goodbye Blues," by the Chocolate Dandies (with BENNY CARTER and COLEMAN HAWKINS).

"Deep Down South" and "I Don't Mind Walkin' in the Rain," by "BIX" BEIDERBECKE and his orchestra.

"Shake It and Break It" and "Stingaree Blues," by "KING" OLIVER.

"Somebody Loves Me," by the FLETCHER HENDERSON Orchestra.

"Song of the Islands," by the Louis Armstrong Orchestra.

"St. James Infirmary," "When You're Smiling," "Hot and Bothered," and "Mood Indigo," by the DUKE ELLINGTON Orchestra.

1931

"Blues in My Heart," by CHICK WEBB.

"Clarinet Marmalade" and "Sugar Foot Stomp," by the FLETCHER HENDERSON Orchestra.

"Creole Rhapsody," by the DUKE ELLINGTON Orchestra.

"Dixie Vagabond" and "Minnie the Moocher," by CAB CALLOWAY.

"Draggin' My Heart Around," by FATS WALLER.

"Go Harlem," by JAMES P. JOHNSON.

"Papa De Da Da" and "I'm Crazy 'Bout My Baby," by "KING" OLIVER.

"Stardust," "Just a Gigolo," "Walkin' My Baby Back Home," and "Georgia on My Mind," by LOUIS ARMSTRONG.

1932

"Between the Devil and the Deep Blue Sea" and "Love, You Funny Thing," by LOUIS ARMSTRONG.

"It's a Great World After All," by DON REDMAN.

"IT DON'T MEAN A THING (IF IT AIN'T GOT THAT SWING)," by the DUKE ELLINGTON Orchestra.

"Moten Swing," by BENNIE MOTEN's band, featuring COUNT BASIE, BEN WEBSTER, and Hot Lips Page.

"Sweetie Dear" and "I've Found a New Baby," by SIDNEY BECHET.

"Tell All Your Daydreams to Me," by BENNY CARTER.

1933

"Dance of the Octopus," by RED NORVO, with BENNY GOODMAN.

"I've Got the World on a String," by LOUIS ARMSTRONG.

"On the Sunny Side of the Street," by CHICK WEBB.

"Raggin' the Scale," by EDDIE LANG and JOE VENUTI.

"Solitude" and "Sophisticated Lady," by the DUKE ELLINGTON Orchestra.

"Symphony in Riffs," by BENNY CARTER.

"Texas Tea Party," by Benny Goodman, featuring JACK TEAGARDEN.

"The Day You Came Along," by COLEMAN HAWKINS.

"TIGER RAG," by ART TATUM.

1934

"Dinah" and "TIGER RAG," by the Quintette of the Hot Club (Paris).

"Don't Be That Way," by CHICK WEBB and his orchestra.

"Ebony Rhapsody" and "Delta Serenade," by the DUKE ELLINGTON Orchestra.

"Hells Bells and Hallelujah," by JOE VENUTI.

"Moonglow" and "Anything for You," by ART TATUM.

"ST. LOUIS BLUES" and "Will You, Won't You Be My Baby?" by LOUIS ARMSTRONG (recorded in Paris).

"Wrappin' It Up," by the FLETCHER HENDERSON Orchestra.

1935

"Chinatown" and "Limehouse Blues," by Stephane Grappelli and DJANGO REINHARDT.

"Get Rhythm in Your Feet," "If I Could Be with You," and "Throwing Stones at the Sun," by the BENNY GOODMAN Orchestra.

"IN A SENTIMENTAL MOOD" and "Reminiscing in Tempo," by the DUKE ELLINGTON Orchestra.

"It's Too Hot for Words" and "If You Were Mine," by BILLIE HOLIDAY.

"The Last Round-Up," by GENE KRUPA and his orchestra.

1936

"China Boy" and "More Than You Know," by the BENNY GOODMAN Trio.

"Corny Rhythm" and "Swingin' for Joy," by MARY LOU WILLIAMS.

"Echoes of Harlem," by the DUKE ELLINGTON Orchestra.

"Flight of a Haybag" and "Somebody Loves Me," by FRANKIE TRAUMBAUER.

"I'm Gonna Sit Right Down and Write Myself a Letter," by FATS WALLER.

"Just for the Thrill," by LIL HARDIN (Armstrong).

"Last Affair" and Darktown Strutter's Ball, by ELLA FITZGERALD and the Savoy 8.

"Moonglow," "Vibraphone Blues," and "My Melancholy Baby," by the Benny Goodman Quartet (with LIONEL HAMPTON).

"The Music Goes Round and Round," by LOUIS ARMSTRONG.

"Pick Yourself Up," "Stompin' at the Savoy," and "Breakin' in a New Pair of Shoes," by the Benny Goodman Orchestra.

"Shoe Shine Boy," by the COUNT BASIE QUINTET.

"Summertime" and "Billie's Blues," by BILLIE HOLIDAY.

"When Ruben Swings the Cuban," by Louis Armstrong, with the JIMMY DORSEY Orchestra.

1937

"Born to Swing" and "Lindy Hop," by LIL ARMSTRONG and Her Swing Band.

"Djangoology," by DJANGO REINHARDT and Stephane Grappelli.

"Gin and Jive" and "Nagasaki," by BENNY CARTER.

"Honeysuckle Rose" and "Pennies from Heaven," by the COUNT BASIE Orchestra.

"I'll Never Be the Same," by BILLIE HOLIDAY, with the Teddy Hill Orchestra, featuring LESTER YOUNG.

"King Porter Stomp," by Teddy Hill's band, featuring DIZZY GILLESPIE (his first recording).

"Swing Guitars," by Django REINHARDT.

"The New East St. Louis Toodle-o" and "Harmony in Harlem," by the DUKE ELLINGTON Orchestra.

"Public Melody Number One" and "Cuban Pete," by the LOUIS ARMSTRONG Orchestra.

"With Plenty of Money and You" and "I've Got My Love to Keep Me Warm," by ART TATUM and his Swingsters.

"You Showed Me the Way" and "I Ain't Got Nobody," by FATS WALLER and his Rhythm.

1938

"A-TISKET A-TASKET," by CHICK WEBB and his orchestra, featuring ELLA FITZGERALD.

"Begin the Beguine," by ARTIE SHAW.

Benny Goodman: Live at Carnegie Hall 1938, by BENNY GOODMAN.

"Get Happy Together" and "Happy Today, Sad Tomorrow," by the LIL ARMSTRONG Orchestra.

"Riding on a Blue Note" and "Lost in Meditation," by the DUKE ELLINGTON Orchestra.

"Satchel Mouth Swing" and "As Long As You Live You'll Be Dead If You Die," by the LOUIS ARMSTRONG Orchestra.

"Weary Blues" and "I Wish I Could Shimmy Like My Sister Kate," by SIDNEY BECHET's New Orleans Feetwarmers.

1939

"BODY AND SOUL," by COLEMAN HAWKINS.

"Drummin' Man," by the GENE KRUPA Orchestra.

"I Had to Live and Learn," by ELLA FITZGERALD and the Savoy 8.

"Jeepers Creepers," by the LOUIS ARMSTRONG Orchestra.

"Jive at Five," by the COUNT BASIE Orchestra.

"London Suite," by FATS WALLER.

"Stairway to the Stars" and "Out of Nowhere," by Ella Fitzgerald and Orchestra.

"Strange Fruit" and "Dream of Life," by BILLIE HOLIDAY.

"Summertime," by the SIDNEY BECHET Quintet.

"Tea for Two," by ART TATUM.

"Two O'Clock Jump" and "Concerto for Trumpet," by the HARRY JAMES Orchestra.

1940

"Black Butterfly" by Cootie Williams and his Rugcutters.

"Body and Soul" and "Falling in Love Again," by Billie Holiday.

"Cotton Tail," by Duke Ellington.

"Deep Forest" and "Easy Rhythm," by the Earl Hines Orchestra.

"Frenesi," by Artie Shaw.

"Gone with What Wind" and "Six Appeal," by the Benny Goodman Sextet, with Charlie Christian.

"Nuages," by Django Reinhardt.

"Sixth Street" and "Riffin' the Blues," by the Lil Armstrong Orchestra.

"Special Delivery Stomp," by Artie Shaw and his Gramercy Five.

"Stormy Weather" and "Sophisticated Lady," by the Duke Ellington Orchestra.

"Sweet Lorraine" and "Honeysuckle Rose," by the Nat King Cole Trio.

1941

"All That Meat and No Potatoes" and "Cash for Your Trash," by Fats Waller.

"Basie Boogie" and "Fancy Meeting You," by the Count Basie Orchestra.

"God Bless the Child," by Billie Holiday.

"The One I Love" and "When My Sugar Walks Down the Street," by Ella Fitzgerald and Orchestra.

"Sheik of Araby," by Sidney Bechet, a solo recording featuring the early use of overdubs.

"Solo Flight," by the Benny Goodman Sextet with Charlie Christian.

"Stompin' at the Savoy," by Charlie Christian.

"Swingmatism," by the Jay McShann Band, featuring Charlie Parker.

"Take the 'A' Train," by Duke Ellington.

1942

"Flying Home," by Lionel Hampton.

"Four Leaf Clover," by Ella Fitzgerald.

"Indiana" and "I Can't Get Started," by Cootie Williams and Nat King Cole.

"Jersey Bounce" and "String of Pearls," by the Benny Goodman Orchestra.

"One O'Clock Jump," by the Count Basie Orchestra.

"Sherman Shuffle," by the Duke Ellington Orchestra.

1943

"Black, Brown, and Beige," "Koko," and "Cottontail," by the Duke Ellington Orchestra.

"I've Found a New Baby," by Dexter Gordon.

"Just You, Just Me" and "I Never Knew," by Lester Young.

"The Man I Love," by Coleman Hawkins.

"Sometimes I'm Happy," by Lester Young.

"Stormy Weather," by Lena Horne.

"Straighten Up and Fly Right," by the Nat King Cole Trio.

"Woke Up Clipped" and "The Horn," by Ben Webster.

1944

"After Theatre Jump" and "These Foolish Things," by Lester Young.

"All The Things You Are" and "Cloudburst," by Erroll Garner.

"Don't Be That Way," by Roy Eldridge.

"Don't Blame Me," by Oscar Pettiford.

"G.I. Jive," by Woody Herman.

"I Got a Date with Rhythm," by the Billy Eckstine Orchestra.

"I'll Get By" and "How Am I to Know?" by Billie Holiday.

"Kansas City Stride," by the Count Basie Orchestra.

"Make Believe" and "Don't Blame Me," by Coleman Hawkins.

"Sleep" and "Linger Awhile," by Sid Catlett.

1945

"Billie's Bounce" and "Warming up a Riff," by Charlie Parker.

"Blow Mr. Dexter" and "Dexter's Deck," by Dexter Gordon.

"If I Had You" and "Takin' Off," by SIR CHARLES THOMPSON.

"Laura" and "Caldonia," by WOODY HERMAN.

"Lester Blows Again," by LESTER YOUNG.

"Little Jazz Boogie," by ROY ELDRIDGE.

"Night and Day" and "Loot to Boot," by ERROLL GARNER.

"Poinciana" and "Love for Sale," by BENNY CARTER.

"Prelude to a Kiss," by the DUKE ELLINGTON Orchestra.

"SALT PEANUTS" and "Be-Bop," by DIZZY GILLESPIE and his All Star Quintet.

"That's the Way It Is," by ELLA FITZGERALD.

"What More Can a Woman Do?" by SARAH VAUGHN.

"Zodiaz Suite," by MARY LOU WILLIAMS.

1946

"Diga Diga Doo" and "Who's Sorry Now?" by BENNY CARTER.

"Good Morning Heartache," by BILLIE HOLIDAY.

"If You Could See Me Now," by SARAH VAUGHN.

"Pam," by WOODY HERMAN's Woodchoppers.

"Things to Come," by DIZZY GILLESPIE.

1947

"Angel Face," by COLEMAN HAWKINS.

"Bikini," by Dexter Gordon.

"Cubana Be, Cubana Bop" and "Manteca," by CHANO POZO and DIZZY GILLESPIE.

"Embraceable You" and "Crazeology," by CHARLIE PARKER.

"Nostalgia," by the Bebop Boys, featuring Fats Navarro.

"Progressive Gavotte," by the DUKE ELLINGTON Orchestra.

"Satchmo," by LOUIS ARMSTRONG, with SID CATLETT and JACK TEAGARDEN.

Genius of Modern Music, "Weel, You Needn't," by THELONIOUS MONK.

1948

"Baby You're Mine for Keeps," by BENNY CARTER.

"Barbados," "Constellation," "Parker's Mood," and "Marmalade," by CHARLIE PARKER.

"EPISTROPHY," "Misterioso," and "Evidence," by THELONIOUS MONK.

"I Can't Go on Without You," by ELLA FITZGERALD.

"'Round Midnight," "Algo Bueno," and "Afro-Cubano Suite," by the DIZZY GILLESPIE Orchestra.

"Tea for Two," "East of Suez," and "Something to Remember You By," by LESTER YOUNG.

"Mucho Macho," "Cubop," and "Mango Mangue," by MACHITO & His Afro-Cuban Salseros.

1949

"Dedicated to You," by SARAH VAUGHN and Billy Eckstine.

"Embraceable You," recorded at CARNEGIE HALL by CHARLIE PARKER, LESTER YOUNG, and ROY ELDRIDGE.

"In the Land of Oo-Bla-Dee," by DIZZY GILLESPIE (written by MARY LOU WILLIAMS).

"Jeru," "Move," and "Godchild," by MILES DAVIS.

Lee Konitz (with Tristano Marsh & Bauer), by Lee Konitz.

"Subconscious-Lee," by LENNIE TRISTANO.

"Tempus Fugit" and "Celia," by the BUD POWELL Trio.

"Willow Weep for Me," by ART TATUM.

"You Can't Lose a Broken Heart," by LOUIS ARMSTRONG and BILLIE HOLIDAY.

1950

All-Star Sessions with Sonny Stitt, by SONNY STITT.

BIRTH OF THE COOL, by the MILES DAVIS Nonet.

"Deception," "Rocker," and "Darn That Dream," by Miles Davis.

Innovations in Modern Music, by STAN KENTON.

"Love You Madly," by the DUKE ELLINGTON Orchestra.

"Nice Work If You Can Get It," by Miles Davis and SARAH VAUGHN.

"Perdido" and "Blues for Blanton," by OSCAR PETTIFORD.

"So Sorry Please," "Get Happy," and "Sometimes I'm Happy," by Bud Powell.

"Too Marvelous for Words," by Lester Young.

"Twisted," by Annie Ross.

1951

"Criss-Cross," by Thelonious Monk.

"Deep Night," and "A Tone Parallel to Harlem," by the Duke Ellington Orchestra.

"I Know," by Sonny Rollins.

"Indiana" and "Baby It's Cold Outside," by the Louis Armstrong All-Stars.

"It's Easy to Remember" and "Pooper," by the Oscar Peterson Trio.

"Lonesome Gal" and "Give a Little, Get a Little," by Ella Fitzgerald.

"Love Me" and "We Love to Boogie," by the Dizzy Gillespie Sextet.

"Morpheus," "Down," and "Conception," by Miles Davis.

"Night in Tunisia," by Bud Powell.

Stan Kenton Presents, by Stan Kenton.

"Star Eyes" and "My Little Suede Shoes," by Charlie Parker.

"Yesterdays," by Miles Davis and Lee Konitz.

1952

"All the Things You Are," by the Modern Jazz Quartet.

"Citizen's Bop" and "Man with a Horn," by Dexter Gordon.

"East of the Sun" and "You Go to My Head," by Billie Holiday.

"Ellington Uptown," by the Duke Ellington Orchestra.

Jazz at Storyville, by the Dave Brubeck Trio and Quintet.

"New Basie Blues" and "Jive at Five," by Count Basie.

The New Benny Goodman Sextet, by the Benny Goodman Sextet.

Pastel Moods, by the Oscar Peterson Trio.

"Precognition" and "Paris in Blue," by Charles Mingus.

"The President Plays," by Lester Young and Oscar Peterson.

Stan Getz Quintet, by the Stan Getz Quintet.

1953

The Amazing Bud Powell, Vol. 2, by the Bud Powell Trio.

Blue Haze, by Miles Davis.

Chet Baker Ensemble, by the Chet Baker Ensemble.

"Deep Purple," by Art Pepper.

Diz & Getz, by Dizzy Gillespie.

Django, by the Modern Jazz Quartet.

"Easy Livin'" and "Hymn to the Orient," by Clifford Brown.

"In the Still of the Night," by Charlie Parker.

Jazz at Massey Hall, by Charlie Parker, Dizzy Gillespie, Charles Mingus, Bud Powell, and Max Roach.

"Let's Call This," by Thelonious Monk.

Mary Lou Williams and Don Byas, by Mary Lou Williams and Don Byas.

Walkin' Shoes, by the Gerry Mulligan Tentette.

"Without a Song," by Art Tatum.

1954

Bag's Groove, by Miles Davis and Thelonious Monk.

Dinah JAMs, by Dinah Washington.

Horace Silver Quintet, Vol. 1, by the Horace Silver Quintet.

"Love for Sale" and "I Love Paris," by Charlie Parker.

Movin' Out, by Sonny Rollins.

A Night at Birdland, by Art Blakey, featuring Clifford Brown.

"Parisian Thoroughfare," by Clifford Brown and Max Roach.

Sarah Vaughn with Clifford Brown, by Sarah Vaughn and Clifford Brown.

Walkin', by Miles Davis.

"The Way You Look Tonight," by Thelonious Monk with SONNY ROLLINS.

1955

Clifford Brown with Strings, by CLIFFORD BROWN.
Concert by the Sea, by ERROLL GARNER.
Contemporary Concepts, by STAN KENTON.
Dexter Plays Hot and Cool, by Dexter Gordon.
The Jazz Messengers at the Café Bohemia, Volumes 1 & 2, by ART BLAKEY and the Jazz Messengers.
Lines, by LENNIE TRISTANO.
Songs from the Heart, by JOHNNY HARTMAN.
"Too Marvelous for Words," by ART TATUM.
The Wailing Buddy Rich, by BUDDY RICH.
Work Time, by SONNY ROLLINS.

1956

A Garland of Red, by Red Garland.
April in Paris, by COUNT BASIE.
BRILLIANT CORNERS, by THELONIOUS MONK.
Count Basie Swings, Joe Williams Sings, by COUNT BASIE.
Ella and Louis, by ELLA FITZGERALD and LOUIS ARMSTRONG.
Jazz Advance, by CECIL TAYLOR.
Lady Sings the Blues, BILLIE HOLIDAY.
New Jazz Directions, by BILL EVANS.
Pithecanthropus Erectus, by CHARLES MINGUS.
"'Round Midnight," by MILES DAVIS with JOHN COLTRANE.
SAXOPHONE COLOSSUS, by SONNY ROLLINS.
Whims of Chambers, by PAUL CHAMBERS.
Workin', Relaxin', Cookin', and Steamin', by the Miles Davis Quintet.

1957

BLUE TRAIN, by JOHN COLTRANE.
Dizzy Gillespie with Sonny Rollins and Sonny Stitt, by DIZZY GILLESPIE with SONNY ROLLINS and SONNY STITT.

Gerry Mulligan Meets Paul Desmond, by GERRY MULLIGAN and Paul Desmond.
"Haitian Fight Song" and "Tijuana Moods," by CHARLES MINGUS.
Miles Ahead, by MILES DAVIS.
Out on a Limb, by CLARK TERRY.
Soulville, by BEN WEBSTER.
Such Sweet Thunder, by DUKE ELLINGTON.
Thelonious Himself, by THELONIOUS MONK.

1958

At the Pershing, by Ahmad Jamal.
Ella in Rome: The Birthday Concert, by ELLA FITZGERALD.
"Fever," by PEGGY LEE.
The Freedom Suite, by SONNY ROLLINS.
Jazz in Silhouette, by SUN RA.
Lady in Satin, by BILLIE HOLIDAY.
Looking Ahead! by CECIL TAYLOR.
MOANIN', by ART BLAKEY and the Jazz Messengers.
Porgy and Bess, by MILES DAVIS and GIL EVANS.
Reflections—Plays Thelonious, by STEVE LACY.
Somethin' Else, by Cannonball Adderley.
The Sermon, by JIMMY SMITH.

1959

At Town Hall, by the THELONIOUS MONK Orchestra.
Beauty and the Beat, by PEGGY LEE.
Ben Webster and Associates, by BEN WEBSTER.
BLUES AND ROOTS, by CHARLES MINGUS.
Change of the Century, by ORNETTE COLEMAN.
Gerry Mulligan Meets Ben Webster, by GERRY MULLIGAN and BEN WEBSTER.
GIANT STEPS, by JOHN COLTRANE.
KIND OF BLUE, by MILES DAVIS.
MINGUS AH UM, by CHARLES MINGUS.
The Monterey Concerts, by Cal Tjader.
THE SHAPE OF JAZZ TO COME, by ORNETTE COLEMAN.
TIME OUT, by the DAVE BRUBECK Quartet.
Unforgettable, by DINAH WASHINGTON.

What a Diff'rence a Day Makes! by Dinah Washington.

1960

"MY FAVORITE THINGS," by JOHN COLTRANE.

Complete Ella in Berlin—Mack the Knife, by ELLA FITZGERALD.

FREE JAZZ, by ORNETTE COLEMAN.

THE INCREDIBLE JAZZ GUITAR OF WES MONTGOMERY, by WES MONTGOMERY.

Live at the Village Gate, by HERBIE MANN.

Mingus Presents Mingus, by CHARLES MINGUS.

OUT THERE, by ERIC DOLPHY.

Outward Bound, by Eric Dolphy.

Sketches of Spain, by MILES DAVIS and GIL EVANS.

Wishes You a Swinging Christmas, by Ella Fitzgerald.

1961

After Hours, by SARAH VAUGHN.

Ballads, by JOHN COLTRANE.

THE BLUES AND THE ABSTRACT TRUTH, by Oliver Nelson.

Bluesnik, by Jackie McLean and FREDDIE HUBBARD.

Clap Hands Here Comes Charlie, by ELLA FITZGERALD.

Doin' Alright, by Dexter Gordon.

Eric Dolphy at the Five Spot, by ERIC DOLPHY.

Hip Twist and Shirley Scott Plays Horace Silver, by SHIRLEY SCOTT.

Nancy Wilson/Cannonball Adderley, by NANCY WILSON and Cannonball Adderley.

Percussion Bittersweet, by MAX ROACH.

WALTZ FOR DEBBY, by BILL EVANS.

1962

BBB & Company, by BENNY CARTER.

Coltrane, by JOHN COLTRANE.

The Comedy, by the MODERN JAZZ QUARTET.

The Composer of "Desafinado", Plays, by ANTONIO CARLOS JOBIM.

"IN A SENTIMENTAL MOOD," by DUKE ELLINGTON and John Coltrane.

Jazz Samba, by STAN GETZ.

Let Freedom Ring, by Jackie McLean.

Night Train, by OSCAR PETERSON.

Undercurrent, by BILL EVANS.

"WATERMELON MAN," by HERBIE HANCOCK.

1963

Conversations with Myself, by BILL EVANS.

Duke Ellington & John Coltrane, by DUKE ELLINGTON and JOHN COLTRANE.

Duke Ellington Presents the Dollar Brand Trio, by Dollar Brand (ABDULLAH IBRAHIM).

GETZ/GILBERTO, by STAN GETZ and João Gilberto.

John Coltrane and Johnny Hartman, by JOHN COLTRANE and JOHNNY HARTMAN.

Live at Newport, by HERBIE MANN.

Midnight Blue, by Kenny Burrell.

Mink Jazz, by PEGGY LEE.

"Mississippi Goddam!" by NINA SIMONE.

Night Lights, by GERRY MULLIGAN.

Shiny Stockings, by ELLA FITZGERALD and COUNT BASIE.

Takin' Off, by HERBIE HANCOCK.

The Sidewinder, by LEE MORGAN.

1964

A LOVE SUPREME, by the JOHN COLTRANE Quartet.

Maiden Voyage, by HERBIE HANCOCK.

Out to Lunch, by ERIC DOLPHY.

SONG FOR MY FATHER, by HORACE SILVER.

Speak No Evil, by WAYNE SHORTER.

Thelonious Monk: Live at the It Club, by THELONIOUS MONK.

Town Hall Concert 1964, by CHARLES MINGUS.

Travelin' Light, by SHIRLEY SCOTT.

1965

Ascension and *First Meditations for Quartet,* by JOHN COLTRANE.

Concert of Sacred Music, by Duke Ellington.
East Broadway Rundown, by Sonny Rollins.
"E.S.P.," by the Miles Davis Quintet.
Herbie Mann Today, by Herbie Mann.
Rip Rig and Panic, by Rahsaan Roland Kirk.
Soul Finger, by Art Blakey and the Jazz Messengers.
Spring, by Tony Williams with Wayne Shorter.
The Heliocentric Worlds of Sun Ra, by Sun Ra.
The Soothsayer, by Wayne Shorter.
Unit 7, by Wes Montgomery.

1966

California Dreaming, by Wes Montgomery.
Cosmic Music, by John Coltrane.
Drums Unlimited, by Max Roach.
Four for Trane, by Archie Shepp.
The Golden Flute, by Yusef Lateef.
Money in the Pocket, by Joe Zawinul.
Of Love and Peace, by Larry Young.
The Rajah, by Lee Morgan.
Sound, by Roscoe Mitchell.
Town Hall Concert, by Bill Evans.
Where Is Brooklyn? by Don Cherry.

1967

A Day in the Life, by Wes Montgomery.
And His Mother Called Him Bill, by Duke Ellington.
Atlantis, by Sun Ra.
Concerto for Herd, by Woody Herman.
El Hombre, by Pat Martino.
Electric Bath, by Don Ellis.
Interstellar Space, by John Coltrane.
Live at the Village Vanguard, by Thad Jones and Mel Lewis.
Lofty Fake Anagram, by Gary Burton.
Mama Too Tight, by Archie Shepp.
Nefertiti, by Miles Davis.
Tender Moments, by McCoy Tyner.
The Gamut, by Chico Hamilton.
The Real McCoy, by McCoy Tyner.

1968

A Genuine Tong Funeral, by Carla Bley and Gary Burton.
A Monastic Trio, by Alice Coltrane.
Bill Evans Alone, by Bill Evans.
Bliss! by Chick Corea.
Communications, by the Jazz Composer's Orchestra.
For Alto, by Anthony Braxton.
Heavy Sounds, by Elvin Jones.
The Inflated Tear, by Rahsaan Roland Kirk.
The Jazz Compositions of Dee Barton, by Stan Kenton.
Live in New Orleans, by Gerry Mulligan and Dave Brubeck.
Mercy, Mercy, by Buddy Rich.
Miles in the Sky, by Miles Davis.
New York Is Now, by Ornette Coleman.
Praxis, by Cecil Taylor.

1969

Cosmos, by McCoy Tyner.
Emergency, by the Tony Williams Lifetime.
Esoteric Circle, by Jan Garbarek.
Extrapolation, by John McLaughlin.
Fat Albert Rotunda, by Herbie Hancock.
Finally, by Betty Carter.
In a Silent Way, by Miles Davis.
Infinite Search, by Miroslav Vitous.
Jewels of Thought, by Pharoah Sanders.
Mu, by Don Cherry.
Super Nova, by Wayne Shorter.
Tutankhamen and *Message to Our Folks,* by the Art Ensemble of Chicago.
Volunteered Slavery, by Rahsaan Roland Kirk.

1970

Afric Pepperbird, by Jan Garbarek.
Bitches Brew, A Tribute to Jack Johnson, and *Live Evil* by Miles Davis.
Blue Bird, by Charles Mingus.
Consummation, by Thad Jones and Mel Lewis.

Devotion and *My Goals Beyond*, by JOHN MCLAUGHLIN.

Gary Burton and Keith Jarrett, by GARY BURTON and KEITH JARRETT.

It's After the End of the World, by SUN RA.

Mwandishi, by HERBIE HANCOCK.

New Orleans Suite, by DUKE ELLINGTON.

Odyssey of Iska, by WAYNE SHORTER.

Ptah, the El Daoud, by ALICE COLTRANE.

Purple, by MIROSLAV VITOUS.

The Trio, by JOHN SURMAN.

1971

Alone at Last, by GARY BURTON.

Crossings, by HERBIE HANCOCK.

Escalator Over the Hill, by CARLA BLEY.

Ethiopian Night, by DONALD BYRD.

Facing You, by KEITH JARRETT.

Great Connection, by OSCAR PETERSON.

Let My Children Hear Music, by CHARLES MINGUS.

Natural Black Inventions, by RAHSAAN ROLAND KIRK.

Orange Lady, by WEATHER REPORT.

Piano Improvisations Volumes 1 & 2, by CHICK COREA.

Under Fire, by GATO BARBIERI.

Wordless, by STEVE LACY.

1972

CONFERENCE OF THE BIRDS, by DAVE HOLLAND.

Crossings, by HERBIE HANCOCK.

Facing You, by KEITH JARRETT.

THE INNER MOUNTING FLAME, by JOHN MCLAUGHLIN and the MAHAVISHNU ORCHESTRA.

Last Tango in Paris, by GATO BARBIERI.

On the Corner, by MILES DAVIS.

Return to Forever, by CHICK COREA.

Sadao Watanabe, by Sadao Watanabe.

Sextant, by Herbie Hancock.

Sonata Erotica, by JEAN-LUC PONTY.

Space Is the Place, by SUN RA.

Tenor Titans, by BEN WEBSTER and Dexter Gordon.

1973

African Sketchbook, by ABDULLAH IBRAHIM (Dollar Brand).

Basie Jam, by COUNT BASIE.

The Crust, by STEVE LACY.

Elevation, by PHAROAH SANDERS.

Fanfare for the Warriors, by the ART ENSEMBLE OF CHICAGO.

Fort Yawuh and *Solo Concerts*, by KEITH JARRETT.

GIANT STEPS, by WOODY HERMAN.

HEAD HUNTERS, by HERBIE HANCOCK.

Hymn of the Seventh Galaxy, by Return to Forever.

Relativity Suite and *The Sonet Recordings*, by DON CHERRY.

Skylark, by Paul Desmond.

Solos, by CECIL TAYLOR.

The Source, by DIZZY GILLESPIE.

Street Lady, by DONALD BYRD.

1974

All the Things We Are, by DAVE BRUBECK.

Belonging, by JAN GARBAREK and KEITH JARRETT.

Carnegie Hall Concert, by GERRY MULLIGAN and CHET BAKER.

Consciousness, by PAT MARTINO.

Hotel Hello, by GARY BURTON.

In the Light, by Keith Jarrett.

In the Tradition, by ANTHONY BRAXTON.

Kogun, by TOSHIKO AKIYOSHI.

Native Dancer, by WAYNE SHORTER.

The Restful Mind, by Larry Coryell.

Satch & Josh, by OSCAR PETERSON and COUNT BASIE.

Thrust, by HERBIE HANCOCK.

Timeless, by JOHN ABERCROMBIE.

Tropic Appetites, by CARLA BLEY.

1975

Afrisong, by MUHAL RICHARD ABRAMS.

Alive in New York, by GATO BARBIERI.

The Best of Two Worlds, by STAN GETZ.

The Brecker Brothers, by the Brecker Brothers.

Bright Size Life, by PAT METHENY.
For the Second Time, by the COUNT BASIE Trio.
Gleam, by FREDDIE HUBBARD.
Live at the Cookery, by MARY LOU WILLIAMS.
No Mystery, by CHICK COREA.
Nucleus, by SONNY ROLLINS.
Panagea, by MILES DAVIS.
Rope-a-Dope, by LESTER BOWIE.
Seven Comes Eleven, by BENNY GOODMAN.
Tales of a Courtesan, by TOSHIKO AKIYOSHI.
The Tony Bennett/Bill Evans Album, by Tony Bennett and BILL EVANS.
Top Hat, by Charlie Byrd.

1976

Air Raid, by Air.
Backgammon, by ART BLAKEY.
Hear and Now, by DON CHERRY.
HEAVY WEATHER, by WEATHER REPORT.
Herbie Hancock VSOP, by HERBIE HANCOCK.
Invitation, by JOANNE BRACKEEN.
Jaco Pastorius, by JACO PASTORIUS.
Journey into Capricorn, by STAN KENTON.
Live in Tokyo, by MARIAN MCPARTLAND.
Passengers, by GARY BURTON.
Sanborn, by DAVID SANBORN.
Silence/Time Zones, by ANTHONY BRAXTON.
Silver n' Voices, by HORACE SILVER.
The Survivor's Suite, by KEITH JARRETT.
Wham, by CLARK TERRY.
Wonderland, by BENNY CARTER.

1977

Blackout, by LIONEL HAMPTON.
Chicago Slow Dance, by GEORGE LEWIS.
Cubia, by CHARLES MINGUS.
For Trio, by ANTHONY BRAXTON.
I Love Brazil, by SARAH VAUGHN.
Look to the Rainbow, by AL JARREAU.
New Rags, by JACK DEJOHNETTE.
Piccolo, by RON CARTER.
Priestess, by GIL EVANS.

Red in New York, by RED NORVO.
Soapsuds, by ORNETTE COLEMAN.
Sophisticated Giant, by Dexter Gordon.
Star Wars, by DON ELLIS.
Supertrios, by MCCOY TYNER.
The Gifted Ones, by DIZZY GILLESPIE and COUNT BASIE.
Tring-a-Ling, by JOANNE BRACKEEN.
Watercolours, by PAT METHENY.

1978

All Star Band at Newport, by LIONEL HAMPTON.
From This Moment On, by MARIAN MCPARTLAND.
Hand Crafted, by Kenny Burrell.
In This Korner, by ART BLAKEY.
Live at Carnegie Hall, by Stephane Grappelli.
The Mad Hatter, by CHICK COREA.
Mirjana, by John Lewis.
New Conversations, by BILL EVANS.
New Steps, by SUN RA.
Parabola, by GIL EVANS.
Passion Flower, by Marion Brown.
Photo With . . ., by JAN GARBAREK.
Rough House, by JOHN SCOFIELD.
Something Like a Bird, by the CHARLES MINGUS Band.
Transfiguration, by ALICE COLTRANE.

1979

African Magic, by MALACHI FAVORS.
African Marketplace, Africa/Tears of Laughter, Echoes from Africa, by ABDULLAH IBRAHIM.
Back Home, by DAVE BRUBECK.
Chair in the Sky, by Mingus Dynasty.
Common Cause, by Attilla Zoller.
Eclipse, by THAD JONES.
Forest Eyes, by STAN GETZ.
Historic Concerts, by MAX ROACH and CECIL TAYLOR.
In a Temple Garden, by YUSEF LATEEF.
In Concert, by CHICK COREA and GARY BURTON.
Magico, by DAVE HOLLAND.
Makin' Whoopee, by DOROTHY DONEGAN.
The Moth and the Flame, by KEITH JARRETT.

Close Enough for Love, by SHIRLEY HORN.
Fleur Carnivore, by CARLA BLEY.
Garrett 5, by KENNY GARRETT.
Live at Sweet Basil, by RANDY BRECKER.
The Majesty of the Blues, by WYNTON MARSALIS.
Mostly Blues, by LIONEL HAMPTON.
Portraits, by CLARK TERRY.
Reunion, by MEL TORME.
Spy vs. Spy: The Music of Ornette Coleman, by JOHN ZORN.
Tribute to Gil, by the GIL EVANS Orchestra.
Trio Jeepy, by BRANFORD MARSALIS.
The Truth Is Spoken Here, by Marcus Roberts.

1989

African River, by ABDULLAH IBRAHIM.
All That Jazz, by ELLA FITZGERALD.
Amandla, by MILES DAVIS.
Anthem, by STEVE LACY.
Duets, by ANTHONY BRAXTON and MARILYN CRISPELL.
Euphoria, by CHICO HAMILTON.
The Hearinga Suite, by MUHAL RICHARD ABRAMS.
In Florescence, by CECIL TAYLOR.
Live at Maybeck Recital Hall, by JOANNE BRACKEEN.
Live in San Francisco, by Marilyn Crispell.
Living on the Edge, by Dewey Redman.
Olé Ola, by MONGO SANTAMARIA.
Opalescence, by HERBIE MANN.
Reunion, by GARY BURTON.
Squeeze Me, by the CLARK TERRY Spacemen.
The Vision's Tale, by COURTNEY PINE.

1990

African Exchange Student, by KENNY GARRETT.
American South Africa, by The ART ENSEMBLE OF CHICAGO.
A Waltz for Grace, by STEVE WILLIAMSON.
The Calculus of Pleasure, by the EITHER/ORCHESTRA.
Droppin' Things, by BETTY CARTER.
Ellis Marsalis Trio, by the Ellis Marsalis Trio.
Live at the 1990 Floating Jazz Festival, by DOROTHY DONEGAN.

Live at the Village Gate, by CLARK TERRY.
The Mediterranean Concerto, by JOHN MCLAUGHLIN.
Naked City, by JOHN ZORN.
Plays the Benny Carter Songbook, by MARIAN MCPARTLAND.
Reflections, by Steve Grossman.
She Who Weeps, by CASSANDRA WILSON.
Within the Realms of Our Dreams, by COURTNEY PINE.
You Gotta Pay the Band, by ABBEY LINCOLN.
You Won't Forget Me, by SHIRLEY HORN.
The Very Big Carla Bley Band, by CARLA BLEY.

1991

Ask the Ages, by SONNY SHARROCK.
The Blessing, by Gonzalo Rubacalba.
Blue Interlude, by WYNTON MARSALIS.
From the Soul, by JOE LOVANO.
Grace Under Pressure, by JOHN SCOFIELD.
Live with Dizzy Gillespie, by the DOROTHY DONEGAN Trio.
Nina Simone, by NINA SIMONE.
People Time, by STAN GETZ.
Power Trio, by John Hicks, Cecil McBee, and ELVIN JONES.
Spirits of Our Ancestors, by Randy Weston.
Stormy Weather, by Grace Night.
Tuskegee Experiments, by Don Byron.

1992

A Handful of Keys, by HANK JONES.
A Tribute to Miles, by HERBIE HANCOCK.
A Walkin' Thing, by SHIRLEY SCOTT.
Black Hope, by KENNY GARRETT.
Code Red, by CINDY BLACKMAN.
Doo Bop, by MILES DAVIS.
Evanescence, by the MARIA SCHNEIDER Orchestra.
Here's to Life, by SHIRLEY HORN.
In This House, On This Morning, by WYNTON MARSALIS.
Mambo Mongo, by MONGO SANTAMARIA.

1993

A Lady in Waiting, by KENNY GARRETT.
Blue Light 'Til Dawn, by CASSANDRA WILSON.
The Brunt, by The EITHER/ORCHESTRA.
Dancing to a Different Drummer, by CHICO HAMILTON.
Desert Lady/Fantasy, by TOSHIKO AKIYOSHI.
Dona Nostra, by DON CHERRY.
Expressions, by CHICK COREA.
Hand on the Torch, by Us3.
Nostalgia in Times Square, by the MINGUS BIG BAND.
Reminiscence, by TOMMY SMITH.
Reunion, by Stephane Grappelli.
Time Remembered, by JOHN MCLAUGHLIN.
Twelve Moons, by JAN GARBAREK.
V As in Victim, by Wayne Horvitz and Pigpen.

1994

At Maybeck, by TOSHIKO AKIYOSHI.
At the Blue Note, by KEITH JARRETT.
Dream a Little Dream, by GERRY MULLIGAN.
Only Trust Your Heart, by DIANA KRALL.
Orange and Blue, by AL DI MEOLA.
Pipe Dreams, by the Rova Saxophone Quartet.
Power Talk, by JOANNE BRACKEEN.
Vernal Fields, by INGRID JENSEN.
We Live Here, by PAT METHENY.

1995

Coming About, by the MARIA SCHNEIDER Orchestra.
Dragonfly, by GERRY MULLIGAN.
Friday Afternoon in the Universe, by Medeski, Martin, and Wood.
Gunslinging Birds, by the Mingus Big Band.
New Moon Daughter, by CASSANDRA WILSON.
One Line, Two Views, by MUHAL RICHARD ABRAMS.
Peace-Song, by D. D. JACKSON.
The Promise, by JOHN MCLAUGHLIN.
Solitude, by CLEO LAINE.
Take Off! by BARBARA DENNERLEIN.
Tone Dialing, by ORNETTE COLEMAN.
Trilogy, by KENNY GARRETT.

1996

1 + 1, by HERBIE HANCOCK and WAYNE SHORTER.
The Brass Orchestra, by J. J. JOHNSON.
Brazilian Sunset, by MONGO SANTAMARIA.
Colors, by ORNETTE COLEMAN.
Coming Home Jamaica, by the ART ENSEMBLE OF CHICAGO.
Conversin' With The Elders, by BETTY CARTER.
Here on Earth, by INGRID JENSEN.
I Don't Know This World Without Don Cherry, by the New York Jazz Collective.
I'm Yours, You're Mine, by Betty Carter.
Into Another Light, by SONNY SHARROCK.
Junkanoo, by BARBARA DENNERLEIN.
Live & More, by MARCUS MILLER.
Modern Day Jazz Stories, by COURTNEY PINE.
The New Standard, by HERBIE HANCOCK.
Oscar Peterson Meets Roy Hargrove and Ralph Moore, by OSCAR PETERSON.
Some Like It Hot, by KIT MCCLURE.

1997

Alone Together, by Lee Konitz.
Blues for the New Millennium, by Marcus Roberts.
Conversations, by GEORGE LEWIS.
Flying Colours, by JOE LOVANO and Ganzalo Rubalcaba.
4 + 1 Ensemble, and *Brand Spankin' New,* by Wayne Horvitz.
Introducing Ruben Gonzalez, by RUBEN GONZALEZ.
Jazz Underground: Live at Smalls, various European artists.
Spaces Revisited, by Larry Coryell.
Trio Fascination, by Joe Lovano.
Underground, by COURTNEY PINE.

1998

Blue Moon Rendevous, by CASSANDRA WILSON.
Both Worlds, by MICHEL PETRUCCIANI.
The Bribe, by JOHN ZORN.
Combustication, by JOHN MEDESKI.

Four Compositions, by ANTHONY BRAXTON.
Friendly Fire, by JOE LOVANO.
Gershwin's World, by HERBIE HANCOCK.
Heard on the Street, by the YOUNGBLOOD BRASS BAND.
Higher Ground, by INGRID JENSEN.
Inner Voyage, by GONZALO RUBALCABA.
Khepera, by Randy Weston.
Like Minds, by GARY BURTON with CHICK COREA and PAT METHENY.
Possible Cube, by the CHICAGO UNDERGROUND TRIO.
Voice in the Night, by Charles Lloyd.
A Week at the Blue Note, by Chick Corea.

1999

All Rise, by WYNTON MARSALIS.
The Art of the Song, by CHARLIE HADEN.
Better Together and Synesthesia, by the CHICAGO UNDERGROUND TRIO.
Blues and Politics, by the MINGUS BIG BAND.
Bump, by JOHN SCOFIELD.
Count's Jam Band Reunion, by Larry Coryell.
From the Round Box, by RAVI COLTRANE.
Momentum Space, by CECIL TAYLOR.
Popsicle Illusion, by JOANNE BRACKEEN.
The Rent, by STEVE LACY.
So You Say, by the JIM CIFELLI New York Nonet.
Timely, by CHICO HAMILTON.
Traveling Miles, by CASSANDRA WILSON.
Works on Canvas, by CINDY BLACKMAN.

2000

Compositions/improvisations 2000, by ANTHONY BRAXTON.
Everything for Love, by CHUCK MANGIONE.
52nd Street Themes, by JOE LOVANO.
Flamethrower, by the CHICAGO UNDERGROUND TRIO.
For Hamp, Red, Bags, and Cal, by GARY BURTON.
Inner Urge, by Larry Coryell.
Invisible Nature, by JOHN SURMAN.
Live on QE2, by CLARK TERRY.
Monk's Dream, by STEVE LACY.

Nearness of You: The Ballad Book, by MICHAEL BRECKER.
New Colors, by FREDDIE HUBBARD.
Nocturne, by CHARLIE HADEN.
Someday, by CINDY BLACKMAN.
Work on Canvas, by Cindy Blackman.

2001

Amaryllis, by MARILYN CRISPELL, Gary Peacock, and Paul Motian.
Ballads: Remembering John Coltrane, by Karrin Allyson.
Dear Louis, by Nicholas Payton.
Footprints Live! by WAYNE SHORTER.
Forestorn, by CHICO HAMILTON.
Future 2 Future, by HERBIE HANCOCK.
Hanging in the City, by RANDY BRECKER.
Happy People, by KENNY GARRETT.
Keith Jarrett/Gary Peacock/Jack DeJohnette: Inside Out, by KEITH JARRETT, Gary Peacock, and Jack DEJOHNETTE.
The Look of Love, by DIANA KRALL.
Matthew Shipp's New Orbit, by Matthew Shipp.
Sigame, by D. D. JACKSON.
Virtuosi, by GARY BURTON.
Viva Caruso, by JOE LOVANO.

2002

African Symphony, by ABDULLAH IBRAHIM.
Afro-Cubism, by The EITHER/ORCHESTRA.
Happy People, by KENNY GARRETT.
Monk's Moods, by STEVE LACY.
No Nonsense, by the John Fedchock New York Big Band.
Speaking of Now, by the PAT METHENY Group.
Time, by HUGH MASEKELA.
Tonight at Noon, by the MINGUS BIG BAND.
Tunnel Vision, by the JIM CIFELLI New York Nonet.
Uberjam, by JOHN SCOFIELD.
Uninvisible, by Medeski, Martin, and Wood.
Verve Remixed, including various archival recordings produced and remixed by Dahlia Ambach Caplin and Jason Olaine.

2003

African Magic, by ABDULLAH IBRAHIM.
Alegria, by WAYNE SHORTER.
Bounce, by Terence Blanchard.
Couldn't Be Hotter, by MANHATTAN TRANSFER.
Extended Play, by the DAVE HOLLAND Quintet.
Extended Play: Live at Birdland, by Dave Holland.
Freak In, by Dave Douglas.
Glamoured, by CASSANDRA WILSON.
Hard Grove, by ROY HARGROVE.
A Little Moonlight, by DIANE REEVES.
Masada Guitars, by JOHN ZORN.
New-Modernism, by the EITHER/ORCHESTRA.
Property of Gordon Goodwin's Big Phat Band XXL, by Gordon Goodwin's Big Phat Band.
Standard of Language, by KENNY GARRETT.
Suite for New York, by D. D. JACKSON.
These Are the Vistas, by THE BAD PLUS.
Thieves and Poets, by JOHN MCLAUGHLIN.
Universal Syncopation, by MIROSLAV VITOUS.

Verve Remixed 2, including various archival recordings produced and remixed by Dahlia Ambach.
With a Heartbeat, by PHAROAH SANDERS.

2004

Avatango, by Pablo Aslan.
Beyond Brooklyn, by HERBIE MANN and Phil Woods.
Coral, by David Sanchez.
End of the World Party (Just in Case), by Medeski, Martin, and Wood.
Even Canadians Get the Blues, by the Boss Brass.
Give, by THE BAD PLUS.
Ivey-Divey, by Don Byron.
Land of the Sun, by CHARLIE HADEN.
The Life of a Song, by Geri Allen.
Live at MCG, by the Bob Mintzer Big Band.
The Lost Chords, by CARLA BLEY.
R.S.V.P, by NANCY WILSON.
Translinear Light, by ALICE COLTRANE.
Tribute to Lester, by MALACHI FAVORS.

Appendix II

Geographical History of Early Jazz (1900 to 1950)

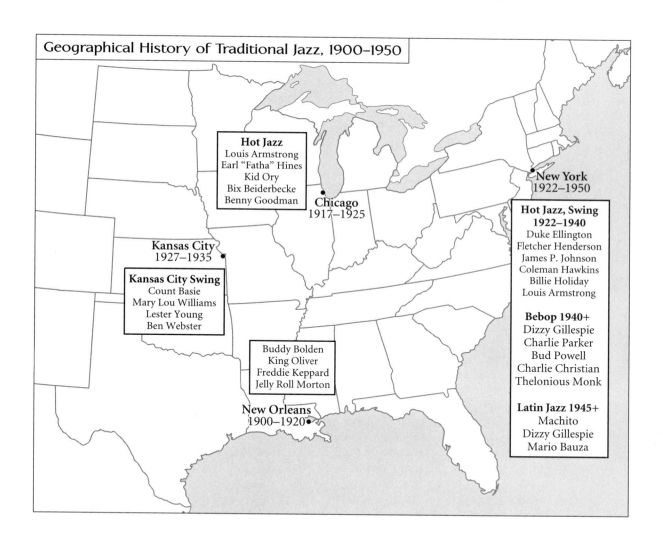

Geographical History of Traditional Jazz, 1900–1950

Hot Jazz
Louis Armstrong
Earl "Fatha" Hines
Kid Ory
Bix Beiderbecke
Benny Goodman

Chicago
1917–1925

New York
1922–1950

Hot Jazz, Swing
1922–1940
Duke Ellington
Fletcher Henderson
James P. Johnson
Coleman Hawkins
Billie Holiday
Louis Armstrong

Bebop 1940+
Dizzy Gillespie
Charlie Parker
Bud Powell
Charlie Christian
Thelonious Monk

Latin Jazz 1945+
Machito
Dizzy Gillespie
Mario Bauza

Kansas City
1927–1935

Kansas City Swing
Count Basie
Mary Lou Williams
Lester Young
Ben Webster

Buddy Bolden
King Oliver
Freddie Keppard
Jelly Roll Morton

New Orleans
1900–1920

Appendix III

Evolution of Jazz Styles

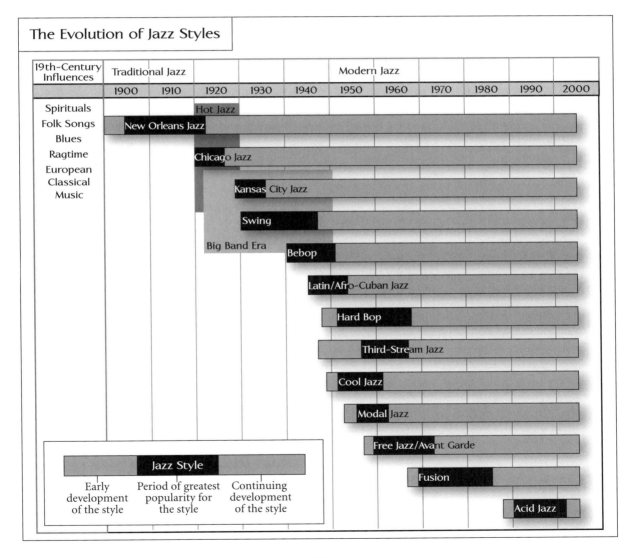

The Evolution of Jazz Styles

Appendix IV

Jazz in the Movies

Jazz stories and performances have been a part of the movies since the early days of jazz. Motion pictures featuring performances of early jazz stars provide a rare look at some of the most influential jazz legends. There have been movies about famous jazz figures, documentaries about jazz, and musical appearances in movies by noted jazz stars. The list below includes selected titles in each of these categories.

In the 1940s and early 1950s, before there were music videos, two film companies produced short motion pictures of jazz performances. SOUNDIES were three-minute, black-and-white films made by the Soundies Distributing Corporation of America, Inc. Designed to be played in coin-operated viewing machines, soundies could be seen in public places such as restaurants and nightclubs. More than 1,800 soundies were distributed in the United States and Canada from 1941 to 1947, but fewer than 100 of these were of jazz artists. The distribution of soundies met with resistance from cinemas and the labor union of motion picture projectionists, two reasons for their eventual demise in 1947. Another company, the Snader Telescriptions Corporation, took up making similar short movies of musical performances from 1950 to 1954. These short black-and-white films were distributed to television stations for broadcasting. Of the 1,100 or so "Snaders" that were made, only a small number featured jazz performances, but some of the best jazz snaders were later compiled into feature-length movies for theaters, including *Basin Street Revue* (1955) and *Jazz Festival* (1955). More recently, snaders were compiled by the Showtime television network into 30-minute programs for the series *Showtime at the Apollo*. Many jazz soundies have been made available on videotape and DVD from a variety of distributors, including Bayside Entertainment, and Efor films, and Idem Home Video, among others. Movies by and about jazz artists reveal the world of jazz in a way that no book can capture. Soundies in particular represent a time capsule of the world of jazz from an era long gone.

The following list of selected movies provides a point of departure for an excursion into jazz history. All of these are available on videotape or DVD. Sources for these and other jazz movies can be located through a quick search on the Internet. Unless otherwise noted, all of the following movies are 60 minutes or longer.

Movies about Jazz and Jazz Legends

Bird (1988), about CHARLIE PARKER.

Bix: Interpretation of a Legend (1990), about "BIX" BEIDERBECKE.

The Benny Goodman Story (1955), about the King of Swing.

The Cotton Club (1984), featuring Richard Gere in a movie about the famous HARLEM nightspot during the 1920s.

The Fabulous Dorseys (1947), about TOMMY and JIMMY DORSEY.

The Gene Krupa Story (1959), with Sal Mineo starring as the SWING drummer and GENE KRUPA "ghosting" the drumming itself for the sound-track.

The Glenn Miller Story (1953), featuring James Stewart in the story of the BIG BAND leader.

Kansas City (1996), director Robert Altman's homage to the KANSAS CITY JAZZ scene of the 1930s.

'Round Midnight (1986), an homage to jazz in 1959 Paris, featuring Dexter Gordon.

Young Man with a Horn (1950), in which Kirk Douglas plays the tragic role of a character much like "Bix" Beiderbecke.

Documentaries about Jazz

A Duke Named Ellington (1988), exploring the life and work of DUKE ELLINGTON.

A Great Day in Harlem (1994), about a reunion of jazz greats from 1958, including QUINCY JONES (Narrator), DIZZY GILLESPIE, SONNY ROLLINS, Buck Clayton, ART BLAKEY, and many others.

Al Jarreau in London (1985), featuring AL JARREAU in concert.

Artie Shaw—Time Is All You've Got (1984), about ARTIE SHAW's life and music.

The Band Parade (1949), a 13-minute film featuring COUNT BASIE and Bobby Brooks.

Benny Carter—Symphony in Riffs (1989), about BENNY CARTER, with concert footage.

Black and Tan (1929), a 19-minute film featuring DUKE ELLINGTON and his COTTON CLUB Orchestra.

Black Music in America—From Then Till Now (1971), 29-minute film featuring interviews and performances with Count Basie, Duke Ellington, and BILLIE HOLIDAY.

Branford Marsalis-Steep (1988), featuring a concert by the Marsalis Quartet.

The Buena Vista Social Club (1999), featuring legendary Afro-Cuban jazz artists such as COMPAY SEGUNDO, RUBEN GONZALEZ, and many others.

But Then, She's Betty Carter (1980), a 53-minute film featuring BETTY CARTER and LIONEL HAMPTON.

Calle 54 (2001), featuring Latin Jazz greats.

The Cry of Jazz (1959), a 29-minute film exploring racial identity and jazz with music by SUN RA.

Different Drummer—Elvin Jones (1979), a 20-minute film about ELVIN JONES.

Dizzy Gillespie (1965), a 24-minute film about "the Diz," who speaks and performs with his Quintet.

Dizzy Gillespie—A Night in Tunisia (1980), a 28-minute film profiling DIZZY GILLESPIE during rehearsals for a CARNEGIE HALL performance.

The Duke (1965), a five-minute film about Duke Ellington featuring performances from 1964.

The Duke—Conversation in Music (1984), a 55-minute film featuring an informal conversation with Duke Ellington from 1964.

The Golden Classics of Jazz, Series (1980), a nine-volume series of feature length films about jazz legends. Volume 1, The Best of Jazz (featuring ART TATUM, Dorsey Brothers, Count Basie, BENNY GOODMAN, Artie Shaw, FATS WALLER, and others); Volume 2, The Best of Jazz II (featuring Count Basie, THELONIOUS MONK, NAT KING COLE, SARAH VAUGHN, Fats Waller, DINAH WASHINGTON, DAVE BRUBECK, CAB CALLOWAY, Lionel Hampton, and others); Volume 3, The Best of LOUIS ARMSTRONG; Volume 4, The Best of the BIG BANDS; Volume 5, The Duke Ellington Story (featuring an Ellington concert from 1962); Volume 6, ELLA FITZGERALD in Concert; Volume 7, Juke Box Saturday Night; Volume 8, Sinatra and Friends; Volume 9, Sinatra Live in Concert.

Great Performances: The Cotton Club Remembered (1986), a 60-minute film including historic clips of early jazz performances.

Great Performances: Miles Ahead (1986), a 60-minute film with interviews and concert clips featuring MILES DAVIS.

Imagine the Sound (1981), about AVANT-GARDE jazz with CECIL TAYLOR, Paul Bley, ARCHIE SHEPP, and others.

International Sweethearts of Rhythm (1986), about the all-female swing band of the same name from the 1940s.

Jammin' the Blues (1944), a classic short film (11 minutes) directed by Norman Granz featuring a JAM SESSION with SID CATLETT, Illinois Jacquet, LESTER YOUNG, and others.

Jam Session (1944), a musical feature with Louis Armstrong, Charlie Barnet, and other bands.

Jazz Casual Series (1963), a series of 30-minute interviews and performances. Featured artists include: CARMEN MCRAE, ART FARMER, Dave Brubeck, Dizzy Gillespie, GERRY MULLIGAN, BEN WEBSTER, JOHN COLTRANE, Cannonball Adderley, the MODERN JAZZ QUARTET, SONNY ROLLINS, WOODY HERMAN, and others.

Jazz Classics (compiled in 1987), this multivolume series includes historic performance clips and SOUNDIES on videotape. Most of the volumes are between 30 and 45 minutes long. Some of the artists represented include Duke Ellington (Volume: 101); Louis Armstrong (Volume: 102); Cab Calloway (Volume: 103); Symphony of Swing (Volume: 104); Nat King Cole (Volume: 106); Fats Waller (Volume: 107); Bessie Smith (Volume: 108); Count Basie (Volume: 109); Harlem Harmonies I (Volume: 110); Harlem Harmonies II (Volume: 111); LENA HORNE (Volume: 112); and Dizzy Gillespie, Jivin' in BEBOP (Volume: 115). Note that newer distributors, including Idem Home Video, have made soundies available on DVD as well.

Jazz on a Summer's Day (1960), award-winning film about the 1958 NEWPORT JAZZ FESTIVAL.

Jazz: A Film by Ken Burns (2000), the celebrated multipart television documentary with WYNTON MARSALIS. It is contained on 10 DVDs.

The King of Jazz (1929), an early color musical featuring PAUL WHITEMAN and his orchestra.

Live at the Village Vanguard (1984), a 57-minute film featuring a club performance with MEL LEWIS and others.

Machito—A Latin Jazz Legacy (1987), a 58-minute film about Afro-Cuban jazz.

Mingus (1968), a profile of CHARLES MINGUS.

Ornette—Made in America (1985), a profile of ORNETTE COLEMAN.

Movie Appearances by Jazz Artists

Cabin in the Sky (1943), featuring LOUIS ARMSTRONG, DUKE ELLINGTON, LENA HORNE, and Ethel Waters.

Follow That Music (1946), an 18-minute feature including performances by GENE KRUPA.

Harlem is Heaven (1932), a 33-minute film with an all-black cast featuring Eubie Blake and others.

Hi De Ho (1947)/*Duke is Tops* (1938), a double feature of all-black musicals featuring CAB CALLOWAY and Duke Ellington.

Murder at the Vanities (1934), features Duke Ellington performing "Ebony Rhapsody."

New Orleans (1947), a fictionalized version of the birth of jazz, with performances by Louis Armstrong and BILLIE HOLIDAY.

Paris Blues (1961), starring Paul Newman and featuring a battle of the horns with Louis Armstrong in this drama.

Reveille with Beverly (1943), a 77-minute film featuring performances by COUNT BASIE, Duke Ellington, and others.

1961	Best Original Jazz Composition	*African Waltz*	Galt MacDermott, composer
1962	Best Jazz Performance, Large Group	*Adventures in Jazz*	STAN KENTON
1962	Best Jazz Performance, Soloist or Small Group	*Desafinado*	STAN GETZ
1962	Best Original Jazz Composition	*Cast Your Fate to the Winds*	Vince Guaraldi, composer
1963	Best Instrumental Jazz Performance, Large Group	*Encore: Woody Herman, 1963*	WOODY HERMAN Band
1963	Best Instrumental Jazz Performance, Soloist or Small Group	*Conversations with Myself*	BILL EVANS
1963	Best Original Jazz Composition	*Gravy Waltz*	Steve Allen and RAY BROWN, composers
1964	Best Instrumental Jazz Performance, Large Group or Soloist with Large Group	*Guitar from Ipanema*	Laurindo Almeida
1964	Best Instrumental Jazz Performance, Small Group or Soloist with Small Group	*Getz/Gilberto*	STAN GETZ
1964	Best Original Jazz Composition	*The Cat*	Lalo Schifrin, composer
1965	Best Instrumental Jazz Performance, Large Group or Soloist with Large Group	*Ellington '66*	DUKE ELLINGTON Orchestra
1965	Best Instrumental Jazz Performance, Small Group or Soloist with Small Group	*The In Crowd*	Ramsey Lewis Trio
1965	Best Original Jazz Composition	*Jazz Suite on the Mass Texts*	Lalo Shifrin, composer
1966	Best Instrumental Jazz Performance, Group or Soloist with Group	*Goin' Out of My Head*	WES MONTGOMERY

1966	Best Original Jazz Composition	*In the Beginning God*	DUKE ELLINGTON, composer
1967	Best Instrumental Jazz Performance, Large Group or Soloist with Large Group	*Far East Suite*	DUKE ELLINGTON
1967	Best Instrumental Jazz Performance, Small Group or Soloist with Small Group	*Mercy, Mercy, Mercy*	Cannonball Adderley Quintet
1968	Best Instrumental Jazz Performance, Large Group or Soloist with Large Group	*AND HIS MOTHER CALLED HIM BILL*	DUKE ELLINGTON
1968	Best Instrumental Jazz Performance, Small Group or Soloist with Small Group	*Bill Evans at the Montreux Jazz Festival*	BILL EVANS Trio
1969	Best Instrumental Jazz Performance, Large Group or Soloist with Large Group	*Walking in Space*	QUINCY JONES
1969	Best Instrumental Jazz Performance, Small Group or Soloist with Small Group	*Willow Weep for Me*	WES MONTGOMERY
1970	Best Jazz Performance, Large Group or Soloist with Large Group	*BITCHES BREW*	MILES DAVIS
1970	Best Jazz Performance, Small Group or Soloist with Small Group	*Alone*	BILL EVANS
1971	Best Jazz Performance by a Big Band	New Orleans Suite	DUKE ELLINGTON
1971	Best Jazz Performance by a Group	*The Bill Evans Album*	BILL EVANS Trio
1971	Best Jazz Performance by a Soloist	*The Bill Evans Album*	Bill Evans
1972	Best Jazz Performance by a Big Band	*Toga Brava Suite*	DUKE ELLINGTON
1972	Best Jazz Performance by a Group	*First Light*	FREDDIE HUBBARD

1972	Best Jazz Performance by a Soloist	*Alone at Last*	GARY BURTON
1973	Best Jazz Performance by a Big Band	*GIANT STEPS*	WOODY HERMAN
1973	Best Jazz Performance by a Group	*Supersax Plays Bird*	Supersax
1973	Best Jazz Performance by a Soloist	*God Is in the House*	ART TATUM
1974	Best Jazz Performance by a Big Band	*Thundering Herd*	WOODY HERMAN
1974	Best Jazz Performance by a Group	*The Trio*	OSCAR PETERSON, Joe Pass, and Niels Pedersen
1974	Best Jazz Performance by a Soloist	*First Recordings!*	CHARLIE PARKER
1975	Best Jazz Performance by a Big Band	*Images*	Phil Woods with Michel Legrand and his Orchestra
1975	Best Jazz Performance by a Group	*No Mystery*	CHICK COREA and Return to Forever
1975	Best Jazz Performance by a Soloist	*Oscar Peterson and Dizzy Gillespie*	DIZZY GILLESPIE
1976	Best Jazz Performance by a Big Band	*The Ellington Suites*	DUKE ELLINGTON
1976	Best Jazz Performance by a Soloist	*Basie and Zoot*	COUNT BASIE
1976	Best Jazz Vocal Performance	*Fitzgerald and Pass Again*	ELLA FITZGERALD
1977	Best Jazz Performance by a Big Band	*Prime Time*	COUNT BASIE and his Orchestra
1977	Best Jazz Performance by a Group	*The Phil Woods Six-Live From the Showboat*	Phil Woods
1977	Best Jazz Performance by a Soloist	*The Giants*	OSCAR PETERSON
1977	Best Jazz Vocal Performance	*Look to the Rainbow*	AL JARREAU
1978	Best Jazz Instrumental Performance, Big Band	*Live in Munich*	THAD JONES and MEL LEWIS

1978	Best Jazz Instrumental Performance, Group	*Friends*	CHICK COREA
1978	Best Jazz Instrumental Performance, Soloist	*Montreux '77 Oscar Peterson Jam*	OSCAR PETERSON
1978	Best Jazz Vocal Performance	*All Fly Home*	AL JARREAU
1979	Best Jazz Fusion Performance, Vocal or Instrumental	*8:30*	WEATHER REPORT
1979	Best Jazz Instrumental Performance, Big Band	*At Fargo, 1940 Live*	DUKE ELLINGTON
1979	Best Jazz Instrumental Performance, Group	*Duet*	GARY BURTON and CHICK COREA
1979	Best Jazz Instrumental Performance, Soloist	*Jousts*	OSCAR PETERSON
1979	Best Jazz Vocal Performance	*Fine and Mellow*	ELLA FITZGERALD
1980	Best Jazz Fusion Performance, Vocal or Instrumental	*BIRDLAND*	MANHATTAN TRANSFER
1980	Best Jazz Instrumental Performance, Big Band	*On the Road*	COUNT BASIE and Orchestra
1980	Best Jazz Instrumental Performance, Group	*We Will Meet Again*	BILL EVANS
1980	Best Jazz Instrumental Performance, Soloist	*I Will Say Goodbye*	Bill Evans
1980	Best Jazz Vocal Performance, Female	*A Perfect Match/Ella and Basie*	ELLA FITZGERALD
1980	Best Jazz Vocal Performance, Male	*Moody's Mood*	George Benson
1981	Best Jazz Fusion Performance, Vocal or Instrumental	*Winelight*	Grover Washington, Jr.
1981	Best Jazz Instrumental Performance, Big Band	*Walk on the Water*	GERRY MULLIGAN and his Orchestra

1981	Best Jazz Instrumental Performance, Group	*Chick Corea and Gary Burton in Concert, Zurich, October 28, 1979*	CHICK COREA and GARY BURTON
1981	Best Jazz Instrumental Performance, Soloist	*Bye Bye Blackbird*	JOHN COLTRANE
1981	Best Jazz Vocal Performance, Duo or Group	*Until I Met You (Corner Pocket)*	MANHATTAN TRANSFER
1981	Best Jazz Vocal Performance, Female	*Digital III at Montreux*	ELLA FITZGERALD
1981	Best Jazz Vocal Performance, Male	*Blue Rondo a la Turk*	AL JARREAU
1982	Best Jazz Fusion Performance, Vocal or Instrumental	*Offramp*	PAT METHENY Group
1982	Best Jazz Instrumental Performance, Big Band	*Warm Breeze*	COUNT BASIE and his Orchestra
1982	Best Jazz Instrumental Performance, Group	*More Live*	Phil Woods Quartet
1982	Best Jazz Instrumental Performance, Soloist	*We Want Miles*	MILES DAVIS
1982	Best Jazz Vocal Performance, Duo or Group	*Route 66*	MANHATTAN TRANSFER
1982	Best Jazz Vocal Performance, Male	*An Evening With George Shearing and Mel Torme*	MEL TORME
1982	Best Jazz Vocal Performance, Female	*Gershwin Live!*	SARAH VAUGHN
1983	Best Jazz Fusion Performance, Vocal or Instrumental	*Travels*	PAT METHENY Group
1983	Best Jazz Instrumental Performance, Big Band	*All in Good Time*	ROB McCONNELL and the boss Brass
1983	Best Jazz Instrumental Performance, Group	*At the Vanguard*	Phil Woods Quartet

1983	Best Jazz Instrumental Performance, Soloist	*Think of One*	WYNTON MARSALIS
1983	Best Jazz Vocal Performance, Duo or Group	*Why Not!*	MANHATTAN TRANSFER
1983	Best Jazz Vocal Performance, Female	*The Best Is Yet to Come*	ELLA FITZGERALD
1983	Best Jazz Vocal Performance, Male	*Top Drawer*	Mel TORME
1984	Best Jazz Fusion Performance, Vocal or Instrumental	*First Circle*	PAT METHENY Group
1984	Best Jazz Instrumental Performance, Big Band	*88 Basie Street*	COUNT BASIE and his Orchestra
1984	Best Jazz Instrumental Performance, Group	*New York Scene*	ART BLAKEY
1984	Best Jazz Instrumental Performance, Soloist	*Hot House Flowers*	WYNTON MARSALIS
1984	Best Jazz Vocal Performance	*Nothin' but the Blues*	Joe Williams
1985	Best Jazz Fusion Performance, Vocal or Instrumental	*Straight to the Heart*	DAVID SANBORN
1985	Best Jazz Instrumental Performance, Big Band	*The Cotton Club–Original Motion Picture Soundtrack*	John Barry and Bob Wilber
1985	Best Jazz Instrumental Performance, Group	*Black Codes from the Underground*	WYNTON MARSALIS Group
1985	Best Jazz Instrumental Performance, Soloist	*Black Codes from the Underground*	Wynton Marsalis
1985	Best Jazz Vocal Performance, Duo or Group	*Vocalese*	MANHATTAN TRANSFER
1985	Best Jazz Vocal Performance, Female	*Cleo at Carnegie (The 10th Anniversary Concert)*	CLEO LAINE
1985	Best Jazz Vocal Performance, Male	*Another Night in Tunisia*	Jon Hendricks and BOBBY MCFERRIN

1986	Best Jazz Fusion Performance, Vocal or Instrumental	*Double Vision*	Bob James and DAVID SANBORN
1986	Best Jazz Instrumental Performance, Big Band	*The Tonight Show Band with Doc Severinsen*	The Tonight Show Band With Doc Severinsen
1986	Best Jazz Instrumental Performance, Group	*J Mood*	WYNTON MARSALIS
1986	Best Jazz Instrumental Performance, Soloist	*Tutu*	MILES DAVIS
1986	Best Jazz Vocal Performance, Duo or Group	*Free Fall*	2 + 2 Plus (Clare Fischer and His Latin Jazz Sextet)
1986	Best Jazz Vocal Performance, Female	*Timeless*	DIANE SCHUUR
1986	Best Jazz Vocal Performance, Male	*Round Midnight*	BOBBY MCFERRIN
1987	Best Jazz Fusion Performance, Vocal or Instrumental	*Still Life (Talking)*	PAT METHENY Group
1987	Best Jazz Instrumental Performance, Big Band	*Digital Duke*	DUKE ELLINGTON Orchestra conducted by Mercer Ellington
1987	Best Jazz Instrumental Performance, Group	*Marsalis Standard Time, Volume 1*	WYNTON MARSALIS
1987	Best Jazz Instrumental Performance, Soloist	*The Other Side of 'Round Midnight*	Dexter Gordon
1987	Best Jazz Vocal Performance, Female	*Diane Schuur and the Count Basie Orchestra*	DIANE SCHUUR
1987	Best Jazz Vocal Performance, Male	*What Is This Thing Called Love*	BOBBY MCFERRIN
1988	Best Jazz Fusion Performance	*Politics*	Yellowjackets
1988	Best Jazz Instrumental Performance, Big Band	*Bud and Bird*	GIL EVANS and the Monday Night Orchestra

1988	Best Jazz Instrumental Performance, Group	*Blues for Coltrane, A Tribute to John Coltrane*	McCoy Tyner, Pharoah Sanders, David Murray, Cecil McBee, and Roy Haynes
1988	Best Jazz Instrumental Performance, Soloist on a Jazz Recording	*Don't Try This at Home*	Michael Brecker
1988	Best Jazz Vocal Performance, Duo or Group	*Spread Love*	Take 6
1988	Best Jazz Vocal Performance, Female	*Look What I Got!*	Betty Carter
1988	Best Jazz Vocal Performance, Male	*Brothers*	Bobby McFerrin
1989	Best Jazz Fusion Performance	*Letter from Home*	Pat Metheny Group
1989	Best Jazz Instrumental Performance, Big Band	*Aura*	Miles Davis
1989	Best Jazz Instrumental Performance, Group	*Chick Corea Akoustic Band*	Chick Corea Akoustic Band
1989	Best Jazz Instrumental Performance, Soloist on a Jazz Recording	*Aura*	Miles Davis (Columbia/CBS)
1989	Best Jazz Vocal Performance, Duo or Group	*Makin' Whoopee*	Dr. John and Rickie Lee Jones
1989	Best Jazz Vocal Performance, Female	*Blues on Broadway*	Ruth Brown
1989	Best Jazz Vocal Performance, Male	*When Harry Met Sally*	Harry Connick, Jr.
1990	Best Jazz Fusion Performance	*Birdland*	Quincy Jones
1990	Best Jazz Instrumental Performance, Big Band	*Basie's Bag*	George Benson featuring the Count Basie Orchestra
1990	Best Jazz Instrumental Performance, Group	*The Legendary Oscar Peterson Trio Live at the Blue Note*	Oscar Peterson Trio
1990	Best Jazz Instrumental Performance, Soloist	*The Legendary Oscar Peterson Trio Live at the Blue Note*	Oscar Peterson

1990	Best Jazz Vocal Performance, Female	*All That Jazz*	ELLA FITZGERALD
1990	Best Jazz Vocal Performance, Male	*We Are in Love*	Harry Connick, Jr.
1991	Best Contemporary Jazz Performance	*Sassy*	MANHATTAN TRANSFER
1991	Best Jazz Instrumental Performance, Group	*Saturday Night at the Blue Note*	OSCAR PETERSON Trio
1991	Best Jazz Instrumental, Solo	*I Remember You*	STAN GETZ
1991	Best Jazz Vocal Performance	*He Is Christmas*	Take 6
1991	Best Large Jazz Ensemble Performance	*Live at the Royal Festival Hall*	DIZZY GILLESPIE and the United Nation Orchestra
1992	Best Contemporary Jazz Performance, Instrumental	*Secret Story*	PAT METHENY
1992	Best Jazz Instrumental Performance, Individual or Group	*I Heard You Twice the First Time*	BRANFORD MARSALIS
1992	Best Jazz Instrumental Performance, Solo	*Lush Life*	JOE HENDERSON
1992	Best Jazz Vocal Performance	*'Round Midnight*	BOBBY MCFERRIN
1992	Best Large Jazz Ensemble Performance	*The Turning Point*	MCCOY TYNER Big Band
1993	Best Contemporary Jazz Performance	*The Road to You*	PAT METHENY Group
1993	Best Jazz Instrumental Performance, Individual or Group	*So Near, So Far (Musings for Miles)*	JOE HENDERSON
1993	Best Jazz Instrumental, Solo	*Miles Ahead*	Joe Henderson
1993	Best Jazz Vocal Performance	*Take a Look*	Natalie Cole
1993	Best Large Jazz Ensemble Performance	*Miles and Quincy Live at Montreux*	MILES DAVIS and QUINCY JONES

1994	Best Contemporary Jazz Performance	*Out of the Loop*	Brecker Brothers
1994	Best Jazz Instrumental Performance, Individual or Group	*A Tribute to Miles*	RON CARTER, HERBIE HANCOCK, Wallace Roney, WAYNE SHORTER and Tony Williams
1994	Best Jazz Instrumental, Solo	*Prelude to a Kiss*	Benny Carpenter
1994	Best Jazz Vocal Performance	*Mystery Lady (Songs of Billie Holiday)*	Etta James
1994	Best Large Jazz Ensemble Performance	*Journey*	MCCOY TYNER Big Band
1994	Best Latin Jazz Performance	*Danzon*	ARTURO SANDOVAL
1995	Best Contemporary Jazz Performance	*We Live Here*	PAT METHENY Group
1995	Best Jazz Instrumental Performance, Individual or Group	*Infinity*	MCCOY TYNER Trio featuring MICHAEL BRECKER
1995	Best Jazz Instrumental, Solo	*Impressions*	Michael Brecker
1995	Best Jazz Vocal Performance	*An Evening with Lena Horne*	LENA HORNE
1995	Best Large Jazz Ensemble Performance	*All Blues*	GRP All-Star Big Band and Tom Scott
1995	Best Latin Jazz Performance	*Antônio Brasileiro*	ANTONIO CARLOS JOBIM
1996	Best Contemporary Jazz Performance	*High Life*	WAYNE SHORTER
1996	Best Jazz Instrumental Performance, Individual or Group	*Tales from the Hudson*	MICHAEL BRECKER
1996	Best Jazz Instrumental, Solo	*Cabin Fever*	Michael Brecker
1996	Best Jazz Vocal Performance	*New Moon Daughter*	CASSANDRA WILSON

1996	Best Large Jazz Ensemble Performance	*Live at Manchester Craftmen's Guild*	COUNT BASIE Orchestra (with The New York Voices); Grover Mitchell, conductor
1996	Best Latin Jazz Performance	*Portraits of Cuba*	Paquito D'Rivera
1997	Best Contemporary Jazz	*Into the Sun*	RANDY BRECKER
1997	Best Jazz Instrumental, Individual or Group	*Beyond the Missouri Sky*	CHARLIE HADEN, and PAT METHENY (Verve Records)
1997	Best Jazz Instrumental, Solo	*Stardust*	Doc Cheatham and Nicholas Payton
1997	Best Jazz Vocal	*Dear Ella*	Dee Dee Bridgewater
1997	Best Large Jazz Ensemble	*Joe Henderson Big Band*	JOE HENDERSON Big Band
1997	Best Latin Jazz	*Habana*	ROY HARGROVE's Crisol
1998	Best Contemporary Jazz	*Imaginary Day*	PAT METHENY Group
1998	Best Jazz Instrumental, Individual or Group	*Gershwin's World*	HERBIE HANCOCK (Verve Records)
1998	Best Jazz Instrumental, Solo	*Rhumbata*	CHICK COREA and GARY BURTON
1998	Best Jazz Vocal	*I Remember Miles*	SHIRLEY HORN
1998	Best Large Jazz Ensemble	*Count Plays Duke*	COUNT BASIE Orchestra
1998	Best Latin Jazz	*Hot House*	ARTURO SANDOVAL
1999	Best Contemporary Jazz	*Inside*	DAVID SANBORN
1999	Best Jazz Instrumental, Individual or Group	*Like Minds*	GARY BURTON, CHICK COREA, Pat Metheny, Roy Haynes, and DAVE HOLLAND (Concord Jazz)
1999	Best Jazz Instrumental, Solo	*In Walked Wayne*	WAYNE SHORTER

1999	Best Jazz Vocal	*When I Look in Your Eyes*	DIANA KRALL
1999	Best Large Jazz Ensemble	*Serendipity 18*	The Bob Florence Limited Edition
1999	Best Latin Jazz	*Latin Soul*	Poncho Sanchez
2000	Best Contemporary Jazz	*Outbound*	Béla Fleck and the Flecktones
2000	Best Jazz Instrumental, Individual or Group	*Contemporary Jazz*	BRANFORD MARSALIS (Columbia Records)
2000	Best Jazz Instrumental, Solo	*(Go) Get It*	PAT METHENY
2000	Best Jazz Vocal	*In the Moment-Live in Concert*	Dianne Reeves
2000	Best Large Jazz Ensemble	*52nd Street Themes*	JOE LOVANO (Blue Note Records)
2000	Best Latin Jazz	*Live at the Village Vanguard*	Chucho Valdés
2001	Best Contemporary Jazz	*M2*	MARCUS MILLER (Telarc)
2001	Best Jazz Instrumental, Individual or Group	*This Is What I Do*	SONNY ROLLINS (Milestone Records)
2001	Best Jazz Instrumental, Solo	*Chan's Song*	MICHAEL BRECKER, soloist
2001	Best Jazz Vocal	*The Calling*	DIANE REEVES (Blue Note Records)
2001	Best Large Jazz Ensemble	*Homage to Count Basie*	Bob Mintzer Big Band (Digital Music Products)
2001	Best Latin Jazz	*Nocturne*	CHARLIE HADEN (Verve Records)
2002	Best Contemporary Jazz Album	*Speaking of Now*	PAT METHENY Group
2002	Best Jazz Instrumental Album, Individual or Group	*Directions in Music*	HERBIE HANCOCK, MICHAEL BRECKER and ROY HARGROVE

2002	Best Jazz Instrumental, Solo	*My Ship*	Herbie Hancock
2002	Best Jazz Vocal Album	*Live in Paris*	DIANA KRALL
2002	Best Large Jazz Ensemble Album	*What Goes Around*	DAVE HOLLAND Big Band
2002	Best Latin Jazz Album	*The Gathering*	Caribbean Jazz Project
2003	Best Contemporary Jazz Album	*34th N Lex*	RANDY BRECKER
2003	Best Jazz Vocal Album	*A Little Moonlight*	DIANE REEVES
2003	Best Jazz Instrumental, Solo	*Matrix*	CHICK COREA
2003	Best Jazz Instrumental Album, Individual or Group	*Alegría*	WAYNE SHORTER
2003	Best Large Jazz Ensemble Album	*Wide Angles*	MICHAEL BRECKER Quindectet
2003	Best Latin Jazz Album	*Live at the Blue Note*	Michel Camilo With Charles Flores & Horacio "El Negro" Hernandez

Appendix VI

Jazz at Lincoln Center Inaugural Hall of Fame Inductees

On September 30, 2004, JAZZ AT LINCOLN CENTER in New York City dedicated its new Ertegun Jazz Hall of Fame with the official induction of its inaugural roster of members. Located within the new home of Jazz at Lincoln Center, the Ertegun Jazz Hall of Fame was named in honor of the late Atlantic Records executive Nesuhi Ertegun.

Inductees were nominated by a 72-person international voting panel, which included musicians, scholars, and educators from 17 countries. The panel was responsible for nominating and selecting "the most definitive artists in the history of jazz" for inclusion in the first group of inductees.[219]

Nomination criteria included "excellence and significance of the artists' contributions to the development and perpetuation of jazz."

The first 14 inductees, representing every decade from the more than 100-year history of jazz, included the following:

Louis Armstrong
Sidney Bechet
Bix Beiderbecke
John Coltrane
Miles Davis
Duke Ellington
Dizzy Gillespie
Coleman Hawkins
Billie Holiday
Thelonious Monk
Jelly Roll Morton
Charlie Parker
Art Tatum
Lester Young

might be held for two, four, or eight beats, but they appear in sequence. The progression is very common in doo-wop music.

blues An African-American vocal and instrumental style that developed in the late 19th to early 20th centuries. The "blues scale" usually features a flattened third and seventh, giving the music a recognizable sound. The classic 12-bar blues features three repeated lines of four bars each, with the first two lines of lyrics repeated, followed by a contrasting line. The chord progression is also fairly standardized, although many blues musicians have found ways to extend and improvise around these rules.

boogie-woogie Boogie-woogie is a way of playing BLUES on the piano that was first recorded in the 1920s. Its chief characteristic is the left-hand pattern, known as eight-to-the-bar (a note is played on every one of the eight possible eighth notes in a measure of four beats), which provides a propulsive rhythm that seems to have been influenced by the sound of trains. Boogie-woogie became a fad after the 1938 and 1939 From Spirituals to Swing concerts, and was adapted into big band swing, pop, and country music. From there it became part of ROCK 'N' ROLL. To boogie in general slang (as in "I've got to boogie now") means to leave somewhere in a hurry. In musical slang, to boogie means to maintain a repetitive blues-based rhythmic foundation, particularly one associated with the style of John Lee Hooker, similar to the figure in his song, "Boogie Chillen."

brass Traditionally, musical instruments whose bodies are made out of brass (although sometimes today they are made out of other metals). Usually used to refer to members of the horn family, including trumpets and trombones.

British invasion Popular groups of the 1960s that dominated the American pop charts. The Beatles led the charge in 1964, but were quickly followed by many soundalike bands, as well as more distinctive groups like the Rolling Stones, The Who, the Kinks, and many others.

cadence A melodic or harmonic phrase usually used to indicate the ending of a PHRASE or a complete musical composition.

capo A metal or elastic clamp placed across all of the strings of a guitar that enables players to change key, while still using the same chord fingerings as they would use without the capo.

CD (compact disc) A recording medium developed in the mid-1980s that enables music to be encoded as digital information on a small disc, and that is "read" by a laser. Various forms of CDs have been developed since to contain higher sound quality and/or other materials (photographs, moving images, etc.)

chord The basic building block of HARMONY, chords usually feature three or more notes played simultaneously.

chord progression A sequence of chords, for example in the key of C: C, F, and G7.

chorus Most commonly used in popular songs to indicate a repeated STANZA that features the same melody and lyrics that falls between each verse. Perhaps because members of the audience might "sing-along" with this part of the song, it came to be known as the chorus (a chorus literally being more than one voice singing at the same time). See VERSE.

clef The symbol at the beginning of a notated piece of music indicating the note values assigned to each line of the STAFF. The three most common clefs used in popular music are the G clef (or treble clef), usually used to notate the melody; the F clef (or bass clef), usually used for harmony parts; and the less-frequently seen C clef (or tenor clef), used for notating instruments with special ranges, most usually the viola.

country and western (C&W) A category developed by the music industry in the late 1940s to distinguish folk, cowboy, and other musical styles aimed at the white, rural, working-class listener (as opposed to R&B, aimed at black audiences, and pop, aimed at urban whites). Later, the *western* was dropped.

cover versions The music business has always been competitive, and even before recordings were possible, many artists would do the same song, as can be seen by the multiple editions of the sheet music for certain hits, each with a different artists' photo on the front. In the 1950s the practice of copying records was rampant, particularly by bigger companies, which had more resources (publicity, distribution, influence) and which used their artists to cover songs from independent labels that had started to show promise in the marketplace. A true cover version is one that attempts to stay close to the song on which it is based. Interpretations of existing songs are often called covers, but when artistry is involved in giving an individual treatment to an existing song, that effort is worthy of being considered more than a cover version.

crescendo A gradual increase in volume indicated in music notation by a triangle placed on its side below the STAFF, like this <.

crossover record A record that starts in one musical category, but has a broader appeal and becomes popular in another category. For example B. B. King's "The Thrill Is Gone" started out as an R&B record, but crossed over to the pop category.

cut a record Recording a record.

decrescendo A gradual decrease in volume indicated in music notation by a triangle placed on its side below the STAFF, as in >.

Delta blues Blues music originating in the Mississippi Delta and typically featuring the use of a slide, intense vocal performances, an aggressive, sometimes strummed guitar style with bass notes "popped" by the thumb for a snapping sound.

diatonic harmony The CHORDS implicit in the major scale. The sequence of triads is I major, II minor, III minor, IV major, V major, VI minor, and VII diminished. Because the diminished chord is unstable, it is virtually never used in this context. Because major chords are more common, many songs use only them: I, IV, and V.

disco A dance form of the 1970s developed in urban dance clubs, consisting of a heavily accented, repeated rhythmic part.

Dixieland jazz Jazz style popularized in New Orleans at the beginning of the 20th century by small combos, usually including three horns: a clarinet, a trumpet, and a trombone. The rhythm section includes a banjo, a tuba, a simple drum set, and a piano, and occasionally a saxophone, string bass, or guitar is added.

DIY (Do-It-Yourself) An emphasis on homemade music and recordings, which began with the PUNK movement but outlived it. The message was that everyone could make their own music, and record and market it on their own, using simple, inexpensive instruments and technology.

DJ (deejay) The person who plays records at a dance club or on a radio station. DJs began to create musical compositions by stringing together long sequences of records, and then further manipulated them using techniques such as backspinning (rapidly spinning a turntable backward while a record is being played) and scratching (moving the turntable back and forth rapidly to emphasize a single note or word).

DVD (digital video disc) A form of optical disc designed to hold video or film, but also sometimes used for higher-quality music reproduction. See CD (COMPACT DISC).

easy listening See MOR (MIDDLE-OF-THE-ROAD).

eighth note See NOTE VALUES.

electronic music Music created using electronic means, including SYNTHESIZERS, SEQUENCERS, tape recorders, and other nontraditional instruments.

falsetto A high register vocal sound producing a light texture. Often used in soul music.

finger-picking A style of guitar playing that keeps a steady bass with the thumb while playing melody on the treble strings.

flat A symbol in music NOTATION indicating that the note should be dropped one-half step in PITCH. Compare SHARP.

flat pick A pick held between the thumb and first finger of the right hand that is very effective for music, this is usually A above middle C, defined as vibrating at 440 vps.

pop music   Any music that appeals to a large audience. Originally, the pop charts featured records aimed at white, urban listeners (as opposed to R&B, aimed at blacks, and C&W or country, aimed at rural, lower-class whites). Today, "pop" is applied to any recording that appeals across a wide range of listeners, so that Michael Jackson or Shania Twain could equally be defined as "pop" stars.

power chords   Played on the low strings of an electric guitar, power chords use only the root and the fifth (and often a repeat of the root an octave higher) of a triad, leaving out the third of the CHORD. With no third, the chord is neither MAJOR or MINOR. With only two notes, it is technically not even a chord, but an interval. The use of power chords was pioneered by Link Wray ("Rumble") and the Kinks ("You Really Got Me"), and used extensively in hard rock (Deep Purple's "Smoke on the Water"), heavy metal (Metallica), and grunge (Nirvana's "Smells Like Teen Spirit").

power trio   Three instruments—guitar, bass, and drums—played at loud volumes.

psychedelic   Popular ROCK style of the late 1960s-early 1970s that featured extended musical forms, "spacey" lyrics, and unusual musical timbres often produced by synthesizers. Psychedelic music was supposed to be the "aural equivalent" of the drug experience. See also SYNTHESIZER; TIMBRE.

punk   A movement that began in England and travelled to the United States in the mid-1970s emphasizing a return to simpler musical forms, in response to the growing commercialization of ROCK. Punk also encompassed fashion (including spiked hair, safety pins used as body ornaments, etc.) and sometimes a violent, antiestablishment message.

quarter note   See NOTE VALUES.

race records   Music industry name for African-American popular music recorded in the 1920s until around 1945.

ragtime   Music dating from around the 1890s and usually composed in three or four different sections. The most famous ragtime pieces were for piano, but the style was also adapted in a simplified form for the banjo and the guitar.

record producer   The person in charge of a recording session.

register   The range in notes of a specific part of a musical composition. Also used to define the range of an individual musical instrument or vocal part.

resonator guitar   Guitars with a metal front and back, often used in playing slide guitar, and prized during the 1930s for their volume.

rhythm   The basic pulse of a musical composition. In 4/4 time, the 4 beats per measure provide the pulse that propels the piece. Compare METER.

rhythm and blues (R&B)   Black popular music that emerged around 1945 and peaked in popularity in the 1960s. It usually included gospel-influenced vocal performances, and a rhythm section of piano, bass, and drums. The lead instruments were often guitar and saxophone.

riff   A short, recognizable melodic phrase used repeatedly in a piece of music. Commonly heard in big band jazz or in electric guitar solos.

rock   An outgrowth of ROCK 'N' ROLL in the 1960s that featured more sophisticated arrangements, lyrics, and subject matter. The BRITISH INVASION groups—notably the Beatles and the Rolling Stones—are sometimes credited with extending the style and subjects treated by rock 'n' roll. Rock itself has developed into many different substyles.

rockabilly   Mid-1950s popular music that combined BLUES and COUNTRY music.

rock 'n' roll   The popular music of the mid-1950s aimed at teenage listeners. Popular rock 'n' roll artists included Elvis Presley, Chuck Berry, Little Richard, and Carl Perkins. Compare ROCK.

royalties   Payments to recording artists based on the sales of their records.

salsa Literally "spice." A form of Latin dance music popularized in the 1970s and 1980s.

scale A succession of seven notes. The most common scales are the MAJOR and MINOR.

score The complete notation of a musical composition.

sequencer An electronic instrument that can record a series of pitches or rhythms and play them back on command.

78 The first form of recorded disc, that revolved on a turntable at 78 revolutions per minute (rpm). The first 78s were 10 inches in diameter and could play for approximately three minutes per side; later, 12-inch 78s were introduced with slightly longer playing times.

sharp A symbol in a piece of music indicating that a pitch should be raised one half-step in PITCH. Compare FLAT.

side One side of a recording disc.

slide guitar Style of guitar in which the player wears a metal or glass tube on one finger or uses a bottle neck to play notes. It creates a distinctive crying sound. Also called bottleneck guitar.

songster A turn-of-the-20th-century musician with a varied repertoire that included different styles of music.

soprano The highest female voice, or the highest pitched instrument in a family of instruments.

soul A black musical style developed in the 1960s that combined elements of GOSPEL MUSIC with RHYTHM AND BLUES.

spirituals Traditional religious music found in both white and African-American traditions.

staff The five parallel lines on which the symbols for notes are placed in a notated piece of music. The CLEF at the beginning of the staff indicates the pitch of each note on the staff.

stanza In poetry, the basic lyrical unit, often consisting of four or six lines. The lyrics to both the VERSE and CHORUS of a popular song follow the stanza form.

strings Instruments that produce musical sound through the vibration of strings, made out of animal gut or metal. Violins and guitars are stringed instruments.

suite In classical music, a group of dances played in succession to form a larger musical composition.

symphony In classical music, a defined form usually consisting of three parts, played Fast-Slow-Fast.

syncopation Accenting the unexpected or weaker BEAT. Often used in RAGTIME, jazz, and related styles.

synthesizer An electronic instrument that is capable of creating different musical pitches and timbres.

tempo The speed at which a piece of music is performed.

tenor The highest male voice.

theme A recognizable MELODY that is often repeated within a musical composition.

thumb picks and finger picks Guitar picks made of metal or plastic worn on the player's right hand fingers and thumb in order to play louder.

timbre The quality of a PITCH produced by a musical instrument or voice that makes it distinctive. The timbre of a guitar is quite different from that of a flute, for example.

time signature In notation, the symbol at the beginning of each STAFF that indicates the basic metric pulse and how many beats are contained in a measure. For example, in 4/4 time, a quarter-note is given one beat, and there are four beats per measure; in 6/8 time, an eighth-note is given one beat, and there are six beats in a measure.

Tin Pan Alley The center of music publishing on West 28th Street in New York City from the late 19th century through the 1930s (so-called because the clatter from competing pianists working in different buildings sounded to passersby like rattling tin pans). Used generally to describe the popular songs of this period.

tone See PITCH.

tremolo The rapid repetition of a single note to give a "quivering" or "shaking" sound. Compare VIBRATO.

turnaround A musical phrase at the end of a verse that briefly outlines the CHORDS of the song before the start of the next verse.

12-bar blues A 12-bar BLUES has 12 measures of music, or bars, and is the most common blues format, though eight bars and 16 bars are also used.

vamp A short segment of music that repeats, usually two or four CHORDS. Two chord vamps are common in GOSPEL and ROCK, especially the I and IV chords (C and F in the key of C).

vanity records Recordings that are conceived and financed by the artists involved. They are called "vanity records" because the motivation comes from the person or group themselves, not from a record company. The reason is to realize a creative project, to promote a career, or just to boost the ego. Previously, singers and musicians would pay to go into a studio and to cover the costs of backup musicians, mixing, mastering, and manufacturing. This continues, but with the rise of home studios, these steps can be done at home, with computerized recording and CD burning. Vanity records now represent perhaps the majority of recordings being made and are more likely to be called independent productions.

verse The part of a song that features a changing lyric set to a fixed MELODY. The verse is usually performed in alternation with the CHORUS.

vibrato A rapid moving up and down slightly in PITCH while performing a single note as an ornament. Compare TREMOLO.

walking bass A style of bass playing that originated in jazz on the upright bass. The bassist plays a new note on every beat, outlining the CHORDS as they pass by in a CHORD PROGRESSION. Chord notes are primary, but passing notes and other decorations enliven the bass line, as well as brief rhythmic variations enliven the bass line. A rock example is Paul McCartney's bass part in the Beatles' "All My Loving" (1964).

whole note See NOTE VALUES.

woodwinds A class of instruments traditionally made of wood, although the term is now used for instruments made of brass or metal as well. Clarinets, flutes, and saxophones are usually classified as woodwinds.

End Notes and Further Reading

1 Marsalis, Wynton. *Jazz for Young People* (New York: Scholastic, 2002), audio disc 1, track 78.

2 Tucker, Sherrie. *Swing Shift: "All-Girl" Bands of the 1940s* (Durham, N.C.: Duke University Press, 2000).

3 ———. "Women in Jazz," Available online. URL://http://www.pbs.org/jazz/time/time_women.htm. Downloaded on October 13, 2004.

4 Abercrombie, John. "Bio," Available online. URL: http://www.johnabercrombie.com/bio.htm. Downloaded on February 11, 2004.

5 Feather, Leonard, and Ira Gitler. *The Biographical Encyclopedia of Jazz* (New York: Oxford University Press, 1999), 5.

6 Byrd, Donald, and Pepper Adams. "The Complete Blue Note Byrd/Adams Studio Sessions," Mosaic Records Web page, Available online. URL: http://www.mosaicrecords.com/prodinfo.asp?number=194-MD-CD&OVRAW=pepper%20adams%20bio&OVKEY=pepper%20adams&OVMTC=advanced.

7 Feather, Leonard, and Ira Gitler, *The Biographical Encyclopedia of Jazz* (New York: Oxford, 1999), 6.

8 Wang, Alice. "Toshiko Akiyoshi," Available online. URL: http://www.duke.edu/~amw6/akio.htm. Posted in 1997.

9 Carr, Ian, Digby Fairweather, and Brian Priestly, eds. *Jazz, The Rough Guide* (London: Penguin Books, 2000), 16.

10 Shapiro, Nat, and Nat Henthoff. *Hear Me Talkin' to Ya* (New York: Dover, 1955).

11 Marsalis, Wynton. *Jazz for Young People Teaching Guide* (New York: Scholastic, 2002), 8.

12 Williams, Mary Lou. "Liner Notes to the Album *Jazz Women: A Feminist Retrospective*," Available online. URL: http://www.jazzmanrecords.com/jazwomlinnot.html. Downloaded on October 13, 2004.

13 Barbieri, Gato. "InterJazz." Available online. URL: http://centralentertainment.com/gato/. Downloaded on February 11, 2004.

14 Rich, Alan. *The Listener's Guide to Jazz* (Dorset, England: Blandford Press, 1980), 11.

15 Crow, Bill. *Jazz Anecdotes* (New York: Oxford University Press, 1990), 225.

16 ———. *Jazz Anecdotes* (New York: Oxford University Press, 1990), 226.

17 O'Brien, R. Barry. "Bandleader Ivy Played on to the End," Available online. URL: http://www.ivybenson-online.com/Information/playedon.htm. Downloaded on October 13, 2004.

18 Winn, Godfrey. "Ivy Benson All Girls Band," Available online. URL:http://www.ivybenson-online.com/Information/godfrey_winn.htm. Downloaded on October 13, 2004.

19 Ibid.

20 Clarke, Stanley. "Going with the Bass-ics," Available online. URL: http://www.innerviews.org/inner/clarke.html. Downloaded on October 13, 2004.

21 Crow, Bill. *Jazz Anecdotes* (New York: Oxford University Press, 1990), 252.

22 Bley, Carla. "Carla Bley Profiles Herself," Available online. URL: http://www.wattxtrawatt.com/carla profilepaper.htm. Downloaded on January 5, 2004.

23 Cook, Richard, and Brian Morton. *The Penguin Guide to Jazz* on CD, 6th ed. (New York: Penguin Books, 2002), 683.

24 Crow, Bill. *Jazz Anecdotes* (New York, Oxford University Press, 1990), 253.

25 ———. "Richard Bona Biography, Bonathology," Available online. URL: http://www.bonatology. com/index_02.html. Downloaded on October 13, 2004.

26 Bowie, Lester. "Lester Bowie," Available online. URL: http://aacmchicago.org/members/Bowie. html. Downloaded on February 11, 2004.

27 Lock, Graham. *Forces in Motion: Anthony Braxton and the Meta-reality of Creative Music* (London: Quartet Books, 1988).

28 Nicholson, Stuart. *Jazz: The 1980s Resurgence* (New York: Da Capo, 1995), 127.

29 Grey, Hillary. "Dizzy Gillespie," Available online. URL: http://www.morganbouldin.com/jazz quotes.html. Downloaded on January 10, 2004.

30 Feather, Leonard. *The New Encyclopedia of Jazz* (New York: Bonanza, 1960), 475.

31 Pfeffer, Murray L. "Jack Hylton Orchestra," Available online. URL: http://nfo.net/brit/bh3. html#JHylton. Downloaded on March 4, 2004.

32 Munn, Billy. Memory Lane website, http://www. memorylane.org.uk/previous_articles.htm, accessed on March 4, 2004.

33 Ward, Geoffrey C., and Ken Burns. *Jazz: A History of America's Music* (New York: Knopf, 2000), 258.

34 Feather, Leonard and Ira Gitler. *The Biographical Encyclopedia of Jazz* (New York: Oxford University Press, 1999), 113.

35 Ibid.

36 Feather, Leonard. Interview (*Down Beat*, May 25, 1961).

37 Carter, Betty. "The Kennedy Center Press Release, March 13, 2003," Available online. URL: http://www.kennedy-center.org/programs/ jazz/jazzahead/. Downloaded on October 13, 2004.

38 Gridley, Mark C. *Jazz Styles: History and Analysis*, 3rd ed. (Englewood Cliffs, N.J.: Prentice Hall, 1988), 302.

39 Feather, Leonard, and Ira Gitler. *The Biographical Encyclopedia of Jazz* (New York: Oxford University Press, 1999), 124.

40 Tanner, Paul O. W., David W. Megill, and Maurice Gerow. *Jazz*, 9th ed. (New York: McGraw-Hill, 2001), 96.

41 Feather, Leonard. *The New Encyclopedia of Jazz* (New York: Bonanza, 1960), 160.

42 Clarke, Stanley. "Going with the Bass-ics," Available online. URL: http://www.innerviews. org/inner/clarke.html. Downloaded on October 13, 2004.

43 Coleman, Ornette. *Free Jazz* liner notes (Atlantic 1364, 1960).

44 ———. "Chick Corea Biography," Available online. URL: http://www.chickcorea.com/bio. html. Downloaded on March 24, 2004.

45 Crow, Bill. *Jazz Anecdotes* (New York: Oxford University Press, 1990), 90.

46 Schoenberg, Loren. *The NPR Curious Listener's Guide to Jazz* (New York: Perigee, 2002), 23.

47 Crow, Bill. *Jazz Anecdotes* (New York: Oxford University Press, 1990), 99.

48 Ibid. 98.

49 Feather, Leonard. *The Jazz Years: Earwitness to an Era.* (New York: Da Capo, 1987), 138.

50 ———. "A Woman with Serious Swing, Ernestine Davis!" Available online. URL: http:// www.aaregistry.com/african_american_history/ 1059/A_Woman_with_serious_SWING_Erne stine_Davis. Downloaded on March 28, 2004.

51 Davis, Miles. *Miles* (New York: Simon & Schuster, 1989), 28.

52 Ibid. 32.

53 Ibid. 73.

54 Al Di Meola. "Al Di Meola Biography," Available online. URL: http://www.hopper-management. com/am_bio_e.htm. Downloaded on April 3, 2004.

55 Gridley, Mark C. *Jazz Styles: History and Analysis*, 3rd ed. (Englewood Cliffs, N.J.: Prentice Hall, 1988), 80.

56 Neely, Mike. "Eric Dolphy: The Complete Prestige Recordings," Available online. URL: http:/www.

allabout jazz.com/php/article.php? id=276. Downloaded on April 10, 2003.

57 Feather, Leonard, and Ira Gitler. *The Biographical Encyclopedia of Jazz* (New York: Oxford University Press, 1999), 186.

58 ———. "Review of Eric Dolphy, Outward Bound," Available online. URL: http://www.down beat.com/artists/artist_main.asp?sect=archives& sub=reviews&su bid=108&aid=189&photo=& aname=Eric+Dolphy. Downloaded on October 13, 2004.

59 Feather, Leonard. *The Encyclopedia of Jazz in the Sixties* (New York: Horizon, 1966), 109.

60 Dolphy, Eric, quoted in Robert Levin's liner notes, *Eric Dolphy in Europe*. Vol. 1 (Prestige 7304).

61 Carr, Ian, Digby Fairweather, and Brian Priestly, eds. *Jazz, The Rough Guide* (London: Penguin Books, 2000), 212.

62 Schuller, Gunther. *The Swing Era* (New York: Oxford University Press, 1989), 677.

63 Ibid. 679.

64 Ibid. 450.

65 Feather, Leonard, and Ira Gitler. *The Biographical Encyclopedia of Jazz* (New York: Oxford University Press, 1999), 205.

66 Feather, Leonard. *The New Encyclopedia of Jazz* (New York: Bonanza, 1960), 474–475.

67 "Rudi Williams, James Reese Europe, Arlington National Cemetery," Available online. URL: http://www.arlingtoncemetery.net/jreurope.htm. Downloaded on June 5, 2000.

68 Feather, Leonard. *The New Encyclopedia of Jazz.* (New York: Bonanza, 1960), 103.

69 Ibid. 490.

70 Gridley, Mark C. *Jazz Styles: History and Analysis,* 3rd ed. (Englewood Cliffs, N.J.: Prentice Hall, 1988), 219.

71 Tompkins, Les. "Bill Evans, Group Dialogue," Available online. URL: http://www.jazzprofes-sional.com/interviews/Bill%20Evans_1.htm. Downloaded on October 13, 2004.

72 Schuller, Gunther. *The Swing Era* (New York: Oxford University Press, 1989), 756.

73 Crow, Bill. *Jazz Anecdotes* (New York: Oxford University Press, 1990), 191.

74 ———. "Malachi Favors Maghostut," Available online. URL: http://www.ecm-records.com/New/Diary/17_malachi.php?cat=&we_start=0&lvre dir=733. Downloaded on February 11, 2004.

75 Crumpacker, Bunny and Chick Crumpacker. *Jazz Legends* (Layton, Utah: Gibbs Smith, 1995), 38.

76 ———. "Bill Frisell, Biography," Available online. URL: http://www.songtone.com/artists/frisell_link.htm. Downloaded on April 9, 2004.

77 Ibid.

78 ———. "Kenny Garrett, Biography," Available online. URL: http://www.kennygarrett.com/. Downloaded on October 13, 2004.

79 ———. "Biography, Astrud Gilberto," Available online. URL: http://www.astrudgilberto.com/biography.htm. Downloaded on October 13, 2004.

80 Feather, Leonard, and Ira Gitler. *The Biographical Encyclopedia of Jazz* (New York: Oxford University Press, 1999), 255.

81 Olsen, Eric B. "Dexter Gordon," The Hard Bop Home Page, Available online. URL: http://members.tripod.com/~hardbop/dex.html

82 Davis, Francis. "Charlie Haden, Bass," Available online. URL: http://www.theatlantic.com/issues/2000/08/davis.htm. Downloaded on October 13, 2004.

83 Gridley, Mark C. *Jazz Styles: History and Analysis,* 3rd ed. (Englewood Cliffs, N.J.: Prentice Hall, 1988), 239.

84 ———. "Charlie Haden main page," Available online. URL: http://www.interjazz.com/haden. Downloaded on October 13, 2004.

85 Gould, Dave. "Jim Hall Interview," Available online. URL: http://www.gould68.freeserve.co.uk/jimhalltext2.html. Downloaded on October 13, 2004.

86 ———. "Full Biography," Available online. URL: http://www.herbiehancock.com/music/biography.html. Downloaded on October 13, 2004.

87 Gridley, Mark C. *Jazz Styles: History and Analysis,* 3rd ed. (Englewood Cliffs, N.J.: Prentice Hall, 1988), 256.

88 Jorgl, Stephanie. "Hancock Explores New Sounds in Concert," Available online. URL: http://www. apple.com/hotnews/articles/2002/08/herbie hancock/index1.html. Downloaded on October 13, 2004.

89 ———. "Roy Hargrove, Biography," Available online. URL: http://www.vervemusicgroup.com/ artist.aspx?ob=art&src=rslt&aid=2905. Downloaded on October 13, 2004. Many attempts to blend hip-hop and jazz do it superficially, using rigid beats and decorative solos that never seem to mesh. Hargrove's approach is successful because it sounds like a group of musicians playing together, grooving together, to make convincing jazz that swings with hip-hop sensibility.

90 Harley, Rufus, liner notes to King/Queens (Atlantic Records, Stereo LP SD 1539, 1970).

91 Esquizito. "Johnny Hartman," Available online. URL: http://www.wwoz.org/html/hartman.html. Downloaded on October 13, 2004.

92 Feather, Leonard, and Ira Gitler. *The Biographical Encyclopedia of Jazz* (New York: Oxford University Press, 1999), 315.

93 Gridley, Mark C. *Jazz Styles: History and Analysis,* 3rd ed. (Englewood Cliffs, N.J.: Prentice Hall, 1988), 348.

94 Crumpacker, Bunny, and Chick Crumpacker. *Jazz Legends* (Layton, Utah: Gibbs, 1995), 15.

95 ———. "Dave Holland Biography," Available online. URL: http://www.daveholland.com/. Downloaded on October 13, 2004.

96 Carr, Ian, Digby Fairweather, and Brian Priestly, eds. *Jazz, The Rough Guide* (London: Penguin Books, 2000), 357.

97 Feather, Leonard, and Ira Gitler. *The Biographical Encyclopedia of Jazz* (New York: Oxford University Press, 1999), 327.

98 Ibid. 330.

99 Gordon, Dick. "Shirley Horn," Available online. URL: http://www.theconnection.org/shows/2002/ 05/20020509_b_main.asp. Downloaded on October 13, 2004.

100 Alexander, Scott. "Alberta Hunter," Available online. URL: http://www.redhotjazz.com/creole. html. Downloaded on October 13, 2004.

101 Yanow, Scott. *Classic Jazz* (San Francisco: Backbeat Books, 2001), 114.

102 Feather, Leonard. *The Jazz Years: Earwitness to an Era* (New York: Da Capo, 1987), 138.

103 Tucker, Sherrie. *Swing Shift: "All Girl" Bands of the 1940s* (Durham, N.C.: Duke University Press, 2000), 149.

104 Ibid. 105–106.

105 Pfeffer, Murray L. "The Great American Big Bands," Available online. URL: http://www.nfo. net/usa/i1.html. Downloaded on June 17, 2004.

106 Tucker, Sherrie. *Swing Shift: "All Girl" Bands of the 1940s* (Durham, N.C.: Duke University Press, 2000), 183.

107 ———. "D. D. Jackson Q & A," Available online. URL: http://ddjackson.com/frame_article1.html. Downloaded on October 13, 2004.

108 Siders, Harvey. "Review of *Suite for New York,*" Available online. URL: http://ddjackson.com/ frame_prquote1.html. Downloaded on October 13, 2004.

109 Davis, Miles. *Miles* (Simon & Schuster, 1989), 178.

110 Atkins, E. Taylor. "Localizing Jazz and Globalizing Identities in Japan" (paper prepared for the Triangle East Asia Colloquium, November 1, 2003), 1.

111 Ibid. 8.

112 Newton, Lynn David. "Keith Jarrett: A Sketch of His Life and Work," Available online. URL: http://www.eecs.umich.edu/~lnewton/music/ JarrettSketch.html#early_history. Downloaded on October 13, 2004.

113 Carr, Ian, Digby Fairweather, and Brian Priestly, eds. *Jazz, The Rough Guide* (London: Penguin, 2000), 384.

114 Ward, Geoffrey C., and Ken Burns. *Jazz: A History of America's Music* (New York: Knopf, 2000), 65.

115 Rogers, J. A. "Jazz at Home" (*The Survey Graphic,* 1925).

[116] Kressman, Mark. "Review of Ingrid Jensen, *Higher Ground*," Available online. URL: http://www.jazzreview.com/cdreview.cfm?ID=2129). Downloaded on March 30, 2003.

[117] Feather, Leonard, and Ira Gitler. *The Biographical Encyclopedia of Jazz* (New York: Oxford University Press, 1999), 366.

[118] Fine, Larry. "Jazz Drummer Elvin Jones of Coltrane Quartet Dies," Available online. URL: http://www.reuters.com/newsArticle.jhtml?type=peopleNews&storyID=5196284. Downloaded on October 13, 2004.

[119] Shapiro, Ben. "Hank Jones Episode, Jazz Profiles from NPR," Available online. URL: http://www.npr.org/programs/jazzprofiles/archive/jones_h.html. Downloaded on October 13, 2004.

[120] Feather, Leonard, and Ira Gitler. *The Biographical Encyclopedia of Jazz* (New York: Oxford University Press, 1999), 371.

[121] Berlin, Edward, A. *A Biography of Scott Joplin,* The Scott Joplin International Ragtime Foundation, 1998.

[122] ———. "Stan Kenton Biographical Information," Available online. URL: http://kenton.52ndstreet.com/. Downloaded on December 19, 2000.

[123] Yanow, Scott. *Classic Jazz* (San Francisco: Backbeat Books, 2001), 128.

[124] Alexander, Scott. "The Original Creole Orchestra," Available online. URL: http://www.redhotjazz.com/creole.html. Downloaded on October 13, 2004.

[125] Fitzgerald, Michael. "Rahsaan Roland Kirk, A Brief Biography," Available online. URL: http://www.eclipse.net/~fitzgera/rahsaan/rrk-home.htm. Downloaded on October 13, 2004.

[126] Ibid.

[127] Henthoff, Nat. "Are Krall and Monheit Jazz Singers?" Available online. URL: http://jazztimes.com/home.cfm?URL=http://jazztimes.com/final_chorus/finalchorus_krall_monheit.cfm?. Downloaded on October 13, 2004.

[128] Lacy, Steve. *Findings: My Experience with the Soprano Saxophone* (Paris: CMAP, 1994).

[129] Martin, Mel. "Steve Lacy." *Saxophone Journal* 16, no. 3 (November/December 1991): 38.

[130] ———. "Singer Peggy Lee Dead of Heart Attack at 81," Associated Press, January 22, 2002.

[131] Baraka, Amiri. "Interview with Abbey Lincoln," Available online. URL: http://www.jazzatlincolncenter.org/jazz/note/lincoln.html. Downloaded on October 13, 2004.

[132] Plaksin, Sally. "Interview with Abbey Lincoln," Available online. URL: http://www.npr.org/programs/jazzprofiles/archive/lincoln.html. Downloaded on November 15, 2002.

[133] ———. "Manhattan Transfer Discography," Available online. URL: http://www.tmtfanclub.com/extens.html. Downloaded on October 13, 2004.

[134] Marsalis, Wynton. *Jazz for Young People Teaching Guide* (New York: Scholastic, 2002), inside cover.

[135] Ibid.

[136] McLaughlin, John. "Influences," Available online. URL: http://www.johnmclaughlin.com/influences/influences.html. Downloaded on October 13, 2004.

[137] Milkowski, Bill. "John McLaughlin: A Candid Chat with a Musical Provateur," Available online. URL: http://www.abstractlogix.com/mclaughlin-mil.php. Downloaded on October 13, 2004.

[138] Miller, Marcus. "Marcus Miller's Biography," Available online. URL: http://www.prarecords.com/artists/miller/bio.html. Downloaded on October 13, 2004.

[139] Gillespie, Dizzy. *To Be or Not to Bop* (New York: Doubleday, 1979).

[140] Gross, Jason. "Roscoe Mitchell Interview," Available online. URL: http://www.furious.com/perfect/roscoemitchell.html. Downloaded on October 13, 2004.

[141] Monk, Thelonious. "Quoted on Monkzone.com," Available online. URL: http://www.monkzone.com/silent/biographyHTML.htm. Downloaded on October 13, 2004.

[142] Morton, Jelly Roll. "I Created Jazz in 1902, Not W.C. Handy," Available online. URL: http://www.

downbeatjazz.com/?sect=stories&subsect=story_detail&sid=317. Downloaded on October 13, 2004.

143 Bean, B. B. "Gerry Mulligan Remembered as Founder of Cool School of Jazz," Available online. URL: http://www.whitman.edu/news/News96-97/gerry.html. Downloaded on October 13, 2004.

144 Schuller, Gunther. *The Swing Era* (New York: Oxford University Press, 1989), 515–516.

145 ———. "Chico O'Farrill Obituary," Available online. URL: http://www.arrangeonline.com/notablePersons/notable.asp?ObituaryID=60726642. Downloaded on October 13, 2004.

146 Charles Mingus, after the death of Charlie Parker, quoted in Ted Gioia's *History of Jazz* (New York: Oxford University Press, 1998).

147 Metheny, Pat. "The Life and Music of Jaco Pastorius," (liner notes, *Jaco Pastorius,* Sony 64977, 2000 reissue of 1976 album).

148 Quoted from "Lore," on Ingrid's Jaco Pastorius Cyber Nest, Available online. URL: http://www.jacop.net/story_bass.html. Ingrid was married to Pastorius from 1979 until their separation in 1985.

149 ———. "Oscar Peterson: The Early Years," Available online. URL: http://www.oscarpeterson.com/op/rootsframe.html. Downloaded on October 13, 2004.

150 Voce, Steve. "Michel Petrucciani: A Very Special Jazz Pianist," Available online. URL: http://www.jazzreview.com/articleprint.cfm?ID=25. Downloaded on October 13, 2004.

151 Feather, Leonard, and Ira Gitler. *The Biographical Encyclopedia of Jazz* (New York: Oxford University Press, 1999), 526.

152 ———. "Courtney Pine," Available online. URL: http://www.ejn.it/mus/pine.htm. Downloaded on October 13, 2004.

153 ———. "Courtney Pine," Available online. URL: http://members.lycos.co.uk/earthdaughta/id64.htm. Downloaded on October 13, 2004.

154 Rich, Alan. *The Listener's Guide to Jazz* (Dorset, England: Blandford Press, 1980), 53.

155 Monk, Thelonious, as quoted at URL: http://www.budpowelljazz.com/book/jazz.html. Downloaded on October 13, 2004.

156 Hancock, Herbie, as quoted at www.budpowelljazz.com. URL: http://www.budpowelljazz.com/book/jazz.html.

157 Feather, Leonard, and Ira Gitler. *The Biographical Encyclopedia of Jazz* (New York: Oxford University Press, 1999), 551.

158 Schuller, Gunther. *The Swing Era* (New York: Oxford University Press, 1989), 367.

159 Feather, Leonard, and Ira Gitler. *The Biographical Encyclopedia of Jazz* (New York: Oxford University Press, 1999), 554.

160 Carr Ian, Digby Fairweather, and Brian Priestly, eds. *Jazz, The Rough Guide* (London: Penguin Books, 2000), 635.

161 Feather, Leonard, and Ira Gitler. *The Biographical Encyclopedia of Jazz* (New York: Oxford University Press, 1999), 581.

162 ———. "Diane Schuur—The Grammy Winning Voice of Jazz," Available online. URL: http://www.arizonamusicscene.com/bios/bio_dianeschuur.htm. Downloaded on October 14, 2004.

163 Carr, Ian, Digby Fairweather, and Brian Priestly, eds. *Jazz, The Rough Guide* (London: Penguin Books, 2000), 684.

164 Reel, Lou. "Jimmy Scott," Available online. URL: http://www.artistsonly.com/scothm.htm. Downloaded on October 14, 2004.

165 ———. "Shirley Scott biography," Available online. URL: http://www.vervemusicgroup.com/artist.aspx?aid=2760. Downloaded on April 1, 2004.

166 Hill, Dannette. "Sonny Sharrock: On Improvisation," Available online. URL: http://www.jazzguitar.com/features/sharrock.html. Downloaded on October 14, 2004.

167 ———. "Biography: Artie Shaw," Available online. URL: http://www.artieshaw.com/bio.html. Downloaded on October 14, 2004.

168 ———. "Biography: Artie Shaw," Available online. URL: http://www.artieshaw.com/bio.html. Downloaded on October 14, 2004.

169 Feather, Leonard, and Ira Gitler. *The Biographical Encyclopedia of Jazz* (New York: Oxford University Press, 1999), 596.

170 Cashman, Scott. "A Dialogue with Archie Shepp," Available online. URL: http://www.archieshepp.com/dialogue.html. Downloaded on October 14, 2004.

171 Jung, Fred. "A Fireside Chat with Wayne Shorter," Available online. URL: http://www.allaboutjazz.com/iviews/wshorter2002.htm. Downloaded on October 14, 2004.

172 Davis, Miles. *Miles* (New York: Simon & Schuster, 1989), 274.

173 Gridley, Mark C. *Jazz Styles: History and Analysis,* 3rd ed. (Englewood Cliffs, N.J.: Prentice Hall, 1988), 306.

174 Jung, Fred. "A Fireside Chat with Wayne Shorter," Available online. URL: http://www.allaboutjazz.com/iviews/wshorter2002.htm. Downloaded on October 14, 2004.

175 Davis, Miles. *Miles* (New York: Simon & Schuster, 1989), 274.

176 Jung, Fred. "My Conversation with Horace Silver," Available online. URL: http://www.allaboutjazz.com/iviews/hsilver.htm. Downloaded on October 14, 2004.

177 Ibid.

178 Sebastian, Tim. "Nina Simone Interview," Available online. URL: http://news.bbc.co.uk/1/hi/entertainment/302438.stm. Downloaded on October 14, 2004.

179 Feather, Leonard, and Ira Gitler. *The Biographical Encyclopedia of Jazz* (New York: Oxford, 1999), 605.

180 Crow, Bill. *Jazz Anecdotes* (New York: Oxford University, 1990), 264.

181 Alexander, Scott. "Bessie Smith," Red Hot Jazz Web site, Available online. URL: http://www.redhotjazz.com/bessie.html.

182 Feather, Leonard, and Ira Gitler. *The Biographical Encyclopedia of Jazz* (New York: Oxford, 1999), 608.

183 Alexander, Scott. "Bessie Smith," (Red Hot Jazz web site, Available online. URL: http://www.redhotjazz.com/bessie. html.

184 Crow, Bill. *Jazz Anecdotes* (New York: Oxford University Press, 1990), 219.

185 Yanow, Scott. *Classic Jazz* (San Francisco: Backbeat Books, 2001), 216.

186 Carr, Ian, Digby Fairweather, and Brian Priestly, eds. *Jazz, The Rough Guide* (London: Penguin Books, 2000), 717.

187 Schuller, Gunther. *The Swing Era* (New York: Oxford University Press, 1989), 359.

188 Gridley, Mark C. *Jazz Styles: History and Analysis,* 3rd ed. (Englewood Cliffs, N.J.: Prentice Hall, 1988), 154.

189 Feather, Leonard, and Ira Gitler. *The Biographical Encyclopedia of Jazz* (New York: Oxford University Press, 1999), 626.

190 Ibid. 626.

191 Schuller, Gunther. *The Swing Era* (New York: Oxford University Press, 1989), 134.

192 Quoted on the Smithsonian National Museum of American History Web site, URL: http://americanhistory.si.edu/archives/de-tour/tr301b02.htm. Downloaded on June 5, 2004.

193 Shore, Michael. "Sun Ra." *Musician Player and Listener* 24 (April/May 1980): 48–51.

194 Carr, Ian, Digby Fairweather, and Brian Priestly, eds. *Jazz, The Rough Guide* (London: Penguin Books, 2000), 742.

195 Schuller, Gunther. *The Swing Era* (New York: Oxford University Press, 1989), 483.

196 Ibid. 478.

197 Lester, James. *Too Marvelous for Words* (New York: Oxford University Press, 1994).

198 Feather, Leonard. *The Encyclopedia of Jazz in the Seventies* (New York: Horizon Press, 1976), 23.

199 Crumpacker, Chick, and Bunny Crumpacker. *Jazz Legends* (Layton, Utah: Gibbs Smith, 1995), 52.

200 Feather, Leonard, and Ira Gitler. *The Biographical Encyclopedia of Jazz* (New York: Oxford University Press, 1999), 664.

201 Ibid. 667.

202 Crumpacker, Chick, and Bunny Crumpacker. *Jazz Legends* (Layton, Utah: Gibbs Smith, 1995), 41.

203 ———. "Fats Waller, Biography," Available online. URL: http://www.pbs.org/jazz/biography/artist_id_waller_fats.htm. Downloaded on May 9, 2004.

204 ———. *Jazz Legends* (Layton, Utah: Gibbs Smith, 1995), 43.

205 Crow, Bill. *Jazz Anecdotes* (New York: Oxford University Press, 1990), 231.

206 Feather, Leonard, and Ira Gitler. *The Biographical Encyclopedia of Jazz* (New York: Oxford University Press, 1999), 678.

207 Alexander, Scott. "Ethel Waters," Red Hot Jazz web site, Available online. URL: http://www.redhotjazz.com/bessie.html.

208 Ibid. 95.

209 Hill, Hal. "Ben Webster Profile," Available online. URL: http://www.jazzcanadiana.on.ca/_Webster.htm. Downloaded on October 14, 2004.

210 Crow, Bill. *Jazz Anecdotes* (New York: Oxford University Press, 1990), 285.

211 Maddix, Melanie. "Mary Lou Williams," Available online. URL: http://www.jazzbrat.com/templates/jpage.php?u_pageid=520. Downloaded on April 28, 2004.

212 Crow, Bill. *Jazz Anecdotes* (New York: Oxford University Press, 1990), 13.

213 Maddix, Melanie. "Mary Lou Williams," Available online. URL: http://www.jazzbrat.com/templates/jpage.php?u_pageid=520. Downloaded on April 28, 2004.

214 Ellington, Duke. *Music Is My Mistress* (New York: Doubleday, 1973), 169.

215 Fordham, John. "Interview with Steve Williamson," Available online. URL: http://www.jazzsite.co.uk/JUK/JUK46/JUK46_12.pdf. Down-loaded on April 27, 2004.

216 Hamilton, Rhonda. "Interview with Cassandra Wilson," Available online. URL: http://www.allaboutjazz.com/php/article.php?id=1107. Posted on January 31, 2004.

217 Boukas, Richard. "A Tribute to Attila Zoller," Available online. URL: http://www.boukas.com/jjgarticles/jjgattila.html#attila1, may 1998. Down-loaded on October 14, 2004.

218 Nicholson, Stuart. *Jazz: The 1980s Resurgence* (New York: Da Capo, 1995), 278.

219 "Jazz at Lincoln Center to Induct Inaugural Class of Musicians into the Ertegun Jazz Hall of Fame," press release, Jazz at Lincoln Center, September 30, 2004.

Editorial Board of Advisers

Richard Carlin, general editor, is the author of several books of music, including *Southern Exposure, The Big Book of Country Music, Classical Music: An Informal Guide,* and the five-volume *Worlds of Music.* He has also written and compiled several books of music instruction and songbooks and served as advisory editor on country music for the American National Biography. Carlin has contributed articles on traditional music to various journals, including the *Journal of Ethnomusicology, Sing Out!, Pickin', Frets,* and *Mugwumps.* He has also produced 10 albums of traditional music for Folkways Records. A longtime editor of books on music, dance, and the arts, Carlin is currently executive editor of music and dance at Routledge Publishers. He previously spent six years as executive editor at Schirmer Books and was the founding editor at A Cappella Books, an imprint of the Chicago Review Press.

Barbara Ching, Ph.D., is an associate professor of English at the University of Memphis. She obtained a graduate certificate in women's studies and her doctorate in literature from Duke University. Dr. Ching has written extensively on country music and rural identity, and she is the author of *Wrong's What I Do Best: Hard Country Music and Contemporary Culture* (Oxford University Press) and *Knowing Your Place: Rural Identity and Cultural Hierarchy* (Routledge). She has also contributed articles and chapters to numerous other works on the subject and has presented

papers at meetings of the International Association for the Study of Popular Music.

William Duckworth is the composer of more than 100 pieces of music and the author of six books and numerous articles, the most recent of which is "Making Music on the Web" (*Leonardo Music Journal,* vol. 9, December 1999). In the mid-1990s he and codirector Nora Farrell began *Cathedral,* a multiyear work of music and art for the Web that went online June 10, 1997. Incorporating acoustic and computer music, live Web casts by its own band, and newly created virtual instruments, *Cathedral* is one of the first interactive works of music and art on the Web. Recently, Duckworth and Farrell created Cathedral 2001, a 48-hour World Wide Web event, with 34 events streamed live from five continents. Duckworth is currently a professor of music at Bucknell University in Pennsylvania.

Kevin Holm-Hudson, Ph.D., received his doctorate of musical arts (composition with ethnomusicology concentration) from the University of Illinois at Urbana-Champaign. He is an assistant professor of music at the University of Kentucky and is an editor/contributor to *Progressive Rock Reconsidered* (Routledge). Dr. Holm-Hudson is also the author of numerous articles that have appeared in such publications as *Genre* and *Ex Tempore* and has presented papers on a wide variety of topics at conferences, including "'Come

Sail Away' and the Commodification of Prog Lite," at the inaugural Conference on Popular Music and American Culture in 2002.

Craig Morrison, Ph.D., holds a doctorate in humanities with a concentration in music from Concordia University (Montreal, Quebec). He is currently a professor of music at Concordia, where he teaches a course titled "Rock and Roll and its Roots." Dr. Morrison is the author of *Go Cat Go! Rockabilly Music and Its Makers* (University of Illinois Press) and contributed to *The Encyclopedia of the Blues* (Routledge). He has presented many papers on elements of rock and roll.

Index

Boldface page numbers indicate major treatment of a subject. Page numbers in *italic* indicate illustrations. Page numbers followed by a *g* indicate glossary entries.

A

AABA form **1,** 19, 23
AAB form **1**
AACM. *See* Association for the Advancement of Creative Musicians
Abercrombie, John **1,** 80, 124, 154, 224
Abrams, Muhal Richard **1–2,** *2,* 7, 46, 122, 197
a cappella 275*g*
accent **2,** 91, 192, 275*g*
acid jazz xxv, **2–3**
   Miles Davis 51
   Roy Hargrove 85
   jazz firsts 117
   Courtney Pine 155
   time line 252
   Steve Williamson 217
Ackley, Bruce 166
acoustic bass. *See* double bass
Acuna, Alex 15
Adams, Pepper **3,** 19
Adderly, Cannonball **3**
   Miles Davis 49
   Barry Harris 86
   Coleman Hawkins 87
   Kind of Blue 113
   Yusef Lateef 121
   Nancy Wilson 218
   Joe Zawinul 223
Aeolian Hall (New York City) 213
Africa 9, 20, 123. *See also* South African jazz
African Americans. *See also specific musicians*
   all-woman bands xxx
   European jazz 64
   Harlem 85
   jazz as soundtrack for xxi

race music 161
race records 161
"African Violets" (Cecil Taylor) 194
"Afro Blue" (Mongo Santamaria) 170
Afro-Cuban jazz. *See* Latin and Afro-Cuban jazz
"Afternoon in Paris" (Sonny Stitt/Bud Powell recording) 188
"Ain't Misbehavin'" (Fats Waller) 210
Akiyoshi, Toshiko **3–4,** *4,* 103
Alabama 63, 84, 189
Alexander, Van 70
Ali, Rashied 41, 46
Alias, Don 15
Allen, Marshall 190
"All the Things You Are" (Art Tatum/Ben Webster recording) 213
"All Too Soon" (Duke Ellington) 213
all-women orchestras 47, 53, 99. *See also* women in jazz
alto 275*g*
alto saxophone
   Cannonball Adderly **3**
   Gato Barbieri 9
   Anthony Braxton **21–22**
   Benny Carter **28**
   Ornette Coleman **36–38**
   Eric Dolphy **54–55**
   Kenny Garrett **73–74**
   Roscoe Mitchell 137
   Out There (Dolphy) 150
   Charlie Parker **151–152**
   Don Redman 162
   David Sanborn **169**
   Artie Shaw 175, 176
   Zoot Sims 182
   Sonny Stitt 187–188, **187–188**
   John Zorn **224–225**
Altschul, Barry 22, 41, 42
Amandla (Miles Davis) 73
Ambrose, Bert 25
American Jazz Museum (Kansas City, Missouri) **4**
American Jazz Music (Wilder Hobson) **4**

Ammons, Gene 188
Andersen, Arild 185
Anderson, Ivie **4,** *5,* 99
Anderson, Reid 9
And His Mother Called Him Bill (Duke Ellington) **4–5,** 189
Ansermet, Ernest 12
Apollo Theater 183, 205
Armstrong, Lil Hardin. *See* Hardin, Lil
Armstrong, Louis xxiii, **5–6**
   Sid Catlett 30
   in Chicago xxiii
   Chicago jazz 32
   cornet 43
   "Dipper Mouth Blues" 52
   Baby Dodds 53
   Johnny Dodds 54
   Roy Eldridge 59
   European jazz 64
   Ella Fitzgerald 70
   Dexter Gordon 77
   Lionel Hampton 81
   Lil Hardin xxx, 84
   "Heebie Jeebies" **88–89**
   Fletcher Henderson 89
   Earl "Fatha" Hines 91
   Billie Holiday 91
   Hot Five and Hot Seven **94**
   Japanese jazz 103
   jazz firsts 116
   Freddie Keppard 113
   Hugh Masekela 129
   Charles Mingus 135
   New Orleans jazz 143
   Newport Jazz Festival 144
   King Oliver 147, 148
   Kid Ory 150
   Ma Rainey 161
   recordings of early jazz 162
   Don Redman 163
   "St. Louis Blues" 187
   scat singing 171
   Artie Shaw 175
   "Singin' the Blues" 182

big band *(continued)*
  swing **192**
  Jack Teagarden 195
  territory bands 196
  Clark Terry 196
  Chick Webb **212**
  Mary Lou Williams 215
  Steve Williamson 217
big band era. *See* swing
big band jazz 275*g*
Billboard magazine 31
Birdland (nightclub) **14–15,** 147, 157
"Birdland" (Joe Zawinul) **15,** 126, 208
Birth of the Cool (Miles Davis/Gil Evans)
  15, 42, 49, 67, 141, 172
Bitches Brew (Miles Davis) **15–16**
  Billy Cobham 35
  Chick Corea 42
  Miles Davis 49
  Jack DeJohnette 51
  fusion 72
  Dave Holland 92
  John McLaughlin 131
  Wayne Shorter 178
  Joe Zawinul 223
"Black and Tan Fantasy" (Duke Ellington)
  16
"Black Bottom Stomp" (Jelly Roll Morton)
  16
Black Byrd (Donald Byrd) 26
Blackman, Cindy **16**
Black Orpheus (soundtrack) 107
Black Swan Records 89, 116, 162, 211
Blackwell, Ed **16–17,** *17, 37*
  Don Cherry 31, 32
  Anthony Cox 44
  Free Jazz (Ornette Coleman) 71
  Charlie Haden 79
Black Woman (Sonny Sharrock) 175
Blakey, Art **17–18.** *See also* Jazz
  Messengers
  Cindy Blackman 16
  Clifford Brown 23
  Donald Byrd 26
  Stanley Clarke 34
  Kenny Garrett 73
  Freddie Hubbard 95
  Japanese jazz 103
  Keith Jarrett 104
  Chuck Mangione 125
  Wynton Marsalis 127
  Moanin' **137–138**
  Lee Morgan 140
  Courtney Pine 155
  Sonny Rollins 165
  Wayne Shorter 178
  Horace Silver 179, 180
  Jimmy Smith 183
  Mary Lou Williams 215
  Steve Williamson 217

Blanton, Jimmy **18,** 137, 154, 193
Bley, Carla **18**
  avant-garde 7
  Gary Burton 26
  Charlie Haden 79
  Steve Lacy 119
  Michael Mantler 126–127
  Pharoah Sanders 170
  Andy Sheppard 177
  Steve Swallow 191, 192
Bley, Paul 72, 191, 224
Bloch, Ray 109
Blood, Sweat, and Tears 22, 90
"Blood Count" (Billy Strayhorn) 5, 189
"Blood on the Fields" (Wynton Marsalis)
  217
Blount, Herman "Sonny." *See* Sun Ra
"Blue Moon" progression 275–276*g*
blue note **18**
Blue Note Records 63, 82, 124, 154, 163,
  183
blues **19,** 276*g*
  AAB form **1**
  Blues and Roots 19
  The Blues and the Abstract Truth 19
  Buddy Bolden 20
  "Dipper Mouth Blues" **52–53**
  Duke Ellington 62
  W. C. Handy **84**
  Fletcher Henderson 89
  Alberta Hunter **95**
  jazz firsts 117
  Eddie Lang 120
  race music 161
  race records 161
  Ma Rainey **161**
  Don Redman 163
  rhythm and blues **164**
  "St. Louis Blues" (Louis Armstrong
    recording) 187
  David Sanborn 169
  Shirley Scott 174
  shuffle rhythm **179**
  Bessie Smith **182–183**
  Mamie Smith **183–184**
  "Straight, No Chaser" 188
  Sun Ra 189
  Jack Teagarden 195
  Stanley Turrentine 200
  12-bar blues 282*g*
  12-bar structure **200**
  Ethel Waters 211
  Cassandra Wilson 217
Blues and Roots (Charles Mingus) **19**
The Blues and the Abstract Truth (Oliver
  Nelson) **19**
Blues Forever (Muhal Richard Abrams) 2
"Blues Up and Down" (Gene Ammons/
  Sonny Stitt recording) 188
Blue Train (John Coltrane) **19**

"Body and Soul" (Coleman Hawkins
  recording) **19,** 87, 88
Bofill, Angela 16
Boland, Francy 34
Bolden, Buddy xxvi, **19–20**
  cutting contest 45
  double bass 56
  jazz firsts 116
  Freddie Keppard 112
  New Orleans jazz 143
  use of string bass in band xxii
Bona, Richard **20,** 152
boogie-woogie **20,** 276*g*
bop. *See* bebop
Bortnick, Avi 173
bossa nova **20,** 74, 75, 107, 117
Bowie, David 68, 169
Bowie, Lester 6, **20–21**
Brackeen, Joanne 17, **21**
Bradford, Perry 184
Brand, Dollar. *See* Ibrahim, Abdullah
brass **21,** 142, 276*g*. *See also specific brass
  instruments*
brass bands 143, 221
Brass Fantasy 21
Braxton, Anthony **21–22**
  AACM 7
  avant-garde 7
  Ed Blackwell 16
  Conference of the Birds 41
  Chick Corea 42
  Marilyn Crispell 44
  Andrew Cyrille 46
  Dave Holland 92
  Leroy Jenkins 107
  George Lewis 122
  third stream jazz 197
Brazil 20, 75, 107, 126
break **22**
Brecker, Michael 20, 22, **22,** 134, 180, 216
Brecker, Randy 20, **22,** 180
Brecker Brothers (band) 169
bridge **23**
Bridgewater, Dee Dee **23**
Brilliant Corners (Thelonious Monk) **23**
British invasion 276*g*
Broadway musicals 61, 93–94
Bronson, Art 219
Brooks, Harvey 15
Brotherhood of Breath 187
Brown, Clifford **23–24,** 81, 211
Brown, James 169
Brown, Ray **24,** 153
Brubeck, Dave **24–25,** 117, 132, 144, 197
Bruce, Jack 131
Brun, Philipe **25,** 64
Bryant, Ray 25
B-3 organ. *See* Hammond B-3 organ
Buchanan, Elwood 48
Buchla synthesizer 192

Buena Vista Social Club (documentary and recording) 76, 174
Burrell, Kenny 30, 44, 183, 200
Burton, Gary **26,** 133, 172, 185, 192
Burton, Ron 98
Bush, George H. W. 81
Butterfield, Paul 169
Byrd, Charlie 74
Byrd, Donald **26**
  Pepper Adams 3
  Paul Chambers 30
  Herbie Hancock 82
  Horace Silver 180
  Stanley Turrentine 200
  Larry Young 219

C

Cabin in the Sky (film) 211
cadence 276*g*
Cadence magazine 27
Cage, John 21, 224
California 139, 142, 150
call-and-response 10, 27, **27**
Calloway, Cab 11, **27,** 75, 210, 213
Canada 67–68, 70, 101, 107, 130, 153
Caplin, Dalia Ambach 3
capo 276*g*
Carnegie Hall **27–28**
  Duke Ellington 61
  James Reese Europe 63
  jazz firsts 116, 117
  Chano Pozo 157
  Diane Reeves 163
  John Scofield 172
  Fats Waller 210
  Mary Lou Williams 215
Carney, Harry 61, 213
"Carolina Shout" (James P. Johnson) 107, 116
Carroll, Barbara **28**
Carter, Benny **28–29**
  Cannonball Adderly 3
  Sid Catlett 30
  Ornette Coleman 36
  Roy Eldridge 60
  Art Farmer 69
  Dizzy Gillespie 75
  Coleman Hawkins 87
  Japanese jazz 103
  JATP 106
  jazz firsts 117
  Abbey Lincoln 122
  Carmen McRae 132
  Diane Reeves 163
  George Russell 166
  saxophone 171
  Chick Webb 212
  Ben Webster 213
  Shadow Wilson 218

Carter, Betty **29,** 51, 81
Carter, Ron **29–30**
  Miles Davis 49
  "E.S.P." 63
  Jim Hall 80
  Chico Hamilton 80
  Herbie Hancock 82
  Out There (Dolphy) 150
  Tony Williams 216
Castle, Vernon and Irene 63
Castro, Fidel 174
Catlett, Sid 30, 157, 169
CD (compact disc) 276*g*
Cele, Willard 187
Celestin, Papa 10
cello 150, 154
cha-cha 76
chamber jazz 24. *See also* Modern Jazz Quartet
Chambers, Paul 19, **30,** 49, 74, 92
Charles, Ray 120, 200
"Charleston" (James P. Johnson recording) **30–31,** 108
chart, music arrangement **31**
chart, sales **31**
Chatterjee, Amit 223
Cherry, Don **17,** **31–32**
  Gato Barbieri 9
  Ed Blackwell 16–17
  Ornette Coleman 36
  Free Jazz (Ornette Coleman) 71
  Jan Garbarek 73
  Charlie Haden 79
  Abdullah Ibrahim 97
  Steve Lacy 119
  pocket trumpet 156
  Pharoah Sanders 169
  The Shape of Jazz to Come 174
  Sonny Sharrock 175
  Archie Shepp 177
Chicago, Illinois
  AACM 7
  Muhal Richard Abrams 1–2
  Louis Armstrong 6
  Art Ensemble of Chicago 6–7
  Lovie Austin 7
  Anthony Braxton 21
  Cab Calloway 27
  Jack DeJohnette 51
  as destination for early New Orleans musicians xxiii
  "Dipper Mouth Blues" 52
  Dixieland jazz 53
  Baby Dodds 53
  Johnny Dodds 54
  Dorothy Donegan 55
  Benny Goodman 76
  Lil Hardin 84
  Alberta Hunter 95
  Jazz Institute of Chicago 106

  Leroy Jenkins 106–107
  Freddie Keppard 113
  New Orleans jazz 143
  recordings of early jazz 162
  Artie Shaw 175
  Sun Ra 189
  traditional jazz (classic jazz) 198
  Lennie Tristano 198
"Chicago Breakdown" (Louis Armstrong Hot Seven recording) 94
Chicago jazz xxiii, **32,** 147, 149
  time line 252
Chicago Underground Trio **32**
Chisholm, George 64
chops **32**
chord **32,** 41, 53, 198, 276*g*
chord changes **32–33**
chord progression 276*g*
chorus 33, 276*g*
Christensen, Jon 208
Christian, Charlie **33**
  Kenny Clarke 34
  Jim Hall 79–80
  Eddie Lang 120
  Wes Montgomery 139
  Bud Powell 156
  "Stompin' at the Savoy" **188**
"The Christmas Song" (Mel Torme) 198
Cifelli, Jim **33**
Circle (Corea/Holland/Braxton/Altschul) 22, 42, 92
circular breathing **33,** 98, 114
Civil Rights movement 181
clarinet **33–34**
  Gato Barbieri 9
  Sidney Bechet 12
  Benny Carter 28
  Johnny Dodds **54**
  in early jazz xxvi
  Bill Frisell 72
  Benny Goodman **76**
  Woody Herman **90–91**
  Courtney Pine 155
  Artie Shaw **175–176**
Clarke, Kenny **34**
  bebop 12
  Andrew Cyrille 46
  Al Di Meola 52
  Minton's Playhouse 137
  Modern Jazz Quartet 138
  Charlie Parker 151
  "Stompin' at the Savoy" (Charlie Christian recording) 188
Clarke, Stanley 17, 18, **34–35,** 43, 163, 216
classical music
  Dave Brubeck 24
  Bobby McFerrin 130
  Charles Mingus 136
  Modern Jazz Quartet 138
  Artie Shaw 175

classical music *(continued)*
   Art Tatum 193
   third stream jazz 196–197
   Time Out (Brubeck) 197
   John Zorn 224
classic jazz. *See* traditional jazz
clef 276g
Cleveland, Ohio 79
Clinton, Bill 29, 81, 138
C melody saxophone 199
Cobb, Jimmy 74, 113
Cobham, Billy **35**
   John Abercrombie 1
   Randy Brecker 22
   Jan Hammer 80
   The Inner Mounting Flame 99
   John McLaughlin 132
   John Scofield 172
Cohen, Avishai 43
Cohn, Al 182
Cole, Nat "King" **35–36**, 153, 154
Coleman, Ornette xxiv, **36–38**, *37*
   Ed Blackwell 16
   Don Cherry 31, 32
   Eric Dolphy 55
   free jazz 71
   Free Jazz **71–72**
   Charlie Haden 79
   Pat Metheny 134
   The Shape of Jazz to Come **174–175**
   Cecil Taylor 195
   Attilla Zoller 224
collective improvisation 71
Colomby, Bobby 152
Coltrane, Alice 16, 38, 40, 41, 107, 170
Coltrane, John **38–41**, *39*
   Cannonball Adderly 3
   Birdland 15
   Blue Train 19
   Donald Byrd 26
   Don Cherry 31
   Alice Coltrane 38
   Ravi Coltrane 41
   Miles Davis 49
   Eric Dolphy 54, 55
   Duke Ellington 61
   Giant Steps (John Coltrane) **74**
   Grammy Awards 78
   Johnny Hartman 86
   Coleman Hawkins 88
   "In a Sentimental Mood" **98**
   Elvin Jones 108–109
   Kind of Blue 113
   A Love Supreme **124**
   Thelonious Monk 139
   Wes Montgomery 139
   multiphonics 142
   "My Favorite Things" **142**
   Courtney Pine 155

George Russell 167
Pharoah Sanders 169
Mongo Santamaria 170
saxophone 171
Archie Shepp 177
Andy Sheppard 177
Wayne Shorter 178
McCoy Tyner 200
Shadow Wilson 218
Lester Young 220
Coltrane, Ravi 41
Columbia Records
   Miles Davis 49
   "It Don't Mean a Thing (If It Ain't Got
     That Swing)" 99
   Mingus Ah Um 136
   recordings of early jazz 161, 162
   "St. Louis Blues" (Louis Armstrong
     recording) 187
   Bessie Smith 183
   Time Out (Brubeck) 197
   Ethel Waters 211
Combelle, Alix 25
combo **41,** 159, 164. *See also* ensemble
comping 41
Complete Communion (Don Cherry) 16,
   31–32
composer **41**. *See also* arranger
   Muhal Richard Abrams **1–2**
   Toshiko Akiyoshi **3–4**
   Lovie Austin **7**
   Bix Beiderbecke 12
   Carla Bley **18**
   Richard Bona **20**
   Joanne Brackeen **21**
   Anthony Braxton **21–22**
   Dave Brubeck **24–25**
   Gary Burton **26**
   Benny Carter 28, 29
   Jim Cifelli **33**
   Stanley Clarke **35**
   John Coltrane **38–41**
   Chick Corea **42–43**
   Eric Dolphy **54–55**
   Duke Ellington **60–62**
   James Reese Europe **63**
   Bill Evans **65–67**
   Gil Evans **67–68**
   Leonard Feather 70
   Bill Frisell **72**
   Jan Garbarek **73**
   Erroll Garner **73**
   Dizzy Gillespie **75**
   Charlie Haden **79**
   Chico Hamilton **80**
   Herbie Hancock **81–83**
   W. C. Handy **84**
   Lil Hardin **84**
   Joe Henderson **90**

Earl "Fatha" Hines 91
D. D. Jackson **101**
Keith Jarrett **104–105**
Antonio Carlos Jobim **107**
James P. Johnson **107–108**
Thad Jones **110**
Scott Joplin **110**
Stan Kenton **111–112**
Steve Lacy **119**
Peggy Lee **121**
Melba Liston **123**
Kit McClure **129–130**
Pat Metheny **133–134**
Charles Mingus **135–137**
Roscoe Mitchell **137**
Thelonious Monk **138–139**
Jelly Roll Morton **140–141**
Gerry Mulligan **141–142**
Chico O'Farrill **147**
Oscar Pettiford **154**
Don Redman **162–163**
Max Roach **165**
George Russell **166–167**
Mongo Santamaria **170**
Maria Schneider **171**
Gunther Schuller **171–172**
Artie Shaw **176**
Andy Sheppard **177**
Wayne Shorter **177–179**
Horace Silver **179–181**
Nina Simone **181–182**
Tommy Smith **185**
Billy Strayhorn **188–189**
Sun Ra **189–191**
John Surman **191**
Cecil Taylor **194–195**
Sir Charles Thompson **197**
Mel Torme **198**
Lennie Tristano **198–199**
Stanley Turrentine **200**
McCoy Tyner **200–201**
Fats Waller **209–210**
Mary Lou Williams **215–216**
women in jazz xxix
Joe Zawinul **223–224**
John Zorn **224–225**
composition. *See* arrangement; composer;
   counterpoint
computer software 134
"Concertino for Jazz Quartet and
   Orchestra" (Gunther Schuller) 172
Conference of the Birds (Dave Holland) **41,**
   92
congas 170
Connecticut 16, 179
Connie's Inn 85
Connors, Bill 43
contemporary jazz **42**. *See also specific
   artists*

Cooder, Ry 174
cool jazz xxiv–xxv, **42**
 Birth of the Cool **15**
 bossa nova 20
 Dave Brubeck 24, 25
 Miles Davis 49
 flute 71
 Stan Getz 74
 Chico Hamilton 80
 Gerry Mulligan 142
 Red Norvo 145
 time line 252
 Lennie Tristano 199
 Attilla Zoller 224
Copenhagen, Denmark 77, 154, 213
Corea, Chick *42,* **42–43**
 Bitches Brew 15, 16
 Art Blakey 17
 Richard Bona 20
 Anthony Braxton 22
 Stanley Clarke 34, 35
 Miles Davis 49
 Al Di Meola 52
 Maynard Ferguson 70
 Jan Garbarek 73
 Dave Holland 92
 Bobby McFerrin 130
 piano 155
 In a Silent Way 98
 Tommy Smith 185
 Steve Swallow 192
 Miroslav Vitous 208
 Joe Zawinul 223
cornet **43**
 Louis Armstrong 6
 Bix Beiderbecke **12**
 Buddy Bolden **19–20**
 Philipe Brun 25
 in early jazz xxvi
 W. C. Handy 84
 Freddie Keppard **112–113**
 King Oliver **147–148**
 "Singin' the Blues" 182
Coryell, Larry 20, 26, 80
Cosby, Bill 174
Costello, Elvis 72, 114
Cotton Club **43–44**, 60, 85, 93
"Cotton Tail" (Duke Ellington) 213
counterpoint 24, **44**
country and western (C&W) 276*g*
cover versions 277*g*
Cox, Anthony **44**
crash cymbal **44**
Crayton, Pee Wee 36
"Crazy Blues" (Mamie Smith recording)
 184
Creole Jazz Band (King Oliver) 53, 54, 84,
 147–148
"Creole Rhapsody" (Duke Ellington) 115

Creoles 150
crescendo 277*g*
Crispell, Marilyn **44–45**, 46
criticism. *See* scholarship
Crosby, Bing 56, 206
Crossings (Herbie Hancock) 83, 117
crossover jazz 13, **45**
Crouch, Stanley 106
Crump, E. H. 84
Cruz, Adam 43
Cuba. *See also* Latin and Afro-Cuban jazz
 Mario Bauzá 11
 Ruben Gonzalez 76
 Latin and Afro-Cuban jazz 121
 Machito 125
 Chico O'Farrill 147
 Chano Pozo 157
 Gonzalo Rubalcaba 166
 Arturo Sandoval 170
 Mongo Santamaria 170
 Compay Segundo 174
"Cubana Be, Cubana Bop" (George
 Russell) 157, 166
Cugat, Xavier 125
cut and record 277*g*
cutting contest **45–46**, 87, 212
cymbal 44, 91, 164–165
Cyrille, Andrew **46**
Czechoslovakia 80–81, 207–208

D

dancing 125, 170–171
Dankworth, John 120
Davis, Art 41
Davis, Eddie "Lockjaw" 174
Davis, Ernestine "Tiny" **47**, 99
Davis, Miles **47–51**, *48, 50*
 Muhal Richard Abrams 1
 acid jazz 2
 Cannonball Adderly 3
 Birdland 15
 Birth of the Cool **15**
 Bitches Brew **15–16**
 Art Blakey 17
 Clifford Brown 23
 Benny Carter 29
 Ron Carter 30
 Paul Chambers 30
 Billy Cobham 35
 John Coltrane 39, 40
 and cool jazz xxiv
 Chick Corea 42
 Jack DeJohnette 51
 Eric Dolphy 55
 Duke Ellington 62
 "E.S.P." **63**
 Bill Evans 65–66
 Gil Evans 67–68

 fusion xxv, 72
 Kenny Garrett 73
 Herbie Hancock 82, 83
 Coleman Hawkins 87
 Dave Holland 92
 Shirley Horn 93
 In a Silent Way **98**
 Ahmad Jamal 102
 Keith Jarrett 104
 jazz firsts 117
 Philly Joe Jones 109
 Thad Jones 110
 Kind of Blue **113**
 John McLaughlin 130–131
 Marcus Miller 134–135
 Charles Mingus 135
 modal jazz 138
 Thelonious Monk 139
 Gerry Mulligan 141
 Charlie Parker 152
 Sonny Rollins 165
 Gunther Schuller 172
 John Scofield 172
 Sonny Sharrock 175
 Wayne Shorter 178, 179
 Horace Silver 180
 Clark Terry 196
 Miroslav Vitous 207
 wah-wah pedal 209
 Tony Williams 216
 Larry Young 219
 Joe Zawinul 223
Davis, Steve 43, 142
Decca Records 7, 84
decrescendo 277*g*
DeFrancesco, Joey **51**
Deitch, Adam 173
DeJohnette, Jack **51**
 John Abercrombie 1
 Bitches Brew 15
 Herbie Hancock 83
 Dave Holland 92
 Charles Lloyd 124
 Pat Metheny 134
 Michel Petrucciani 154
 John Surman 191
 Miroslav Vitous 207
Delta blues 277*g*
DeLucia, Paco 52, 132
de Marky, Paul 153
Dennerlein, Barbara **51–52**
Dennis, Willie 19
Desmond, Paul 21, 24, 197
Detroit, Michigan
 Pepper Adams 3
 Donald Byrd 26
 Paul Chambers 30
 Alice Coltrane 38
 Barry Harris 86

Detroit, Michigan *(continued)*
   Joe Henderson 90
   Yusef Lateef 121
diatonic harmony 277*g*
Dibango, Manu 20
"Digression" (Lennie Tristano) 199
Di Meola, Al 43, **52,** 81, 132
"Dipper Mouth Blues" (King Oliver)
   52–53, 147
disco 277*g*
dissonance **53,** 139, 194
Diva 53
Dixieland jazz 9, **53,** 91, 277*g*
DIY (Do-It-Yourself) 277*g*
DJ (deejay) 277*g*
DJ Logic 133
Dludlu, Jimmy 187
Dodds, Baby 52, **53–54,** 147
Dodds, Johnny 52, **54,** 94, 147
Dolphy, Eric *54,* **54–55**
   Ed Blackwell 16
   The Blues and the Abstract Truth 19
   John Coltrane 40
   Free Jazz (Ornette Coleman) 71
   Chico Hamilton 80
   Freddie Hubbard 95
   Charles Mingus 136
   Out There 150
   George Russell 167
   saxophone 171
   Steve Swallow 191
   Tony Williams 216
   Lester Young 220
Donaldson, Lou 183, 219
Donegan, Dorothy 55
"Don't Worry, Be Happy" (Bobby
   McFerrin) 130
Doo Bop (Miles Davis) 2, 51, 117
Dorham, Kenny 180
Dorsey, Jimmy **55–56,** 56, 134, 163, 214
Dorsey, Tommy **56**
   Jimmy Dorsey 55
   Fletcher Henderson 89–90
   Glenn Miller 134
   Ma Rainey 161
   Buddy Rich 164
   Paul Whiteman 214
   Mary Lou Williams 215
Dorsey Brothers Orchestra 55
double bass **56**
   Jimmy Blanton **18**
   Ray Brown **24**
   Ron Carter **29–30**
   Paul Chambers **30**
   Stanley Clarke **34–35**
   Anthony Cox **44**
   in early New Orleans jazz xxii
   Malachi Favors **69**
   Charlie Haden **79**

Dave Holland **92**
   Charles Mingus **135–137**
   Oscar Pettiford **154**
   rhythm section 164
   Steve Swallow 191–192
   Miroslav Vitous **207–208**
double time 19, **56**
Down Beat magazine 55, **56–57,** 142
"Down Hearted Blues" (Alberta Hunter
   recording) 95
"Downhearted Blues" (Bessie Smith
   recording) 183
"Down Home Blues" (Ethel Waters) 162
Drew, Kenny 19
drug abuse 49, 67, 140, 152, 157
drums **57.** *See also* percussion
   Cindy Blackman **16**
   Ed Blackwell **16–17**
   Art Blakey **17–18**
   Sid Catlett **30**
   Kenny Clarke **34**
   Billy Cobham **35**
   crash cymbal **44**
   Andrew Cyrille **46**
   Jack DeJohnette **51**
   Baby Dodds **53–54**
   Chico Hamilton **80**
   Lionel Hampton **81**
   hi-hat cymbal **91**
   Elvin Jones **108–109**
   Philly Joe Jones **109**
   Gene Krupa **114–115**
   Mel Lewis **122**
   rhythm section 164
   Buddy Rich **164**
   ride cymbal **164–165**
   ride rhythm **165**
   Max Roach **165**
   George Russell 166
   shuffle rhythm **179**
   Zoot Sims 182
   Chick Webb **212**
   Tony Williams **216**
   Shadow Wilson **218**
Duke, George 104, 172
Dutrey, Honore 52, 147
DVD (digital video disc) 277*g*

E

early jazz. *See* traditional jazz
*Early Jazz: Its Roots and Musical
   Development* (Gunther Schuller) **59**
early jazz recordings. *See* recordings of
   early jazz
Eastman School of Music 29, 125, 171
East St. Louis, Illinois 47
Eastwood, Clint 86
easy listening 277*g*

Easy Mo Bee 51, 117
Eckstine, Billy
   Miles Davis 48
   Dexter Gordon 77
   Johnny Hartman 86
   Earl "Fatha" Hines 91
   Hank Jones 109
   Quincy Jones 110
   Charlie Parker 151
   Sonny Stitt 187
   Sarah Vaughn 205
ECM Records 41, 72, 73, 104–105, 191,
   208
Edna Croudson's RhythmGirls 13
educators
   AACM **7**
   Muhal Richard Abrams **2**
   Berklee College of Music **14**
   Gary Burton **26**
   Donald Byrd 26
   Benny Carter 29
   Don Cherry 32
   Andrew Cyrille 46
   Barry Harris **86**
   Stan Kenton 112
   Yusef Lateef 121
   Melba Liston 123
   Wynton Marsalis 128–129
   Marian McPartland **132**
   George Russell **166–167**
   Gunther Schuller 172
   Lennie Tristano 199
   Attila Zoller 224
Either/Orchestra 59
El Corazón (Don Cherry/Ed Blackwell)
   16–17
Eldridge, Roy 34, 45, **59–60,** 76, 137, 197
electric bass (bass guitar) **10–11**
   Richard Bona **20**
   Stanley Clarke **34–35**
   Marcus Miller **134–135**
   Jaco Pastorius **152**
   Steve Swallow **191–192**
Electric Bath (Don Ellis) 62
electric guitar. *See* guitar
electric piano 42, 155
electronic keyboards 134, 190. *See also*
   synthesizer
electronic music 122, 277*g*
Electronic Wind Instrument (EWI) 22
Ellington, Duke xxiii, *5,* **60–62,** *61*
   Ivie Anderson 4
   And His Mother Called Him Bill (Duke
   Ellington) **4–5**
   Louis Armstrong 6
   bebop xxiv, 12
   Tony Bennett 13
   "Black and Tan Fantasy" **16**
   Jimmy Blanton 18

Buddy Bolden 20
Carnegie Hall 27–28
Benny Carter 28
Cotton Club 44
European jazz 64
Gil Evans 67
Abdullah Ibrahim 97
"In a Sentimental Mood" **98**
"It Don't Mean a Thing (If It Ain't Got
    That Swing)" **99**
Japanese jazz 103
jazz firsts 116
Cleo Laine 120
Melba Liston 123
Charles Mingus 136
Newport Jazz Festival 144
New York City 144
Oscar Pettiford 154
Django Reinhardt 164
Savoy Ballroom 171
South African jazz 186
Billy Strayhorn 5, 188, 189
"Take the 'A' Train" (Billy Strayhorn)
    193
Clark Terry 196
third stream jazz 197
Ben Webster 213
Ellington, Mercer 61, 73, 132
Ellis, Don **62,** 70
Ellis, Herb 153
Encyclopedia of Jazz (Leonard Feather) **62,**
70
Ennis, Skinnay 67
ensemble **62.** *See also* combo
    arrangement 6
    big band **14**
    combo **41**
    instrumentation in early jazz xxvi
    quartet **159**
    quintet **159**
    rhythm section **164**
"Epistrophy" (Thelonious Monk) 34,
    62–63, 218
Ervin, Booker 19
Escalator Over the Hill (Carla Bley) 18, 127
"E.S.P." (Miles Davis) **63**
"Eternal Triangle" (Dizzy Gillespie/Sonny
    Stitt recording) 188
Europe, American jazz musicians in
    Chet Baker 9
    Sidney Bechet 12
    Benny Carter 28
    Don Cherry 31
    Kenny Clarke 34
    Miles Davis 51
    Eric Dolphy 55
    Duke Ellington 60–61
    James Reese Europe 63
    Dexter Gordon 77

Coleman Hawkins 87
    JATP 106
    Thad Jones 110
    Steve Lacy 119
    Stuff Smith 184
Europe, James Reese **63,** 116, 162, 207
European jazz **63–65**
    Richard Bona 20
    Philipe Brun **25**
    Jan Garbarek **73**
    Dave Holland **92**
    Hot Club de France **94**
    John McLaughlin **130–132**
    Jean Luc Ponty **156**
    Django Reinhardt **163–164**
    Tommy Smith **185**
Evans, Bill **65–67,** 66
    Tony Bennett 13
    The Blues and the Abstract Truth 19
    Jim Hall 80
    Herbie Hancock 82
    Philly Joe Jones 109
    Kind of Blue 113
    George Russell 167
    David Sanborn 169
    Lennie Tristano 199
    Waltz for Debby 210
Evans, Gil **67–68**
    John Abercrombie 1
    Miles Davis 49, 51
    Steve Lacy 119
    Gerry Mulligan 141
    progressive jazz 158
    Maria Schneider 171
    Gunther Schuller 172
    Andy Sheppard 177
    Tony Williams 216
Evers, Medgar 181
Everybody Digs Bill Evans 65
EWI. *See* Electronic Wind Instrument 22
Extrapolation (John McLaughlin) 191

F

Facing You (Keith Jarrett) 105
Fairfax, Frankie 218
falsetto 277*g*
"Far Away" (Chet Baker/Astrud Gilberto
    recording) 75
Farmer, Addison 69
Farmer, Art **69**
    Jim Hall 80
    Lionel Hampton 81
    Chico O'Farrill 147
    Horace Silver 180
    Billy Strayhorn 189
    Steve Swallow 192
    Miroslav Vitous 207
    Nancy Wilson 218

Farrell, Joe 43
Favors, Malachi 6, **69**
Feather, Leonard 62, **69–70,** 172
Featherstonhaugh, Buddy 64
"Feels So Good" (Chuck Mangione)
    125
Fender, Leo 10
Fender bass. *See* electric bass
Ferguson, Maynard **70**
    Pepper Adams 3
    Stan Kenton 112
    Oscar Peterson 153
    Wayne Shorter 178
    Dinah Washington 211
    Joe Zawinul 223
festivals. *See* jazz festivals
"Fever" (Peggy Lee recording) 121
52nd Street, New York City 184, 213
fill **70**
Fillmore West 124
films. *See* movies
finger-picking 277*g*
Fitzgerald, Ella **70–71**
    "A-Tisket A-Tasket" 7
    Ray Brown 24
    Duke Ellington 61
    Dizzy Gillespie 75
    Jim Hall 80
    Chico Hamilton 80
    Japanese jazz 103
    JATP 106
    Hank Jones 109
    Oscar Peterson 153
    Savoy Ballroom 171
    scat singing 171
    Clark Terry 196
    Dinah Washington 211
    Chick Webb 212
    Shadow Wilson 218
Five Spot (New York City) 36
Flack, Roberta 135
Flanagan, Tommy 74, 185
flat 277*g*
flat pick 277–278*g*
flip side 278*g*
Florida 3, 152, 170
flugelhorn **71**
    Chet Baker 9
    Art Farmer **69**
    Freddie Hubbard 95
    Thad Jones **110**
    Chuck Mangione **125–126**
    Clark Terry 196
flute 54–55, **71,** 114, 121, 124, 126
"Flying Home" (Lionel Hampton
    recording) 81, 101
folk music 19, 278*g*
For Alto (Anthony Braxton) 22
form. *See* song form

Hammer, Jan 65, **80–81,** 99, 131, 192, 207
Hammond, John 158
Hammond B-3 organ 51, 92, 133, 148, 183
Hampton, Lionel **81**
   Betty Carter 29
   Art Farmer 69
   Benny Goodman 76
   Dexter Gordon 76
   Illinois Jacquet 101
   Quincy Jones 109
   Charles Mingus 135
   Wes Montgomery 139
   Oscar Peterson 153
   Jimmy Scott 173
   Sir Charles Thompson 197
   Dinah Washington 211
   Shadow Wilson 218
Hancock, Herbie 50, **81–83,** *82*
   Richard Bona 20
   Michael Brecker 22
   Ron Carter 30
   Miles Davis 49
   "E.S.P." 63
   Headhunters **88**
   Joe Henderson 90
   Dave Holland 92
   In a Silent Way 98
   jazz firsts 117
   Bobby McFerrin 130
   Jaco Pastorius 152
   piano 155
   Diane Reeves 163
   "Rockit" **165**
   synthesizer 192
   Miroslav Vitous 207
   "Watermelon Man" 211
   Tony Williams 216
   Attilla Zoller 224
Handy, John 19
Handy, W. C. **84,** 187
hard bop xxiv, **84**
   Pepper Adams 3
   Cannonball Adderly **3**
   Art Blakey **17–18**
   The Blues and the Abstract Truth **19**
   Blue Train **19**
   Clifford Brown 24
   Donald Byrd 26
   Jim Cifelli 33
   Chick Corea 42
   Art Farmer 69
   Roy Hargrove 84
   Joe Henderson 90
   Elvin Jones 108
   Chuck Mangione 125
   Moanin' (Blakey) **137–138**
   Lee Morgan **140**
   prominent artists xxxii
   Sonny Rollins 165

Wayne Shorter 177
Horace Silver **179–181**
Sun Ra 190
time line 252
Mary Lou Williams 216
Hardin, Lil **84**
   "Dipper Mouth Blues" 52
   Baby Dodds 53
   Hot Five and Hot Seven 94
   Alberta Hunter 95
   King Oliver 147
   women in jazz xxx
Hardwicke, Otto 60
Hargrove, Roy **84–85**
Harlem **85**
   Cotton Club **43–44**
   Billie Holiday 91
   Minton's Playhouse **137**
   Savoy Ballroom **170–171**
   Mamie Smith 184
   "Stompin' at the Savoy" (Charlie Christian recording) 188
   Chick Webb 212
Harlem Hellfighters 63
Harlem Playgirls 47
Harlem Renaissance **85**
Harley, Rufus **85–86**
"harmolodics" 37
harmony 12, 53, 278*g. See also* chord; chord changes
harp 38
Harris, Barry **86**
Harris, Craig 44
Harris, Eddie 1
Harrison, Jimmy 195
Hart, Billy 83
Hartman, Johnny **86**
Hauser, Tim 126
Havana, Cuba 76, 174
Hawkins, Coleman *87,* **87–88**
   "Body and Soul" **19**
   Benny Carter 28
   cutting contest 45
   Andrew Cyrille 46
   Miles Davis 49
   Roy Eldridge 60
   Duke Ellington 61
   European jazz 64
   Dizzy Gillespie 75
   Barry Harris 86
   Fletcher Henderson 89
   Hank Jones 109
   Oscar Pettiford 154
   Max Roach 165
   Sonny Rollins 165
   saxophone 171
   Horace Silver 179
   Mamie Smith 184
   Jack Teagarden 195
   Sir Charles Thompson 197

   Ben Webster 212
   Lester Young 219, 220
Hayes, Edgar 34
Haynes, Roy 19, 40
Hayton, Lennie 80
head **88**
head arrangement **88**
Headhunters (Herbie Hancock) 81, 83, **88**
headliner **88**
The Hearinga Suite (Muhal Richard Abrams) 2
Heath, Percy 138
heavy metal 278*g*
Heavy Weather (Weather Report) 15
"Heebie Jeebies" (Louis Armstrong) 6, **88–89,** 116, 162
Hefti, Neal 90
Hell Divers 47
Henderson, Fletcher **89,** **89–90**
   Benny Carter 28
   Sid Catlett 30
   Roy Eldridge 59
   Dexter Gordon 77
   Coleman Hawkins 87
   jazz firsts 116
   Ma Rainey 161
   recordings of early jazz 162
   Don Redman 163
   Savoy Ballroom 171
   Bessie Smith 183
   Sun Ra 189
   Jack Teagarden 195
   Sir Charles Thompson 197
   Fats Waller 209
   Ethel Waters 211
   Ben Webster 213
Henderson, Joe 16, **90,** 140, 154, 180
Hendricks, Jon 120
Hendrix, Jimi 68, 209, 219
Henry, Ernie 23
Hentoff, Nat 114, 213
Herman, Woody **90–91**
   Tony Bennett 13
   Stan Getz 74
   Joe Lovano 124
   Oscar Pettiford 154
   Tito Puente 158
   Zoot Sims 182
   Shadow Wilson 218
heroin 49
Herzog, Arthur, Jr. 76
Heywood, Eddie 76
Higgins, Billy 31, 36, 71, 174, 211
hi-hat cymbal **91**
Hill, Teddy 59, 137
Hilliard Ensemble 73
Hines, Earl "Fatha" 86, **91,** 94, 218
hip-hop 278*g*
   acid jazz **2–3**
   The Bad Plus 9

Miles Davis 51
    New Birth Brass Band 143
    Courtney Pine 155
    "Rockit" **165**
    Andy Sheppard 177
Hobson, Wilder 4
Hodges, Johnny 39, 61, 212
Holder, Terrence 215
Holiday, Billie **91–92**
    Barbara Carroll 28
    Miles Davis 48
    "God Bless the Child" **76**
    Savoy Ballroom 171
    Artie Shaw 176
    Lester Young 220
Holland, Dave **92**
    John Abercrombie 1
    Bitches Brew 15
    Anthony Braxton 22
    Conference of the Birds **41**
    Chick Corea 42
    Anthony Cox 44
    Miles Davis 49
    Charles Lloyd 124
    John McLaughlin 131
    In a Silent Way 98
Holmes, Richard "Groove" **92,** 129, 148
holy blues 278*g*
hook 278*g*
Hopps, Jimmy 98
Horn, Paul 80
Horn, Shirley **93,** 93
Horne, Lena 80, **93–94,** 117, 176, 211
Hornsby, Bruce 127
Horvitz, Wayne 72
hot **94**
Hot Chocolates (revue) 27, 210
Hot Club de France **94**
Hot Five and Hot Seven xxiii, **94**
    Louis Armstrong 6
    Baby Dodds 53
    Johnny Dodds 54
    Lil Hardin 84
    "Heebie Jeebies" **88–89**
    Earl "Fatha" Hines 91
    recordings of early jazz 162
hot jazz xxiii, xxxii, 47, 94, **94–95,** 144, 163
house band **95,** 212
Howard Theater (Washington, D.C.) 99
Howard University 99
Hubbard, Freddie **95**
    Art Blakey 17
    The Blues and the Abstract Truth 19
    John Coltrane 40
    Malachi Favors 69
    Free Jazz (Ornette Coleman) 71
    Kenny Garrett 73
    Joe Henderson 90
    Michel Petrucciani 154

Diane Reeves 163
    Miroslav Vitous 207
    "Watermelon Man" 211
Humphrey, Bobbi 135
Hungary 224
Hunter, Alberta 7, **95,** 209
Hussain, Zakir 132
Hutchinson, Gregory 185
Hylton, Jack 25, 87

I

Ibrahim, Abdullah **97,** 186, 187
"I Loves You Porgy" (Nina Simone recording) 181
improvisation xxviii, **97,** 185, 192
Impulse! Records 124
"In a Mist" (Bix Beiderbecke) 144
"In a Sentimental Mood" (Duke Ellington/John Coltrane recording) **98**
In a Silent Way (Miles Davis) **98**
    Chick Corea 42
    Miles Davis 49
    Dave Holland 92
    jazz firsts 117
    John McLaughlin 131
    Joe Zawinul 223
Incognito 2
The Incredible Jazz Guitar of Wes Montgomery **98**
The Inflated Tear (Rahsaan Roland Kirk) **98,** 114
inflection **98**
The Inner Mounting Flame (John McLaughlin and the Mahavishnu Orchestra) **99**
instrumental background 165
integration 196
interaction xxix
"Interlude in B-flat" (Artie Shaw) 176
International Association of Jazz Educators 196
international jazz groups 117
International Sweethearts of Rhythm xxx–xxxi, 47, **99,** 130
interval 278*g*
In the Light (Keith Jarrett) 105
"Intuition" (Lennie Tristano) 199
"I Put a Spell on You" (Nina Simone recording) 181
Irakere 170
"It Don't Mean a Thing (If It Ain't Got That Swing)" (Duke Ellington) 4, **99,** 116
Iverson, Ethan 9

J

Jack Johnson (Miles Davis) 131, 175
Jackson, D. D. **101**
Jackson, Michael 109, 110, 183

Jackson, Milt 62, **90–91,** 123, 138, 188
Jackson, Mississippi 217
Jackson, Paul 88
Jacquet, Illinois 81, 86, **101,** 197
Jagger, Mick 81
JALC. *See* Jazz at Lincoln Center
jam **102**
Jamal, Ahmad **102**
jam bands 132, 173
James, Harry 48, **102,** 198
jam session **102**
    Birdland 15
    Jimmy Blanton 18
    Carnegie Hall 28
    Charlie Christian 33
    cutting contest **45–46**
    Keith Jarrett 104
    JATP **106**
    Minton's Playhouse **137**
    Mary Lou Williams 216
Japan 3–4, 116, 126, 197
Japanese jazz **102–103**
Jarman, Joseph 6
Jarreau, Al **103–104**
Jarrett, Keith *104,* **104–105**
    Art Blakey 17
    Jack DeJohnette 51
    Jan Garbarek 73
    Charlie Haden 79
    Charles Lloyd 124
JATP. *See* Jazz at the Philharmonic
jazz **105**
    brief history of xxii–xxv
    definition xxi
    jazz firsts 116–117
    in movies. *See* movies, jazz in
    time line 252
Jazz Advance (Cecil Taylor) 194
the Jazz Age xxiii, **105–106,** 144, 188–189, 206
Jazz at Lincoln Center (JALC) x–xi, **106,** 128
Jazz at Lincoln Center Hall of Fame **273**
Jazz at Massey Hall (Charlie Parker/Dizzy Gillespie/Bud Powell/Charles Mingus/Max Roach) 157
Jazz at the Philharmonic (JATP) **106**
    Ray Brown 24
    cutting contest **45–46**
    Roy Eldridge 60
    Dizzy Gillespie 75
    Coleman Hawkins 87–88
    Illinois Jacquet 101
    Japanese jazz 103
    Hank Jones 109
    Gene Krupa 115
    Oscar Peterson 153
    Ben Webster 213
    Lester Young 220
jazz clubs 14–15

Metheny, Pat *133*, **133–134**
    Richard Bona 20
    Michael Brecker 22
    Gary Burton 26
    guitar synthesizer 78
    Jim Hall 80
    Dave Holland 92
    Jaco Pastorius 152
    Still Life Talking **187**
    Tony Williams 216
    Attilla Zoller 224
Miami Vice (theme music) 81
Middle Eastern music 121
MIDI (Musical Instrument Digital
    Interface) **134,** 279*g*
Miles Ahead (Miles Davis/Gil Evans) 68
Miles Davis and the Modern Jazz Giants 139
Milestones (Miles Davis) 3
Miley, Bubber 16, 184
Milhuad, Darius 24
Miller, Glenn 55, **134,** 195
Miller, Marcus 50, 74, **134–135,** 152
Mills College (Oakland, California) 22, 24
Mingus, Charles **135–136,** *136*
    Pepper Adams 3
    Toshiko Akiyoshi 4
    Jimmy Blanton 18
    Blues and Roots **19**
    Eric Dolphy 54, 55
    double bass 56
    Duke Ellington 61
    Chico Hamilton 80
    Lionel Hampton 81
    Illinois Jacquet 101
    Rahsaan Roland Kirk 114
    Yusef Lateef 121
    Mingus Ah Um **136**
    Red Norvo 145
    Charlie Parker 151, 152
    Gunther Schuller 172
    John Scofield 172
    third stream jazz 197
Mingus, Sue 137
Mingus Ah Um (Charles Mingus) **136**
Mingus Big Band 107, 136, **136–137**
Minimoog 192
minor 279*g*
minstrel 279*g*
Minton, Henry 137
Minton's Playhouse **137**
    Jimmy Blanton 18
    Kenny Clarke 34
    Miles Davis 48
    Harlem 85
    Thelonious Monk 139
    Bud Powell 156
Mississippi 99, 219
"Mississippi Goddam!" (Nina Simone) 181
"Misty" (Erroll Garner) 73, 92
Mitchell, Blue 42

Mitchell, Joni 22, 83, 152, 178
Mitchell, Red 31
Mitchell, Roscoe 6, 20, 21, 122, **137**
Moanin' (Art Blakey and the Jazz
    Messengers) **137–138**
Mobley, Hank 86, 180, 219
modal jazz xxiv, **138**
    John Coltrane 40
    Miles Davis 49
    Bill Evans 65
    Kind of Blue **113**
    "My Favorite Things" **142**
    George Russell 166
    Sun Ra 190
    time line 252
    McCoy Tyner 200
    Larry Young 219
modern jazz xxiv–xxv
Modern Jazz Quartet 34, **138,** 172, 197
modes 279*g*
Moffett, Charnett 83, 175
Moholo, Louis 187
Monk, Thelonious **138–139**
    bebop 12
    Birdland 15
    Ed Blackwell 16
    Art Blakey 17
    Brilliant Corners **23**
    Donald Byrd 26
    Kenny Clarke 34
    John Coltrane 40
    "Epistrophy" **62–63**
    Dizzy Gillespie 75
    Barry Harris 86
    Coleman Hawkins 87
    Steve Lacy 119
    Minton's Playhouse 137
    Charlie Parker 151, 152
    Oscar Pettiford 154
    Bud Powell 156
    Sonny Rollins 165
    "Stompin' at the Savoy" (Charlie
        Christian recording) 188
    "Straight, No Chaser" **188**
    tone cluster 198
    McCoy Tyner 200
    Mary Lou Williams 216
    Shadow Wilson 218
Monogram Theater (Chicago) 7
Monroe, Clark 85
Monterey Jazz Festival 4, 139, **139,** 156
Montgomery, Wes 30, 72, 81, 98, 129, **139**
Montreal Jazz Festival 166
Montreux Jazz Festival **139,** 166, 191
"Mood Indigo" (Duke Ellington) 60
Moog synthesizer 192
Moreira, Airto 43, 52
Morello, Joe 24
Morgan, Edwin 185
Morgan, Lee 19, 86, 137, 138, **140**

MOR (middle-of-the-road) 279*g*
Morton, Jelly Roll (Ferdinand Joseph La
    Menthe) *140,* **140–141**
    "Black Bottom Stomp" **16**
    definition of jazz xxii
    Baby Dodds 53
    Scott Joplin 110
    New Orleans jazz 143
    Kid Ory 150
    piano 155
    ragtime 161
    Stuff Smith 184
Moses, Bob 26
Moten, Bennie 10, 111, **141,** 212–213
"Moten Swing" (Bennie Moten) 213
Motian, Paul 65, 104, 124, 210
movement 279*g*
movies, jazz in 255–257
    Benny Carter 29
    Jimmy Dorsey 56
    Duke Ellington 61
    Chico Hamilton 80
    Herbie Hancock 82
    Lena Horne 93
    Peggy Lee 121
    soundies **185**
Mulligan, Gerry *141,* **141–142**
    Pepper Adams 3
    Chet Baker 9, 80
    Birth of the Cool **15**
    Dave Brubeck 25
    Gil Evans 67
    Art Farmer 69
    Chico Hamilton 80
    Mel Lewis 122
    Gunther Schuller 172
    John Scofield 172
    Lester Young 220
multi-instrumentalists
    Rahsaan Roland Kirk **113–114**
    Yusef Lateef **121**
    Roscoe Mitchell **137**
multiphonics **142**
"Mumbles" (Clark Terry) 196
Murphy, Jess 173
museums 4
Musica Electronica Viva 119
music videos 83, 185
mute 51, **142**
"My Baby Just Cares for Me" (Nina
    Simone recording) 181
"My Favorite Things" (John Coltrane
    recording) 40, **142**

N

Nance, Ray 189
National Association of Jazz Educators
    163
National Medal of Arts 29, 81

National Public Radio (NPR) 23, 218
Natural Black Inventions (Rahsaan Roland Kirk) 114
Navarro, Fats 81
NBC 196
Nelson, Oliver 19
New Air 217
New Birth Brass Band 143
New England Conservatory of Music 28, 167, 172, 208
New Jersey 10
New Music Distribution Service (NMDS) 127
New Orleans jazz (classic) xxii–xxiii, **143,** 229
   Louis Armstrong 6
   banjo 9
   Emma Barrett **10**
   Sidney Bechet 12
   "Black and Tan Fantasy" 16
   "Black Bottom Stomp" **16**
   Buddy Bolden **19–20**
   Chicago jazz 32
   cutting contest 45
   Dixieland jazz 53
   Baby Dodds 53–54
   Johnny Dodds **54**
   double bass 56
   W. C. Handy 84
   hot jazz **94–95**
   jazz firsts 116
   Freddie Keppard **112–113**
   "Livery Stable Blues" **124**
   Jelly Roll Morton 140, **140–141**
   King Oliver 147–148
   Original Dixieland Jazz Band 148–150
   Kid Ory 150
   Preservation Hall, New Orleans **157–158**
   prominent artists xxxii
   recordings of early jazz 162
   Storyville **188**
   time line 252
   traditional jazz 198
   trombone 199
New Orleans jazz (contemporary) 16, 127, 143
New Orleans Jazz & Heritage Festival 143
Newport Jazz Festival **143–144**
   Dave Brubeck 25
   Coleman Hawkins 88
   Abdullah Ibrahim 97
   jazz firsts 117
   Charles Mingus 136
   Cecil Taylor 194
   Joe Venuti 206
New York City **144**
   Pepper Adams 3
   Cannonball Adderly 3
   Mario Bauzá 11

bebop 11–12
Birdland **14–15**
Carla Bley 18
Carnegie Hall **27–28**
Benny Carter 28
Billy Cobham 35
Duke Ellington 60
James Reese Europe 63
Bill Evans 65
Dizzy Gillespie 75
Dexter Gordon 77
Harlem. *See* Harlem
JALC **106**
James P. Johnson 107
Yusef Lateef 121
Mel Lewis 122
Machito 125
Charles Mingus 135
Mingus Big Band 136
Minton's Playhouse **137**
Chico O'Farrill 147
recordings of early jazz 162
Max Roach 165
Pharoah Sanders 169
Artie Shaw 175–176
Horace Silver 179–180
Mamie Smith 184
Stuff Smith 184
Lennie Tristano 198
Joe Venuti 206
Tony Williams 216
Cassandra Wilson 217
John Zorn 224–225
New York Contemporary Five 31, 177
New York Philharmonic 215
Ngqawana, Zim 187
Nichols, Red 206
A Night at the Village Vanguard (Sonny Rollins) 166
nightclubs and ballrooms 14–15, 43–44, 170–171
Nighthawk Syncopators 59
NMDS. *See* New Music Distribution Service
nonet 15, 49, 67, **144**
Norvo, Red 135, **144–145,** 224
Norway 73
notation 279*g*
note values 279*g*
Novosel, Steve 98
NPR. *See* National Public Radio
"Nuages" (Django Reinhardt) 164

O

oboe 121
Ochs, Larry 166
octave 279*g*
Odyssey of Iska (Wayne Shorter) 178
O'Farrill, Chico **147**

"Oh Daddy" (Ethel Waters) 162
OKeh Records 6, 162, 184
Oklahoma 33
Olaine, Jason 3
Old and New Dreams 16, 79
Oliver, Joseph "King" **147–148,** *148*
   Louis Armstrong 6
   in Chicago xxiii
   cornet 43
   "Dipper Mouth Blues" **52–53**
   Baby Dodds 53, 54
   Johnny Dodds 54
   Lil Hardin xxx, 84
   Alberta Hunter 95
   New Orleans jazz 143
   Kid Ory 150
   recordings of early jazz 162
On the Corner (Miles Davis) 2, 50
Onyx Club 184
opus 279*g*
organ 148. *See also* Hammond B-3 organ
   Count Basie 10
   Joey DeFrancesco **51**
   Barbara Dennerlein **51–52**
   Groove Holmes **92**
   John Medeski 133
   Shirley Scott **173–174**
   Jimmy Smith **183**
   Sun Ra 190
   Sir Charles Thompson 197
   Fats Waller 209
   Larry Young **219**
Original Dixieland Jazz Band **148–150,** *149,* 229
   Dixieland jazz 53
   jazz 105
   jazz firsts 116
   "Livery Stable Blues" **124**
   recordings of early jazz 162
Original Tuxedo Jazz Band 10
Origin (Chick Corea band) 43
Ornstein School of Music 38
Ory, Kid 94, 116, 135, 147, **150,** 162, 229
Oscar Awards 121
Out There (Eric Dolphy) 55, **150**
Out to Lunch (Eric Dolphy) 55, 216
Outward Bound (Eric Dolphy) 55
overdubbing **150**
Oxley, Tony 130

P

Pace, Harry Herbert 116, 162
Page, Oran "Hot Lips" 15, 109
Palomar Ballroom, Los Angeles 76
Panama 35
Paradise in Harlem (film) 184
Paramount Records 7, 162
Paris, France 119, 157, 177
Paris Opera 191

Rollins, Sonny (continued)
    Courtney Pine 155
    Saxophone Colossus 171
    Lester Young 220
Ross, Annie 120
Ross, Diana 123
'Round Midnight (film) 77, 82
Rova Saxophone Quartet 51, 166
royalties 280g
Rubalcaba, Gonzalo 52, 124, 166
Russell, Curly 169
Russell, George 166–167
    Don Ellis 62
    Bill Evans 65
    Jan Garbarek 73
    modal jazz 138
    Courtney Pine 155
    Gunther Schuller 172
    Andy Sheppard 177
    Steve Swallow 191
    third stream jazz 197

S

Sahara (McCoy Tyner) 201
St. Cyr, Johnny 94
St. Louis, Missouri 196
"St. Louis Blues" (W. C. Handy) 84, 188
"St. Thomas" (Sonny Rollins) 171
sales chart. See chart, sales
salsa 280g
"Salt Peanuts" (Dizzy Gillespie) 34, 63, 75,
    152, 169
Sanborn, David 135, 169
Sanders, Pharoah 16, 34, 41, 169–170,
    175, 219
Sandoval, Arturo 170
San Francisco 90, 166
Santamaria, Mongo 42, 170
Santana, Carlos 178
Sargeant, Winthrop 106
Saud, Sulaimon. See Tyner, McCoy
Savoy Ballroom 27, 45, 170–171, 212
saxophone 142, 171. See also multi-instru-
    mentalists; specific saxophones
Saxophone Colossus (Sonny Rollins) 166,
    171
scale 171, 280g
scat singing 171
    Louis Armstrong 6
    Cab Calloway 27
    Betty Carter 29
    Ella Fitzgerald 70
    "Heebie Jeebies" 88–89
    jazz firsts 116
    recordings of early jazz 162
    Stuff Smith 184
    Clark Terry 196
    Mel Torme 198
    Cassandra Wilson 217

Schifrin, Lalo 9
Schneider, Maria 107, 171
scholarship 4, 59, 62, 106
Schuller, Gunther xxiv, 15, 59, 72,
    171–172, 197
Schuur, Diane 172
Scofield, John 172–173, 173
    Gary Burton 26
    Anthony Cox 44
    Bill Frisell 72
    John Medeski 133
    Steve Swallow 192
score 281g
Scotland 185
Scott, Jimmy 35, 173
Scott, Ronnie 92
Scott, Shirley 148, 173–174, 200
Scott, Tony 30, 65
Scranton, Pennsylvania 56
segregation 85, 186
Segundo, Compay 174
sequencer 281g
session 174, 193
set 174
78 (78 RPM record) 6, 61, 99, 281g
Sextant (Herbie Hancock) 83
Shakti 132
Shankar, L. 132
The Shape of Jazz to Come (Ornette
    Coleman) 174–175
sharp 281g
Sharrock, Sonny 175
Shaw, Artie 91, 175–176, 176, 182, 197,
    198
Shaw, Woody 73, 219
Shearing, George 26, 170
"sheets of sound" 40
Shepp, Archie 31, 177, 217
Sheppard, Andy 177, 192
Sheppard, Bob 43
Shorter, Wayne 50, 177–179, 179
    "Birdland" 15
    Bitches Brew 15
    Art Blakey 17
    Miles Davis 49
    "E.S.P." 63
    Maynard Ferguson 70
    Herbie Hancock 82, 83
    In a Silent Way 98
    Bobby McFerrin 130
    Jaco Pastorius 152
    saxophone 171
    Horace Silver 180
    Tony Williams 216
    Joe Zawinul 223
shuffle rhythm 179, 192
side 281g
sideman 179
The Sidewinder (Lee Morgan) 86, 140
Siegel, Janis 126

Silver, Horace 179–181, 180
    Art Blakey 17
    Randy Brecker 22
    Paul Chambers 30
    Stanley Clarke 34
    Billy Cobham 35
    Art Farmer 69
    Joe Henderson 90
    Oscar Peterson 154
    Wayne Shorter 177–178
    Song for My Father 185–186
Simmons, John 62
Simon, Paul 22, 129
Simone, Nina 181, 181–182
Sims, Zoot (John Haley Sims) 182
    Tony Bennett 13
    Dexter Gordon 77
    Woody Herman 90
    Stan Kenton 112
    Steve Swallow 192
Sinatra, Frank 56, 102, 110, 164
Sing a Song of Basie (Lambert, Hendricks,
    and Ross) 120
singers. See vocalists
"Singin' the Blues" (Frankie Trumbauer/
    Bix Beiderbecke recording) 182, 199
Singleton, Zutty 57
Sissle, Noble 93
Sketches of Spain (Miles Davis/Gil Evans)
    49, 68
Skies of America (Ornette Coleman) 37
slap bass 56
slaves and slavery 9, 19
slide guitar 281g
slide trombone 199
Small's Paradise 85
Smith, Bessie 182–183
    Fletcher Henderson 89
    Billie Holiday 91
    Alberta Hunter 95
    Ma Rainey 161
    Don Redman 163
    Fats Waller 209
Smith, Jimmy 51, 148, 183, 200
Smith, Leo 7
Smith, Lonnie Liston 135
Smith, Mamie xxx, 87, 116, 183, 183–184,
    229
Smith, Stuff 184, 207
Smith, Tommy 26, 185
Smith, Willie "the Lion" 28, 45, 184
smooth jazz 125–126, 185, 187
Snowden, Elmer 60
Soft on the Inside Big Band 177
solo 19, 22, 162, 185
Solo Concerts (Keith Jarrett) 105
Something Else! (Ornette Coleman) 36
song form
    AAB 1
    AABA 1

bridge **23**
call-and-response **27**
chorus **33**
Song for My Father (Horace Silver)
  185–186
songster 281*g*
soprano 281*g*
soprano saxophone
  Sidney Bechet **12**
  John Coltrane 38–41
  Ravi Coltrane 41
  Jan Garbarek 73
  Kenny Garrett 73–74
  Abdullah Ibrahim 97
  Steve Lacy **119**
  Branford Marsalis 127
  Roscoe Mitchell 137
  Courtney Pine 155–156
  Don Redman 162
  David Sanborn 169
  Andy Sheppard 177
  Wayne Shorter 177–179
  John Surman 191
soul jazz 200
soul music 3, 281*g*
Sound (Roscoe Mitchell) 137
soundies **185**
soundtracks. *See* movies, jazz in
South, Eddie 207
South African jazz 97, 129, **186–187**
South Carolina 75
Southern Syncopated Orchestra 12, 64
Soviet Union 124
"So What" (Miles Davis) 113
Speaking of Now (Pat Metheny) 20, 134
spirit, vs. style x
spirituals 281*g*
Spivak, Charlie 55
Springsteen, Bruce 169
staff 281*g*
stanza 281*g*
State Department, U.S. 75
Steely Dan 185
Steps Ahead 22
Stewart, Slam 194
Still Life Talking (Pat Metheny) 134, **187**
Sting 68, 74, 127, 171
The Sting (soundtrack) 172
Stitt, Sonny 85, 86, **187–188**
Stockhausen, Karlheinz 21
"Stompin' at the Savoy" (Charlie Christian
  recording) **188**
Stone, Jesse 87
Stormy Weather (film) 93
Storyville **188**
"Straight, No Chaser" (Thelonious Monk)
  188
"Strange Fruit" (Billie Holiday recording)
  92
Strayhorn, Billy 4–5, **188–189**, 193

stride piano **189**
  Count Basie 10
  "Charleston" **30–31**
  Erroll Garner 73
  James P. Johnson **107–108**
  Thelonious Monk 139
  piano 155
  Art Tatum 193
  Fats Waller 209, 210
string bass. *See* double bass
strings 281*g*
stritch 114
style, spirit vs. x
styles. *See* jazz styles, evolution of
suite 281*g*
Sullivan, Ira 152
Summers, Bill 88
Sun Ra xxiv, 169, **189–191**, *190*, 192
SUNY-Buffalo 177
Surman, John 92, 130, **191**, 208
Swallow, Steve 26, 152, **191–192**
swing xxiii, **192**
  Count Basie 10
  big band **14**
  "Black and Tan Fantasy" 16
  Sid Catlett 30
  Baby Dodds 54
  Jimmy Dorsey **55–56**
  Tommy Dorsey **56**
  Roy Eldridge **59–60**
  Erroll Garner 73
  Benny Goodman **76**
  Harlem 85
  Fletcher Henderson **89**
  Woody Herman 90
  International Sweethearts of Rhythm **99**
  "It Don't Mean a Thing (If It Ain't Got
    That Swing)" 99, **99**
  Harry James **102**
  jazz firsts 117
  Kansas City jazz **111**
  Glenn Miller **134**
  Red Norvo 144
  Oscar Peterson 153
  prominent artists xxxii
  Don Redman **163**
  "St. Louis Blues" (Louis Armstrong
    recording) 187
  Artie Shaw **175–176**
  shuffle rhythm 179
  Stuff Smith **184**
  Cecil Taylor 195
  Sir Charles Thompson 197
  time line 252
  Chick Webb **212**
The Swing Era (Gunther Schuller) 172
Switzerland 139
symphony 281*g*
Symphony for Improvisers (Don Cherry)
  16, 31–32

syncopation 161, 192, **192**, 281*g*
synthesizer xxvi, **192**, 281*g*
  Michael Brecker 22
  Barbara Dennerlein 52
  Gil Evans 68
  guitar synthesizer **78**
  Jan Hammer 80–81
  Herbie Hancock 83
  jazz firsts 117
  John McLaughlin 132
  John Surman 191
  Joe Zawinul 223–224
Szabo, Gabor 80

T

Tabackin, Lew 4
"tailgate" trombone style 150
take **193**
"Take Five" (Paul Desmond; Dave Brubeck
  Quartet recording) 25, 197
"Take the 'A' Train" (Billy Strayhorn) 189,
  193
Takin' Off (Herbie Hancock) 82
Tampa Red 161
tango 76
Tatum, Art **193–194**
  Dorothy Donegan 55
  Charles Mingus 135
  Oscar Peterson 154
  piano 155
  Bud Powell 156
  "Tiger Rag" 197
  Lennie Tristano 199
  McCoy Tyner 200
  Ben Webster 213
Taylor, Billy, Sr. 18
Taylor, Cecil **194–195**, *195*
  avant-garde 7
  Andrew Cyrille 46
  Leroy Jenkins 107
  Steve Lacy 119
  Michael Mantler 126
  Archie Shepp 177
  third stream jazz 197
Taylor, Chad 32
Taylor, John 208
Tchicai, John 177
Teagarden, Jack **195**, 214
technique 32, 33, 142, **195**
Teddy Joyce and the Girlfriends 13
television 29, 109, 110
tempo **196**, 281*g*
"Tenderly" (Sarah Vaughn recording) 205
Tennessee 23
tenor 281*g*
tenor saxophone
  Gato Barbieri **9–10**
  Michael Brecker **22**
  John Coltrane **38–41**

tenor saxophone *(continued)*
    Ravi Coltrane **41**
    Jan Garbarek **73**
    Stan Getz **74**
    Dexter Gordon **76–77**
    Coleman Hawkins **87–88**
    Joe Henderson **90**
    Illinois Jacquet **101**
    Yusef Lateef 121
    Charles Lloyd **124**
    Joe Lovano **124**
    Branford Marsalis **127**
    Courtney Pine 155–156
    Sonny Rollins **165–166**
    Pharoah Sanders **169–170**
    Archie Shepp **177**
    Andy Sheppard **177**
    Wayne Shorter **177–179**
    Zoot Sims **182**
    Tommy Smith **185**
    Sonny Stitt 187–188
    Stanley Turrentine **200**
    Ben Webster **212–213**
    Steve Williamson 216–217
    Lester Young **219–221**
territory bands xxiii, 134, 141, 184, **196,** 197
Terry, Clark 23, 81, 163, 192, **196,** 211
Texas 110
Thad Jones—Mel Lewis Orchestra 3, 23, 109, 110, 122
Thelonious Monk Institute of Jazz 82
theme 88, 281*g*
Thiele, Bob 158
Thigpen, Ben 184
third stream jazz xxiv, 171–172, **196–197,** 252*t*
Thomas, Leon 170
Thompson, Gail 155
Thompson, Sir Charles **197**
Thornhill, Claude 67
Thriller (Michael Jackson) 109
thumb picks and finger picks 281*g*
Tiberi, Frank 91
"Tiger Rag" (Art Tatum recording) 193–194, **197**
timbales 158
timbre 281*g*
Time magazine 24–25
Time Out (Dave Brubeck Quartet) 24, 117, **197**
time signature 25, 62, 197, **198,** 281*g*
Timmons, Bobby 137
Tin Pan Alley 281*g*
"Tin Tin Deo" (Dizzy Gillespie) 157
Tjader, Cal 158
TOBA (Theater Owners Booking Association) 7, 182, 183
"To Be Young, Gifted, and Black" (Nina Simone recording) 181

Tokyo, Japan 102
tone cluster 194, **198**
Tonight Show Orchestra 127, 196
Torme, Mel 130, **198**
Town Hall (New York) 4
traditional jazz (classic jazz) 190, **198.** *See also* Chicago jazz; New Orleans jazz (classic); recordings of early jazz; *specific musicians*
map 251
tremolo **198,** 282*g*
Trent, Alphonso 184
tres (Cuban guitar) 174
Tri-Centric Ensemble 22
Tristano, Lennie 15, **198–199**
trombone **199**
    Tommy Dorsey **56**
    in early jazz xxvi
    George Lewis **122**
    Melba Liston **123**
    Kit McClure **129–130**
    Rob McConnell **130**
    Glenn Miller **134**
    Kid Ory **150**
    Jack Teagarden **195**
The Trouble with Cinderella (Artie Shaw book) 176
Trumbauer, Frankie 182, **199,** 214
trumpet **199–200.** *See also* cornet; flugelhorn; pocket trumpet
    Louis Armstrong **5–6**
    Chet Baker **9**
    Mario Bauzá **11**
    Lester Bowie **20–21**
    Randy Brecker **22**
    Clifford Brown **23–24**
    Philipe Brun **25**
    Donald Byrd **26**
    Benny Carter **28**
    Don Cherry **31–32**
    Jim Cifelli **33**
    Ornette Coleman 37
    Ernestine "Tiny" Davis **47**
    Miles Davis **47–51**
    Roy Eldridge **59–60**
    Don Ellis **62**
    Art Farmer **69**
    Maynard Ferguson **70**
    Dizzy Gillespie **75**
    Roy Hargrove **84–85**
    Freddie Hubbard **95**
    Harry James **102**
    Ingrid Jensen **107**
    Quincy Jones 109
    Thad Jones **110**
    Wynton Marsalis **127–129**
    Hugh Masekela **129**
    Lee Morgan **140**
    mute 142
    pocket trumpet **156**

Arturo Sandoval **170**
Clark Terry **196**
tuba xxvi, 56, 67
turnaround 282*g*
Turner, Lana 176
turntable 155
Turrentine, Stanley 35, 174, 183, **200**
Tutu (Miles Davis) 135
12-bar blues 282*g*
12-bar structure 19, **200**
"Twisted" (Lambert, Hendricks, and Ross) 120
Tyner, McCoy 40, 41, 124, 142, 163, **200–201**
Tzadik (record label) 225

U

"U.M.M.G" (Billy Strayhorn) 5
unison **203**
Unit Structures (Cecil Taylor) 195
University of Massachusetts, Amherst 121, 177
upright bass. *See* double bass
U.S. Army 90, 177–178, 220
U.S. Naval School of Music 55
U.S. Navy Band 38, 176
Us3 3

V

valve trombone 130, 199
vamp 282*g*
vanity records 282*g*
variation xxviii–xxix
vaudeville 182, 184
Vaughn, Sarah 80, 109, *205*, **205–206**
Venuti, Joe 120, **206,** 207, 214
verse **206,** 282*g*
verse-chorus song form **206**
Verve Records 90, 93, 123
vibraphone **206**
    Gary Burton **26**
    Lionel Hampton **81**
    Red Norvo **144–145**
    Tito Puente 158
    rhythm section 164
vibrato 206, **207,** 282*g*
Victor Records 16, 124, 161, 162, 210
Village Vanguard 93, 104, 110, 122, 210
Vinayakaram, T. H. 132
Vinson, Eddie "Cleanhead" 38
violin **207**
    Ornette Coleman 37
    Leroy Jenkins **106–107**
    Jean Luc Ponty 156
    Stuff Smith **184**
    Joe Venuti **206**
Visiones 171
Vitous, Miroslav *207*, **207–208**

vocalese 29, 120, 126, 171, **208**
Vocalion Records 162
vocalists
   Ivie Anderson **5**
   Chet Baker **9**
   Tony Bennett **12–13**
   Richard Bona **20**
   Dee Dee Bridgewater **23**
   Cab Calloway **27**
   Betty Carter **29**
   Nat "King" Cole **35–36**
   Ella Fitzgerald **70–71**
   Lionel Hampton **81**
   Johnny Hartman **86**
   Billie Holiday **91–92**
   Shirley Horn **93**
   Lena Horne **93–94**
   Alberta Hunter **95**
   Al Jarreau **103–104**
   Diana Krall **114**
   Cleo Laine **119–120**
   Lambert, Hendricks, and Ross **120**
   Peggy Lee **121–122**
   Abbey Lincoln **122–123**
   Machito **125**
   Bobby McFerrin **130**
   Carmen McRae **132**
   Ma Rainey **161**
   Diane Reeves **163**
   Savoy Ballroom **171**
   Diane Schuur **172**
   Jimmy Scott **173**
   Nina Simone **181–182**
   Bessie Smith **182–183**
   Mamie Smith **183–184**
   Jack Teagarden **195**
   Mel Torme **198**
   Sarah Vaughn **205–206**
   Fats Waller **209–210**
   Dinah Washington **211**
   Ethel Waters **211**
   Cassandra Wilson **217–218**
   Nancy Wilson **218**
   women in jazz xxix
Voight, Andrew 166

W

wah-wah pedal 51, **209**
Waldron, Mal 19
"Walkin' and Swingin'" (Mary Lou
  Williams) 216
walking bass 56, **209**, 282g
Waller, Fats **209–210**
   Count Basie 10
   Benny Carter 28
   James P. Johnson 107
   recordings of early jazz 162
   stride piano 189
   Art Tatum 193

Waltz for Debby (Bill Evans Trio) **210**
Warren, Butch 211
Washington, D.C. 60, 63, 93
Washington, Dinah 81, **211**, 223
Watanabe, Sadao 80
"Watermelon Man" (Herbie Hancock) 82,
  88, 170, **211**
Waters, Ethel 7, 89, 162, 163, **211**
Watkins, Doug 180
Watson, Bobby 185
Wayne State University, Detroit 90
Weather Report
   "Birdland" **15**
   Bitches Brew 16
   European jazz 65
   Jaco Pastorius 152
   Wayne Shorter 178
   Miroslav Vitous 207, 208
   Joe Zawinul 223, 224
Webb, Chick **212**
   "A-Tisket A-Tasket" 7
   Mario Bauzá 11
   cutting contest 45
   Ella Fitzgerald 70
   Savoy Ballroom 171
Webster, Ben **212–213**, *213*
   Cab Calloway 27
   cutting contest 45
   Duke Ellington 61
   Groove Holmes 92
   Bennie Moten 141
   Archie Shepp 177
   "Take the 'A' Train" (Billy Strayhorn)
    193
"Wednesday Night Prayer Meeting"
  (Charles Mingus) 19
Wein, George 144
We Insist! Freedom Now Suite (Max Roach)
  123
Wesleyan University 16, 22
Westbrook, Mike 191
West Coast jazz xxiv–xxv, 9, 24–25, 80,
  142. *See also* cool jazz
West Philadelphia Music School 200
Whetsol, Arthur 60
Whims of Chambers (Paul Chambers) 30
White, Lenny 15
Whiteman, Paul **213–215**, *214*
   Bix Beiderbecke 12
   Jimmy Dorsey 55
   Tommy Dorsey 56
   Red Norvo 144
   Don Redman 163
   Jack Teagarden 195
   third stream jazz 197
   Frankie Trumbauer 199
   Joe Venuti 206
   violin 207
Whitlock, Bob 142
Williams, Buster 30, 83

Williams, Clarence 209
Williams, Cootie 61, 156
Williams, Joe 81
Williams, John 215
Williams, Mary Lou *215*, **215–216**
   Lovie Austin 7
   Barbara Carroll 28
   Andrew Cyrille 46
   Kansas City jazz 111
   Mary Lou Williams Women in Jazz
    Festival 129
   women in jazz xxx
Williams, Tony **216**
   Cindy Blackman 16
   Ron Carter 30
   Miles Davis 49
   "E.S.P." 63
   fusion 72
   Herbie Hancock 82
   In a Silent Way 98
   John McLaughlin 131
   Diane Reeves 163
   Larry Young 219
Williamsburg Bridge (New York) 165
Williamson, Steve **216–217**
Wilson, Cassandra 16, **217–218**
Wilson, Nancy 211, **218**
Wilson, Rossiere "Shadow" 62–63, **218**
Wilson, Steve 43
Wilson, Teddy 76, 81, 213
Winburn, Anna Mae 99
The Wire magazine **218**
Wisconsin 221
The Wiz (Broadway musical) 23
Wolff, Francis 158
women in jazz xxix–xxxi. *See also* all-
  women orchestras
   Toshiko Akiyoshi **3–4**
   Ivie Anderson **5**
   Lovie Austin **7**
   Emma Barrett **10**
   Ivy Benson **13–14**
   Cindy Blackman **16**
   Carla Bley **18**
   Joanne Brackeen **21**
   Dee Dee Bridgewater **23**
   Barbara Carroll **28**
   Betty Carter **29**
   Alice Coltrane **38**
   Marilyn Crispell **44–45**
   Ernestine "Tiny" Davis **47**
   Barbara Dennerlein **51–52**
   Diva **53**
   Dorothy Donegan **55**
   Ella Fitzgerald **70–71**
   Lil Hardin **84**
   Billie Holiday **91–92**
   Shirley Horn **93**
   Lena Horne **93–94**
   Alberta Hunter **95**

women in jazz *(continued)*
    International Sweethearts of Rhythm **99**
    Ingrid Jensen **107**
    Diana Krall **114**
    Cleo Laine **119–120**
    Peggy Lee **121–122**
    Abbey Lincoln **122–123**
    Melba Liston **123**
    Kit McClure **129–130**
    Marian McPartland **132**
    Carmen McRae **132**
    Ma Rainey **161**
    Diane Reeves **163**
    Maria Schneider **171**
    Diane Schuur **172**
    Shirley Scott **173–174**
    Nina Simone **181–182**
    Bessie Smith **182–183**
    Mamie Smith **183–184**
    Sarah Vaughn **205–206**
    Dinah Washington **211**
    Ethel Waters **211**
    Mary Lou Williams **215–216**
    Cassandra Wilson **217–218**
    Nancy Wilson **218**
Wonder, Stevie 83, 169
Wood, Chris 133
wood blocks 54
"Woodchopper's Ball" (Woody Herman) 90
woodwinds 71, **218**, 282*g. See also specific woodwinds*
"Woody 'n' You" (Dizzy Gillespie) 75
Workman, Reggie 40, 46
Work Time (Sonny Rollins) 166
world music xxvi, **218**
    Richard Bona 20
    Lester Bowie 21
    Don Cherry 31, 32
    Al Di Meola 52
    Either/Orchestra 59
    Malachi Favors 69
    Herbie Mann 126
    Courtney Pine 155
    Pharoah Sanders 170
World War I 63
World War II
    Toshiko Akiyoshi 3
    and all-women big bands xxx–xxxi
    Ivy Benson 14
    Philipe Brun 25
    Ernestine "Tiny" Davis 47
    Coleman Hawkins 87
    Hot Club de France 94
    Alberta Hunter 95
    International Sweethearts of Rhythm 99
    Japanese jazz 103
    Glenn Miller 134
    Django Reinhardt 164
    Artie Shaw 176
    Lester Young 220
Wright, Gene 24
writers, on jazz 69–70, 171–172
Wylie, Austin 175

X

xylophone 144

Y

Yale University 102, 122, 129, 191
Yamekraw (James P. Johnson) 210
Young, Larry **219**
    Bitches Brew 15
    Barbara Dennerlein 51–52
    John McLaughlin 131
    organ 148
    Tony Williams 216
Young, Lester **219–221**, *220*
    Count Basie 10
    Birdland 15
    cutting contest 45
    Stan Getz 74
    Dexter Gordon 77
    Chico Hamilton 80
    Kansas City jazz 111
    Modern Jazz Quartet 138
    Charlie Parker 152
    Oscar Peterson 153
    saxophone 171
    Zoot Sims 182
    Sir Charles Thompson 197
    Lennie Tristano 199
    Frankie Trumbauer 199
    Ben Webster 212
Youngblood Brass Band **221**

Z

Zappa, Frank 156
Zawinul, Joe **223–224**
    Cannonball Adderly 3
    "Birdland" **15**
    Bitches Brew 15
    Richard Bona 20
    Miles Davis 49
    European jazz 65
    Maynard Ferguson 70
    In a Silent Way 98
    Jaco Pastorius 152
    piano 155
    Wayne Shorter 178
    Dinah Washington 211
Zodiac Suite (Mary Lou Williams) 215
Zoller, Attilla **224**
Zorn, John **224–225**